VICTORY FEVER ON GUADALCANAL

Number 147: Williams-Ford
Texas A&M University Military History Series

VICTORY FEVER ON GUADALCANAL

JAPAN'S FIRST LAND DEFEAT ★★★ OF WORLD War II ★★★

William H. Bartsch

FOREWORD BY RICHARD B. FRANK

Texas A&M University Press

College Station

First edition

This paper meets the requirements of ANSI/NISO Z39.48-1992
(Permanence of Paper).
Binding materials have been chosen for durability.
♾ ♲

Library of Congress Cataloging-in-Publication Data

Bartsch, William H., 1933– author.
Victory fever on Guadalcanal: Japan's first land defeat of World War II / William H. Bartsch; foreword by Richard B. Frank.—First edition.
pages cm—(Williams-Ford Texas A&M University military history series; number 147)
Includes bibliographical references and index.
ISBN 978-1-62349-184-0 (cloth: alk. paper)—ISBN 978-1-62349-220-5 (ebook)
1. Guadalcanal, Battle of, Solomon Islands, 1942–1943. I. Title. II. Series: Williams-Ford Texas A&M University military history series; no. 147.
D767.98.B37 2014
940.54'265933—dc23

2014011246

This book is dedicated to the memory of
Lt. Gen. Edwin A. Pollock, USMC
March 21, 1899–November 5, 1982

Contents

ILLUSTRATIONS

MAPS

Foreword

THE BATTLE OF THE TENARU, August 20–21, 1942, stakes a strong claim for being the smallest American battle of World War II with the greatest effects. The Japanese reacted to the Marine landing on Guadalcanal by dispatching the Ichiki Detachment with aspirations to recapture the island or at least to prevent completion of the airfield. Col. Kiyonao Ichiki took the first echelon of his regimental command, numbering 916 men, ahead in six destroyers. After landing east of the US perimeter, Ichiki marched most of his men to attack the Americans at the eastern extremity of their position, a tidal lagoon known as Alligator Creek to the locals but misnamed the Tenaru River on Marine photomaps (the Marines never had a true map during the Guadalcanal campaign). During the night of August 20–21, Ichiki hurled multiple assaults at Marine positions. In wild and desperate fighting the green Marines held. The next day, a Marine counterattack came close to annihilating the men Ichiki brought to the "Tenaru."

William Bartsch has assembled an incredibly vivid retelling of the battle as it appeared to the participants on both sides. Those familiar with Bill's prior sterling work will expect and find the rewarding fruits of his diligent research from the accounts and memories (judiciously culled) of the US Marines—particularly the enlisted men, for this is a bottom up, not a top down, narrative. What is especially remarkable is Bartsch's feat of bringing to life the views of the Japanese participants. Given the catastrophic casualties sustained by the Ichiki Detachment, this is astonishing. The nature of the surviving Japanese accounts presented particular challenges, but the author is well up to the task of avoiding the numerous pitfalls this body of evidence presented. While personal accounts are the hallmark of this work, there is no lack of equally patient work through the formal records on both sides.

After the Battle of the Tenaru seemed over, Marines and navy corpsmen swept over terrific scenes of carnage, attempting to take prisoners and treat the few wounded survivors. The refusal of the overwhelming majority of the Japanese to be taken prisoner, and the attempts of some to kill their Marine and sailor Samaritans, transmitted with tremendous shock the realization that Japanese warriors down to the rank and file would not surrender. This came only a few days after the survivors of the ambushed Goettge Patrol returned with the news that the Japanese were not taking prisoners. These twin events, but above all the Tenaru, cast a shadow that extended for the rest of the war. Before the Tenaru, the only Americans who had fought the Japanese on land were dead or prisoners of the Japanese. It was at the Tenaru that American fighting forces came to understand the terms on which the Japanese insisted that the war in the Pacific would be fought. And contrary to the view advanced in some of the literature that there was something distinct or even unique about the racially charged manner in which Americans and Japanese fought, we now know that these were the same terms on which the Chinese and Japanese had battled since 1937. It is the creation of this enduring template for the rest of the war that is ultimately why the Tenaru deserves the top-notch account Bill Bartsch delivers in the following pages.

Richard B. Frank
Annandale, Virginia
September 2013

Preface

THIS BOOK REPRESENTS the culmination of a fourteen-year effort to reconstruct the events of one of the most significant clashes of the Pacific War. Fought by the 1st Marine Division against a Japanese reinforced battalion, known as the Ichiki Detachment, on the late night and morning of August 20–21, 1942, on Guadalcanal, it has gone down in history as the Battle of the Tenaru. Despite its significance as the first major land defeat of the Japanese in the Pacific War, it has previously never received the coverage it deserved, from either the Japanese or the American side.

The idea for this book originated following my research into a relatively unknown engagement during the Battle of Bloody Ridge of mid-September 1942, in which I reconstructed the experiences of K Company, 1st Marines, and those of the second echelon of the Ichiki Detachment in their deadly confrontation. The reconstruction effort was published in the *Marine Corps Gazette* in its September 1997 issue as "Crucial Battle Ignored." From this delving into the details of the combat experiences of the two sides, I developed a keen interest in the Ichiki Detachment and decided to probe into its first echelon's experience in the attempt to recapture Guadalcanal's vital airfield a month earlier.

As for my *Gazette* article, I wanted to present the story from the human standpoint—American and Japanese alike. This approach meant that I would have to identify, locate, and contact as many surviving participants as possible, or, failing that, their families. While my efforts proved relatively successful on the American side, they would not be so on the Japanese side: the virtual annihilation of Ichiki's force at the Battle of the Tenaru left only a few of the actively engaged participants alive, and many of them had since died. Fortunately, a member of their 7th Division Engineer Regiment who was not a participant and who survived the war had decided to try to reconstruct the experiences of the detachment based on interviews of survivors living at the time. From a translation made of the Japanese text of his book, I was able to piece together—aided by a few other sources—the experiences of these survivors to get a picture, albeit incomplete, of the detachment's operations that night and the following morning.

Juxtaposing the accounts of each side within a detailed time frame proved a greater challenge. Fading memories of Marine and Japanese participants alike produced in some cases unlikely scenarios that had to be resolved. Few of the Americans and none of the Japanese survivors had kept diaries covering their battle experiences, nor did either side recall exact times of events in their memoirs—not surprising, considering the life-or-death conditions they were facing during the entire battle. From analysis of what fragmented information I was able to glean from participants' accounts and other previously unknown sources, I have developed a timetable that I believe is accurate, though not necessarily 100 percent so.

Another example of the somewhat confused nature of documentation of this first encounter of the Marines against the Japanese on Guadalcanal is the misnaming of the site of the fighting. Because of either incorrect information provided to the Marine command prior to the landing on August 7, 1942, by a former manager of the Lunga/Tenaru plantations, or an error of a member of Vandegrift's staff using that information, Alligator Creek and its extension upstream, the Ilu River, were mismarked on maps as "the Tenaru," while the actual Tenaru River was a little over two miles to the east and incorrectly labeled "the Ilu." But historians have opted against renaming such a historic battle, known from the outset as the Battle of the Tenaru, a position I support also.

I refer to the Battle of the Tenaru as the first major defeat on land by the Japanese Army in World War II. It might be argued that the Battle of the Points in January 1942 on Bataan in the Philippines was actually the first defeat, but I maintain that that was a tactical defeat by a smaller battalion-sized unit in an isolated operation, not one to attain a major strategic goal: the reoccupation of Guadalcanal and its airfield.

Acknowledgments

THIS RECONSTRUCTION OF THE EVENTS of the Battle of the Tenaru derives mainly from the accounts of experiences of those men who participated in it, Americans and Japanese alike. Thus, my overwhelming debt of gratitude goes to those individuals—or, in the case of the deceased, their families—who shared such personal information with me via correspondence, interviews, or provision of diaries or memoirs. In the case of Japanese participants, however, such information was primarily gleaned from statements made to Susumu Sugawara for his 1979 privately published book *Ichiki Shitai zenmetsu* (Annihilation of the Ichiki Detachment), translated for me by Edward Rasmussen, for whose invaluable service I am grateful.

On the American side, it was two battalions of the 1st Marine Regiment, 1st Marine Division, that were mainly responsible for the destruction of Colonel Ichiki's first-echelon detachment, as supported by a battery of the division's 1st Special Weapons Battalion, a company of the 1st Tank Battalion, and a battalion of the 11th Marines (artillery). While various official reports written on the performances of these units during the battle provided me a basic picture of the engagement, it was the firsthand accounts of participants—officers and enlisted men—that gave me the detailed human dimension of the story I sought that would otherwise have been lost to history.

For the experiences of Lt. Col. Edwin A. Pollock's 2nd Battalion, 1st Marines, which bore the brunt of the fighting, I am particularly indebted to (then) 2nd Lt. A. William Larson, the operations officer of the battalion, who unearthed and shared with me records he had kept over the past seventy years, including unpublished maps and unit reports he had prepared himself. Three of Colonel Pollock's platoon leaders also stand out for their strong commitment to my efforts: 2nd Lts. George Codrea (G Company), Ed Craig (F Company), and Bill Whorf (H Company), whose tireless efforts to recall details in response to my persistent queries I wish to acknowledge. It would be impractical to cite here all the other officers, NCOs, and enlisted men who also helped me piece together the 2nd Battalion's side of the story, but correspondence and interviews with them are cited in the Notes, and their memoirs are listed in the Sources. However, I would be remiss not to acknowledge the particular perseverance of ten enlisted men in responding to my requests for information. Here I mean to thank Charley Royer (E Company); B. J. Wilson and Charley Gambrell (F Company); Harry Horsman, Al Schlemmer, and John Joseph (G Company); and Sid Phillips, John "Deacon" Tatum, Clyde Lucas, and George Parker (H Company).

The 1st Battalion, 1st Marines, contributed to the victory in its cleanup of the remaining Japanese troops who had not been committed to cross the Tenaru. For providing me with detailed information about the key role of C Company in this operation, I wish to acknowledge the dedicated cooperation of its commanding officer, Capt. Nikolai "Nick" Stevenson, with whom I had almost daily conversations in August 2010. It is to my heartfelt regret that he passed away at the age of ninety-three just before I completed my writing.

The 1st Battalion's A Company is also featured in this account, particularly for the role of its 1st Platoon during the so-called Brush Patrol that wiped out Colonel Ichiki's large reconnaissance party shortly before the Battle of the Tenaru. The platoon's commanding officer, 2nd Lt. John Jachym, along with several of its enlisted men, among whom stands out Hugh "Stub" Morse, helped me piece together its experiences. Others of the 1st Battalion who helped with their personal experiences are cited in the Notes and Sources.

If it were not for the inputs of several men of the 1st Special Weapons Battalion's B Battery, the story of its key contribution to the victory would have gone unknown. I wish to acknowledge the sustained support of four of its former members: Jim Olliff, Clair Hume, Glen Campbell, and Mel Berge. Similarly, for information on their experiences as members of the 3rd Battalion, 11th Marines,

I am grateful in particular to 2nd Lt. Nat Mewhinney and Sgt. Bob Askey. As in the case of other units, all who helped are cited in the Notes and Sources.

Although his K Company, 3rd Battalion, was not engaged in the Battle of the Tenaru, its commanding officer at the time, Capt. Robert Putnam, provided me with a copy of his "Guadalcanal Memoirs," written in 1942, which proved a good source of information for the August 7–20 period. For that I am indebted to him (as well as for his unstinting support for my *Marine Corps Gazette* article). Similarly, Michael Santoro's A Battery, 1st Battalion, 11th Marines, was not a participant in the Tenaru battle, but he was an invaluable source of information about the characteristics of 75 mm pack howitzers and 37 mm antitank guns employed in the fighting, for which I am grateful to him, too.

In addition to surviving participants at the time I researched this story, family members of many of the deceased responded to my requests for information on their experiences, which I wish to acknowledge here. Colonel Pollock's grandson, Edward Appel, kindly made a copy available to me of Colonel Pollock's previously unknown personal diary held by the family. Jon Small—the son of 2nd Lt. Gilbert Small, Jr., then a forward observer for I Battery, 11th Marines—provided me a copy of his father's 1942 correspondence and journal, of invaluable importance in my reconstruction of events before the Tenaru battle. Mary Anne Kampmann, the daughter of 2nd Lt. Bayard Berghaus, a platoon leader of L Company, 3rd Battalion, 1st Marines, located the diary of her father covering the February–August 1942 period of his experiences that allowed me to provide detailed pre-Tenaru sections of the book. For copies of the prebattle correspondence of his great uncle, 2nd Lt. Irving "Perry" Perine, who as the intelligence officer of the 1st Battalion, 1st Marines, was killed in the cleanup operation, I am grateful to John Collins. At the level of enlisted men, I would particularly like to thank the relatives of two H Company, 2nd Battalion, men: Jim Donahue, Jr., for a copy of the personal diary of his father, and Bill Freedman for copies of the early 1942 correspondence of his uncle, Jack Rivers.

As noted earlier, the experiences of most of the few surviving Japanese participants in this story have been derived from the Japanese-language book of Susumu Sugawara, who was personally linked to the men of Colonel Ichiki's detachment as a nonparticipant member of the 7th Engineer Regiment, which was based, like the detachment's 28th Infantry Regiment, at Asahigawa, Hokkaido. I regret that he passed away before I initiated my research, and thus I could not thank him for his invaluable effort in honor of the regiment. I am grateful to his family for giving me permission, through the kindness of an intermediary at Hokkaido University Library, Hiroyuki Chiba, to quote freely from his book.

Similarly, thanks to the efforts of Akio Tani we have access to the personal experiences of surviving former sergeant Sadanobu Okada of Ichiki's headquarters staff, who translated Okada's memoir, partly published in *Guadalcanal Echoes*. Indeed, from 1989 to the time of his death in 1994, Tani-san tirelessly searched for and dug out any documentation he could find and tracked down surviving members of the whole Guadalcanal campaign for me. His correspondence with me fills twenty binders of my Guadalcanal material on the Japanese side.

My best source of information on the Ichiki Detachment from May 1942 up to just before the landing on Guadalcanal of its first echelon was the diary of former second lieutenant Genjirou Inui of its second echelon, made available on the internet by his son, Itirou Inui, who also responded to my requests for further information and photos of his father. I am also grateful for the assistance of second-echelon adjutant 2nd Lt. Hajime Yamamoto, who in addition to providing information as the main input for my *Gazette* article on his echelon's September 1942 experiences, also included details relevant to the operations of the first echelon at the earlier Battle of the Tenaru.

I would finally like to express my appreciation for the support given me by persons other than the participants and their families. The archivist of the Marine Corps' Parris Island Museum, Stephen Wise, kindly provided me with copies of papers from Lieutenant General Pollock's collection that included many items of importance for reconstructing the battle, including the unpublished account of the 1st Marines' intelligence officer, 2nd Lt. George Hunt. The historian of the 1st Marine Division Association, Tom McLeod, had an equal interest in seeing this story told and provided leads and support throughout. But assistance came from far away, too, including from Peter Flahavin and Annika Korsgaard in Australia and Ewan Stevenson in New Zealand—like Tom McLeod, enthusiasts of the Guadalcanal Campaign and keen to see this story of its first battle known.

Almost all of those participants who helped me with this account have since passed away and thus regrettably will not have the opportunity to read this story and their role in it. If I had started the research for the book ten years later than I did, I would not have been able to write it. Indeed, the curtain has fallen for this participant-based type of World War II story that reminds us of the personal sacrifices made by friend and foe alike in that most traumatic event of the twentieth century.

VICTORY FEVER ON GUADALCANAL

Prologue

BARELY WEEKS AFTER Brig. Gen. Alexander A. Vandegrift had reported in at Marine Barracks New River, North Carolina, in November 1941 to take up his new assignment as assistant commander of the 1st Marine Division, he was faced with an immense task. The Japanese had attacked Pearl Harbor, plunging the United States into war. In response, the division—formed only ten and a half months earlier from the 1st Marine Brigade and, with a strength of 7,389 men, existing "more in paper than in fact"—would be more than doubling in size to reach its authorized strength of 19,514. Vandegrift would be responsible for the training essential to mold his new command into a powerful fighting unit.[1]

As he surveyed his new domain, which would be designated on February 17 as the home base of the division, the fifty-five-year-old career Marine appreciated the immensity of the task that awaited him. New River "was largely wasteland," 111,710 acres of "water, coastal swamp, and plain" that had been inhabited "largely by sandflies, ticks, chiggers, and snakes" when the Marine Corps bought it in 1941. Now a billeting area, referred to as Tent Camp One, was rapidly being built of pyramidal tents to house the thousands of new recruits that would soon be flooding in. But the camp had few firing ranges, almost no roads, and few wooden buildings.[2]

Parris Island, some 350 miles to the south by troop train, would be providing the men to flesh out the division's enlisted strength. President Roosevelt had authorized on December 16 the expansion of the authorized strength of the Marine Corps from 75,000 to 104,000 by March 1, 1942. Since the actual strength of the Corps was only 66,319 at the time, it would be accepting some 38,000 young men from the numbers thronging Marine Corps recruitment stations nationwide, incensed to fight after Pearl Harbor. None draftees, all would be volunteers, keen to join the elite Marine Corps with its proud tradition.[3] Already in December 1941, 10,224 had signed up and would be heading for boot camp, either at Parris Island or at San Diego, to begin the process that would convert them into fighting men.

But the fivefold surge in numbers recruited in December, from 1,978 in November, was overwhelming the facilities at the two training depots, forcing a hard decision on the part of Marine Corps headquarters. From January 1 the training period would be reduced from the prewar level of eight weeks—the length regarded as providing minimum quality of training—to five weeks. In January the number recruited doubled, to 22,686, and only in February did it taper off to 12,037 as the Marine Corps reached the strength authorized for March 1. Headquarters was now able to expand the length of training to six weeks from February 15, a slight improvement.[4]

Of these totals, some ten thousand men passing through Parris Island would be assigned to Vandegrift's 1st Marine Division. From early February, "odd lots" began arriving almost daily by train from Yemassee Junction, South Carolina, having completed their training in the recruit battalions. "They were a motley bunch," one veteran Marine recalled. But they had undergone the rigorous training and "psychological transformation" that had converted them from civilians to proud Marines.[5]

But who would be commanding them and providing the follow-up training they all required to become effective fighting men? Except for senior officers—mostly Reservists called to active duty in 1940—the 1st Marine Division, from division headquarters down to its three infantry regiments and one artillery regiment, then down to the three battalions in each regiment, and finally the four companies in each battalion, had no officer personnel. Vandegrift would have to rely on the limited number of noncommissioned officers—the "old breed of Marine," some of whom had served as far back as World War I—to lead the men and provide their training.

The problem was not lost on Marine Corps headquarters. As a first step, on

February 6, 1942, it called to active duty all the second lieutenants who had graduated from college and been commissioned in the Reserves from eastern platoon leaders classes dating back to 1937 and ordered them to Basic School at the Philadelphia Navy Yard for further training, including three weeks in the use of infantry weapons at Indiantown Gap, Pennsylvania. To speed up the operation, the training was cut back from twelve to ten weeks. More drastically, even those relatively large numbers of members of the platoon leaders classes who were not scheduled for graduation from college until June 1942 were given their commissions on February 6, put on active duty with the others, and sent with them to Basic School for their training. Under this revised schedule, some 119 second lieutenants (and two first lieutenants) would be ready to join the 1st Marine Division and be assigned in mid-April 1942 to fill its vacant platoon leader positions.[6]

But the other peacetime source of procurement of junior officers was also being speeded up. Already in fiscal 1941 (July 1940–June 1941) the Officers Candidate Class (OCC) and follow-on Reserve Officers Class (ROC) had turned out 67 percent of the officers commissioned in the Reserve. Under this two-stage program, beginning in November 1940, college graduates enlisted as privates first class in the Reserve and spent three months at OCC, with those succeeding put on active duty and assigned to the ROC as second lieutenants for an additional three months of training. But now the 7th ROC, originally scheduled for training from February 1 through April 30, 1942, was ordered cut short, and the 319 members were moved up to graduate on April 1 instead, with orders to report immediately to their new stations.[7]

When the 7th ROC officers arrived at New River for their assignments at the beginning of April, a new division commander welcomed them. On March 23, Vandegrift had been promoted to major general and given command of the division. Training was now not his only concern; overseeing the division's expansion was his responsibility, too. More recruits were flooding in and fleshing out his division's enlisted strength. With the arrival of the Platoon Leaders Class (PLC) second lieutenants three weeks later, every platoon in his division would finally have an officer to command it.

But developments arose that frustrated Vandegrift's efforts too. Only weeks after he assumed command, one of his three infantry regiments—the 7th Marines—was ordered detached to form the nucleus of the 3rd Marine Brigade to be deployed to Western Samoa. When it left New River and sailed from Norfolk on April 10, it took with it "an undue proportion of the Division's best fighting talent." Vandegrift was not informed when it would be returning to his command, if ever.[8]

The second blow fell on April 15. Marine Corps headquarters had framed a plan, dubbed Operation Lone Wolf, that spelled finis to further training and equipping of Vandegrift's division at New River. The division was being ordered to ship out to New Zealand as soon as possible as an emergency move to serve as the landing force for a newly established South Pacific Amphibious Force. To ease the impact of the order, Vandegrift was given assurance that the division would not be expected to go into combat before January 1, 1943. Following arrival in Wellington, New Zealand—designated a "forward amphibious training base"—it would be given six more months of training to bring it up to a satisfactory state of readiness for amphibious operations.[9]

Pursuant to his new orders, Vandegrift and his staff, along with the 5th Marines and supporting units, left New River for Norfolk. This first echelon boarded the transport *Wakefield* (formerly the SS *Manhattan*). By May 15 the cargo ships *Electra* and *Del Brazil* were loaded, and four days later they set sail for New Zealand.[10]

Now alone at New River, the 1st Marines and other division supporting units were awaiting orders to leave next. Finally, on June 12 the official word arrived from division headquarters. The regiment would be moving to New Zealand as the second echelon, completing the division's deployment overseas. Kept in the dark about high-level plans, the men—except for the NCO veterans—were "apprehensive about what was going to happen next." They had every reason to be so.[11]

The Japanese rampage through Southeast Asia and the Pacific was common knowledge to all the men. Beginning on the first day of the war with the surprise attack on Pearl Harbor, the near destruction of MacArthur's Far East Air Force in the Philippines, and the capture of Guam, followed on December 23 by the seizure of Wake Island, the shocks generated by the unbroken Japanese victories continued unabated. The successes of the Japanese army in overwhelming the British defenders in Malaya, culminating with the surprisingly quick fall of their bastion of Singapore on February 15, 1942, coupled with the forced evacuation of American and Filipino forces from Luzon to Bataan for a last-ditch resistance against the Japanese, dominated the news during the first three months of the Pacific War. On March 7 the Japanese attained their main objective of Southern Operations: the seizure of Java and the oil riches of the Dutch East Indies after

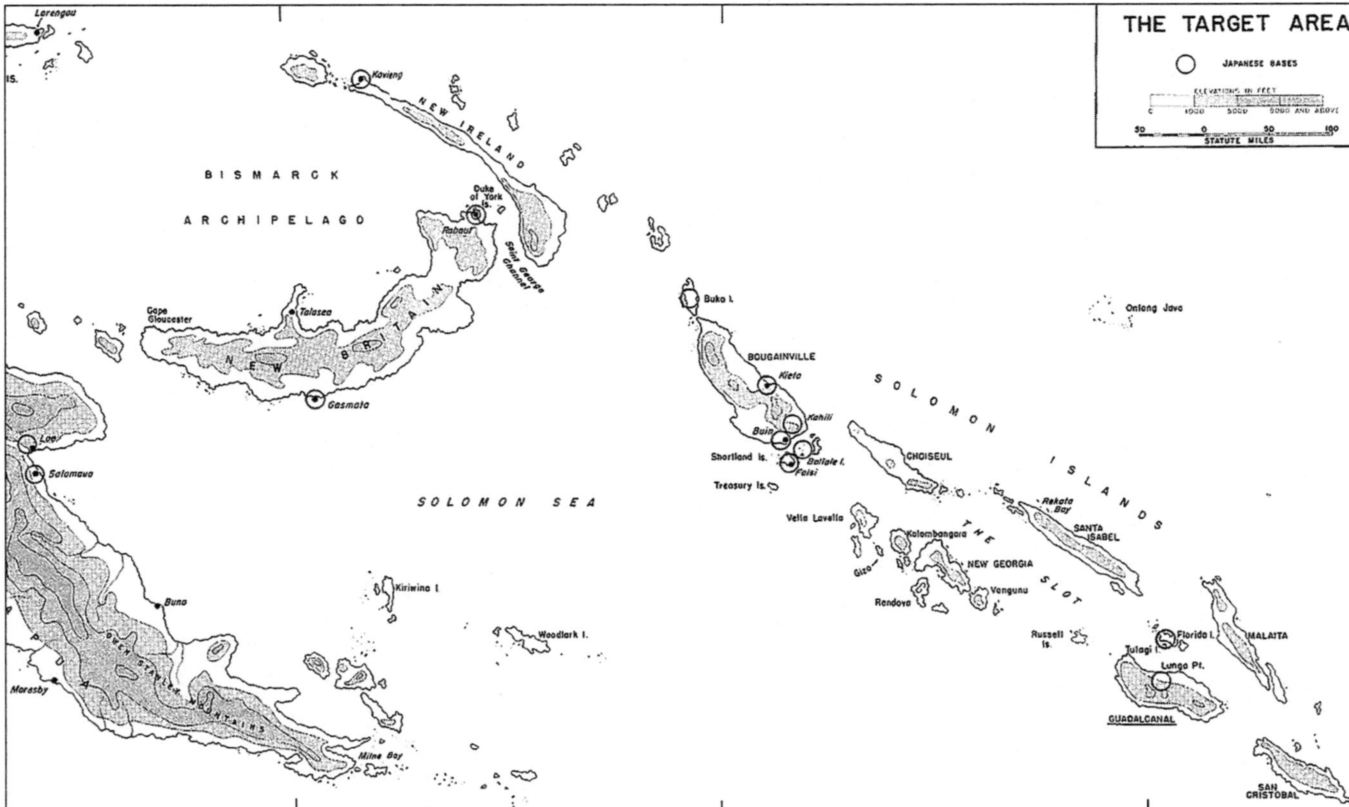

Japanese bases in the Solomons, New Guinea, and New Britain, July 1942. *Army Map Service; Map III in John Miller, Jr.,* Guadalcanal: The First Offensive.

step-by-step advances through the outer islands of the colony. The biggest blow to American morale followed the next month, when Bataan finally succumbed on April 9 after three months of dogged resistance. The fall of Corregidor and the capture of Mindanao to the south the following month marked the end of American presence in the Philippines.

In addition to their Southeast Asia drives, the Japanese had also struck eastward into the islands of the South Pacific, including northern New Guinea, New Britain to its north, and Bougainville in the upper Solomons. With the seizure of strategically important Rabaul on New Britain in late January and Bougainville in March, it had become apparent that the Japanese intended to continue spreading eastward from the Solomons. Such movements threatened American lines of communication and supply with Australia and New Zealand as well as American island outposts in the New Hebrides and Tonga. Then on May 4 the Japanese occupied Tulagi, across from the island of Guadalcanal in the lower Solomons. Their only setback was the blocked attempt to land an invasion force at Port Moresby in southern New Guinea when in the May 7–8 Battle of the Coral Sea, American carrier aircraft fought to a standstill enemy carriers supporting the invasion force, thus forcing the Japanese to postpone their Port Moresby occupation plans.

To combative Adm. Ernest J. King, US Fleet commander, the situation in the South Pacific had become intolerable. As early as February, as an exception to the "Germany First" policy that informed American war strategy, King had aggressively argued for taking the offensive to halt the Japanese encroachment. In early March he formulated plans for a step-by-step general advance through the New Hebrides, the Solomons, and the Bismarck Archipelago, using amphibious troops to occupy strong points. Then in a first move to operationalize his plans, King informed the Marine Corps commandant on April 10 that his 1st Marine Division would be transferred in May from its New River base to the South Pacific.[12]

The decisive American victory at the Battle of Midway in the beginning of June, which heavily damaged the Japanese Navy's air capabilities, strengthened King's position. Having gained the support of the Joint Chiefs of Staff (JCS), King on June 25 advised Adm. Chester W. Nimitz, commander-in-chief of the Pacific Fleet, and Nimitz's subordinate, Vice Adm. Robert L. Ghormley, commander of South Pacific Force, that an offensive would be launched against Japanese forces in the lower Solomons. Specifically, the Santa Cruz Islands, Tulagi, and "adjacent areas" in the Solomons were to be seized, with a target D-Day of August 1. Ghormley was ordered to begin planning for the operation immediately, using his South Pacific forces. Then on July 2 a JCS directive spelled out the offensive plans in more detail and specified that Task 1 would be the operation that Ghormley had been ordered by Nimitz and King to execute.[13] The ambitious amphibious operation would necessarily have to be carried out by the only qualified and ready force available to Ghormley on such short notice, Vandegrift's 1st Marine Division, the forward echelon of which was currently in New Zealand and the second echelon of which was expected within two weeks.

Timing of the operation became critical on July 6 when intelligence reports from the Australian coastwatcher on Guadalcanal indicated that a large force of construction workers had been landed on the northern part of the island on July 2 with the obvious intention of building an airfield on the Lunga Plain. For the first time, Guadalcanal became the focal point for the Marine landing, when on the same day Admirals King and Nimitz agreed to drop the Santa Cruz Islands from Task 1 and designate Guadalcanal instead.[14]

Neither the Japanese activity on Guadalcanal nor American plans to counter them were known to the men of the 1st Marine Regiment in the rear echelon of the division as they put ashore from their three transports at Wellington on July 11. Like the men of the forward echelon that had landed a month earlier, they were as uninformed about what lay ahead as they had been when they left New River in June. They assumed they would be undergoing further training—cut short at New River following the movement order—but there was disturbing talk about engaging in large-scale maneuvers with the forward echelon. However, there was no indication of plans for impending combat. Only a deeply concerned Vandegrift and his staff were privy to such information.[15]

1

"You Shitheads Are Here to Learn to Fight!"

AT 1215 ON A "clear, cold, but very windy day," twenty-three-year-old Bayard S. Berghaus was dropped off by his father and younger brother at the entrance to Marine Barracks, Philadelphia Navy Yard, after a ninety-six-mile trip east from the little town of Marietta, Pennsylvania. It was Monday, February 2, 1942, just eight weeks after the Japanese attack on Pearl Harbor. Called to active duty, 2nd Lieutenant Berghaus had been ordered to Marine Corps Basic School at the Navy Yard for twelve weeks of instruction to prepare him for assignment to a combat unit.[1]

After saying goodbye to his father—the Episcopalian minister in his hometown—and brother, Berghaus collected a footlocker containing helmet, gas mask, belt, and holster, headed over to Barracks 101 of the school, and entered room 3. One of his new roommates, Maurice Ahearn, a graduate of Tufts University, was already settled in, but the other had not shown up yet. Berghaus knew the second roommate wouldn't be his Washington and Lee University classmate Richard W. Smith, though. They were the only two W&L '41 graduates who had signed up for the Marine Corps' Eastern Platoon Leaders Class in 1938 and had spent six weeks each summer following their sophomore and junior years in basic training. Commissioned as Reserve second lieutenants upon graduation, Berghaus and

Smith were now together again for further training at the Navy Yard as members of the 2nd Basic School Reserve Officers Class.[2]

Instruction began two days later. Berghaus, who was serious, quiet, and reserved by nature, was wondering how the school would be able to "pack so much in so little time"—just three months for what he thought should be a nine-month course. When informed originally that he was going to Basic School, he had expected a much longer period of instruction that he felt was needed to prepare him as a platoon leader.[3]

Two days before Berghaus and the other 189 members of his battalion began their classes on February 4, 2nd Lt. George Codrea commenced his own active-duty training as a member of the 7th Reserve Officers Class at Quantico, Virginia. Unlike the PLC officers at the Basic School, however, Codrea had no prior Marine Corps instruction during summers while a student at Akron University in Ohio. After a stint with B. F. Goodrich following his graduation in June 1940, the twenty-four-year-old of Rumanian heritage had signed up for the Marine Corps officers candidate class that began at Quantico on November 1, 1941, and along with the 318 other survivors of the three-month qualifying course was now a second lieutenant in the Marine Corps Reserve and assigned to an additional three months of training in the ROC.[4]

"Mud, mud, and more mud!" Jack Rivers muttered to himself on the morning of February 18, 1942, as he poked his nose outside. It was biting cold. Only the smoking kerosene stove on the wooden floor provided any warmth for Rivers and his squad mates in the tent hut that was now his home at the Marine Barracks, New River, North Carolina.[5]

But Rivers was not really complaining. Life was proving much easier than it had been at Parris Island, where the twenty-three-year-old recruit had endured five weeks of grueling boot camp before reporting in at New River on February 13, 1942. After graduating from high school and gaining employment at Bethlehem Steel, Rivers had taken up professional boxing and was in tip-top physical shape when he enlisted in the Marine Corps shortly after Pearl Harbor and reported in at Parris Island on January 5. Dubbed in the boxing world "Indian Johnny Rivers," he could take any punishment the Marine Corps could dish out.[6]

Raised in a Lutheran orphans' home, Rivers now had a family for the first time: his buddies in the squad to which he'd been assigned and who shared the hut with him. Particularly close was Al Schmid, with whom he'd bonded from the time they together boarded the train from New Jersey that would take them to Parris Island. Both were assigned at New River on reporting in to a machine gun platoon, one of the three such platoons in H Company, 2nd Battalion, 1st Marine Regiment, following reactivation of the battalion on February 11, 1942.[7]

In another hut in the H Company area, twenty-one-year-old Bob Leckie was wondering why he, a sports writer before he enlisted on December 8, 1941, had been selected as a machine gunner. On his arrival the night before, he was perfunctorily assigned to the 1st Marine Regiment, and the next day the H Company commander—whom Leckie would refer to as "Captain High-Hips"—in his very British manner assigned Leckie to a squad in a machine gun platoon. Unknown to Leckie, the moustached Capt. John Howland, a thirty-one-year-old graduate of Harvard University—BA in 1932 and LLB in 1936—had spent a year at Exeter College, Oxford, where he had evidently picked up his British mannerisms before enlisting in the Marine Corps and being called to active duty in 1940.[8]

Howland's H Company—the weapons company of the 2nd Battalion—was comprised of three machine gun platoons, a mortar platoon, and a platoon of 37 mm antitank guns and .50-caliber machine guns. But for the time being the company had no officers other than Howland. Its veteran noncommissioned officers would be providing the training on the company's weapons and molding Rivers, Leckie, and the others into fighting men.[9]

For seventeen-year-old Sid Phillips, being assigned to H Company's mortar platoon on his arrival by train from Parris Island appeared an arbitrary decision, too. He was just a high school kid from Mobile, Alabama, who like the others had survived the five weeks of "conceived nightmare" at Parris Island. On arrival at New River on February 13, Phillips and the others with him were marched off to stand in ranks outside a lighted hut that served as an office and then called in one at a time and interviewed by NCOs inside the hut. To Sid, it was "silly," because everyone was assigned to the 1st Marines. He was then additionally ordered to H Company's mortar platoon and to gun squad 4, which to his delight turned out with one exception to be comprised entirely of fellow southerners.[10]

Sid Phillips may have thought that the formalities of assigning everyone to the 1st Marines was inane, but then he and the others reporting in with him to the 1st Marine Division were ignorant of the plight of the regiment in early February 1942. It had just been reactivated at New River and was being built up from scratch to meet the needs of the division for a third regiment other than just on paper. At the time of its reactivation, it had consisted of only 160 key personnel, just senior officers and veteran NCOs. Its 1st Battalion was the first to be reactivated, on February 7, followed by the 2nd Battalion on February 11 and the 3rd Battalion on February 16.[11]

Pvt. John Joseph from Cambridge, Massachusetts, felt that his mastering of the M1903 Springfield rifle at Parris Island explained why he was assigned on February 13 to G Company, one of the three rifle companies of the 2nd Battalion. A self-described "city slicker," he had never fired a weapon other than a Daisy air rifle before enlisting in the Marine Corps. But instead of being selected for one of the rifle platoons, he had drawn G Company's Weapons Platoon, equipped with .30-caliber air-cooled machine guns and 60 mm mortars. He was pleasantly surprised to find that the platoon was being run by Cpl. Willis Accord, his old drill instructor at Parris Island, and another "Old Breed" NCO, Cpl. Stanley Necikowski. In fact, the only officer in G Company was the CO, Capt. James Sherman, a 1936 graduate of Tufts College from Somerville, Massachusetts, a Reservist, who had worked in the private sector for four years before being called to active duty in 1939.[12]

Buddies Hugh Morse, from Auburn, Indiana, and Jack Gardner, from Syracuse, New York, were selected as Browning automatic rifle (BAR) men in a rifle platoon of the 1st Battalion's A Company. It was an assignment both sought to avoid, but they had qualified as sharpshooters on the BAR during their Parris Island boot training despite their best efforts to avoid the distinction. They knew "damned well that anyone who qualified was going to get stuck with carrying one of those monsters in a rifle company" when assigned afterwards to a unit. Hoping to boost the other's score and lower his own, Morse had fired on Gardner's target while Gardner fired on Morse's, but their strategy failed when *both* got top marks.[13]

To the south of the 1st Marine Regiment's site, near Verona, the camp of the 3rd Battalion, 11th Marine Regiment—the artillery unit of the 1st Marine Division—looked to Pvt. Bill White like a Civil War encampment on his arrival there to take up his assignment in late January 1942. The sixteen-year-old native of Clarksdale, Mississippi, had lied about his age when he enlisted in September 1941 and now found himself assigned to the battalion's Headquarters Battery after finishing boot camp at Parris Island and training in telephone communications at Quantico. He found the living conditions at the camp primitive: no shower facilities, water trucked in, limited electricity. To fend off the bitter cold, he and the others were wearing overcoats over long johns, using towels for earmuffs, and sometimes blankets as covers.[14]

"They're putting us through the mill all right," Jack Rivers wrote to his sister in mid-March. Training for the men of the 2nd Battalion in the flat, swampy area of New River was becoming more intense. "And the weather is getting hot as heck," he added.[15]

Pvt. John Rivers during his visit home on leave from New River, May 1942. *Courtesy of William Freedman.*

Rivers, Al Schmid, and the others were now sharing the hut with their newly appointed squad leader, Cpl. LeRoy Diamond. Promoted from private first class on March 9, Diamond was then transferred to H Company's 3rd Machine Gun Platoon from his old G Company, 2nd Battalion, 7th Marines. Still in its rebuilding process, the 1st Marine Regiment needed more NCOs.[16]

Over in H Company's 1st Machine Gun Platoon, newly promoted Pfc. Bob Leckie had become good friends with Pvt. Lewis Juergens, whom he would refer to later as "Chuckler" for his good-natured chortling. They were learning the mysteries of the heavy, water-cooled M1917A1 Browning machine gun. Juergens, as the gunner, would carry the fifty-four-pound tripod, and Leckie, as assistant gunner, the forty-pound gun. By mid-March the two had mastered use of the gun and could even take it apart and reassemble it blindfolded.[17]

As was the case for all the other platoons in the 2nd Battalion, and in fact for the whole 1st Regiment, there still was no second lieutenant to lead the platoon. Sgt. Frank Stewart was in charge of them. Despite being only three months older than Leckie, he was a world apart in experience, having already served over three years as a regular since enlisting in September 1938 when he turned eighteen. Leckie would later refer to him as "Sgt. Thinface."[18]

Sid Phillips and the other "stovepipers" of his squad in H Company's mortar platoon had now also mastered their weapon, the 81 mm mortar, with which they were now equipped some two weeks after being assigned to the platoon. Before then, they had had to make do with "imaginary weapons of lumber" in their training. By mid-March they could even quote the manual for the mortar by heart. Every day, all day, they were marching several miles out from their hut for gun drill and field problems, then marching back to their huts for the evening.[19]

As Leckie had noted for his own squad, Phillips and his comrades regarded their squad as different from any other. It was its almost exclusive composition of Southerners that set their "rebel squad" apart from the others. In fact, in Leckie's view, the only common denominator of all the squads in H Company was their dislike of "officers and discipline."[20]

Over at the 37 mm antitank platoon of H Company, Cpl. George Parker was continuing his earlier training as a 37 mm gun crewman, firing on the special range for the weapon. The twenty-year-old native of Cameron, West Virginia, had enlisted back in September 1940 and after Parris Island had been assigned to the 1st Marine Division at Guantanamo Bay, Cuba, then moved on to Quantico, where he had begun his training on the 37 mm.[21]

In the 2nd Battalion's G Company, Pvt. John Joseph and the men of his Weapons Platoon had graduated from refresher training on their Springfield '03s and bayonet use to operation of the air-cooled .30-caliber light machine guns and the platoon's two 60 mm mortars. There was a lot of simulated firing and drilling. But Joseph himself was mainly occupied as a runner between the platoon and G Company headquarters.[22]

Communications exercises were keeping Pvt. Bill White busy three times a week at Headquarters Battery, 3rd Battalion, 11th Marines. It was hard work for the sixteen-year-old, laying telephone lines and setting up radio circuits for artillery exercises. And when everything was in place and working, White and the others would have to take it all down and start over again.[23]

On the afternoon of Monday, March 23, 2nd Lt. Bayard Berghaus received orders transferring him on temporary duty from Basic School at the Philadelphia Navy Yard to the State Military Reservation, Indiantown Gap, Pennsylvania, ninety miles northwest of Philadelphia, for "instruction in the practical use of infantry weapons." All 190 members of his 2nd Basic School ROC were to report in at the Marine Corps encampment there on March 29 to begin training that would extend over three weeks, topping off the eight weeks of basically classroom instruction at the school. This schedule implied that the twelve weeks' duration of the Basic School course was being shortened by a week.[24]

For George Codrea and his 318 classmates at Quantico, it was a similar story. On his battalion's return on a Saturday morning from a field exercise, they "found a bit of astounding news waiting." Their three-month 7th Reserve Officers Class, scheduled to end on April 30, was being shortened by a full month. As they stood to receive their diplomas in the Quantico Marine Corps base on April 1, they realized that this was indeed no April Fool's joke. Codrea and most of the others were now being ordered immediately to New River, North Carolina, to join the 1st Marine Division.[25]

"You shitheads are here to learn to fight!" Capt. Martin F. Rockmore bellowed as he swaggered up and down the line in front of Don Moss, an artist in civilian life, and the other assembled E Company men on April 6, 1942. They had just completed six weeks of basic training at Parris Island before reporting in to the 1st Marine Division at New River and being assigned to E Company, 2nd Battalion, 1st Marines, one of the battalion's three rifle companies. Private Moss had just completed art school and was working for a printing company when he had enlisted in the Marine Corps.[26]

After glowering at his new charges, Rockmore—a thirty-four-year-old graduate in economics from Saint Lawrence University, Canton, New York, and a Reservist now on active duty—turned Moss and some forty of the others in the platoon over to 2nd Lt. Dean Stover, who had just arrived at New River, too, and had been assigned to lead E Company's 1st Rifle Platoon. The twenty-three-year-old native of Salina, Pennsylvania, had graduated from Penn State University in June 1940 and had decided to leave his shipping clerk job to join the Marine Corps and enter Officer Candidate Class to avoid being drafted.[27]

Stover and the other second lieutenants accompanying him to New River from Quantico on April 5—graduates of the 7th Reserve Officers Class at Quantico—were finally providing the 1st Marine Division, and in Stover's case its 1st Marine Regiment, with many of the junior officers sorely needed to lead the platoons in each of the companies of the battalions. In addition to Stover, the 2nd Battalion was assigned six others, while another ten were ordered to the 1st Battalion.[28]

Two of the newly arrived graduates of the 7th ROC going to the 1st Battalion were assigned to 1st Lt. Nick Stevenson's C Company. Until then, C-1-1 was without any platoon leader officers. John Rentz, from Lancaster, Pennsylvania, and Jim Wagner, from Richmond, Virginia, were each given a rifle platoon to lead, leaving the positions of 3rd Rifle Platoon leader, Weapons Platoon leader, and executive officer (following the departure of 2nd Lt. Clarence Mabry) still to be filled.[29]

2nd Lt. Nikolai S. Stevenson in April 1941 as a member of the Fourth Reserve Officers Class, Quantico (March 1–June 1, 1941). *Courtesy of Nanette Stevenson.*

Stevenson, who was two weeks short of his twenty-third birthday, had been appointed CO of C Company only weeks earlier, when the only officer in the Company was the executive, Lieutenant Mabry (a January 31, 1942, graduate of the 6th ROC). A 1940 graduate of Columbia University, Stevenson had signed up for OCS that fall, and on graduation from the 4th ROC on June 1, 1941, he had been assigned as a platoon leader in the 3rd Battalion, 7th Marines, at Parris Island. When his commanding officer, Lt. Col. Julian N. Frisbie, was transferred to command the 1st Marine Regiment at New River on March 23, 1942, he brought Stevenson and two other junior officers from his 3rd Battalion with him to the 1st Marines. Frisbie gave Stevenson a company command position despite the fact that Stevenson was still only a second lieutenant, a problem of rank that would be rectified on April 14 when Stevenson was promoted to first lieutenant.[30]

Another junior officer Frisbie took with him to the 1st Marines was twenty-seven-year-old Charles H. Brush, already a first lieutenant in Frisbie's 3rd Battalion. Brush was appointed commanding officer of A Company on April 1, four days before the next two officers assigned to A Company arrived: 2nd Lts. John Jachym and Victor Valente, fresh out of the 7th ROC.[31]

The forty-seven-year-old Frisbie was well known as "the Bull" because of his huge frame—he weighed over 230 pounds—and the loud manner in which he shouted commands.[32] When his 3rd Battalion had been hived off from the 1st Marine Division and ordered to Samoa with the rest of the 7th Marines, Frisbie had apparently elected to remain behind to take command of the newly reformed 1st Marine Regiment from Lt. Col. James F. Moriarty. It was a temporary assignment only until Col. Clifton Cates could wind up his assignment as director of the Basic School in Philadelphia to take permanent command.

With the war underway, Cates was anxious to be given a regiment to command and had so asked the Marine Corps commandant, Maj. Gen. Thomas Holcomb, who had served as Cates's battalion commander in World War I, during a visit of

Holcomb in March to Indiantown Gap, where Berghaus and the other members of the 2nd Basic School ROC were undergoing weapons training. "I'll see what I can do for you," Holcomb had responded. Back in Washington, Holcomb had kept his word and orchestrated the command change in the 1st Marines.[33]

The influx of the new batch of recruits for the 1st Marine Division that arrived with Don Moss at New River brought the 1st Regiment and its three battalions nearly up to authorized strength, except for about half of the junior officer positions still vacant after the assignment of the second lieutenants of the 7th ROC. In the case of the 2nd Battalion, some 870 officers and men were now assigned, of which 180 were in Moss's E Company. Maj. William Chalfant III, a Reserve officer, had been transferred from his position as executive officer of 1st Battalion, 7th Marines, to the 2nd Battalion to serve—evidently temporarily—as its commanding officer.[34]

Rockmore and Stover soon had the new E Company recruits marching for miles on the hot, dusty red clay transformed from winter's mud, trudging under the weight of their combat packs. To Moss and the others, Rockmore seemed merciless, but they respected him as he set a blistering pace by his own leadership. As they crawled under barbed wire cradling their Springfield '03s and pulling themselves forward on their elbows, live ammunition was being fired over their heads. After they got past the wire, the command came to throw grenades. Finally, at the end of the day, covered with mud and sweat, and totally exhausted, they were marched back to their huts. But Moss for one felt that he was getting stronger physically and mentally as the days went by. He was proud to be succeeding as a Marine.[35]

Over at G Company, 1st Platoon leader George Codrea was under scrutiny by his senior noncoms. But Codrea already had his own ideas on how to win the support of the men he would now lead. Thus, when on this, his first day, he was being put on the spot by Sgt. Charlie Spakes, who was offering him chewing tobacco, he knew just how to respond. Familiar with chewing tobacco from his Akron days at B. F. Goodrich before joining the Marines, Codrea took the cut proffered and, closely watched by Spakes, chewed it with no problem. From that moment on, Spakes, who had enlisted in the Marine Corps in May 1935, bonded with his leader, at twenty-four one year younger than him. It was the same with Sgt. Jim Hancock, the other senior NCO in Codrea's platoon.[36]

While Codrea and the other 7th ROC officers were adjusting to their new

Noncommissioned officers (NCOs) of 1st Platoon, G Company, 1st Marines, at New River tent camp, North Carolina. *Front row, left to right:* Cpls. Peter J. Falbo and Joseph J. Faso. *Back row, left to right:* Cpl. Thomas E. Bailey, Sgt. James W. Hancock, and Plat. Sgt. Charlie F. Spakes. *Courtesy of George Codrea.*

commands in the 1st Marine Division at New River, 2nd Lt. Bayard Berghaus and his fellow junior officers in the 2nd Basic School ROC were making their own adjustments at Indiantown Gap Military Reservation. After the relative luxury of his urban accommodations in the Marine barracks at the Philadelphia Navy Yard, 2nd Lt. Bill Sager, a June 1941 graduate of the University of Virginia, found the "rough wooden barracks" to which he had been assigned in the Marine Corps encampment "very chilly," with muddy conditions outside. But the infantry weapons training, scheduled for the three weeks ending on April 18, was proving practical after the academic nature of the instruction at the Basic School. In addition to rifle range practice with their Springfield '03s, Berghaus, Sager, and the others were becoming familiar with the operation of the .30-caliber heavy machine gun and even were benefiting somewhat from very elementary instruction on the 60 mm and 81 mm mortars.[37]

"We're moving out to the boondocks! Enlisted men will fall out tomorrow morning in full marching gear." Sgt. Frank Stewart's order on April 24 was not greeted with enthusiasm by Bob Leckie and the others in H Company's 1st Machine Gun Platoon. But the men were not planning to prepare for the move without confirmation from the 2nd Battalion's new commanding officer.[38]

Much to the disappointment of the men, Lt. Col. Edwin A. Pollock authorized the order the next morning. The forty-three-year-old career Marine officer, from Augusta, Georgia, with almost twenty-two years in the service after graduation from The Citadel in 1921, had arrived two days earlier at New River from his previous post at the Marine Corps Schools, Quantico, to take up his new assignment, replacing Maj. William Chalfant III, who was shifted down to serve as Pollock's executive officer. Pollock was wasting no time in stepping up training.[39]

Loaded down with some twenty pounds on their backs, plus their weapons, Leckie and his platoon mates set out on their ten-mile trek over a narrow dirt road through pine woods. The whole battalion was on the march, with Leckie's platoon somewhere in the center.[40]

When Leckie and the others finally reached a canal that led out to the sea, they saw Higgins boats waiting for them. Ordered to climb aboard the thirty-six-man landing craft, they positioned themselves before the coxswains headed the plywood boats out to sea. As the boats rose and fell in the offshore surf, half of the men in Leckie's boat threw up. Then the assembled boats circled before they spread out in an assault line and headed to shore. When the craft ground to a halt on Onslow beach, Leckie and the others jumped out and began marching to their new camp, a mile inland. In a cold rain they began setting up the pup tents that would be their homes for the next weeks of maneuvers in the boondocks.[41]

Three days into their field exercises, Leckie's platoon was finally assigned an officer to lead it. Twenty-two-year-old Hugh Corrigan, along with 118 other Reserve second lieutenants, had just arrived at New River from Basic School, following orders issued on April 13 to report to the First Marine Division "on or about April 20th" for new duty. Corrigan had graduated in January 1942 from Dartmouth, just in time to receive his Reserve commission and be sent to Basic School on February 2 for eleven weeks of further training.[42]

In addition to Corrigan, sixteen other PLC graduates were assigned platoon leader positions in the 2nd Battalion, seventeen in the 1st Battalion, and eighteen in the 3rd Battalion. Now for the first time since the three battalions of the 1st Regiment were reactivated over two months earlier, all their junior officer positions were filled.

Joining Corrigan in the 2nd Battalion's H Company, Robert "Porky" Molloy found himself in charge of the 2nd Machine Gun Platoon and Bill Whorf the 3rd Platoon, while George Swinston—like Whorf a senior at Amherst College when commissioned—drew the 37 mm antitank gun platoon. Both Whorf and Swinston had been in the class of June 1942 but had their education aborted when they were commissioned and called to active duty in February.[43]

In Don Moss's E Company, twenty-year-old John Williams, a Dartmouth man from Orange, New Jersey, also set to graduate in June 1942, was assigned to the 3rd Rifle Platoon. Leadership of the Company's weapons platoon fell to A. William "Monk" Larson, who had also graduated from Dartmouth, but in June 1941, when he was commissioned.[44] Over at F Company, Ed Craig, slated to graduate in June 1942 from Columbia University, was assigned a rifle platoon. Similarly, Luther Jordan's education at Washington and Lee University in the class of June 1942 was cut short when he was commissioned in February 1942, and he now was taking over G Company's 3rd Rifle Platoon.

Three of the PLC graduates assigned to the 1st Battalion reported in to Nick Stevenson's C Company. Maurice Ahearn, from Marshfield, Massachusetts, and a graduate of Tufts College, was put in charge of the 3rd Rifle Platoon. Bob Fowler, a Dartmouth graduate in the Class of 1941, was appointed leader of the Weapons Platoon. Irving "Perry" Perine took over the 2nd Rifle Platoon as John Rentz shifted up to company executive officer.[45] All officer positions in C Company were now filled.

Assigned to the 3rd Battalion, Bayard Berghaus, one year Jordan's senior at Washington and Lee, found himself given command of one of the three rifle platoons in L Company. Three of his classmates at Basic School—Jay Griffith, William Fitzhugh, and Alfred Minervini—took over the other two rifle platoons and the weapons platoon.[46] All the junior officer positions thus fell to PLC graduates except that of the executive officer, to which Lou Shine, a 7th ROC graduate, was assigned.

Also sent to the 3rd Battalion, Bill Sager and his University of Virginia roommate, Herman Abady, were assigned leadership of the 1st and 3rd Rifle Platoons of K Company, under Capt. Bob Putnam. Phil Wilheit, second in seniority among the three based on date of commission, drew the 2nd Rifle Platoon. Before heading off to the boondocks to take over their new positions, they set themselves up in their new accommodations—small compartments in the wooden barracks just adequate for a cot, small table, and footlocker. At least the living quarters for the junior officers at New River were superior to those for the enlisted men in their pyramidal tents.[47]

Over at the 11th Marine Regiment's encampment, yet another Dartmouth man checked in on April 27 with the other PLC graduates. At twenty-five years, Gil Small was older than the others, having graduated and been commissioned in June 1938. At the time the Wayland, Massachusetts, native was called to active duty on February 6, he was working on his PhD in chemistry, so he was clearly the most highly educated of the 119 second lieutenants reporting in for duty. He was pleased to find himself assigned to I Battery, 3rd Battalion, as he didn't want an infantry platoon leadership position. But with no previous training in field artillery, he felt he was being "rushed into war."[48]

But Gil Small was not the oldest of the group. That distinction fell to the thirty-three-year-old Irving V. G. "Perry" Perine from East Orange, New Jersey. Perine's situation was markedly different from that of the others. He had joined the Marine Corps Reserve back in 1931, following graduation from Princeton University the year before, and had been ordered to Indiantown Gap with the much younger PLC graduates just for a refresher course in use of infantry weapons. On reporting in to New River, Perine, still a bachelor, was assigned as leader of a rifle platoon in the 1st Battalion's C Company. Despite his advanced age and tame civilian experience as an insurance underwriter, Perine—unlike Small—was pleased to get an assignment with an infantry unit, and a platoon leader's position was just the ticket, he figured.[49]

The field training was continuing apace in early May 1942, much to the displeasure of Pvt. John Joseph in G Company. He regarded the boondocks, with copperhead snakes and soot everywhere due to frequent burning of the trees, as a "God forsaken place." Under the command of their new platoon leaders, Joseph and the other men of the 2nd and 3rd Battalions were spending most of their time in exercises consisting of drills in scouting and patrolling and setting up surprise ambushes, as well as further instruction in the care and maintenance of their weapons.[50]

Along with their platoon second lieutenants, the men were also still practicing amphibious operations, this time using a wooden mock-up of the side of a transport that had been positioned on a bank of the Inland Waterway. They were ordered to climb up the stairs of the structure, then go down the cargo nets that hung over the sides and jump into Higgins boats. When the boats were loaded,

Men of G Company, 1st Marines, resting during field exercises at New River, May 1942. *Courtesy of Shirley Samaj.*

the coxswains would take them out into the open sea, assemble, and then speed in for landings on Onslow Beach.[51]

In addition to the daytime landing exercises, one was scheduled for night during the week allotted for the amphibious landing practice. During the night exercise, Bill Sager's K Company platoon managed to land right on target in their Higgins boat. However, his was the only one in the 3rd Battalion to reach its designated beach area. The others "screwed up" and became confused after missing their intended sections of Onslow Beach, wandering around in the dark and not knowing where they were.[52]

Gil Small was out in the boondocks, too, preparing himself to serve as a forward observer for his I Battery. In early May he found himself "running around in the pine woods, sweating and covered with soot from previous forest fires" while working on a communications problem. He was now joined as I Battery's other forward observer by newly minted 2nd Lt. Brooks Johnson, a native of Tupelo, Mississippi, promoted from sergeant and transferred to Small's I Battery from 3rd Battalion's Headquarters Battery.[53]

But the rumors were now flying among the men of the 1st Marine Division that they would be moving out soon from New River. Their suspicions were confirmed when on the night of Saturday, May 16, the sister 5th Regiment suddenly left its camp. The regiment's departure was preceded a day earlier by that of General Vandegrift himself and his 1st Marine Division headquarters, followed by some supporting units. But no one knew where they were going, except that it was an overseas deployment.[54]

On the other side of the world, at Moji Harbor, Kyushu, Japan, on May 19, 2nd Lt. Genjirou Inui was "struck dumb with surprise." He had just returned with the others of his 8th Independent Anti-Tank Company from operations on Java when they were ordered this day to embark immediately for another overseas assignment. They were now to be part of the Ichiki-shitai, under Col. Kiyonao Ichiki, commander of the 28th Infantry Regiment.[55]

Genjirou Inui after being appointed second lieutenant in the Imperial Japanese Army, August 15, 1940. *Courtesy of Genjirou Inui.*

Inui felt it an honor to be attached to the 28th Regiment, reputed to be the most highly skilled and best-trained of the Japanese Army's regiments at the outset of the Pacific War. It had been formed in 1900 mostly from farmers and laborers of Asahigawa, on Hokkaido, the northernmost island of Japan. As part of the 7th Division, the 2nd Battalion of the 28th had engaged in heavy fighting against the Russians during the Nomonhan campaign of June–September 1939, in which it had suffered 80 percent casualties.[56]

Slowly brought back to strength following its return to Japan from Manchuria, the 28th was put under the command of Ichiki in July 1941 on his transfer from his instructor position in Tokyo at the army's infantry school. A 1916 graduate of the Imperial Army's Military Academy (Rikugun Shikan Gakko), Ichiki had graduated from the infantry school in 1934. He was well known as a mercurial leader for his involvement as a battalion commander in northern China in the July 1937 incident that led to the Sino-Japanese war, although it was his regimental commander who had decided to escalate the fighting.[57]

At 1330 Inui and the other officers of the Ichiki-shitai assembled in the customs house of Moji for a meeting with their commander. Colonel Ichiki informed them that they were being ordered to capture Midway Island. Inui joined the others in giving three "Banzai!" for the Japanese empire and for the success of their new duty. Following the meeting, they all proceeded down to the harbor, where Inui's company boarded the transport *Zenyou Maru,* destination Saipan, where the detachment was to hold practice drills for the Midway operation.[58]

Col. Kiyonao Ichiki, commander of the 28th Infantry Regiment, Imperial Japanese Army. *USMC, Department of Defense, photo 150993.*

Back at New River, the 1st Marines men were assembled beside the Inland Waterway and the transport mock-up on May 26 to hear Secretary of the Navy Frank Knox address them on this the last day of the boondocks exercises. Bob Leckie for one felt that Knox had come down from Washington just to reassure himself that the 1st Marine Division—or what still remained of it at New River—actually existed. As soon as Knox finished his talk and reboarded the launch for the return trip from the waterway, the men broke camp and headed back to the previously unappreciated "comforts" of Tent City.[59]

Three days later, on Friday, Captain Rockmore assembled his E Company men for his own announcement. "You have 72 hours of leave. I want each and every one of you back here at 0900 on Monday. Dismissed." The COs at the other 2nd Battalion encampments were giving their men the same leave, too, as were those of the 1st and 3rd Battalions. To Sid Phillips in H Company, when newly appointed Capt. James Ferguson made the same announcement, it was "a sure sign we would be moving soon." The men were not to go beyond five hundred miles, but few were respecting the rule, as Phillips and many others set out hitchhiking to their distant homes.[60]

On the day before, the 2,559 men of the Ichiki-shitai were on the move, too, but it was no leave for them. After just having completed drills on Saipan for the Midway operation, they had boarded transports for their mid-Pacific destination. Plans called for the men to land on the southern shore of Eastern Island from barges, each carrying one hundred men. After halting at the reef, they would disembark and wade some two hundred yards through the lagoon and onto the beach in their assault on the Americans.[61]

The appointment of Ferguson, a 1936 graduate of the Naval Academy, to take over H Company from Captain Howland, who was shifting to command F Company, as of April 23 was the only company command change in a spate of reassignments in the 1st Marine Regiment in anticipation of the move. Also in his H Company, Acting Plat. Sgt. Carl Benson was promoted to second lieutenant and put in charge of the mortar platoon, assisted by 2nd Lt. Don Wheaton, a graduate of the 7th Reserve Officers Class the previous month.[62]

But the most important new assignment was that of Col. Clifton Cates, who took command of the entire regiment on May 3 from Lt. Col. Julian Frisbie, who now became his executive officer. For the forty-five PLC graduates assigned to the 1st Regiment, Cates was a familiar face; at the Navy Yard in Philadelphia he had been in charge of their ten-week Basic School training from February to April. He was now free to take up his regimental command. To 2nd Lt. Tom Barry of L Company, 3rd Battalion, Cates "always looked as if he'd stepped out of a bandbox with his FDR-type cigarette holder down to the spit shine on his shoes."[63]

Training had now slacked off following the return of the men from their Memorial Day weekend leave. In early June, rosters were being made up for train assignments for the trip all knew they would soon be taking. The Atlantic Coast Line Railroad was soon keeping Pvt. John Joseph and the others awake at night with its "eerie whistles" as it shunted cars into position at the New River base. Then on June 12 the men got the long-awaited word: they were to move out immediately.[64]

Like Vandegrift and those of the already deployed 5th Regiment, the commanders of the 1st Regiment's three battalions would have considered as regrettable the high-level decision taken in Washington to move their men out of New River before they were combat ready. It was bad enough that the boot camp training at Parris Island for their privates first class and privates—almost all Pearl Harbor recruits and now comprising some three-fourths of their battalions' strength—had been reduced from the prewar level of eight weeks to five to six weeks. (Experience would prove that the minimum length without sacrificing quality was eight weeks.) But now they would have to abort further training at New River and wait until after arrival at their new, undisclosed destination for it to resume.[65]

Some one hundred miles southwest of Midway Island, the convoy carrying the Ichiki-shitai was making a U-turn on June 9 to head back, destination Guam. Lt. Genjirou Inui and the others were simply informed that the Midway landing operations were "put off." Colonel Ichiki's assault force was ordered dissolved, and the men were transferred to the direct control of the Second Fleet. Five days earlier, the transports of the convoy had undergone an attack by nine American planes, but that was the only thing the officers and men knew for sure about the now-aborted Midway operation. They were being kept in the dark about the outcome of the naval battle of Midway.[66]

2

"Vandegrift, I Have Some Very Disconcerting News"

AFTER OVER THREE WEEKS AT SEA, 2nd Lt. Genjirou Inui and the rest of the Japanese Army's Ichiki-shitai welcomed the prospect of a "life on shore" as their transports entered Apra Harbor, Guam, on Saturday, June 13. But they were distressed to learn for the first time of the "crushing defeat" at Midway. Now they understood why they had been ordered to turn away from Midway Island four days earlier.[1]

As Inui and his comrades explored their new base, they were impressed by how well the Imperial Japanese Navy was governing the island, which had been seized from the Americans in December.[2] "Peace and order" prevailed everywhere. The islanders even left their houses unlocked.

They were also pleased with their new quarters: barracks on a slope overlooking the town of Apra that had formerly been occupied by the American Marines defending the island. The view of the ocean from the barracks was beautiful. Climbing up fifteen hundred meters through coconut groves, they were proud to see the Rising Sun ensign fluttering on the rooftop of the navy headquarters building below.

While the Ichiki-shitai was settling in at their new station, men of the 1st Marine Regiment were leaving theirs this Saturday. First-class Pullman cars in a long line were backed up at the New River rail spur of the Atlantic Coast Railroad, preparing to take on board the approximately sixteen hundred men of the regiment's 2nd and 3rd Battalions. Although their ultimate destination was secret, 2nd Lt. Tom Barry of the 3rd Battalion's I Company and other officers had been informed that they would be spending several months training in a "mild climate." The deployment thus appeared to be a station-to-station movement, not to a combat zone. But this scanty information did not filter down to the enlisted men, whose privates first class and privates were kept "in ignorant bliss."[3]

At 1705, at the head of his platoon, 2nd Lt. Bayard Berghaus left the 3rd Battalion's camp and, as the Marine band played, marched with his forty-one men in ranks the few blocks to the station, where they boarded the wagons to which they had been assigned. The men located their seats—twenty-six to a wagon—and stowed their rifles and combat packs overhead in the racks. Berghaus himself and his fellow L Company platoon leader Bill Fitzhugh merited a small private compartment with bathroom at the end of the wagon, as did all the officers shipping out. This train was carrying K and L Companies of the 3rd Battalion, and K Company's commanding officer, Capt. Bob Putnam, was serving as train commander.[4]

"From the halls of Montezuma to the shores of Tripoli"—the refrain from the Marine Corps hymn being played by the band—sent a "strange thrill" down Berghaus's spine as he stood in the passageway with his men and they were waved off by the rest of the battalion. But the sight of Captain Putnam's wife sobbing uncontrollably as the train pulled out at 1730 "made you sort of hurt inside," a feeling Fitzhugh shared with Berghaus.[5]

One hour earlier, Pfc. Sid Phillips and the other fifty-five men of his oversized mortar platoon of H Company, 2nd Battalion, had managed to fit into a wagon of the train carrying their battalion. They were in the last car of the train, and attached right behind it was the caboose with the train's crew. This was going to be the first really long train ride for most of the Depression-era kids, and they intended to enjoy it. The last to climb aboard was the battalion commander, Lieutenant Colonel Pollock, along with his headquarters company.[6]

At dinnertime, Phillips and his buddies proceeded to the wagon in the middle of the train for a "great meal." Their "high style living" continued as uniformed porters—one to a wagon—converted the sitting areas for the enlisted men into sleeping quarters, folding out the upper and lower berths. Phillips and his best friend, John "Deacon" Tatum, shared the lower berth.[7]

It was hot and the train was not air conditioned. Most of the sweating men opened their windows to catch some breezes, but this allowed in dust, soot, and cinders from the coal-burning steam locomotives.[8] No one complained, however; their first-class Pullman accommodations sure beat their tents at New River and in the boondocks.

At 0745 the next morning, the 3rd Battalion's troop trains arrived at Greenville, South Carolina. In the train carrying two batteries of the 11th Marines, 2nd Lt. Gil Small was amused at the appearance of his Basic School comrade 2nd Lt. Ray Winey, who had been sleeping in the lower bunk with the window down. Covered with soot, Winey looked "like a Welsh coal miner" to Small.[9]

That day it was the turn of the 1st Battalion, 1st Marines, to depart New River, the last remaining unit of the 1st Marine Division to leave. Most of the battalion's recently assigned platoon leaders were looking forward to their overseas deployment, but not C Company's Perry Perine. He was in a foul mood due to a switch in his position made by Lieutenant Colonel Cresswell, the 3rd Battalion's CO, just before boarding the train. He was being forced to give up his 2nd Rifle Platoon to become 1st Lieutenant Stevenson's executive officer. "They have taken my platoon away, and I have a full-time job as E.O. I didn't want it and didn't like it, and screamed, yelled, kicked, and bit like a yowling cornered bobcat, but they made it stick," he wrote his parents.[10] His new assignment as C Company's executive officer took away the opportunity to engage in direct combat as a platoon leader, his prime objective in serving in the Marine Corps.

As the troop trains headed west with the three battalions of the 1st Marines, the officers and men had little to do but enjoy the changing scenery. Lieutenants Berghaus and Fitzhugh also whiled away the time playing cards and throwing dice on and off during the day in the compartment that Lieutenants Sager and Herman Abady shared on their 3rd Battalion train. The only official duty they had was to disembark when their train reached a station and stand on the platform to prevent any civilians from boarding.[11]

On Guam, 2nd Lieutenant Inui and the others of the Ichiki-shitai were also enjoying a leisurely life in mid-June. They spent their time watching movies at the navy's lecture hall, including newsreels depicting the victory at Corregidor, biking around the island, and fishing. The only duty Inui had was to supervise the swimming training of the thirty-three men who didn't know how to swim. "I wish I could be stationed here forever," Inui confided to his diary.[12]

At 0840 on Thursday morning, June 18, Bayard Berghaus woke up to find himself in California. It was hard for him to believe that they were three thousand miles from New River. But he was glad the trip was soon ending. "Everyone is black" from the dirt and cinders, and he had no clean shirts.[13]

At 1338 his 3rd Battalion arrived in Oakland, its last stop. Berghaus and the others disembarked and boarded buses that took them across the Oakland Bay Bridge to the San Francisco waterfront. At Pier 44, a large ocean liner painted dark gray awaited them. They were informed that it was the former Swedish American Lines' *Kungsholm,* now rechristened the *John Ericsson* and in the service of the US government as a troopship. Berghaus was disappointed to find that his assigned stateroom on B deck didn't have a porthole and was only big enough for one person, though he, Al Minervini, and Abady would have to share it. It was made all the more crowded by their luggage.[14]

Sid Phillips also was unhappy about his accommodations on the transport *George F. Elliott,* to which his 2nd Battalion, 1st Marines, had been assigned. He and the other enlisted men didn't rate a stateroom, however small, but were instead crowded together in an open space, with wire racks as bunks, five high, side by side. Toilet facilities for all were in one room—a "head"—twenty toilet seats side by side and a few steel urinals some twenty feet long. "Forget privacy, forget odors, forget everything, sleep with your weapons, sleep with your pack, sleep with your life jacket, no sheets, just green USMC blankets, sleep in your clothing," Phillips recalled years later. And the gray-painted troopship was designated AP-13, "an ominous number we did not particularly care for."[15]

To the officers and men of the 1st Battalion boarding the USS *Barnett* (AP-10), the ship was "an old bucket of bolts with little character or outward grace about her." When the enlisted men descended below, they discovered how she could ingest the whole battalion and its equipment and supplies. The navy was stacking them on berths five high between seven-foot stanchions, "rather like cows at feeding except we were lying down in stacks," an A Company man complained.[16]

But the personnel of the three battalions of the 1st Marines did not have to spend much time aboard their three transports during the days the ships were being loaded. The 2nd Battalion commander, Lieutenant Colonel Pollock, was very generous in allowing liberty until the day the *Elliott* should sail. However, on a pay of only twenty-one dollars a month, most of which was spent on leave just before leaving New River, Phillips and his fellow privates first class and privates were too broke to really enjoy the sights of San Francisco.[17]

At least Phillips and the others in H Company's mortar platoon did not have to handle the loading of cargo ships carrying the 1st Marines' equipment, ammunition, and other supplies to the undisclosed destination, unlike the situation for George Codrea and his rifle platoon in G Company, among others. He had been ordered to supervise his men in loading some nine thousand tons of ammunition—small arms, hand grenades, mortar shells—from trucks into the largest hold of one of the attack cargo ships (but not according to combat loading procedures, another indication that the convoy was not heading for a combat zone). Using innovative albeit unorthodox methods, Codrea managed to reduce by two-thirds the ammunition his men had to manhandle, gaining for him the approbation of Lieutenant Colonel Pollock and freeing up some of his men for liberty.[18]

For the second lieutenants on the *Ericsson,* the free time was spent more pleasantly. Berghaus went into town the first day with Herman Abady, Bill Sager, Al Minervini, Bill Fitzhugh, and Phil Wilheit and took two rooms at the Saint Francis Hotel. After eating in Chinatown, Berghaus and Abady picked up some girls back at the hotel lounge and had "a fine time" that evening. Of the 11th Marines' officers on the *Ericsson*, Gil Small was spending his liberty visiting with old Dartmouth classmates and their families living in San Francisco.[19]

At 1550 on Monday, June 22, the MV *John Ericsson* finally weighed anchor and began heading west into the Pacific "for parts unknown," the largest of the three transports departing San Francisco. More than five thousand troops were jammed on board, including Lt. Col. Bill McKelvy's 3rd Battalion, the 3rd and 5th Battalions of the 11th Marines, the 11th's H&S Battery, the 1st Pioneer Battalion (minus A Company), and other supporting units of the 1st Marine Division.[20]

To Berghaus, the situation on board was "a mess." The men of his L Company were sleeping in four-deep bunks on the closed-in promenade deck "in virtual darkness," and their chow situation was keeping them in line waiting "almost all day." For the 11th Marines, it was taking "almost four hours to feed everybody," 1st Sgt. Abe Felber complained in his diary.[21]

On board the *George F. Elliott* carrying the 2nd Battalion, 1st Marines, conditions were similar, although the transport was much smaller than the *Ericsson.* In addition to crowded quarters, the food was "terrible and sparse," with only two meals a day, leaving the troops "hungry all the time," as Sid Phillips found. As the *Elliott* passed by Alcatraz Island on its starboard, one 2nd Battalion man, facetiously expressing the views of those on board, waved to a man on the dock and shouted, "Hey, lucky, want to trade places?"

After passing under the Golden Gate Bridge and entering the open sea, Berghaus noted that the *Ericsson* was now being joined in a convoy of "about six ships." His estimate was off—there were actually nine vessels, including the *Elliott* and the other transport, the *Barnett,* carrying the sister 1st Battalion and Headquarters and Service (H&S) Company of the 1st Marines. Only one warship was escorting them, the light cruiser *Boise,* carrying two seaplanes to observe for submarines.[22]

On the third day into the voyage, June 24, Berghaus noted that the convoy was heading in a southwesterly direction and was now off the coast of Mexico. The mystery of their destination was now solved—Vandegrift in New Zealand had sent a message informing them that they were going to Wellington, New Zealand, "and admonishing us about our behavior."[23]

To improve morale, the band of the *Ericsson* was playing music every morning and afternoon on the fantail to good effect. On the evening of June 25, the troops were treated to a concert on the bow, closing with the Marine Corps hymn, to which all rose and most sang along. To Berghaus, "The men seem more like kids when listening to the music, not as tough as they pretend."[24]

At his headquarters in the Hotel Cecil in Wellington, Major General Vandegrift was also relaxed this day, largely engaged in official calls and other matters of protocol. The training of the 5th Marines and other units of the first echelon of his 1st Marine Division that had arrived eleven days earlier, on Sunday, June 14, was proceeding according to plan. Even the radioed dispatch he had just received from his US Navy superior, Vice Adm. Robert L. Ghormley, COMSOPAC, asking Vandegrift to come up immediately to his Auckland headquarters, did not faze him. Vandegrift figured it was just for the official call on Ghormley, who had himself just taken up his position in Auckland as commander, South Pacific, on June 19. Ghormley had delayed the request days past the arrival of Vandegrift.[25]

After flying up to Auckland the following day with his staff, Vandegrift was "hustled directly to Ghormley's headquarters." This was not going to be just a protocol visit. In a brusque manner not characteristic of the "intelligent, quiet, most gracious individual" he knew, Ghormley immediately brought up the matter on his mind.[26]

"Vandegrift, I have some very disconcerting news," Ghormley announced.

"I'm sorry to hear that, Admiral," Vandegrift replied.

Handing Vandegrift a "top secret dispatch," Ghormley responded, "You will be more sorry when you read this."[27]

It was a secret dispatch dated June 24 (Washington time) from Adm. Ernest King, US Navy commander-in-chief, to Adm. Chester Nimitz, CINCPAC, that had been copied to Ghormley for his information. The JCS had directed that an offensive be launched against Japanese forces in the lower Solomons. Santa Cruz Islands to the east were to be seized and occupied, as were Tulagi and adjacent areas in the Solomons. The target date of the offensive was set for "about 1 August."[28]

Reading the dispatch, Vandegrift was shocked into disbelief. This was in effect a warning order that directly affected his 1st Marine Division as the only amphibious landing force under SOPAC's command. Vandegrift didn't even know what islands were in "the lower Solomons" or where Tulagi was. And his division was "spread over hell's half acre"—the 7th Regiment in Samoa, the 5th there in New Zealand, and the 1st still at sea.

"I just don't see how we can land anywhere by August 1st," Vandegrift told Ghormley.

In agreement, Ghormley replied, "I don't see how we can land at all, and I am going to take it up with MacArthur." He would ask for a temporary delay in the landing, but in the meantime, Vandegrift would "have to go ahead as best we can."[29]

Returning to Wellington the same day, Vandegrift began taking the initial steps in preparation for the operation thrust on him. Since its success would depend on surprise, all preparations would have to be carried out in "utmost secrecy." Those shouldering the heavy responsibility would mainly be Pearl Harbor enlistees rushed through abbreviated Parris Island recruit training and aborted New River training and most recently idled by the long sea voyage to New Zealand. First, his 5th Regiment, which had settled into its camp at Paekakariki and was undergoing "rigorous training" following its arrival on June 14, would reembark on three assault transports, ostensibly for preparing for "amphibious training" to disguise its real purpose. The 5th Marines along with the 2nd Battalion of the 11th Marines and other supporting units were designated Combat Group A, and the yet-to-arrive 1st Marines, supported by the 3rd Battalion, 11th Marines, and other units, were named Combat Group B. Working parties would unload ten cargo vessels and combat load the supplies and heavy equipment on twenty-three

Major General Vandegrift (*left*) greeting Brigadier General Rupertus and his rear echelon on their arrival at Pipitea Wharf, Wellington, New Zealand, July 11, 1942. *Courtesy http://www.ww2gyrene.org/photo_1.htm.*

transports and cargo ships, leaving behind tentage, trucks, and other vehicles and reducing fuel and food to sixty day's supply and ammunition to ten days of fire.[30]

In very high wind, low clouds, and rain, Bayard Berghaus watched from the deck as the *John Ericsson* approached Wellington Harbor and at 1320 tied up at Pipitea wharf. It was Saturday, July 11. The nineteen-day voyage from San Francisco to New Zealand was finally at a welcomed end.[31]

The band was the first off the *Ericsson*; it was to play the Marine Corps hymn on the dock as Major General Vandegrift and his operations officer, Major Jerry Thomas, boarded to greet the assistant division commander, Brig. Gen. William H. Rupertus, who was in charge of the rear echelon. Many of the men on the *Ericsson* were throwing packs of cigarettes to New Zealand soldiers on the docks, who "scrambled like kids after coins."[32]

On board the *George F. Elliott*, which had reached the wharf just after the *Barnett* with his 2nd Battalion, 1st Marines, Lieutenant Colonel Pollock was distressed about the change of plan for the rear echelon that he had received just before arrival. There would be no period in New Zealand to complete training. He had understood that it was to have included "landing practices in Wellington." Instead, they were to unload all ships and reload for combat on arrival. His nine-hundred-man battalion, reinforced with H Battery, 11th Marines, and a platoon each from the 1st Engineers, 1st Pioneers, and 1st Amphibious Tractor battalions, was being designated Combat Team 5 in Combat Group B. Pollock would command the team.[33]

Pfc. Sid Phillips was also disturbed by the plans for the battalion just after its arrival. Barely hours before the *Elliott* reached the Wellington docks, he'd heard an announcement that the battalion was going to engage in "large and extensive maneuvers" with the 5th and 11th Regiments. The men were to remain aboard the ship; there would be no liberty for his H Company men or the others.[34] But there was no word about any impending combat or the real reason they would be remaining on board, information to which only Vandegrift and his staff and senior commanders were privy.

But unlike the 2nd Battalion on the *Elliott* and the 1st Battalion on the *Barnett,* the 3rd Battalion as well as the other units on the *Ericsson* would not be held on board their ship. The *Ericsson* was not a combat transport, like the others, and had been used only to transport rear-echelon troops to their New Zealand destination.

The following morning, after their last official meal on the *Ericsson,* Berghaus and the others of Lieutenant Colonel McKelvy's 3rd Battalion picked up their combat packs and marched about a mile to Aotea Quay, where the attack transport USS *McCawley* awaited them for boarding. Berghaus and his fellow junior officers of L Company were pleasantly surprised on entering their assigned stateroom, number 18. It was a "vast improvement" over their room on the *Ericsson.*[35]

Gil Small and other officers and men of I Battery, 3rd Battalion, 11th Marines, were also headed towards Aotea Quay to board the *McCawley,* which they found out had been berthed there three weeks after its arrival from Tonga. Small would be sharing a stateroom with five other junior officers, all from his I Battery except for one infantry officer. He felt his new quarters were "immaculately clean" compared to those he had on the *Ericsson.*[36]

Small was also informed that his I Battery was being attached to the 3rd Battalion, 1st Marines. Unknown to him, the battery was now part of newly designated Combat Team 6, Combat Group B, under Lieutenant Colonel McKelvy. In addition to the artillery unit, the 3rd Battalion would also be supported with platoons of Pioneers, Amphibian Tractors, and Engineers.[37]

During the following days, Sid Phillips and the other privates and privates first class spent their time unloading the transports and cargo vessels berthed at Aotea Quay. It was hard physical labor carried out in constant and penetrating cold and rain. Boxes of supplies were simultaneously being off-loaded from vessels to form high stacks on the quay and, after being moved to other locations, reloaded on the attack transports and cargo vessels according to combat loading rules.[38]

Despite the nearness of the war to New Zealand, the unionized civilian dock workers had refused to do the work because of the foul weather, leaving Vandegrift with no other option than to order his own men to do it. Phillips and the other lowest-ranking enlisted men were angry that the New Zealand dock workers had forced them into performing such physical labor. They also resented that in the Marine Corps all such heavy labor was to be performed by privates and privates first class alone.[39]

Berghaus, Small, and the other junior officers and NCOs were assigned supervisory roles for the twenty-man working parties in unloading the *Ericsson* and reloading on the *McCawley*. For the low-ranking enlisted men, it was a brutal schedule: four hours on and four hours off, twenty-four hours a day. "They really hate to get up at night," Berghaus noted in his diary.[40]

Phillips wondered why they were combat-loading the *Elliott* if they were just going on "maneuvers." This seemed ominous to them, occasioning "endless rumors of what was in the making."[41] It appeared that even the junior officers didn't know what was behind the frenzied activity.

Phillips's working party was under the command of Sgt. Vester Albritton of his own mortar platoon, a fellow Southerner from Mississippi. Unlike the junior officers, he stayed with his men the whole time as he supervised the four-hour shifts. Since it was "too cold and noisy" to sleep aboard the *Elliott,* Phillips and his men slept under a thick canvas tarp on the floor in a corner of a warehouse on the quay.[42]

During their four hours off, when they weren't sleeping, Phillips and his contingent would walk a few blocks across the quay into downtown Wellington for a meal or a movie (to keep warm). They saw few young New Zealand men, almost all of whom were in military service overseas. At night the town was "browned out," with only a few lights showing.[43]

To Gil Small, the enlisted men now shifted to the *McCawley* surprisingly didn't seem to be that keen on the abundantly available females, who were "more than ready to be companionable." He often heard from a man just back from his four-hour shore leave: "If that's liberty, give me death!" Small himself, always highly observant, was put off during his frequent visits to town when he noticed that many girls of eighteen had complete sets of false teeth, which he attributed to the lack of calcium in the water and soil. Cosmetics were little used. But he found the people in general to be very friendly, and he enjoyed listening to them talk in their cockney accent.

Unloading the *Ericsson* was supposed to be completed by 1600 on July 16, with departure on the *McCawley* set for the following morning, Small was informed. But he doubted this schedule could be adhered to. "Confusion still reigns with the infantry from Col. [McKelvy] and Major [Walker Reaves] on down," he observed, compared to the efficiency of his I Battery in the loading process, in his estimation. On the afternoon of July 15, the battery's gear had begun coming on board.[44]

There was still no definite word yet on where they would be sent, but it didn't look like it would be for maneuvers. Small had heard that "an Admiral from the States" would be coming aboard, "so we feel no doubt we are 'loading for bear.'"[45]

Unknown to Small and the other junior officers and enlisted men, Major General Vandegrift this day was meeting in Auckland with that same admiral and Vice Admiral Ghormley. Rear Admiral Richard Kelly Turner, Vandegrift's superior as commander of the amphibious force in the envisaged landings, had just arrived earlier that day. At the conference, the irascible Turner objected to aspects of the plan that Vandegrift's operations officer, Lt. Col. Gerald C. Thomas, had developed, but with no plans of his own he could not stop Ghormley from going ahead with it, now code-named Watchtower. Thomas had learned earlier that Guadalcanal should be the focus for the operation, as had Turner at the same time. Intelligence had indicated that the Japanese were building up an airfield base on the lower Solomons island.[46]

But Vandegrift explained that because of the heavy rains, loading of the vessels for the operation was delayed, and thus he couldn't meet the original sailing date (set for the next day). Turner agreed; his naval forces would not be able to keep to the original schedule either. To facilitate meeting the August 1 target landing date, Vandegrift offered to forego the rehearsal practice planned in the Fijis from July 27, but Turner decided to go ahead with the Fiji practice anyway and reset the departure date from New Zealand as July 21, a delay of five days. With the rehearsal now confirmed, and taking into consideration the delayed departure

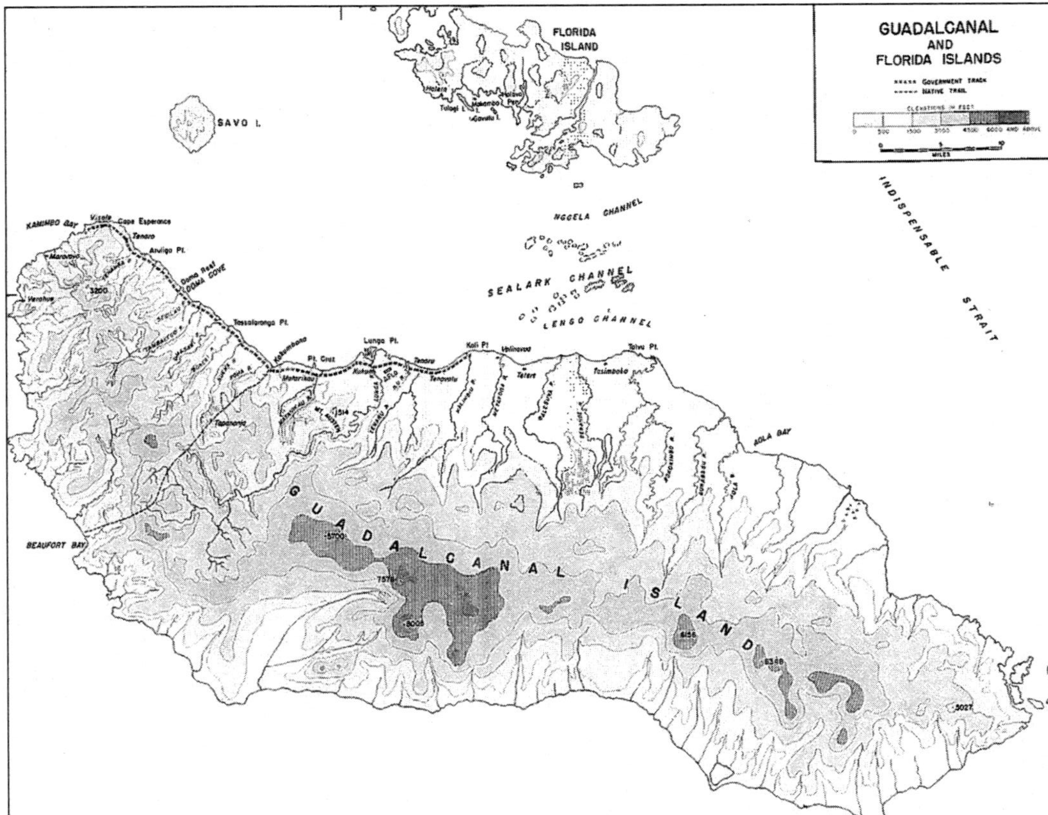

Guadalcanal and Florida Islands. *Army Map Service; Map IV in John Miller, Jr.,* Guadalcanal: The First Offensive.

date, Vandegrift secured Ghormley's approval to set the landing date for six days later. Nimitz and King concurred, and a new date of August 7 was subsequently incorporated into Ghormley's Operation Order 1-42.[47]

On the following day, Thursday, July 16, regimental and battalion commanders of both echelons were brought into the picture for the first time. Vandegrift had called them together for a division conference at his headquarters in the Hotel Cecil in Wellington to brief them on the operations plan. Col. Clifton Cates's 1st Marines, along with Col. Leroy Hunt's 5th Marines, would be landing "on the Japanese-occupied island of Guadalcanal," with Brig. Gen. William Rupertus taking one battalion from the 5th Marines along with a battalion of the 2nd Marines plus the 1st Raider and Parachute Battalions to land on Tulagi—across from Guadalcanal—and its neighboring islets.[48]

"Guadalcanal? Never heard of it before," Lieutenant Colonel Pollock reacted when informed of the objective for his 2nd Battalion. With members of his staff, he now went over the orders, a map, and photos given them before being handed the orders for his Combat Team 5. The key map was one of the northern coast of Guadalcanal, a primitive rendering drawn on July 14, 1942, based on a local's memory.[49]

Back on board the *Elliott,* Pollock met with his staff to begin making preparations for the landing on Guadalcanal. Earlier, on July 10, while still at sea, Pollock had shaken up his staff and brought in a new battalion operations officer. He had replaced the incumbent, 2nd Lt. Billy Pierce, with E Company's executive officer, Bill Larson, who had earlier been moved up from his initial weapons platoon position. Pierce, a fellow PLC graduate with Larson, was reassigned to take over Larson's old weapons platoon job in E Company.[50]

Larson had been taken by surprise by Pollock's decision and was not happy about leaving his old company, but "I had no choice in the matter." He figured that Pollock had been impressed with Larson's work in handling the billeting of his 2nd Battalion on the *Elliott* in San Francisco, a special task Pollock had assigned him. In his new capacity as Bn-3, Larson would now be working closely in planning for the Guadalcanal landing with the battalion intelligence officer, George Stratton, yet another fellow PLC graduate.[51]

While Vandegrift and his commanders were absorbed this day with planning and preparation for the forthcoming landings on Guadalcanal and Tulagi, the junior officers and enlisted men were continuing the loading of the transports and cargo ships on Aotea Quay in cold and rain. Gil Small of the 11th Marines' I Battery, along with the 2nd Battalion's Herman Abady of K Company and Larry Hennessy of M Company, spent the entire afternoon assisting Lieutenant Colonel McKelvy in supervising the movement of shells from the ammunition dump to the side of the *McCawley* for loading. Small was unhappy with the poor organization and execution of the job. They had to supervise men not of their own units and "whom we didn't even know," resulting in poor control over them. In his view, NCOs, rather than second lieutenants, should have been assigned the job and could have more properly provided the supervision.[52]

The next day it was the turn of Bayard Berghaus and fellow L Company officer Jay Griffith to supervise working parties in the loading of the *McCawley.* McKelvy's executive officer, Maj. Walker Reaves, had assigned them watch periods for their supervision assignment. "Not much fun," Berghaus complained after putting in his first watch, 2200 to 0200. "Hardest part is rousing the men to go out," he felt.[53]

The next watch for Berghaus and Griffith was from 1200 to 1700 the following day, supervising the loading of the cargo vessel *Libra* (AK-53). But at least the sun had finally made an appearance, easing the task, although it was still "plenty cold, standing in the wind." Then on the night of July 18/19, they had to get up for a 0200 to 0600 watch. Berghaus was so drowsy that he slept through breakfast and lunch after he returned to his stateroom. The next day he had to get up at 0530 to join Griffith in supervising the procurement and moving of grenades from the ammo dump to be loaded on the *Libra,* and they were not relieved until 1200.[54]

If the supervisory work was a pain for Berghaus and his fellow junior officers, it was proving downright exhausting for Sid Phillips and the lowly enlisted men tasked with providing the physical labor. Phillips and the 2nd Battalion men on the *Elliott* were spending days and nights on Aotea Quay in freezing cold and drizzle, mostly stacking cases of grenades and clover leaves of artillery and mortar shells and moving rolls of barbed wire to be loaded on the *Elliott* for their infantry battalion and supporting Pioneer and Engineers platoons and H Battery of the 11th Marines' artillery. But on Tuesday, July 21, their ordeal was over. Combat loading of the *Elliott* was finally completed after nine days of round-the-clock labor, "the roughest duty" Phillips and the others would ever endure in the Marine Corps.[55]

On the sister transport *McCawley,* loading work was also finished that day, ending all dock working parties, much to the relief of Berghaus and his fellow junior officers. At 1625, "we cast off the hawsers and pushed out into the stream and dropped the hook" for the night layover in Wellington harbor. All liberty had been canceled. Two days earlier, Gil Small had noted many "high ranking officers" coming aboard, and on the day before leaving they were joined by Major General Vandegrift and his staff. Indeed, as confirmation to Small, it appeared that the *McCawley* was going to be the flagship of "the expeditionary task force." In the harbor with the *McCawley* he noted the presence of other transports, supply ships, cruisers, and destroyers.[56]

That night, Sid Phillips and his buddy Pfc. John "Deacon" Tatum were up on the deck of the *Elliott* as she lay in Wellington Harbor, "talking about the future and what it might hold in store for us." The sea was quite rough and a cool, strong wind was blowing. "Where are we going?" Phillips and Tatum wondered. No one knew but Lieutenant Colonel Pollock, he figured.[57]

On a "beautiful, fair day," the morning of Wednesday, July 22, 1942, Gil Small observed the "impressive panorama" of the low, steep hills surrounding Wellington Bay as the *McCawley* moved out of the landlocked harbor at the head of the column of eight transports and four cargo ships. Outside the harbor, five cruisers and seven destroyers picked them up to form the convoy, now heading northeast. The last land view was of the "large, snow clad peaks" on the South Island. Just before noon, cruising positions were taken up, with three cruisers in the lead, three columns of transports and freighters, four abreast, and the two other cruisers in the rear, with the destroyers around the edges. It was a formidable force, but for 1st Sgt. Abe Felber of H&S Battery, 11th Marines, on board the *Hunter Liggett,* "I would feel safer if there was an aircraft carrier or two to join us."[58]

As he departed Wellington on board the *George Elliott,* Lieutenant Colonel Pollock was more preoccupied with the state of his supplies and equipment than the view or the security of the convoy. He had had "an awful time getting enough together" to outfit his 2nd Battalion for its upcoming landing on Guadalcanal. It was very upsetting for him that most of his equipment was left behind in Wellington.[59]

It was not only Pollock's battalion that was leaving for a combat operation inadequately equipped and supplied. Because of "extreme shortage" of shipping, Vandegrift was forced to order that "only that which is necessary to fight and live" should be taken. As a result, bulk consumables—fuels, lubricants, and food—were cut to sixty days of supply and ammunition allowance to ten days of fire for all weapons, while less than half of the motor transport that had been authorized for the division was loaded. Part of the 1st Tank Battalion and the entire 4th Battalion of the 11th Marines, with its 155 mm howitzers, had to be left behind, too.[60]

When Bayard Berghaus and his fellow 3rd Battalion comrades on board the *McCawley* awoke on the morning of Thursday, July 23, they found themselves "in a man-sized storm, with rain, high wind, and huge waves." Chairs had to be roped together "to keep us from sliding all the way across the ward room and back." Gil Small was the exception in not becoming seasick. Conditions were "pretty rugged" for his I Battery men, quartered in the foremost compartment, what with all the "pitching, rolling, and water washing over the well deck above them."[61]

But at least the suspense was now over about their combat destination. It was Guadalcanal. The junior officers and men were given "the dope" on their first operation. Berghaus felt that arrangements seemed "ok." "We'll have a lot of support," he felt.[62]

The next day sea conditions were no better: wind, rain, and huge waves. "The ship is rolling like the devil and the waves are coming over the bow and sides." Berghaus had a difficult time inspecting the sentries on his guard duty: "Many were seasick and having a tough time to keep on their feet." On board the *Hunter Liggett,* 1st Sergeant Felber was forced to take to his bunk. "The ship was plunging and wallowing in great long swells, . . . the decks were awash . . . the seas striking against the *Liggett* with a noise like battery rams."[63]

That evening, on the *Barnett,* 2nd Lt. Irving Perine was too worked up to worry about keeping his balance in the rough weather. The 1st Battalion's commander, Lieutenant Colonel Cresswell, had called him into his office with some startling news. He told Perine that "for some time" he'd wanted Perine on his staff, and now the time had come. He was to be transferred from his executive officer position with C Company to become the battalion intelligence officer. "It's flattering and definitely a promotion," Perine wrote to his parents, though he would have to serve out the year to get his silver first lieutenant bar. While he felt inadequate at present for the promotion, "I am determined to learn fast and do a good job," he wrote in his letter.[64] But it seemed his aspirations to participate in combat operations were now fading further away.

When day broke on Sunday, July 26, the troops on board the transports were relieved to find that the storm had finally run its course, the sea was now calmer, and their ships steadier. At 1230 Felber spotted a group of war vessels on the horizon approaching their convoy. Straining to make them out, it looked to Berghaus as if there were thirty to fifty of them, including two carriers, "said to be the *Enterprise* and the *Saratoga*," and "oodles of cruisers and destroyers." Gil Small made out three carriers, including the *Wasp*. As far as the eye could see from the *McCawley*, "there were ships all over the sea, even to the horizon, a very impressive sight," he noted in his diary.[65]

By midday Monday, July 27, the mountainous islands of Fiji were sighted, and cruising speed diminished. They were now in the Koro Sea, with calm waters, "blue and extremely clear and transparent, more than I have ever seen," Berghaus noted. Most of the warships in the convoy had left the transports and cargo vessels, reportedly to go ahead and meet them where the rehearsals would be staged. On the *Hunter Liggett*, Felber had read a dispatch circulated on the ship: "The landing rehearsals this week involve landing through reefs on coral beaches on Koro Island." Most of the men were busy making up packs for the landing. On the *Elliott*, Deacon Tatum, just appointed acting corporal in his mortar squad, was getting everything ready to disembark at 1600 the following day with his buddy Sid Phillips and the others in the Higgins boat to which they had been assigned. On the *McCawley* there were drills in the morning and afternoon for assembly in preparation for debarkation. Gil Small spent most of the afternoon in the wardroom, preparing a grid sheet for the Koro landing, making use of "what little drafting ability I have."[66]

At 0600 on Tuesday, July 28, Gil Small was awakened for an early breakfast on the *McCawley* but spent most of the rest of the morning waiting around for the Koro landing exercise to commence. Finally, at 1145, the order was given and he went over the side with the others, clambered down the cargo nets and jumped into the bobbing Higgins boat assigned him as a forward observer for his I Battery.[67]

After milling around at the line of departure until 1400, Small's wave finally began speeding in a line abreast towards the section of the northern shore of Koro—code-named Red Beach—designated as the landing area for the three battalions of the 1st Marines. But shortly into the thirty-five-hundred-yard dash to the beach, the engine of Small's boat began overheating, and the coxswain was forced to abort the attempt. The Higgins boat was towed back to the *McCawley*, where Small and the other thirty-six occupants were transferred to a ramp boat and set out again for Koro. But the day's frustrations were not over for them.

About halfway to the shore they met the *McCawley*'s first wave, carrying Berghaus and the others in the rifle companies of the 3rd Battalion. It had been ordered back without landing because its boats had encountered large coral heads that could have damaged their propellers if they had continued on. So it was back to the *McCawley* for Small's boat too.[68]

With a few exceptions, it was the same story for the *Elliott* and the *Barnett*, carrying the other battalions of the 1st Marines. They, too, were prevented from going ashore because of the coral menace. However, some boats of the 2nd Battalion's E and F Companies in the first wave off the *Elliott* did manage to continue all their way in to the shore, avoiding the coral heads. The coxswain of the Higgins boat carrying 2nd Lt. Ed Craig and his F Company platoon managed to get the boat right up on the beach, where the men jumped overboard onto *terra firma*. But when 2nd Lt. Dean Stover in E Company saw the men in the Higgins boat just ahead of him jumping overboard into water over their heads and struggling to get back on board, he refused to let his platoon's men repeat that performance and held them in the boat until he was informed that the landing operation had been canceled and the boats ordered to return to the ship. However, the ramp boats carrying forward observer Nat Mewhinney and the H Battery artillerymen in the third wave off the *Elliott* were able to get in closer than Stover's boat and disembarked in water only waist deep.[69]

Sid Phillips, Deacon Tatum, and their fellow mortarmen in H Company were in the fifth wave off the *Elliott* and were approaching the shore, having eluded the coral up to that point. But some one hundred yards short of their landing location they were ordered to abort and head back to their transport. Phillips and many of the others were sorely disappointed: they were looking forward to going ashore on a tropical island for the first time in their lives. It was the second upsetting development for Phillips and his platoon. During the loading of their boat, a fifty-pound roll of communications wire fell from the deck into the boat, striking Pfc. Earl Jontiff a grazing blow that broke his arm. Without the quick intervention of Deacon Tatum, who saw the falling wire just in time and pulled Jontiff to the side, their comrade most likely would have been killed.[70]

The following morning, at 0905, the *Elliott* sent out boats to pick up those officers and men of E and F Companies and H Battery who had spent the night on Koro. When they came on board again, they regaled their envious 2nd Battalion comrades with descriptions of the "coconuts, lemons, and bananas, and chicken" they had eaten the previous day and evening. "Our mouths were watering for that delicious fruit we were missing," Deacon Tatum recorded in his diary that day. Separated from the others of his F Company, Ed Craig had stumbled into a big barbecue being put on that evening by several platoons of the 5th Marines as they roasted pigs and chickens left behind by the natives. The party was broken up when the CO of the 5th Marines discovered this violation of orders. Pvt. B. J. Wilson and the others in F Company's 1st Platoon, however, enjoyed no barbecue that evening. They had spent a sleepless night on the ground, kept awake by the noise of the engines of Higgins boats and shouts of coxswains trying to free their landing craft from the coral heads on which they were stuck.[71]

For the officers and men on the *McCawley,* July 29 proved a boring, hot, and humid day. With no men to pick up on Koro, the flagship just lay off the island all day, with nothing but a boat drill and a school lecture to break the monotony. Gil Small spent most of the day "in the sack" but did note that "staff, divisional, and intelligence officers" from other ships were coming on board and were engaged "in deep discussions."[72]

To International News Service (INS) correspondent Richard Tregaskis, on board the *McCawley,* the flagship "was practically insane with activity, clogged with Marine officers anxious to get their orders and settle their plans." They needed to review their regiment- and battalion-level plans as based on the division's Operation Order 7-42 issued in New Zealand on July 20 before their departure for Koro as well as the discussions held that day on the *McCawley.*[73]

On the third day of the exercise, Thursday, July 30, the officers and men on board the *McCawley*, *Elliott*, and *Barnett* repeated the first day's landing operation, except that as per orders they proceeded in their boats only to a line two thousand yards short of Red Beach, arriving between 1230 and 1300. To go further was to run the risk of hitting coral heads. The half-attempt was synchronized with naval bombardment and aerial attacks on the shore. While waiting for the order for his wave to return to the *McCawley,* Gil Small scanned the shore with his field glasses and was able to distinguish the primitive huts of villagers along the coastline. So far, he was unimpressed with the organization for the operation; he felt that the "long wait imposed on the men at the assembly areas" prior to debarkation from the *McCawley* was "quite demoralizing."[74]

The next day the *McCawley* was experiencing engine trouble, which Berghaus and Small took as the reason the flagship was just lying off Koro all day. They did not know that no further landing exercises were scheduled for that final day of the operation except for the landing of the 2nd Marines on another beach. For Berghaus, the only interesting item of the day was when the antiaircraft cruiser *San Juan* passed near their stationary flagship; he was impressed with how "very up to date" she was.[75]

On the *Elliott,* Sid Phillips, Deacon Tatum, and the other enlisted men of the 2nd Battalion got the word on the objective of their up-coming amphibious assault—an island called Guadalcanal. The Japanese were building an airfield on it and had to be stopped. But their battalion and the other two of the regiment would have to cross three rivers. The "high grass, swamps, old plantation, and coconut trees" would provide "good cover for Japs."[76] The going would be easier for the 5th Marines, ordered to head due west and hug the shoreline on their mission to seize the airfield.

The information that the 2nd Battalion men were provided derived from two documents: the 2nd Battalion operation order drawn up three days earlier by the battalion's operations officer, 2nd Lt. Bill Larson, and the intelligence note prepared on July 29 by the intelligence officer of the regiment, 2nd Lt. George P. Hunt. According to the battalion operations order, after landing on Beach Red, about five miles east of Lunga Point, at 0 + 50 on D-Day, E and F Companies would head west-southwest on an azimuth of 240 degrees, followed by G and H Companies, with the objective of seizing a "grassy knoll" about four miles south of Lunga Point. They would first ford the Ilu River, cross the corner of the Tenaru Plantation, then traverse a grassy plain before crossing the headwaters of the Tenaru River into dense woods, and finally cross the Lunga River. This "direction of attack" was marked on a map that Hunt had prepared that day as traced from an aerial photo.[77]

At about 1700 that afternoon of July 31, the *Elliott* and other ships in the task force stood out to sea, their next destination the Solomons. On the *McCawley,* as he went below for dinner, Major General Vandegrift was reflecting on the poor execution of the rehearsal for the Guadalcanal landing, which he regarded as a "bust." "I shuddered to think what would happen if those beaches turned out to have been defended in strength," he recalled in his autobiography.[78]

Not privy to the worries of their commanding general about the chances of his men against a strongly defended beachhead, Tatum, Phillips, and W. O. Brown were spending the night sharing their own anxieties about the upcoming operation on Guadalcanal as the Fijis faded further and further away. "This dope on the island has brought a queer feeling over us all. . . . We can either meet our doom or else victory," Tatum confided to his diary that night.[79]

When Bayard Berghaus came up on the deck of the *McCawley* on the morning of Saturday, August 1, he could no longer see Koro to the east, and even the larger islands of Fiji they had passed late the night before "were only dim shadows on the horizon." He found it hard to believe that in a few days he would be in battle. While he had felt depressed about the thought when the *McCawley* pulled out of Wellington ten days earlier, now he actually looked forward to entering into combat with the Japanese on Guadalcanal.[80]

The following days on board the transports heading slowly for Guadalcanal proved monotonous. For Deacon Tatum on the *Elliott* it was even "a drudgery." Tatum and his buddy Sid Phillips were spending much of their time on deck singing and talking. On Monday, their H Company commander, Captain Ferguson, briefed them and their machine gun platoon counterparts on what they could expect when they entered battle with the Japanese. He bolstered the mortar platoon's morale by emphasizing the "essential role" the platoon would play with its 81 mm mortars.[81]

Shells for their mortars were issued on the morning of August 5, along with .30-caliber ammunition for the machine gun crews of the Company. Jack Rivers and the others in the three machine gun platoons loaded belts with a hand-cranked loader until their belts and boxes were full, alternating ball, tracer, and armor-piercing ammunition. The ammunition carriers of the mortar platoon were issued "huge, green canvas poncho-like contraptions" with three pockets each, to be worn over their full packs and loaded with six rounds of mortar shells, "a staggering load" for the men.[82]

On board the *McCawley,* Berghaus was busy all the following day supervising the issue of .30-caliber ammunition to his L Company riflemen. But he was concerned that the men "had lost their hardness" since leaving New River seven weeks earlier. "Our cramped quarters and hurry had left us no space or time for exercise," he lamented.[83]

Later that Thursday, August 6, just before nightfall, Major General Vandegrift was up on the deck of the *McCawley,* standing by the rail and worrying about the chances for his men in the momentous operation that lay ahead for them the next morning. Many of his Marines were "but boys a few months out of boot camp." Their planned New Zealand training had been aborted, and they had only ten days' supply of ammunition. He could have listed "a hundred reasons why the operation would fail."[84]

But he had "prowled the decks" of the flagship the days since leaving Koro, observing the young officers and veteran sergeants under his command as they prepared the men for the vicious combat they could expect. They were all Marines, he reasoned, and they were fighting men, his "secret weapon." He knew that "if the job can be done, we somehow were going to do it."[85]

As Vandegrift's men made final preparations early the evening of August 6 for disembarking from their transports for battle the next day, Colonel Ichiki and his twenty-five-hundred-man detachment on Guam were preparing to board their transports, but not for a combat zone destination. The Ichiki-shitai had been ordered back to Japan. At 1720, 2nd Lt. Genjirou Inui and the others went aboard the *Daifuku Maru* and *Boston Maru* in Apra harbor. Inui was happy to be returning to his homeland and to see his parents and fiancée again, but he would miss Guam and the pleasant lifestyle he'd experienced on the tropical island the past two months.[86]

3

"I'm Beginning to Doubt Whether There's a Jap on the Whole Damned Island"

ON BOARD THE *BARNETT*, 2nd Lt. George P. Hunt was up before dawn on Friday, August 7. A rising star in the Corps, the Amherst graduate had turned twenty-four three weeks earlier, and, only four months out of his 7th Reserve Officers Class at Quantico, he was already the 1st Marine Regiment's intelligence officer (R-2) on the staff of Colonel Cates. After finishing his breakfast of steak and fried eggs, Hunt went up on deck and in the early light took his first look at Guadalcanal. He could make out what he believed was Grassy Knoll on the operation map, and Lunga Point—two key features of the operation in which he was participating—and identified the Lunga River flowing into the sea. As the sun began to rise, the eight-inch guns of the cruiser ahead of the *Barnett* roared, belching "fire and black smoke," followed by shelling by other cruisers and destroyers in the column steaming down the north coast of the island. Then SBD Dauntless dive bombers and Grumman Wildcats from the carriers tore into Japanese defenses.[1]

Hunt was pleased to see that division Operation Order 7-42 was going according to plan so far. Next on the timetable was for the 5th Marines (less one battalion) at zero hour (set at 0910) to head from the line of departure for landing on Beach Red, the sixteen-hundred-yard stretch of beach to the east of the Lunga designated as the landing site, followed fifty minutes later by his 1st Marines off the *Elliott, McCawley,* and *Barnett.* They would land in a column of battalions, with Lieutenant Colonel Pollock's 2nd Battalion in the lead, followed by Lieutenant Colonel McKelvy's 3rd Battalion and finally Lieutenant Colonel Cresswell's 1st Battalion.[2] Hunt himself, along with Colonel Cates and the regiment's headquarters company, would leave the *Barnett* with the 1st Battalion.

"Get ready, boys," 2nd Lt. Bill Whorf cried out to his 3rd Machine Gun Platoon huddled together on the deck of the *Elliott.* The first waves carrying the riflemen of E, F, and G Companies had left the transport, and now it was the turn of his H Company (weapons) to form part of the fourth wave. Pvt. Al Schmid, the forty-pound tube and water jacket of his .30-caliber heavy machine gun slung over his shoulder, lowered himself down the cargo net and jumped into the bobbing Higgins boat assigned to Whorf's machine gun platoon. Pvt. Jack Rivers followed with the fifty-four-pound tripod, then the squad's other men passed the gun parts down, boxes of ammunition and steel carts following afterwards. Even more loaded down were H Company's mortarmen, struggling to get their tubes, bipods, base plates, and shells over the side while also lugging their rifles and back packs as they worked their way down into ramp boats.[3]

Nearby, 2nd Lt. Hugh Corrigan's machine gun platoon was assembled and waiting the word to go when Gunny Sgt. James Blalock bellowed, "First platoon over the side! Down the cargo nets!" Pfc. Robert Leckie, lugging his .30-caliber M1903 Springfield and combat pack, hung on the end of the cargo net, then jumped, managing to land in the Higgins boat before it rolled away. When the landing craft was loaded with its thirty-seven occupants plus three-man crew, the coxswain detached it from the *Elliott* and joined up with the other boats in the wave. To Leckie, the circling boats looked like "monster water bugs on frolic." Crouching below the gunwales with his platoon buddies, he felt the boat swing slowly around to face the shore. Then its vibrations increased as the coxswain applied power, and it began its dash from the line of departure for the shore some five thousand yards away in a line of boats abreast. Praying, Leckie was sure that this was going to be his last act on earth.[4]

After speeding over the water at twelve knots for some twelve minutes, Leckie's boat "struck the shore, lurched, then came to a halt." Instantly, Leckie and the others were up and over the side. In Al Schmid's boat nearby, halted just short of the beach, Bill Whorf was the first man over. Jack Rivers jumped into water up to his chest and caught the tripod a squad mate tossed to him. He was followed by Al Schmid, holding the tube over his head as he waded to the beach. After sprinting to the spot assigned to them on the beachhead, Schmid, Rivers, squad leader Cpl. LeRoy Diamond, and the others "flopped down in the sand," then got their Browning machine gun set up. But after only a few minutes, Whorf ordered them to move and set up further inshore.[5]

In the ramp boat carrying a section of H Company's mortar platoon, Sid Phillips endured the wisecracks of the platoon's "comedians" about enjoying "the last few minutes of your life" before the coxswain applied full power on the 225-horsepower diesel engine and joined the others in the dash to the beach. Looking over the side, Phillips developed a lump in his throat when he saw the American flags "streaming out" from the sterns of the boats that "seemed to stretch to eternity." Bracing themselves as their boat slid up on the beach, Phillips, his buddy Deacon Tatum, and the others "charged out, ready to do or die," only to be greeted by riflemen of the first wave, "laughing at us and opening coconuts."[6]

The ramp boat carrying Pfc. Les Clark's section of H Company's mortar platoon also beached itself near Phillips's boat. When the ramp was lowered, Clark and the others "stormed ashore, crouching and dodging to avoid expected hostile fire." Splashing through knee-deep surf, Clark raced across the sandy beach with his comrades to a coconut grove, where they regrouped.[7]

After leaving the *McCawley* with the 1st Marines' 3rd Battalion, following the departure of the 2nd Battalion's men from the *Elliott,* 2nd Lt. William "Holly" Whyte was also surprised when he jumped out of his command boat onto the beachhead with Lieutenant Colonel McKelvy. "Where are the Japanese?" the battalion intelligence officer wondered. Looking up and down the long, "gently shelving" and sandy beach, Whyte—like Hunt another graduate of the 7th Reserve Officers Class—marveled at the wise choice that the division had made for the landing site.[8]

Earlier, back on the *Barnett,* Hunt had been watching through his field glasses as boats from the *McCawley* headed for the assembly area. It was now their turn to join the others. He descended below deck to the battalion's assembly area to find the men crowded together in their compartments, loaded down with "combat packs, rifles, bayonets, cartridge belts, bandoliers, heavy and light machine guns, mortars, and automatic rifles." Hunt was appalled by their appearance: "faces paled by days of inactivity, of being cooped up in the hold, dripping perspiration" from the heat. Wet with sweat, a stench emanating from their bodies, they were also under terrible nervous strain. One man screamed "in hysterical gibberish," only to be cut off by another: "Shut the hell up, you crazy bastard!"[9]

But now a messenger appeared and informed Hunt that the regimental command boat was ready for departure. Returning to the main deck, he swung over the gunwale, climbed down the net, and jumped into the waiting Higgins boat. "Move aft there, sit down, goddamn it, you're rocking the boat," a sergeant yelled at them. "Make way for the Colonel!" Then Colonel Cates went over the gunwale and joined Hunt and the other headquarters company officers in the boat.[10]

As all hands crouched low beneath the gunwale, the coxswain applied power, and they crossed the line of departure, banging the waves. Exceptionally standing, next to the coxswain, Cates peered through his field glasses as they neared the shore, then turned around to announce to Hunt and the other officers, "There's no opposition at the beach!" Minutes later, their boat hit the sand at full speed and lurched backwards. Hunt, Cates, and the others jumped over the side into knee-deep water, then moved quickly through coconut groves and high kunai grass to the spot chosen for the regiment's first command post, a corner of a deserted coconut plantation.[11]

At 1100, the 2nd and 3rd Battalions of the 1st Marines had come ashore on Beach Red, followed by the 1st Battalion, and had begun forming up for the move inland. Soon Pollock's and McKelvy's men were passing through the lines of the 5th Marines on their right just off the beach. Their objective was Grassy Knoll, while the 5th Marines were to take the airfield at Lunga. Pollock's 2nd Battalion was to lead off, followed by McKelvy's 3rd Battalion, with Cresswell's 1st Battalion in the rear, all on an azimuth heading of 260 degrees. According to the azimuth line marking in red on the map, prepared a week earlier by Hunt's R-2 section, Grassy Knoll was 5.6 miles to the southwest, 3 miles south of Lunga Point.[12]

As Pollock prepared to set out southwest in the direction of Grassy Knoll, he spoke briefly at the 1st Marines' temporary command post in the coconut grove with Colonel Cates and his executive officer, Lt. Col. Julian Frisbie. They wished him good luck. Cates and his regimental headquarters company would be moving forward about a mile to set up a new command post in the next coconut grove.[13] Behind Pollock's battalion, the 3rd and 1st Battalions were echeloned in columns, ready to follow.

After starting out at about 1330, the 2nd Battalion found the going relatively easy in the beginning as it passed through coconut groves and then patches of tall

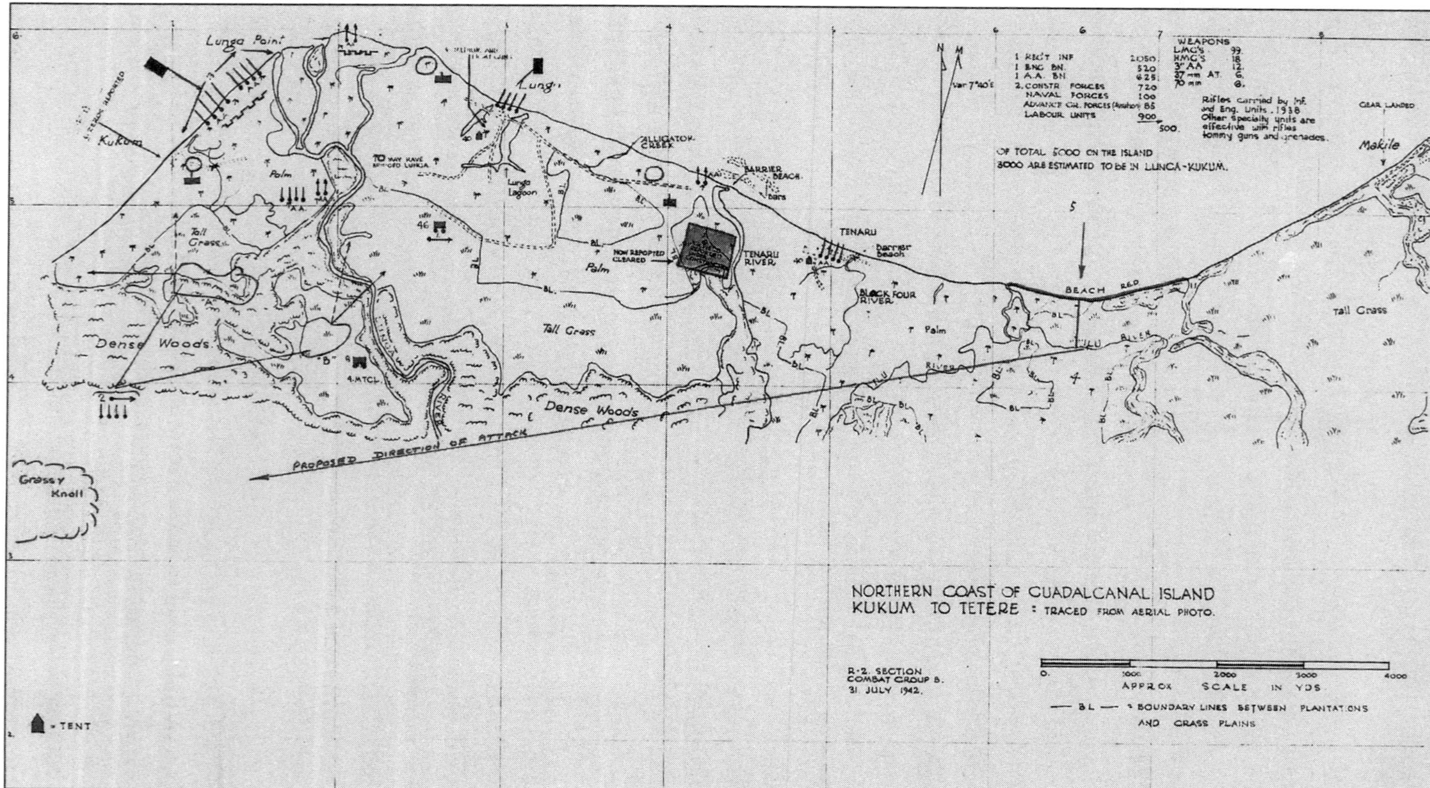

Map prepared by Intelligence Section, 1st Marine Regiment, July 31, 1942, with an overlay marking the azimuth of attack of Marines from Red Beach, August 7, 1942. Note the error in locating Alligator Creek. *National Archives of Australia, A1196, 37/501/167, Attachment 7.*

Men of 2nd Battalion, 1st Marines, resting during their trek to "Grassy Knoll," August 7, 1942. Sid Phillips, with the mortar vest, stands with his back to the camera, above right. Bill Coggin, H&S Company, 2nd Battalion, is lying down in the foreground, hands behind his head. *US National Archives photo 80-G-20683.*

kunai grass. But when the men entered the dense jungle some twenty-five hundred yards from their starting point, hot and sweaty from the heat in the kunai grass, their poor physical condition began taking its toll. Control began breaking down. The battalion split into two groups, with part of battalion headquarters, E and F Companies, and part of H Company in one group, and with G Company and the rest of H and Headquarters Companies in the other. It was taking the riflemen of F Company, cutting through the jungle with machetes, an hour to cover just half a mile. Cpl. Jim McCutcheon, off to the side, passed out and was left behind, never to be seen again.[14]

Still, F Company was going too fast for Bill Whorf's machine gun platoon in H Company, the men loaded down with their .30-caliber Browning heavies and ammunition carts. Unable to get direct footing as he tried to climb slippery slopes, Al Schmid would grab ropes tied to trees and pull himself up the incline, holding the machine gun tube in his left hand, a performance he had to repeat several times, never allowing the gun to touch the ankle-deep mud in the rain forest. Frustrated, Whorf sent his runner, Pfc. Harry McConville, to find the F Company CO, Capt. John Howland, and tell him his platoon could not keep up with F Company's riflemen.[15]

In Hugh Corrigan's machine gun platoon, the men were still drenched with sweat after passing through the kunai patches. Robert Leckie and the others were experiencing thirst from the heat and the dehydrating effect of the jungle after having walked over three hours. Suddenly, they encountered a swift-flowing stream. They plunged into the water, joined by Corrigan in a lapse of discipline. Despite their CO's warning that the water could be poisoned, they "went ahead with the orgy, drinking, drinking, drinking" before rejoining the march.[16]

But having lost contact with F Company ahead, the two machine gun platoons were lost. Like Whorf, Corrigan didn't know where they were, though he did not want to admit it to the men. All Corrigan would reply when asked where they were heading was "Grassy Knoll, up ahead, where the Japs are."[17]

Behind and out of sight of the first group of the battalion, Sgt. Willis Accord, wielding a bayonet, and Sgt. Rene Bolduc, with a machete, were leading the men of G Company's Weapons Platoon as they hacked their way through the kunai grass that trapped fierce heat. After they exited the kunai and entered the dense jungle, the sweat streaming down their faces attracted "all kinds of insects." Pvt. John Joseph, his hands blistered and bleeding, cursed the order that prevented them from deviating the slightest from the "damn azimuth" that was supposed to lead them to Grassy Knoll.[18]

Pfc. Les Clark and the others of H Company's mortar platoon were also using machetes and bayonets to hack through the "twisting vines and choking underbrush" impeding their progress. Giant trees overhead shut out the sun but did not reduce the overwhelming humidity.[19] Lugging the heavy 81 mm mortars, shells, and ammunition carts made the going as exhausting as the machine gun platoons had found it.

By late afternoon, Clark, Sid Phillips, and the others in the H Company mortar platoon had reached the banks of the "swift flowing stream" that Leckie and his comrades in Corrigan's machine gun platoon had encountered. It was too deep to ford, but two amtracs, or landing vehicles tracked (LVTs), had arrived carrying lumber for a makeshift bridge to span what Vandegrift's staff thought, according to their primitive map, was the Ilu River but was actually the mislabeled Tenaru River. "Bunched up like a herd of stupid cattle," the mortar men watched while engineers lay single pieces of planks across the amtracs from each side of the river, using the amphibious tractors as pontoons. They and others of the 2nd Battalion arriving at the location would spend the night on the east bank of the river and cross the following morning.[20]

Following some distance behind the second group of the 2nd Battalion, 2nd Lt. Bayard Berghaus and his L Company, 3rd Battalion, had also been struggling through the jungle in a single line towards Grassy Knoll in the late afternoon. 2nd Lt. Gil Small was with L Company too, assigned to set up an observation post (OP) for fire support from the 11th Marines' I Battery. I Company was ahead of them and K Company behind. [21]

After landing on Beach Red that morning with the rest of the 1st Battalion, C Company's commanding officer, newly promoted Capt. Nikolai Stevenson, had been ordered by the battalion's CO, Lieutenant Colonel Cresswell, to move his company inland two hundred yards. That put his men in the thick kunai grass, where they awaited further orders. But only in late afternoon did new orders come through—"push on" to the adjoining jungle. Trudging on in single file, they had bumped into an unknown group—Putnam's K Company, bringing up the rear of the 3rd Battalion. When word was passed to Stevenson that the rest of the 1st Battalion was ahead of his C Company, he decided to try to catch up with the others. But just after his men had managed to work their way past K Company on the narrow and slippery foot trail cut by those ahead of them, darkness suddenly descended. Then came the command to halt. It was too dark to see in the jungle. The men prepared to spend the night on the ground next to each other, I and C Companies in front of K Company and behind L Company.[22]

It was 1600 before Major General Vandegrift and his operations officer, Lt. Col. Jerry Thomas, had come ashore at Red Beach and headed for the division's advanced command post, which Vandegrift's chief of staff, Col. W. Capers James, and his assistant operations officer, Lt. Col. Merrill "Bill" Twining, had set up one hundred yards inland earlier in the day. Concerned about the progress being made by his 1st and 5th Regiments, Vandegrift set out on foot to investigate the situation firsthand, accompanied only by his orderly.[23]

When they reached the command post of the 1st Marines, Vandegrift and Thomas learned that Colonel Cates's battalions were evidently bogged down in the "immense rain forest" while heading for Grassy Knoll, although Cates had no news from their commanders—the radios were not working.[24] But Vandegrift had earlier realized by observation from his flagship *McCawley* that their objective, Grassy Knoll, was much further away than their Australian advisor had indicated on the rough map that served as their guide. Vandegrift confirmed the order sent from the *McCawley* and repeated by Twining earlier, when he met Cates ashore, that Cates should disregard the part of the original order directing him to seize Grassy Knoll and stop his advance for the night and dig in.[25]

Returning to his command post beneath coconut palms, Vandegrift downed a "hasty meal of cold rations," then just before nightfall "held court" and listened to the reports of his two regimental commanders on developments so far. Both were frustrated in reporting no contact with the enemy. "I'm beginning to doubt whether there's a Jap on the whole damned island," Vandegrift replied.[26]

Cates acknowledged that he "didn't quite know" where his 2nd and 3rd Battalions were in the dense rain forest. Pollock's 2nd Battalion "had advanced so rapidly" that he had completely lost contact with it and was reduced to asking for help from a liaison plane off the USS *Astoria* to locate it for him. In concluding the meeting, Vandegrift made a change in the orders. Cates's men the following morning should pivot to the right and head west out of the jungle for the high ground south of the airfield in order to protect the left flank of the 5th Marines that now occupied it. The 1st Battalion was now to advance almost due west, link up with the 5th Marines in occupying the airfield, and establish positions along the eastern bank of the Lunga River. The 2nd and 3rd Battalions should advance to the Lunga River and set up positions along its eastern bank south of the 1st Battalion's location.[27]

Night had descended when Cates returned to his own command post. He needed to get the new orders to his battalion commanders, but without any radio contact with them, he would need to rely on his staff to deliver the directive. Although it was now completely dark, he ordered his intelligence officer, 2nd Lt. George Hunt, to search for Cresswell's 1st Battalion and give them the message. Cates would not be able to get the new orders to his 2nd and 3rd Battalions until the next day, given the lateness of the hour and their greater distance from his command post.[28]

Leaving the command post, Hunt set out with a "tough California corporal" as his scout, following the approximate azimuth heading the 1st Battalion would have followed on its trek. Soon the two entered a strip of jungle where the night shapes appeared eerie to the young officer. Eventually they came out in an open field, and on the other side they found Cresswell and his men and gave the 1st Battalion CO his new orders.[29]

Further south in the jungle, Lieutenant Corrigan's men of Pollock's H Company were cold and dispirited as they settled in for the night after having set up their four machine guns on top of a hill. Ignorant and fearful of their surroundings and the whereabouts of the Japanese, they imagined that every sound from a jungle "alive with the noise of moving things" indicated that the enemy was moving closer. Suddenly, "a burst of gunfire shattered the night"—then silence.[30]

All was serene early that night where the 3rd Battalion was camped out with C Company of the 1st Battalion. But at about 0100 one of the men—evidently having a nightmare—suddenly jumped up and screamed, "The Japs!" All hell broke loose. Bullets began flying and hitting all around Putnam's K Company, lying on the ground higher up the hill. At first Putnam feared they had been ambushed. After sporadic firing continued for a while, Putnam and the other officers, as well as Stevenson and his platoon leaders in C Company, managed to get the men quieted down, but about an hour later the firing started up again, "even worse." When finally calm was restored, it was found that C Company and I Company had been shooting it out.[31]

Col. Takushirō Hattori, chief, Operations Section, Imperial Japanese Army General Headquarters, Tokyo. *Courtesy US Army; http://homepage2.nifty.com/ijn-2600/hattori.html.*

At Japanese Army General Headquarters in Tokyo, Col. Takushirō Hattori was taken aback as he read the reports that had just arrived from Seventeenth Army headquarters on Rabaul. An American force had landed on Guadalcanal and Tulagi in the Solomon Islands. The reports were vague—they had merely been relayed from navy units at the scene of the action—but there was no mistaking the import of the development.[32]

Many of the other officers of the forty-one-year-old Hattori's Operations Section did not even know where Guadalcanal was. Even those who did had no knowledge of the presence of the Japanese Navy on the island and that it was building an airfield on Guadalcanal's northern coast. Most of the staff officers never expected the Americans to launch an offensive as early as

August 1942. The second half of 1943 was their consensus for the timing of such an offensive.[33]

Immediately, Hattori and his fellow officers met with their navy counterparts in Imperial General Headquarters (IGHQ) to prepare an estimate of the situation for the approval of Gen. Hajime Sugiyama, chief of the Army General Staff, and Adm. Osami Nagano, who headed the Navy General Staff, as an agreed IGHQ position. The estimate concluded that in view of the Americans' current military strength, the landing could not be more than a reconnaissance operation. However, even if it were a counteroffensive, it would not be difficult for the Japanese Army and Navy to recapture Guadalcanal and Tulagi, because at this early stage, American preparations for mounting a counteroffensive would not yet be complete. Nevertheless, since American use of the airfield would "seriously affect our future operations," an operation to recapture the island "must be launched immediately."[34]

At dawn on Saturday, August 8, Robert Leckie and the others in Corrigan's H Company platoon discovered the consequences of the gunfire they'd heard the night before. The medical corpsman from battalion headquarters in their group, HA2C William F. Buchman, had been shot and killed by his own men. Evidently he had botched calling out the password that night and had been shot by the sentry who challenged him when he returned from relieving himself in the jungle. After scraping a hole with their entrenching tools, his comrades sadly lowered him into the primitive grave.[35]

Dawn at the bivouac site of the 3rd Battalion revealed a similar tragedy. The previous night's exchange of fire between I Company and C Company had resulted in the deaths of two Marines, including C Company's Pfc. Oscar J. Grover. Two were wounded, including C Company's Pvt. James F. Crotty.[36]

As 2nd Lt. Bill Sager and his K Company platoon early that morning passed in single file through where C Company had slept the night before in front of them, he was shocked to see the body of a Marine killed by friendly fire, "covered with neither a blanket nor a poncho." Someone told him that the dead Marine was from C Company. "And he'd been shot not more than 20–30 feet in front of where Gunny Sgt. Robert Brooks and I had been sleeping," Sager reflected. Reluctantly, C Company commander Nick Stevenson had decided to leave Grover's body behind as he set out anew at daylight for the Lunga River. He had no stretchers with him, and his men were too weakened from the trek and loaded down to carry a body. He would arrange for medics to return to the site with a stretcher to bring Grover's remains to their next fixed position.[37]

By early morning, Stevenson had led C Company out of the jungle, only to encounter yet another field of kunai grass, where he formed his men into a skirmish line at its edge. But as they moved through the high grass, heading in the direction of the airfield they were ordered to occupy, they spotted the tops of steel helmets and "heard the click of rifle bolts, coupled with cries of 'Who goes there?'" Stevenson's men approached warily. It was with relief they discovered that the challenge emanated from men of D Company, also heading west to 1st Battalion's new objective. "Minutes, possibly seconds, had kept us from repeating in broad daylight last night's tragedy," Stevenson realized.[38]

Camped out further south on the eastern bank of what apparently was the real Tenaru River, H Company's Deacon Tatum "felt fine" as he arose that morning. His 2nd Battalion group had not experienced any promiscuous firing the night before. But there was "a lot of confusion" as they prepared to cross over on the makeshift bridge the engineers had erected. At 0800 the mortar platoon men in single file nervously put their feet on the narrow planks, which "bounced and jiggled" as they made their way over the river. Phillips was wondering what he would do if he should fall off the bridge into the water.[39]

Safely on the other side, the 2nd Battalion group entered a grassy field, and after progressing some eight hundred yards once more entered the jungle some twenty-eight hundred yards south of the airfield, still on a heading to Grassy Knoll. Reaching another narrow river—actually, the upper reaches of the Ilu—they managed to ford it by 1030 and continued on. By early afternoon the column broke out of the jungle and began climbing up a steep incline, from which they could see the heights of Grassy Knoll and the commanding mountain.[40]

But by now the men were totally exhausted. The grade was too difficult for the mortarmen to get their loaded ammo carts over it, so they had unloaded the 81 mm shells and carried them instead, a cloverleaf of four shells over each shoulder, and abandoned the carts. All along the way, Pvt. Jim Donahue was upset as he watched many of the men in the column discarding their combat packs, rifles, mess gear, "and everything imaginable" in their effort to keep going.[41]

Lieutenant Corrigan's H Company platoon was "squirming" up the side of hills "like a sand crab," then sliding down the reverse slopes. The gunners "cursed weakly . . . as the tripods banged against the back of their heads." Once again, Bill Whorf's platoon nearby realized they were lost in the jungle and turned back to the Tenaru. "To hell with the Japs!" Whorf thought as he plunged into the river with his exhausted and frustrated men, then sat on its bank to have a lunch of their rations.[42]

The men of McKelvy's 3rd Battalion had also reached their limits after crossing the Tenaru. Climbing up and down ridges, Putnam's K Company was "discarding gear, ponchos, mosquito nets, pogey bait, and clothes," leaving a trail of litter behind them as they struggled on, like the men of the 2nd Battalion able to move forward at a rate of only one-third of a mile an hour. The number of heat prostration cases was mounting, too; there "wasn't a salt pill on the island" Putnam could offer his men.[43]

It was 1320 when L Company's 2nd Lt. Bayard Berghaus and the other men of the battalion were distracted by a sight overhead. As they looked to the northeast, they could make out Japanese aircraft attacking their transports off Red Beach. One of the transports had been hit and was sending up smoke and fire.[44]

At the head of the first group of his 2nd Battalion, Lieutenant Colonel Pollock was also watching. The transport had suddenly burst into flames and smoke. "It's probably our ship, the *Elliott*," he cynically joked with the others around him. He knew that if his supposition were correct, all the battalion's gear on the *Elliott* would be lost. Only high-priority items would have been unloaded by then: weapons, ammunition, combat packs.[45]

When he had come ashore the day before, Pollock had only one pair of socks and one suit of underwear with him. Trudging through the jungle, he had developed blisters on his feet due to wearing hunting boots and heavy socks. He could now barely walk.[46]

But the lack of ability to communicate with regimental headquarters bothered him more than his personal situation. He had only the hand-cranked two-man field radios with him and "couldn't talk from one side of the tree to the other with them," he complained. The day before, he had no other choice but to send a runner to Cates's command post, but the runner had not come back to him with any reply to his message.[47]

However, the message apparently had gotten through to Cates, for at about 1600 Cates's intelligence officer showed up. After having set out that morning to give Pollock the new plan, 2nd Lt. George Hunt had found the colonel in the jungle some twenty-three hundred yards due south of the airfield. Lt. Col. McKelvy was with him, advancing abreast with Pollock, heading westward with their men along the same trail.[48]

Ahead of Pollock and McKelvy, Hunt was appalled to find advance units of the two battalions lying "flopped to the ground, . . . exhausted, hungry, thirsty." Their canteens were empty, and only a few packs of D-rations were left. Many had fallen due to heat prostration. "Up and down the column came the cries, 'Corpsman forward!' 'Corpsman to the rear!'"[49]

Hunt moved forward to the head of the column where the scouts were clearing the trail with bayonets and machetes. He found that they had cut to the edge of a steep knoll and were now lying on the ground, smoking as they rested. One of them had climbed to the top of the knoll to take a look; he thought he had heard water. Hunt looked up at him and saw him "gesticulating wildly," then screaming, "A river—water!" The word "spread through the column like wildfire."[50]

Doubling back three hundred yards, Hunt rejoined Pollock and McKelvy, both "dripping perspiration, their khaki shirts soaked through," and told them about the river up ahead. The two battalion commanders were not sure what river it was. "Was it the Lunga?" Pollock wondered. McKelvy had been expecting to meet it ever since the day before. When standing on the "tough, red-earthed ridges," Hunt had made out the airfield in front of them and figured it was indeed the Lunga.[51]

At the same hour that Hunt had found Pollock and McKelvy, to the north Stevenson and his C Company men in assault formation had emerged from the jungle and raced across cleared land to approach their objective, the partially completed airfield. As darkness began to descend, they halted on the east bank of the Lunga, just southwest of the edge of the airfield. Earlier, they had been fired on by what they assumed was a small group of Japanese, but Lt. Robert Fowler's weapons platoon had fired back with their .30-caliber light machine guns and had repelled them.[52]

Men of Capt. Charley Brush's A Company had earlier reached the airfield and by 1600 had occupied it. They also had encountered Japanese resistance just before occupying the field. Pvt. James Gorman and others in Vic Valente's 2nd Platoon had spotted eight men in the jungle and had taken them "by surprise," but those prisoners and others captured around the airfield turned out to be unarmed laborers, "scared out of their wits." Brush turned them over to the 1st Battalion's command post for transport to division D-2 (intelligence).[53]

To the south, as darkness set in, the men of the 2nd and 3rd battalions spread themselves out on the ground for the night. They were on the east bank of the upper Lunga River, "with woods all around with huge trees," some forty-five hundred yards south of the airfield. K Company's Captain Putnam was appalled to see some sixteen hundred men jammed together "in a 300 yard area."[54]

Black clouds were forming, and shortly after nightfall rain began coming down, increasingly heavy as the hours wore on. Asleep in their ponchos, the Marines were awakened about 0100 by the sound of a plane buzzing overhead, then suddenly the whole sky lit up in white, red, and green light. Flares were dropping down in little parachutes. The bivouac area was bathed in the eerie light as well as the entire airfield up ahead.[55]

Hunt knew it meant a naval battle was coming up. Soon they heard the sound of heavy guns firing in Sealark Channel in flashes of red and white light, followed by huge explosions. The ground beneath the men trembled. The salvos were coming with increased intensity, seemingly ever closer, followed each time by a few moments of silence. Finally, at about 0300, the cannonading came to a halt.[56]

Obviously, a sea battle had been going on. But was our navy winning, or was it the Japanese? And if the Japanese had won, they "could be ashore before morning and we would have to fight for our lives," INS correspondent Richard Tregaskis feared.[57]

Way to the north that evening, Lt. Genjirou Inui and the two thousand officers and men of the Ichiki-shitai on the transports *Daifuku Maru* and *Boston Maru* were proceeding towards the Japanese naval base of Truk, a completely unexpected destination for them twenty-four hours earlier. Headed north for home in the two transports on the afternoon of August 7, they had been called back abruptly by Army General Headquarters in Tokyo and ordered to await their next command at Guam. They had been singing songs as they were making for Japan, but now the men became dispirited.[58]

Back at Guam, the two transports didn't need to be unloaded. The new orders for the Ichiki-shitai awaited them: proceed to Truk. That afternoon they had weighed anchor for their new destination, 640 miles to the southeast. They were still ignorant of what Army General Headquarters had in mind for them.[59]

Inui was philosophical about their reversal of fortune. "Only a life with a sublime duty to carry out will be worth living," he reflected in his diary.[60]

The officers and men of the 2nd and 3rd Battalions were "a miserable bunch" when they awoke on the morning of Saturday, August 9. They were all "soaked to the skin and stiff as boards from all the hiking" and sleeping on the ground on the east bank of the upper Lunga River. After drinking and washing in the Lunga, they prepared to set out again, now in the direction of the airfield to the north.[61]

But their battalion commanders were not with them. Lieutenant Colonels McKelvy and Pollock had been summoned to attend a meeting at Vandegrift's new command post, due north of their position, at the northwest edge of the airfield. The men were to await their return before setting out.[62]

It was 0900 when McKelvy, Pollock, and Cresswell, along with Colonel Cates and the other colonels, lieutenant colonels, and majors of the 1st, 5th, and 11th Marine Regiments, were assembled "around the dripping bamboo and vine-laden trees along the coral ridge that protected the command post." To Vandegrift, they appeared "a sorry-looking lot, with bloodshot eyes and embryonic beards and filthy dungarees" as they "slumped to the ground and huddled over their knees against rain hissing on a pathetic fire."[63]

Vandegrift was not going to withhold the bad news. Grimly, he spoke of the major naval battle fought the night before, whose outcome he did not know yet, but it did not look good: the sight of small boats landing survivors burned and black with oil from sunken ships was enough to dampen their spirits. The carriers that had supported their landing had "precipitately" retired, and that meant the transports would be leaving too, two days ahead of schedule, with some half of their equipment, including all the heavy items, still on board. Vandegrift did not know when they could expect aerial protection or supporting warships. Concluding, he ordered the assembled senior officers to relate the facts of the situation to their junior officers, NCOs, and men but to emphasize that this was not going to be another Bataan or Wake Island—they would get through the tough situation as Marines had done in the past.[64]

Vandegrift's operations officer, Lt. Col. Jerry Thomas, then took over the briefing to give orders for their next immediate tasks. A main line of resistance was to be set up, the airfield construction completed, and supplies still on the beach moved to dispersed inland dumps. With the waters off the north coast now under Japanese control, Vandegrift and Thomas particularly feared an enemy landing on the beaches that would threaten occupation of the vital airfield. The 5th Marines would defend the coast and perimeter west of the Lunga River, while the 1st Marines were assigned the coast east of the Lunga extending to the mouth of the Tenaru River (actually, Alligator Creek).[65]

For McKelvy's 3rd Battalion and Pollock's 2nd, the new orders for the Tenaru Sector were spelled out in Operations Order 5-42, which Cates issued follow-

Col. Clifton Cates with his 1st Regiment battalion commanding officers. *Left to right:* Lt. Col. Lenard Cresswell, Lt. Col. Edwin A. Pollock, Cates, Lt. Col. William McKelvy. Cates's R-3, Lt. Col. William Stickney, is at the far right. *Courtesy USMC, Quantico Audiovisual Branch, Alfred M. Gray Library.*

ing the meeting. Their battalions would be the ones to organize and defend the beaches from the mouth of the "Tenaru" west to the east branch of the Lunga. Pollock would be responsible for the eastern subsector, protecting the right flank of the Tenaru Sector, with his 2nd Battalion reinforced with B Battery of the division's 1st Special Weapons Battalion plus a platoon from its C Battery. McKelvy was assigned the west subsector, reaching to the Lunga, and would liaise with the 5th Marines to his west. His 3rd Battalion would be reinforced with the 2nd Platoon of C Battery of the special weapons battalion.[66]

Cates also assigned the CO of the special weapons battalion, Maj. Robert Luckey, to be in charge of the reserve. In addition to his headquarters battery of the battalion, he was given the 75 mm gun platoon of the 1st Marines' Weapons Company, along with the 1st Marines' Headquarters and Service Company, the 2nd Platoon of its D Company, and a 75 mm gun platoon from the 11th Marines. These units were to be prepared to counterattack in support of the 2nd and 3rd Battalions and establish outposts covering the entire Tenaru sector.[67]

And what orders for Cresswell's 1st Battalion? It was to move into a defensive position in division reserve in the vicinity of the Tenaru Sector. Its C Company was ordered detached to a position in defense of the beachhead.[68]

On reporting back to their troops, Pollock and McKelvy briefed their junior officers and disseminated their new orders. They would not be setting up defenses on the Lunga River as ordered the day before. To the men, it meant they would be pulling back to the beach and taking up positions extending from the Lunga to the mouth of the "Tenaru" (actually, Alligator Creek).[69]

Pollock's battalion was now intact again; the second group had now caught up with the first. As they set out with the 3rd Battalion, heading north to the beaches, they found traversing the hills "really improbable" after the rains of the night before. For Pvt. John Joseph and the rest of G Company, wading down the Lunga, hugging the east bank, it was a "miserable withdrawal," with many of the men "on the verge of dropping out." Joseph was carrying the rifles of two of his buddies, Whitey McTernan and Arthur Hiltz, both suffering from heat exhaustion.[70]

At about noon, they reached the plains area and spotted an amtrac waiting for them. When Bob Leckie and the rest of H Company reached the LVT, they were handed water and C-rations that it had been carrying for the exhausted men, their "mud-caked formless green twill" adhering to their bodies. In Deacon Tatum's mortar platoon of H Company, eight men had already fallen out.[71]

After eating their first meal since the evening before, they were off again. Lieutenant Colonel McKelvy came up in a jeep and told Putnam and the other company commanders of the 3rd Battalion that they and their men were to march to the beach, where guides would take them to their defensive positions.[72]

A depressing sight greeted the men of the two battalions when they finally reached the beach about 1500: "wrecked and smoking ships." H Company's mortar platoon arrived just as the cruiser *Chicago* was creeping slowly by just offshore, minus her bow, looking "short and stubby." There were no intact ships to be seen. It was then that the men realized that the naval battle the night before had gone badly and that their navy was now gone.[73]

As dusk began enveloping the area, the men of H Company plodded like zombies up the silent beach in darkness to their assigned defensive positions, dug shallow foxholes, and fell asleep. They were about three hundred yards west of the mouth of the "Tenaru" (Alligator Creek). "No chow tonight," Deacon Tatum recorded in his diary.[74]

Captain Putnam's K Company had turned to the left with the rest of the 3rd Battalion to set up defensive positions on their section of the beach. They fully expected a Japanese attack. The men of L Company had passed by the airfield on their way north, heading for their bivouac area for the night on the beach. On the way many had managed to procure bottles of Japanese beer left behind by the previous occupants of the airfield.[75]

Already at the airfield were men of the 1st Battalion. To 1st Sgt. Abe Felber of the 11th Marines, they appeared "a hard and dirty-looking lot." They had carted off "blankets, wine, .25 caliber bullets, paper money and coins, and other Japanese souvenirs."[76]

Captain Stevenson's C Company had only arrived at the airfield that morning, having spent the previous night in the jungle just beyond the western edge of the airstrip. They had been fired on earlier that morning by a Nambu light machine gun situated between the airstrip and their position. It was just after this engagement that a runner from 1st Battalion headquarters arrived with orders for them to shift to the east and take up a beach defensive position in reserve in the vicinity of the "Tenaru" (Alligator Creek).[77]

On board the *Daifuku Maru,* Lt. Genjirou Inui was practicing singing martial songs after dinner on August 9, his second night out from Guam on the way to Truk. He and the others in the Ichiki-shitai had received the news about the Japanese Navy's smashing victory in the naval battle off Guadalcanal the night before. But they were still in the dark about their new combat assignment.[78]

But later that night, Colonel Ichiki received a cable from Imperial General Headquarters in Tokyo. "When you arrive at Truk, you will be under the command of Lt. General Hyakutake's 17th Army," it stipulated.[79] Ichiki would have to wait until his detachment had arrived before obtaining information on what IGHQ and Hyakutake had in mind for him.

On the morning of Sunday, August 10, Lieutenant Colonel Pollock had everyone in his 2nd Battalion busy, digging foxholes and gun emplacements in his subsector on the north coast extending two thousand yards west from the mouth of the Tenaru (actually Alligator Creek) to where it joined up with McKelvy's 3rd Battalion. He was emphasizing placement of H Company's twelve .30-caliber heavy machine guns as the best means of repelling any Japanese landing from the sea, deploying the men of his three rifle companies, with their Springfield '03s and BARs, in foxholes along the line to protect the machine gun squads. Giving extra strength to his coast defense, to fire on any Japanese boats attempting to land on the beach, Pollock now had twelve 37 mm antitank guns and six .50-caliber machine guns assigned to him from B Battery of the 1st Special Weapons Battalion.[80]

About three hundred yards inland from the beach and three hundred yards west of the mouth of Alligator Creek, Lieutenant Benson was emplacing the four 81 mm mortars of his H Company mortar platoon in a line parallel to the beach. Sid Phillips, Deacon Tatum, and the other four in their number 4 gun crew were on the far right, closest to the creek, just behind coconut palms. Lt. Bill Whorf had assigned the two .30-caliber heavy machine guns of his platoon's second section to support the stovepipers.[81]

Pollock had established his battalion command post about two hundred yards west of Alligator Creek and one hundred yards south of the beach, to the northeast of H Company's mortar platoon. To provide protection, Whorf had moved his first section of two machine guns to the site. The other two machine gun platoon leaders of H Company, Hugh Corrigan and Bob Molloy, had emplaced their .30-caliber weapons near the shoreline, where their men were digging shallow emplacements for the guns.[82]

To the west, in the 3rd Battalion's subsector, Bob Putnam's K Company was also digging that morning about one hundred yards in from the beach and six hundred yards east of the mouth of the Lunga. His 3rd Battalion could count on the support of the 75 mm pack howitzers of I Battery, 3rd Battalion, 11th Marines, clustered with the guns of G and H Batteries to the south of Putnam's position. The battalion's Headquarters Battery was positioned in a coconut grove to the east of the airfield, just inside the jungle. Moving the heavy weapons to their assigned locations had been a slow process; hauling them over the beach trail was the only possible transport for them.[83]

Lt. Col. James Keating's 3rd Battalion, 11th Marines, had been assigned in direct support of Cates's 1st Marines, ready to fire in any direction in the regiment's defensive subsector. G Battery was to support Cresswell's 1st Battalion, H Battery was assigned to Pollock's 2nd Battalion, and I Battery was in support of McKelvy's 3rd Battalion. The forward observers of each of the three batteries were already with the battalions to which they had been assigned, including Gil Small with L Company, 3rd Battalion, and 2nd Lt. Nat Mewhinney with E Company, 2nd Battalion. They were ready to call in fire from the 75 mm pack howitzers if and when needed.[84]

Up on the beach, the early afternoon digging efforts of the men of Pollock's and McKelvy's battalions were suddenly interrupted by yells of "Condition Red!"

Looking up into the cloudless sky, Bob Leckie and others in H Company could make out twin-engined aircraft flying in a V high above them, about twenty to twenty-three of them. But unexpectedly, they did not drop bombs. Leckie and his comrades "shouted and danced about in derision" at the Japanese bombers as they departed. Pollock surmised that they were dropping food to the men of the construction battalions driven out of the airfield area by the Marines and now scattered inland.[85]

But the three Zeros escorting the bombers were more deadly in their intentions. Flying just some seven hundred feet high, they fired on Deacon Tatum and his H Company comrades but hit no one. At the airfield to the south, other Zeros flying as low as fifty feet above the coconut palms strafed the men of the 1st Engineer Battalion working on the runway.[86]

Excited as they were by the raid, Leckie and others in his squad were simply "delirious" that day when they discovered a log and thatch warehouse west of their position piled to the brim with "quarts of Japanese beer and balloon-like flasks of Japanese sake." There was food there, too—"huge tins of flour and rice and smaller cans of fish heads," but Leckie's buddies went for the alcohol instead, "pushing rickshaws" piled high with their loot back to their position. However, Deacon Tatum, a teetotaler, and his mortar platoon comrades hauled off food instead—"enough chow to last a lifetime"—as well as bedding rolls to make for a more comfortable sleep.[87]

McKelvy's 3rd Battalion had made the discovery, too. Gil Small, like Tatum a teetotaler, eschewed the alcohol, but others in L Company hauled off cases of beer and sake. K Company's CO, Bob Putnam, planned to check out the warehouse and the Japanese camp the next day.[88]

Leckie and his squad mates buried their sake and beer in the sand deep enough down where the sea water could keep it cool. It was their own private cache; they allowed no one else to touch it. Early that evening they drank in turns, pushing the sake bottles to each other "like the Indians smoke the peace pipe." "What a delicious way to fight a war," Leckie felt. They were getting "gloriously drunk." And they figured their supply would last them for a week.[89]

At Imperial Japanese Army (IJA) headquarters in Tokyo on August 10, Col. Takushirō Hattori had no intelligence informing him that provisions intended for the needs of the two construction battalions building the airfield on Guadalcanal were now meeting the subsistence requirements, albeit partly liquid, of the very men he was determined to annihilate. He was engaged on high-level matters: assignment of army units to the Seventeenth Army at Rabaul for the retaking of Guadalcanal. In addition to the Ichiki-shitai, the Aoba Detachment—previously transferred to the Fourteenth Army in the Philippines and made up mainly of the 4th Infantry Regiment of the 2nd Division—would be returned to the Seventeenth Army.[90]

Hattori's Army Operations Section had also drafted a new document, the "Army-Navy Central Agreement on Operations in Eastern New Guinea and the Solomon Islands Area in Accordance with the Changed Situation." It was now approved on both sides and issued to the commander in chief of the Combined Fleet and the commanding officer of the Seventeenth Army. According to its provisions, it called for a joint operation to be "promptly launched" to "recapture strategic points in the Solomon Islands" by taking advantage of the Japanese Navy's victory at Savo Island. For this task, some thirteen infantry battalions assigned to the Seventeenth Army, including the South Seas Detachment, the 41st Infantry Regiment, the Ichiki Detachment, the 35th Infantry Brigade, and the Aoba Detachment, along with the navy's Southeast Area Force (the 8th Fleet, the 11th Air Fleet, and part of the 2nd and 3rd Fleets) would take part in the operation.[91]

Those units of the Seventeenth Army that were ready to depart immediately—in effect only the Ichiki-shitai—were to cooperate with the navy "to destroy enemy forces on Guadalcanal and recapture strategic points—especially the airfield." Efforts were also to be made to recapture Tulagi, too, as soon as possible. In addition, the earlier-planned operation to seize Port Moresby in New Guinea would also be carried out simultaneously with that in the Solomon Islands.[92]

4

"May I Retake Tulagi Too?"

AFTER A "NOCTURNAL DRINKING BOUT" with his H Company squad, Pfc. Robert Leckie collapsed into his shallow dirt foxhole on the evening of Monday, August 10. But at about 2000 his serenity was interrupted by the sound of insects flying over his chest. Half awake, he realized that the "insects" were actually bullets being fired from the rear. "The Japanese must have gotten behind us," he figured, then he dropped off again in his sake-induced slumber.[1]

Over at the command post of his 1st Regiment, a sober 2nd Lt. George Hunt was also awakened by the sound of bullets—and the sight of bright tracers flying through the coconut palms around him. Transfixed, he listened to the "heavy banging" of .50-caliber machine guns and the "deep staccato" of the .30s. "Have the Japanese attacked us in force?" he wondered.[2]

Behind Hunt, at his command post in the 2nd Battalion area, Lt. Col. Pollock and his communications officer, 1st Lt. Bill Ward, were pinned down on the ground next to the boards that served as their beds. Only a can of raisins served to protect them from the tracers that were flying around. They could hear everyone in the vicinity yelling "Hallelujah!"—the password for the day—and shooting.[3]

At dawn, after the sleepless night, a check showed that miraculously no one had been killed or even wounded. But what had happened? Regimental intelligence officer Hunt concluded that Marines in the southern defense perimeter had opened fire on what they believed was a Japanese patrol in the middle of the field to the north of them, but inadvertently were shooting into Marines on the north edge of the field, who in turn were firing back. It was an "absurd situation," he felt.[4]

Sgt. George Dennis in the 1st Battalion's D Company also felt the Japanese were responsible for the "dreadful night." He had heard that a Japanese patrol "of about 25 men" had gotten inside their lines to create the confusion.[5]

But someone gave another explanation to Leckie. Evidently two companies of the "trigger-happy" 5th Marines to the west had been firing on each other, each mistaking the other for the enemy. Or, he wondered, was the shooting actually triggered by his own regiment's "tipsy sentries," at that late hour still under the influence of sake and beer?[6]

Further along the coast to the west of Leckie's 2nd Battalion position, Lt. Gil Small, serving with the 3rd Battalion's L Company as forward observer for I Battery, 11th Marines, had spent over five sleepless hours during the all-night firing confined to a kneeling-depth foxhole at his forward observation post number 1. Although his left knee was still lame and stiff, by midmorning he managed to walk over to the other side of Lunga Lagoon to the 3rd Battalion's I Company to pay a visit on forward observation post number 2, also manned by his I Battery. He found his fellow forward observer, Lt. Brooks Johnson, and other members of his post quartered in "an old plantation cottage, a bit shot-up but cool."[7] With no Japanese vessels near, the two young officers had not been called on for direct fire from I Battery's 75 mm pack howitzers.

The 3rd Battalion's commanding officer, Lt. Col. Bill McKelvy, was on a visit this day, too, but not under his own initiative. He, Pollock, and Cresswell had been summoned again to Vandegrift's command post, along with their commander, Colonel Cates, and thirty-six other majors, lieutenant colonels, and colonels. In a confidential talk, Vandegrift summed up the situation and expressed his satisfaction over their performance so far. He assured his field-grade officers that the navy would be returning and Marine Corps aircraft would arrive, which, along with Colonel del Valle's artillery and the 3rd Defense Battalion's coastal guns, would crush any Japanese direct amphibious assault on the Lunga perimeter. After concluding his briefing, Vandegrift assembled his commanders for a group photo, all "grim-faced in their stained gray-green dungarees."[8]

The photo session concluded, Vandegrift's senior officers headed back to their respective command posts. Pollock's had been moved to the center of his Tenaru subsector defense area, now about six hundred yards from the sea. Colonel Cates and his executive officer, Lieutenant Colonel Frisbie, had given Pollock some clothes to replace his tattered apparel, and he now had a tarpaulin for his tent, too.[9]

That evening, the 2nd Battalion commander stretched out on boards covered with straw and bags acquired from Japanese stocks, an upgrade of his sleeping arrangements. He was hoping that this evening would not be a repeat of the night before. Colonel Cates had issued "strict orders" that no one was to fire a shot. If any Japanese approached the regiment's men, the Marines were to use their bayonets instead of their rifles or machine guns.[10]

Although Pollock was anticipating a restful sleep this night, it was not to be. At 0520—before daylight—he was rudely awakened by the explosion of a heavy shell that landed just fifty yards to the rear of his command post. Fortunately, it did not cause any damage, except to his nerves. But over the next ten minutes what subsequently was identified as a Japanese submarine kept firing at the defense area of the 2nd and 3rd Battalions, fragments of shells from its deck gun flying in all directions throughout the area.[11]

In the 3rd Battalion area to the west of Pollock's command post, the heavy gunfire had also awakened Gil Small at his forward observation post with L Company. Was it one of the 75 mm pack howitzers firing, "or what?" he wondered. He could see flashes in three distinct places to his north. Only later was he informed that it was a Japanese submarine firing at them.[12]

Small's first guess may have been partially correct. Positioned in his forward observation post for the 2nd Battalion at the edge of the coconut grove just behind the beach, 2nd Lt. Nat Mewhinney had spotted the submarine firing high-velocity rounds over his head. Excited to be going into action for the first time, he contacted his H Battery with a maximum range adjustment for its 75 mm howitzers. The rounds fell short but were close enough to oblige the submarine to dive and clear the area.[13]

But the perceived threat to the airfield was not only from the sea. The numerous reports of the presence of Japanese to the south of the Tenaru subsector had convinced Vandegrift's command of the importance of setting up a perimeter defense to the southeast in order to secure the airfield from any enemy approaches from that direction. On this day of Wednesday, August 12, Pollock was ordered to form this perimeter defense with 150 men from his 2nd Battalion augmented with 145 other Marines drawn from McKelvy's 3rd Battalion. No more than two men were to be drawn from any squad.[14]

That afternoon, squad mates Pvts. Marvin L. Scoggins and Billy J. Wilson, along with other F Company men selected for the duty, were sent out from the 2nd Battalion area to form the defense perimeter. After reaching their destination, the line captain in charge assigned them to a two-man "dishpan-deep foxhole" facing a long, open field. "One man awake at all times!" he yelled at them.[15]

As darkness descended, the moon was already overhead. Soon after nightfall, the moon set, and it became pitch dark. They were sure the Japanese were beginning to probe their position, and they fired their Springfields in response. His heart pounding, Wilson kept saying to himself, "A coward dies a thousand deaths, a brave man only once." Each time the Marines' fire died down, the Japanese would send "a stream of tracers" over their heads, and the firing would resume. Finally, near daylight, the firing subsided. A relieved Wilson figured they had used up one-tenth of all their ammunition.[16]

Back at the 2nd Battalion's command post, the night's mission was deemed "successfully completed," since the enemy "had failed to reach us with harassing fire."[17] But they had no intelligence on who the Japanese were who were provoking them.

Later that morning Lt. George Hunt at the 1st Marines' regimental command post recorded that "the Japs tried their usual tricks, sneaked out of the jungle into the field and opened fire with a light machine gun." They had "advanced no further than the field, and seeing that their attempts to start another inter-Marine war were ineffective, crept back into the jungle."[18]

"What a quiet lagoon," Lt. Genjirou Inui reflected as he surveyed Truk Lagoon early on the morning of Thursday, August 13, from the upper deck of his transport. He and the others of the Ichiki-shitai had finally made it to their destination at 1800 the evening before after a four-day voyage from Guam. Their two transports had not been able to make more than nine and one-half knots during the uneventful trip.[19]

As he looked around at the small islands in the lagoon, overgrown with palms, only patrol planes flying overhead reminded him that he was indeed in a war zone. His impression of the surroundings did not include the many warships of the Combined Fleet that had arrived the previous month in what was now, and unknown to him, the formidable forward naval base of the Japanese in the South Pacific.

At Rabaul, 690 miles to the south, staff officers of Seventeenth Army headquarters this morning were still trying to decide on the second day of deliberations how the combat order to the Ichiki-shitai should be framed. Disagreement on the size of the American force on Guadalcanal was causing the delay in issuing the order.

The day before, a senior naval staff officer of Rabaul's 8th Base Force, after having observed Lunga Point from ten thousand feet in a Mitsubishi G4M1 twin-engine bomber, and noting few Marines around the airfield and only a few ships in the water, had concluded that the main body of the Marines had been withdrawn from the island. However, the Seventeenth Army's chief of staff, Maj. Gen. Akisaburō Futami, disagreed with his assessment, estimating the number of Marines at from seven thousand to eight thousand. Other staff members felt that Futami's figure was exaggerated and argued that Ichiki's detachment should be adequate under prevailing conditions, at least to halt completion of the airfield by the Americans. At any rate, Ichiki could be reinforced by the 35th Infantry Brigade within ten days. When the vice chief of the Army General Staff in Tokyo in a radiogram that day urged prompt action using Ichiki, the Seventeenth Army's commander, Lieutenant General Hyakutake, agreed to Tokyo's course of action.[20]

At 1530 the order to Ichiki was finally drafted, to be hand-delivered to him by staff officer Col. Hiroshi Matsumoto, ordered to fly to Truk the next day. Matsumoto was also to enter into detailed discussions with Ichiki and naval staff on how the Ichiki-shitai's assignment was to be carried out. The August 13 order read:

> The strength of the enemy which landed in the Solomons area is still unknown, but there is no enemy activity as we had expected. Even to this day, August 13, it is certain that they are not utilizing the airfield there.
>
> The Army will cooperate with the Navy and quickly attack and destroy the enemy in the Solomons while the enemy is trying to complete the occupation. It will recapture and maintain these vital places.
>
> The Ichiki Detachment will cooperate with the Navy and quickly recapture and maintain the airfield on Guadalcanal.
>
> If this is not possible, the Detachment will occupy a part of Guadalcanal. For this purpose, a spearhead unit of approximately 900 troops

will be organized and loaded on six destroyers that are near at hand and will advance towards Guadalcanal by a direct route.[21]

Back on Guadalcanal, Lieutenant Colonel Pollock was growing weary of the continual air raid warnings and the attacks that usually followed. The first one of this Friday, August 14, was at 0730, when the 90 mm antiaircraft guns of the 3rd Defense Battalion went into action for the first time, but their fire was inaccurate against the twenty-one high-flying Japanese bombers, while the accompanying machine gun fire was too low to be effective. "Everyone is wondering about our planes—where are they?" Pollock wrote in his diary that evening.[22]

This day also saw new orders issued to Pollock and his Combat Group B, cited as (Regimental) Operation Order 6-42. Colonel Cates instructed Pollock to rearrange his defenses in the Tenaru subsector by shifting his men around from the beach to extend also seventeen hundred yards up the Tenaru River (actually Alligator Creek, or the Ilu) from its mouth. The 1st Marines' commander wanted this easternmost perimeter to be ready "in the event of an attack from the east" as well as a landing from the sea, previously considered the most likely threat. "Selected positions and installations will be dug in and prepared to occupy as the Main Line of Resistance at the earliest possible date," Cates directed.[23]

In the meantime, Pollock's 2nd Battalion was continuing to mount a "close-in" perimeter defense in a "persistent effort" to stop (perceived) Japanese infiltration from the south. This night, it was the turn of H Company to form part of the nocturnal patrol of about one hundred men.[24]

Leaving his machine gun emplacement, Pfc. Bob Leckie joined some thirty other H Company men in the late afternoon as they marched away from the beach, through the coconut grove, and across the kunai grass to the position assigned them beyond the airfield, bayonets fixed on their Springfield '03s. It was still light when Leckie and the others entered "the gloom of the jungle." To Leckie, scraping foxholes out of the jungle floor was "like digging into a compost heap 10,000 years old." Darkness descended just as they finished their excavations, into which they now crawled and waited in the "impenetrable darkness." Leckie recalled years later, "I couldn't see, only hear, the enemy everywhere about me, whispering to each other." Only when daylight finally arrived the next day did Leckie regain his normal composure.[25]

For Deacon Tatum, Sid Phillips, and the other men of H Company's mortar section also assigned perimeter defense that evening, their commanding officer,

Mid-1930s view of Alligator Creek looking north towards its mouth. *Courtesy British Museum, Collection of Robert Lever, copyright Trustees of British Museum.*

Lt. Carl "Benny" Benson, was almost more to be feared than any Japanese infiltrators. He warned his group that anyone who was on top of the ground would be considered Japanese and would be shot. If anyone needed to relieve himself that night, he should use his helmet and empty it in the morning. And to back up his order, Benny positioned himself behind them, his BAR on full automatic.[26]

Through the night, Tatum and his foxhole mate Phillips alternated sleeping, taking two-hour shifts. Not having had any supper before setting out, they found no need to relieve themselves and thus were not faced with Benson's dictum. As for Leckie in his two-man foxhole nearby, the night hours were nerve-wracking but proved uneventful, at least until near daybreak. Then suddenly near daybreak the mortarmen were nearly hit twice by machine gun tracers. From his foxhole Tatum let loose with two hundred rounds from his BAR in the direction of the hostile fire, finally "silencing" the would-be infiltrators.[27]

After arriving on the morning of August 14 at the bomber airfield on Moen Island in Truk Lagoon on their flight from Rabaul, Col. Hiroshi Matsumoto and staff members of the Japanese Navy's 8th Base Force at Rabaul immediately met with Colonel Ichiki. Matsumoto handed him the orders of Lieutenant General Hyakutake, which corresponded to those the 8th Base Force officers carried for this joint army-navy operation. Although Hyakutake's orders indicated uncertainty about the number of Marines on Guadalcanal that Ichiki would encounter, Matsumoto told him that their activity had not been "vigorous" since landing and that they might actually be "withdrawing to Tulagi." On the other hand, the Americans might be at division strength of ten thousand, in which case Ichiki should await reinforcements before launching an attack, as per Hyakutake's order.[28]

In response to this assessment, Ichiki exuded supreme self-confidence. "Don't worry, we can take the airfield. May I retake Tulagi too?" Taken aback by Ichiki's brashness, Matsumoto politely told him to wait until Maj. Gen. Kiyotaki Kawaguchi and his 35th Brigade arrived to join him. Although Matsumoto didn't hint it to Ichiki, Seventeenth Army headquarters was skeptical that Ichiki's detachment alone could recapture the airfield.[29]

To Matsumoto, it was clear that Ichiki intended to attack using only the nine hundred men of his "spearhead" unit that he'd been ordered to form by Hyakutake. The order did not spell out whether Ichiki should launch his assault with this first-echelon force only or wait until the arrival of his second echelon before attacking. Left to his own decision, Ichiki was opting for the first course of action.[30]

Ichiki now faced the question of how he should select the 900 officers and men of his 2,000-man detachment to form his first echelon. Hyakutake's August 13 order stipulated that the 900 members would be transported to Guadalcanal in six destroyers. The fact that each destroyer was capable of carrying only 150 troops was the constraining factor in determining the size of the first echelon. Ordering destroyers as the means of transport automatically eliminated the three units of Ichiki's detachment equipped with 75 mm howitzers or 37 mm antitank guns [the Regimental Gun Company (152 officers and men), the Rapid Fire Gun Company (140 officers and men), and the 8th Independent Anti-Tank Gun Company (136 officers and men)] since the destroyers had neither the means to transport nor to offload such weapons. Only the Battalion Gun Platoon (48 officers and men) could be taken, as its two 70 mm guns could be disassembled.[31]

But excluding the 400-plus men of these gun units still left Ichiki with a surfeit for his first echelon. He was obliged to cut down on the number of men in his detachment's other units. Accordingly, each of his four infantry companies was stripped of 73 men—reduced from 178 to 105—while the Machine Gun Company went from 191 to 110 men and the Engineer Company from 228 to 150. His regimental headquarters was cut in half, and his battalion headquarters was reduced by 90 percent, from 266 to 23. Those who survived the cuts were considered the most combat-capable men of their units.[32]

Ichiki now confronted his next challenge. How were the relatively lightly armed men selected for the first echelon to be landed from the destroyers? Two of them, the *Arashi* and the *Hagikaze*, were already at Truk, having escorted the *Daifuku Maru* and *Boston Maru* from Guam, while three others—the *Tanikaze, Hamakaze,* and *Urukaze*—were due in this day.[33] Landing from a large transport was easy, but the army had no experience in landing troops from a destroyer.[34]

The detachment's Engineer Company had brought thirty-six small, motorless, folding landing boats with it on the transports. This would be an adequate number to land his nine hundred troops, Ichiki felt. Motorboats carried on the destroyers could tow such troop-laden boats to shore, he figured. Practices carried out later in the day confirmed that this landing method would work. A motorboat from each destroyer would pull three of these collapsible boats joined together to the reef, from where the men on board would row the boats onto the shore and disembark.[35]

To Lt. Genjirou Inui it was "really thrilling" to hear of the arrangements made to land the echelon in high-speed destroyers. "This will be how landing operations are carried out in the future," he thought. But the other four officers in his 8th Independent Anti-Tank Gun Company did not share his enthusiasm. They were bitterly disappointed to learn that they would not be going out with the first echelon.[36]

There was disappointing news the following morning for the men of Lieutenant Colonel Pollock's 2nd Battalion on Guadalcanal, too, although it affected their stomachs rather than any combat aspirations they might have. They were being put on battalion mess from that day.[37]

The day before, Pollock's executive officer, Maj. William Chalfant III, had driven his jeep through the coconut palm area of their beach defenses and stopped at the location of the mess of each of the battalion's squads to commandeer the food supplies they had built up the past four days. "Our brief escape from battalion authority was ended," Bob Leckie lamented. But Chalfant found little food to haul off to add to the stock of the newly established battalion mess, which mainly consisted of rice captured from an abandoned Japanese warehouse.[38]

Lined up at the pyramidal tent pitched two hundred yards back of the beach, Leckie, Tatum, and the other men of H Company glumly downed their tasteless and unsatisfying breakfast that morning from wooden Japanese bowls. It was the first of twice-daily meals of rice they would be served from then on, with the second repast set to be dished out for supper. "Reckon we will starve now," Tatum figured.[39]

The new feeding regime was ill-timed, the men felt. They were going to need a higher calorie intake for the heavy physical exertion required of them to carry out the new assignment awaiting them that morning. At 1050 Pollock received an order from Vandegrift's division headquarters backing up Cates's order of the day before: the 2nd Battalion was to shift its dug-in positions and extend its defenses seventeen hundred yards from the mouth of the Tenaru (Alligator Creek) up its west bank, while the 1st Battalion was to lengthen the defense line a further fifteen hundred yards south. This new task "will have priority over further work on beach defenses," Vandegrift emphasized. Pollock was to report progress to division headquarters at 1900 each day.[40]

The new emphasis on building up a defense line on the Marines' eastern perimeter along the Tenaru was apparently triggered by a message from Rear Admiral Turner the day before that warned Vandegrift that the Japanese "were planning an attack in force on the perimeter."[41] The message gained credence when the district officer Martin Clemens reported to Vandegrift's command post the same day that he had received news of the presence of a Japanese radio station near Taivu, nineteen miles east of the mouth of the Tenaru.[42]

Similar news had been picked up by a 1st Battalion patrol sent out on the morning of August 12 to provide security for engineers who had been ordered to carry out a survey for a possible new airfield in the Tetere area ten miles to the east. When Capt. Charley Brush, the A Company commander, the day before had called for volunteers to escort the engineers, his 1st Platoon leader, 2nd Lt. John Jachym, had volunteered himself and his men. They were to be accompanied by two Australian surveyors as well as the 1st Battalion's intelligence officer, 2nd Lt. Irving "Perry" Perine.[43]

A day into the patrol, as they passed through Tetere, a Catholic priest told Jachym and Perine of rumors of a Japanese force further east along the coast. In view of the significance of the account, and with the survey mission's work completed, Jachym decided to shorten the scheduled three-day patrol and return to the perimeter to report the disturbing news. Meeting with Brush as night descended on August 13, the highly regarded Jachym told his commanding officer that he was prepared to return to the area with a larger body to verify the report

Aerial view of east and west banks of Alligator Creek and the airfield, August 23, 1942. *US National Archives photo 80-G-10543.*

should division headquarters deem it necessary to do so. But in the coastal area extending from the Marine perimeter to Tetere, Lieutenant Perine could report to Lieutenant Colonel Cresswell at the 1st Battalion's command post that there were no Japanese. At least in "this quarter" Vandegrift's command now felt "secure."[44]

On August 15 the light cruiser *Jintsu,* accompanied by the destroyer *Kagero,* entered Truk Lagoon after four days' steaming from Yokosuka on the mainland, joining the other *Kagero*-class destroyers *Arashi, Hagikaze, Tanikaze, Hamakaze,* and *Urukaze* already anchored there. On board the *Jintsu,* his flagship, was Rear Adm. Raizo Tanaka. A veteran commander of destroyer squadrons, the fifty-year old Tanaka had received orders to rush to Truk, where he was to await further instructions. Just before reaching his destination, he had been designated by Combined Fleet Headquarters as commander of the Guadalcanal Reinforcement Force.[45]

With no new orders forthcoming, Tanaka spent the rest of the day supervising the loading of supplies on the *Jintsu* and *Kagero.* But as evening descended, he found that he had visitors. Col. Hiroshi Matsumoto of Seventeenth Army headquarters and staff officers of Rabaul's 8th Naval Base Force had come aboard to meet him. Matsumoto showed Tanaka the order to Ichiki from Hyakutake, and the 8th Base officers handed him a detailed order from the 8th Fleet commander at Rabaul.[46]

Reading the 8th Fleet order, Tanaka was shocked. He was being ordered to transport the nine hundred soldiers of Ichiki's first echelon to Cape Taivu on Guadalcanal, leaving first thing the following morning. Furthermore, he would be responsible for transportation arrangements for eleven hundred more of Ichiki's men of his second echelon, also to depart the next morning at the same time.[47]

"How could 8th Fleet Headquarters issue such an order without taking my own views as commander of the Reinforcement Force into consideration?" Tanaka fumed. "There must be great confusion in the headquarters of the 8th Fleet" to order him to carry out "the most difficult operation in war—landing in the face of the enemy." With no rehearsal by Ichiki's detachment nor preliminary study carried out, the operation "could never succeed," in Tanaka's estimation. [48]

But Tanaka realized that his negative reaction to the order counted for nothing now. The operation had been sanctioned at higher level and was already initiated, with Ichiki's men waiting for transportation. With the boarding time set for 0500, there was no time to argue further about it.

That night Tanaka and his staff worked feverishly to supply the *Jintsu,* the destroyers, and the two transports that would carry the troops of both echelons to Guadalcanal. The first-echelon men were to be unloaded at Taivu on the night of August 18, and the second-echelon troops in the slow transports were scheduled to reach Taivu four days later. There were also "complicated and endless details" to take care of before making any naval sortie.[49]

Ichiki had been busy this day, too. He had drafted and issued his Order No. 4 earlier, outlining his plan for the landing operation. His first echelon on the six destroyers "will make the initial attack," while the second echelon, under Maj. Eiji Mizuno, would join the first echelon on its arrival and with it "prepare to annihilate" the rest of the defenders on Guadalcanal. In the words of Ichiki, the first echelon would "in an invincible manner attack the airfield and extend its gains."[50]

Each of the six *Kagero*-class destroyers now at Truk was assigned 150 officers and men of the first echelon. Ichiki and his detachment headquarters, along with a platoon of engineers, would board the *Arashi.* His battalion commander, Maj. Nobuo Kuramoto, and his small 22-man staff, were being sent to the *Tanikaze,* along with 90 of the 105 members of the greatly reduced 4th Company plus a platoon of engineers. The 1st, 2nd, and 3rd Companies of 105 officers and men each, along with 20-man sections of the Machine Gun Company, were to go to the *Kagero*, *Urukaze*, and *Hagikaze*, respectively. The other 50 men of the Machine Gun Company were listed against the *Hamakaze,* along with the 48 men of the Battalion Gun Platoon with their two 70 mm guns.[51]

Late that night, Rear Admiral Tanaka boarded the *Arashi* to discuss the operation that Ichiki planned. He knew Ichiki from the Midway operation, for which he had provided the destroyer escort. Exuding confidence, Ichiki told Tanaka that he intended to use the same tactics on Guadalcanal that he had planned for the Midway landing: his men would use their bayonets, not fire their rifles, as they surged forward to overwhelm the defenders on the third night after landing. Only after having entered the airfield would his men use their rifles, for which each man would carry 150 rounds of ammunition, along with five days' worth of rations.[52]

Tanaka was dismayed to hear Ichiki holding forth on such tactics, though he did not express his skepticism to Ichiki. He knew that Ichiki would have no heavy weapons to support his attack, with his 37 mm and 75 mm guns left behind with the second echelon, and now he did not intend even to use his men's 7.7 mm

Arisaka rifles. Such "bamboo spear" tactics would prove hopeless against an enemy equipped with modern heavy weapons, he was sure.[53]

Nevertheless, right on schedule—at 0500 on August 16—Destroyer Division commander Capt. Yasuo Satō on the *Arashi* began leading the six destroyers under his command out of Truk Lagoon. Crammed on board the *Kagero*-class warships under "difficult conditions" were the 916 officers and men of Colonel Ichiki's first echelon who had boarded late the night before. Following behind, the transports *Daifuku Maru* and *Boston Maru,* along with the old converted destroyers Patrol Boats 34 and 35, carried the balance of Ichiki's men, the eleven hundred of the second echelon, comprised of men of the 37 mm and 75 mm gun companies with their heavy weapons plus those men of the four infantry companies and machine gun company who had not been selected for the first echelon. The *Boston Maru* was also loaded with most of the food and ammunition of both echelons, including the replenishment needs for the first echelon. Rear Admiral Tanaka, in his flagship *Jintsu,* sortied from the south channel, then moved eastward to take command of the entire force.[54]

On board the *Daifuku Maru,* Lt. Genjirou Inui with his 8th Independent Anti-Tank Gun Company found that the destroyers were soon passing from his view. Within hours they were completely out of sight as they steamed due south at twenty-five knots, far ahead of the lumbering transports, which made only 8.5 knots on the zigzag course they were ordered to follow by Tanaka. "How reliable and enviable they look," Inui thought.[55]

To afford better observation of the water off the north coast this morning, 2nd Lt. Gil Small was evacuating his old foxhole, set up as his forward observation post number 1, to another location nearer the beach. Attached to Colonel McKelvy's 3rd Battalion, Small needed to keep an eye out for Japanese submarines intending to shell the airfield area. The past four days they had fired on the Marines with their deck guns, but without causing any damage, although they did get on everyone's nerves.[56]

Excavating a new foxhole for his new post proved "some of the hardest digging ever" for the 11th Marines' forward observer. Finally, sweating profusely after his exertions, Small managed to get in a short swim and washed, then changed his clothing in time for supper. "What a treat just to stand and eat chow in clean underwear," he recorded in his diary that evening.[57]

To Small's east, in the 2nd Battalion's Tenaru subsector, Pfc. John "Deacon" Tatum and three of his comrades in the mortar section of H Company had supplemented their meager supper fare with food that had escaped Major Chalfant's attention two days earlier, but any such pleasure was offset by orders they received afterwards. Tatum and fellow Pfcs. Murray Battles, Carl Ransom, and Clyde Lucas were being assigned a night patrol on both banks of the Tenaru River. Crossing over to the east bank, they found themselves making their way in "the most dense jungle ever." Soon they heard "Japanese signaling with their coconut shells," then one of them "tried to ambush us from behind." Tatum fired on him five times with his BAR before the Japanese jumped into the river. In the pitch darkness the petrified Marines had no idea "who and how many they were," but no more showed up. The rest of the night was spent "in terror of being bayoneted."[58]

At about 1030 the following morning, Monday, August 17, the six destroyers carrying Colonel Ichiki's first echelon passed the equator, heading due south for Guadalcanal. So far, they had encountered no enemy planes. The men on board were enjoying themselves as they played *go* and *shogi* (a kind of chess). To navy officer Tomojiro Kurahashi on the *Hagikaze,* the men of 1st Lt. Magozō Maruyama's 3rd Company crowded on his destroyer seemed very high-spirited. "Seasoned men indeed," he felt.[59]

On board the lead destroyer *Arashi,* Ichiki had every reason to feel encouraged about his forthcoming operation. He had received a report that was based on information sent to Imperial General Headquarters by the Japanese military attaché in Moscow. The August 15 message of the attaché cited sources that indicated that the enemy on Guadalcanal numbered only two thousand and were apparently retiring toward Tulagi.[60]

Lt. Genjirou Inui and the others on board the *Daifuku Maru* were not privy to this intelligence. At any rate, Inui's main concern was rest: he had spent the past twenty-four hours on duty watch, and sleep was now "the biggest event" of his day.[61]

Now considerably behind the fast destroyers, the *Daifuku Maru* and the sister *Boston Maru* carrying Major Mizuno's second echelon had not encountered any patrolling American planes either. In anticipation of the possibility, however, two of the 37 mm antitank guns of Inui's company had been set up on the *Daifuku*

Japanese destroyer *Arashi*, which landed Colonel Ichiki and his headquarters at Taivu Point on the night of August 18, 1942. *Courtesy Kure Maritime Museum, via http://en.wikipedia.org/wiki/Japanese_destroyer_Arashi.*

Maru to provide antiaircraft defense. They could also be adjusted to fire on any submarines that should approach.[62]

In the early afternoon, Pvt. Richard W. "Bill" Harding and his buddies in G Company reached the northern end of Alligator Creek after having set out that morning from their 2nd Battalion defensive positions on the beach. "That damn walking sure got me down," the seventeen-year-old from Adamstown, Pennsylvania, complained. They were under 2nd Battalion orders to cut away the brush along the west bank of Alligator Creek so that the men would have a clear field of fire from the defense positions they would be setting up against a possible Japanese attack from the east.[63]

Except for a skeleton force left on beach defenses, all of Lt. Col. Pollock's men had turned out for the heavy work, scheduled for 0630 to 1500 this day, August 17. At 0800 they took a break from the heavy physical labor when their breakfast meal was brought to them from the battalion mess on the beach.[64]

By the time the 2nd Battalion men knocked off for the day, they had made good progress in clearing the brush for the fields of fire. Some work had also been completed in setting up emplacements along the northern part of the defense line, near the mouth of Alligator Creek. Further work extending the positions to the south was scheduled for the next day.[65]

Under orders from 2nd Lt. Bill Whorf, two machine gun emplacements were being prepared for manning by a section of his H Company platoon. About one hundred yards upstream from the mouth of the creek, men of Cpl. LeRoy Diamond's squad had begun building "a good nest" for their .30-caliber heavy machine gun, the northernmost of the platoon's scheduled positions. Cpl. Diamond and the five men under his command—Pvts. Jack Rivers, Al Schmid, Whitney Jacobs, Bob Coombs, and one other—were tackling the first job: to dig a semicircular trench around the back of the planned emplacement. By the end of the day they had excavated the trench to a depth of four feet and a width of two feet. The ground in the center was left level for the gun platform.[66]

Although 2nd Lt. Bob Molloy's 2nd Machine Gun Platoon was stationed up on the beach about five hundred yards west of Alligator Creek, his men were also ordered to clear brush and make machine gun emplacements along its west bank. Pvt. Tom Brown and the others "griped and groaned" when their working party headed down to their designated area: "It was hot work and we thought it was kind of stupid." No one had told them the purpose of their work.[67]

To check on progress in implementing his August 14 order, Col. Clifton Cates had arrived on the scene. Accompanied by Pollock, the 1st Marine Regiment's CO inspected the right flank along Alligator Creek. Lt. Col. Bill McKelvy also paid a visit on Pollock; the two battalion commanders were coordinating maximum disposition of strength along the main line of resistance extending from the beach and up the creek.[68] Accordingly, McKelvy's beach defenses to Pollock's west were being moved further east to cover the transfer of most of Pollock's defenses up Alligator Creek.

For Gil Small, the shifting of the 3rd Battalion's L Company beach position three hundred yards to the east meant having to set up yet another location for his forward observation post number 1. After lugging their phone, rations, and baggage to the new position, he and his team began digging through the same hard-packed soil. The captured Japanese pick they were using was a "sad excuse" for an excavating tool, he complained. After completing the laborious task that afternoon, Small had his men break out cans of field rations to supplement their supper of "short rations" of fish, rice, and beans.[69]

Deacon Tatum and his mortar squad buddies were up early on Tuesday, August 18, and just getting ready to have their skimpy breakfast when the call came in. They were being ordered to join one of the working parties at the Tenaru

(Alligator Creek) to clear fields of fire and dig new defensive positions where the brush had been cut away. Already at 0630, 2nd Battalion men were occupied all along the defensive perimeter in the heavy work.[70]

Some one hundred yards south of the mouth of the creek, LeRoy Diamond's squad had made good progress in preparing its machine gun position. Al Schmid, Jack Rivers, and the others had stacked sandbags in front of and all around the semicircular trench they had dug, then plastered the bags with river mud. Next would be to put big palm tree logs across the bags to make a roof to protect them against mortar fire.[71]

Considerably further south of Diamond's emplacement, Pfc. Luther Hayes and his squad mates were starting to dig away for another machine gun position.[72] It was going to be the second of section chief Sgt. John Cross's two machine gun emplacements being set up in Lt. Bill Whorf's platoon. Clearing the brush earlier had created a good field of fire for the heavy water-cooled machine guns when installed in their nests.

While Whorf's platoon was being relocated to the west bank of Alligator Creek, Captain Ferguson's other two machine gun platoons, under Lts. Hugh Corrigan and Bob Molloy, remained in defensive positions on the beach. To their west, the H Company commander was consulting with his 3rd Battalion counterpart, Capt. Bill McNulty of M Company, and his superior, Lt. Col. McKelvy, to ensure that machine gun fire of both weapons companies would be coordinated on the beach.[73]

But it was the new defensive arrangements on the west bank of the "Tenaru" (actually, Alligator Creek and its extension upstream, the Ilu River) that most concerned the 1st Marines' CO, Colonel Cates. To check on the situation, Cates had sent his executive officer, Lt. Col. Julian Frisbie, to carry out a reconnaissance of the 2nd Battalion's right flank. Lieutenant Colonel Pollock's operations officer, Lt. Bill Larson, accompanied Frisbie on his inspection of proposed positions along the line and facing east on the Tenaru (Alligator Creek).[74]

On the right of the far end of the 2nd Battalion's defense line, new positions were also being prepared by men of the 1st Battalion, extending a further fifteen hundred yards up the west bank of the Tenaru (now the Ilu), as per the August 14 regimental order. As was the case for the 2nd Battalion, these positions were not to be occupied until orders were received from Colonel Cates. They included four machine gun emplacements of Lt. John Speaks's 2nd machine gun platoon of D Company, attached to B Company, that were being set up this day too. But except for the positions for Speaks's platoon, little progress had been made by the end of the day because of the heavy clearing work required.[75]

Cates had also ordered a regimental intelligence observation post set up on the point where the mouth of Alligator Creek met the ocean, responsible to report to his intelligence officer, Lt. George Hunt. Likewise, Colonel Pollock had established his own observation post, situated on the beach two hundred yards west of Cates's OP. Colonel McKelvy had also set up an OP for his 3rd Battalion further along to the west on the beach in his area of defense responsibility.[76]

Anticipating a possible Japanese attack from the east, Pollock was sending out twenty-five-man patrols twice a day to cover the area between the "Tenaru" (Alligator Creek) and the "Ilu" (the real Tenaru) Rivers. The men sent out at dawn this day had reported back at 1000. At 1430, the second patrol headed out, but when it returned from its two-mile trek eastward at 1730, like the first patrol it reported "nothing of importance" to Pollock and Larson.[77]

While there was no sign of Japanese ground activity to the east of their defensive position, overhead their adversaries were keeping the Marines' nerves jumping. At 1315 that day a formation of eight G4M1 "Betty" bombers began unloading on the airfield, now designated Henderson Field by Vandegrift, for the first time in large numbers. For Deacon Tatum, Clyde Lucas, and Carl Ransom, hunkered down in the same trench near the field, it was a "close call." Fragments from the exploding bombs that were "strewn all about our trench" barely missed them. Other Marines were less lucky; one man was fatally hit by a bomb, and seven others were injured by fragments. Three hits were scored on the runway. To Tatum it appeared that the 3rd Defense Battalion's 90 mm antiaircraft guns had struck one of the G4M1s, but it managed to fly away.[78]

Over at the command post of A Company late in the day, Capt. Charley Brush was meeting with his 1st Platoon leader. Brush had summoned John Jachym to ask how Jachym's men were recuperating after the forced march back from Tetere five days earlier. When Jachym indicated they were in good shape, Brush told him that Cates had instructed him, on orders from division headquarters, to send a combat patrol of Jachym's platoon back to Tetere and on to Taivu Point to destroy the Japanese unit that Jachym had reported hearing about on his August 12–13 patrol. But this time Brush was going along, too, and adding men with two of their 60 mm mortars from his weapons platoon as well as a section of twelve men with their two heavy machine guns from the 1st Battalion's D Company, its weapons company. With Jachym's forty-two-man platoon, the armed patrol would now total over sixty men.[79]

"We're leaving tomorrow morning," Brush told Jachym. When informed of the patrol assignment, Jachym's men were excited to be going out again. It appeared that they were all keen finally to get into combat with the elusive Japanese.[80]

Meanwhile, at the division command post, Vandegrift was more concerned about a larger threat to his forces. Rear Admiral Turner, commander of Task Force 62, had just sent him a message reporting that Turner had information of the possibility of an attack on the Cactus-Ringbolt (Guadalcanal-Tulagi) area "within next forty eight hours."[81] But the message did not indicate *where* the attack would take place.

What further information if any *did* Turner pass to Vandegrift? It was not recorded in Vandegrift's operations journal. The source of Turner's communication to Vandegrift was the "ultra secret" message CINCPAC had sent to Ghormley in New Zealand at 2047 on August 17 from Pearl Harbor (August 18, New Zealand and Guadalcanal time) and copied to Turner signaling that "intelligence at hand indicates ORANGE decision reoccupy Guadalcanal and Tulagi bases" and that "escorted convoy carrying Army shock troops originally destined Midway last June departed Truk 9 hours 17th destined CACTUS." The message concluded: "Attack day can be as early as 20 August but actual date not indicated."[82]

Under bright moonlight, six Japanese destroyers approached the coastal area of Guadalcanal to the immediate west of Taivu Point just before 2300 on the evening of Tuesday, August 18. Following the plan, the *Arashi, Hagikaze, Kagero,* and *Tanikaze* heaved to about eight hundred meters offshore, while the *Hamakaze* and *Urakaze* milled about at each end of and behind the line of the other four as a flanking screen. Then the crews of each of the four anchored destroyers began lowering their motorboats and seven collapsible landing craft, into which 150 men of Colonel Ichiki's first echelon descended.[83]

In one of the collapsible boats being towed by an *Arashi* motorboat, twenty-three-year-old Sadanobu Okada, a clerk in Colonel Ichiki's headquarters detachment, was relieved to find that there appeared to be no American opposition to the landing. To his left, the *Hagikaze* was disembarking the 105 men of 1st Lt. Magozō Maruyama's 3rd Company, while next over, 1st Lt. Yusaku Higuchi from the

Sgt. Sadanobu Okada of Ichiki Detachment headquarters. *Author's collection.*

Kagero was in a boat with part of his 1st Company. Battalion commander Maj. Nobuo Kuramoto and his small headquarters detachment of twenty-two men were heading to the shore from the *Tanikaze,* with other boats from the destroyer carrying 90 of the 105 men of 1st Lt. Toshirō Chiba's 4th Company. The four destroyers were also landing 106 men of 1st Lt. Hideo Gotō's Engineer Company, while 40 men from 1st Lt. Shigeneo Komatsu's Machine Gun Company were also among those disembarking from the *Hagikaze* and *Kagero*—20 from each destroyer.[84]

When the boats had reached shallow water, they were uncoupled from the motorboats, and the men rowed their small craft to shore. Okada and the others were pleasantly surprised to find the seven men of the Port Taivu observation post waiting to help them come ashore. Their unit evidently had been in radio communication with the landing force using a prearranged code as the destroyers approached the shore.[85]

After all 600 men from the four destroyers had safely landed, the *Hamakaze* and *Urakaze* moved in from their screening positions in the second phase of the operation to discharge their 300 soldiers, while the first-phase destroyers switched with them to take up flank screening duties. In westernmost position for the landing, the *Hamakaze* began disembarking the balance of 15 men of Chiba's 4th Company, plus Lieutenant Komatsu with 49 of his Machine Gun Company, 2nd Lt. Tetsuharu Hanami's 48-man Battalion Gun Platoon and its two 70 mm guns, 22 more engineers, and 15 more from headquarters detachment. At the far eastern end, Capt. Tetsurō Sawada's 105 men of his 2nd Company, with 20 men of Komatsu's Machine Gun Company attached, along with 22 more engineers and three more men from the headquarters detachment, climbed into the collapsible boats of the *Urakaze* and began heading for a landing immediately west of Taivu Point.[86]

By 0100, all the officers and men of Ichiki's first echelon were ashore, the two-hour operation completed as planned. There were no casualties. Colonel Ichiki now requested the captain of the *Arashi* and the naval communications men at the Point Taivu observation point to radio headquarters at Rabaul that the landing was a success. He added that he intended to retake the airfield soon.[87]

Like the others in the detachment, Okada was in high spirits. They were all confident that they would annihilate the Marine defenders "instantly." After they had grouped on the landing area, Ichiki ordered his men to start out immediately for the west on a night march. There would be no rest period. Okada was not disappointed—he felt there was no need for rest, as they were already acclimated to tropic weather from their two-month stay on Guam.[88]

Heading in the direction of Tetere, Okada and the others walked hurriedly. They were being guided by two of the men of the observation post. The cool breeze off the sea was making the march pleasant. They all felt that they had already won the battle that lay ahead of them.[89]

5

"The Bastards Are in the Trees!"

ABOUT TWO HOURS INTO THEIR westward trek in the middle of the night along the northern Guadalcanal shoreline from their landing site at Taivu Point, some 875 officers and men of Colonel Ichiki's detachment were now confronted with their first physical obstacle: a deep river flowing north into the sea blocked their progress. It was the Berande River, situated four miles west of Taivu Point. In full uniform and loaded down with their equipment and weapons, including two disassembled 70 mm mountain guns, the men entered into the water and found it up to their chests, but not deeper. They forded the river to the western bank in pitch darkness. It was now after 0300.[1]

But the Berande was not the only river they would have to cross as they moved slowly in the direction of their objective. Two miles further on, they reached the eastern bank of the Balesuma River. Once again, the fatigued and drowsy men plunged into the water and made their way across the mouth of the river to the other side.

Struggling over the soft sands of the coastline had proved wearying for the men. The lack of a firm foundation underfoot hampered their progress. But now about one and a half miles after leaving the Balesuma, they reached the eastern terminus of a coastal track that made the going easier.[2]

After proceeding along the track a further one and one-half miles, they found themselves entering an area they identified as Tetere. There, Colonel Ichiki decided to call a halt. It was somewhat before 0600, and day would soon be breaking. Ichiki didn't want to risk enemy observation of his conspicuous force by air or sea. He would let his men take a rest until evening. Dog-tired and fighting sleep after the nearly five hours' march from Taivu Point, they individually headed into the adjoining jungle, out of sight of enemy observation, spread tarpaulins on the ground, and flopped down.[3]

But for Capt. Yoshimi Shibuya, the rest would be brief. Colonel Ichiki had summoned the leader of his communications unit, as well as his battalion commander, Maj. Nobuo Kuramoto, and his Engineer Company CO, 1st Lt. Hideo Gotō, to his temporary command post, set up under a large palm tree. There, Ichiki told them that he had decided to dispatch a large patrol to the "Nakagawa area" (what he called the area around Alligator Creek) to investigate the enemy situation and reconnoiter positions and the lay of the land. Then Ichiki outlined the organization he wanted for the patrol and identified officers he wanted to participate in it before giving Shibuya orders to plan for its departure at the earliest.[4]

Unlike the decision to mount the patrol, the selection of Shibuya to head it up had not been an easy one for Ichiki. During that night's march he had discussed the question of sending out a patrol with his adjutant, Capt. Yokichi Togashi. Togashi had concurred with his commander's assertion that "the enemy situation is unclear" and that the detachment should obtain as much intelligence as possible "as soon as possible." To Ichiki, this called for a reconnaissance in force, led by his most capable officers. To lead the party, Togashi had argued for the commander of the 2nd Company, Capt. Tetsurō Sawada, as the most battle-experienced officer, rather than Captain Shibuya, his second choice. But both knew that the selection of Sawada would be opposed by Major Kuramoto, who would not want to risk losing his battle-hardened veteran of the 1939 Nomonhan campaign against the Russians. The battalion commander had Sawada in mind to succeed him should Kuramoto become a casualty in the fighting that lay ahead. In the end, Ichiki and Togashi agreed on Shibuya, who had also been at Nomonhan with the 28th Infantry but who had missed most of the combat due to a head wound.[5]

Ichiki and Togashi had also decided who should lead the squads of the party that they had identified and now discussed their selections and squad sizes with Shibuya, Kuramoto, and Gotō. Shibuya himself was to take along thirteen men from the wireless radio and wire communications (telephone) sections of his

Second Lt. Masami Hagiuda, 1st Platoon leader, 2nd (Sawada) Company, Ichiki Detchment, killed in action August 19, 1942. *Courtesy of Akio Tani.*

communications unit. From Ichiki's headquarters staff, 2nd Lt. Kenji Matsumoto would head up a five-man intelligence collection squad. The leader of the 1st Platoon of 1st Lt. Yusaku Higuchi's 1st Company, 1st Lt. Shōji Tate, and 2nd Lt. Masami Hagiuda, 1st Platoon leader in Captain Sawada's 2nd Company, would each lead five-man reconnaissance squads charged with reconnoitering enemy positions at Nakagawa. A third reconnaissance squad, also of five members, to be headed by Prov. 2nd Lt. Shigeru Wada, 3rd Platoon leader of Lieutenant Gotō's Engineer Company, would identify enemy positions while reconnoitering the lay of the land. Two navy men from the 81st Guadalcanal Guard Unit at Taivu Point who had been attached to Ichiki's detachment were chosen as guides. Two military police completed the thirty-eight-man party. Other than Shibuya, none of the officers had any combat experience, although some of the men under them did.[6]

After their meeting with Ichiki, the three commanders joined the others in the jungle for a rest, but for Shibuya it was very brief. He had to meet with the junior officers selected for the patrol, who in turn had to select the enlisted men to join them. For Cpl. Tomoteru Asahi, one of the squad leaders in 1st Lieutenant Higuchi's company, the process led to disappointment, because although he originally was selected to go with Lieutenant Tate, he was later replaced by another squad leader in the Company, Cpl. Kiyonobu Akasaka, who unlike Asahi had combat experience in the fighting at Nomonhan.[7]

Capt. Yoshimi Shibuya, commander of the communications unit, Ichiki Detachment, and leader of the reconnaissance party, killed in action August 19, 1942. *Courtesy of Akio Tani.*

At 0830 Shibuya reported back to Ichiki and informed his CO that his reconnaissance party was ready to depart. Standing before Shibuya, Ichiki reminded him of the importance of the mission. They were to ascertain the enemy's strength and disposition in the Lunga area, propose the best approach route, and indicate a location from which the detachment should lead off for the attack. After assuring Ichiki that they would fulfill everything expected of them, Shibuya saluted and gave the order to set out to the assembled men, taking his place in the lead as they moved forward.[8]

After leaving Tetere, the two navy men moved twenty to thirty yards out in front of the column to act as guides, being familiar with the Guadalcanal terrain. Shibuya had positioned Lieutenant Tate slightly behind himself, with Lieutenants Hagiuda, Matsumoto, and Wada strung out behind them with their men. Near the rear of the party were the thirteen men of Shibuya's communications unit with radios, telephone equipment, and spools of wire. Finally, the two military police were at the very end. Not anticipating any combat on the patrol, their only weapons, other than the swords the officers were carrying, were their 6.5 mm Type 38 (1905) or later model 7.7 mm Type 99 Arisaka bolt-action rifles.[9]

It was 0700 this morning when Capt. Charley Brush at his A Company position to the south of the 2nd Battalion's Tenaru defense line gave the order to the sixty-five men of his combat patrol to move out. Following the same route as that of his patrol a week earlier, 2nd Lt. John Jachym and the forty-one men of his platoon, along with twelve men from a machine gun section of D Company and eleven from the mortar section of A Company's Weapons Platoon, began trudging along northwards on Alligator Creek's west bank. Shouts of "You'll be sorry!" from the 2nd Battalion men in their gun emplacements taunted them as the patrol passed by. "This isn't going to be a practice hike," Pfc. Hubert "Stub" Morse in Jachym's BAR squad reflected.[10]

When the men reached the mouth of Alligator Creek, they turned to the right, crossed over the sandbar, and entered the palm grove on the other side. At the head of the line, Daniel Pule, the "purply-black" head scout of Martin Clemens, and three other natives led the way as they moved along the sandy coastline heading to the east. Concerned that his men were too bunched up, keen as they were to "shoot the breeze" and "pass the latest scuttlebutt," Jachym yelled, "Keep down, out of sight! Stay five paces behind each other!" The NCOs joined in: "Spread out—one shell will get you all!"[11]

As the morning wore on, the men, their BARs and Springfield '03s constantly held at the ready, began getting tired. It was tough going with the loose sand seeping into their shoes and rubbing sore spots on their feet. Walking had become "a real chore." "We trudged along, cursing the heat, the insects, and the guy who dreamed up the whole damned deal," Stub Morse recalled. As the sun rose higher in the sky, Morse and the others in Jachym's platoon became drenched in sweat while gnats attacked their eyes.[12]

Unable to keep up with Morse and the others, the men of the two machine gun squads from Lt. Franklin Sill's platoon in D Company were struggling to pull carts, one with their .30-caliber heavy Browning machine guns and the other with twenty-six units of .30-caliber ammunition in boxes. Unsympathetic, Captain Brush kept yelling at Cpl. Chet Sliva, one of the squad leaders, and his men to speed it up and keep pace with Jachym's platoon. Sliva wondered why Brush had ordered them to join his patrol in the first place with their heavy defensive weapons instead of his own machine gun squads from his weapons platoon with their light, air-cooled .30-caliber machine guns, so much better suited for an offensive operation.[13]

But soon walking conditions improved somewhat when the native guides led the men a few yards off the beach and into the jungle, where a trail paralleled the shoreline. Although it was easier moving forward on this government track, there was little air circulation, and the insects were proving worse.

By noon, Morse and the others were "foot-weary, bone-tired, and hungry." Brush decided to call a break for chow. But before they could break open their rations, the native scouts told them that there was an orange grove about two miles further on. Jachym knew about it, too; during his earlier patrol in the area he had found the orange grove in a little village. The prospect of getting some fresh fruit was enough to get the men to their feet again and on the move with the approval of Brush and Jachym.[14]

Some three and one-half hours after leaving Tetere, Captain Shibuya's reconnaissance party had covered only three miles in their trek westward. Since the government track that had led them into Tetere did not extend beyond the village, the thirty-eight officers and men had no recourse but to make their way again along the sandy beach, which slowed their progress. Just beyond Tetere they had been forced to cross yet another river—Cavaga Creek—and then about a mile further on, the Metapona River. Just after passing Volanavua on the other side of the Metapona, Shibuya noticed a village about fifty yards inland and decided to call a halt. His loaded-down men, weary and drenched in sweat, needed a rest. "The reconnaissance party will rest in that village for one hour," Shibuya announced. "We will eat our noon meal there. Tend to your feet."[15]

As the officers and men entered the village, they were surprised to find that not a single native was to be seen, although chickens and pigs were still there. It seemed to them that the inhabitants must have fled in a hurry. But almost all were too exhausted to dwell on the matter.[16]

After settling down in the shade of a dwelling or a coconut palm and unbuttoning their tunics, the men pulled out some dry bread they had brought with them to ease the pangs of hunger. Soon the whole party dozed off, except for four or five who were shaking a tree of a type they had not seen before to dislodge its fruit. It was a welcome addition to their meager rations.

But Provisional Lieutenant Wada was uneasy. While the men in his squad slept, he was looking around the village area. His inability to pick up signs of the natives was giving him a bad feeling. Similarly, in Lieutenant Tate's squad, Nomonhan veteran Cpl. Kyonobu Akasaka felt the others should not be napping under such suspicious circumstances. Finding no one in the village seemed ominous to him, like they were nearing a battlefield. "We should be checking the area for signs of why the inhabitants have taken refuge," he felt.[17]

After about an hour, the men were awakened and ordered to move out by Shibuya. Falling into formation again, they retraced their steps the fifty meters to the overland track and headed westward once more. The two navy guides again led the way, followed by Captain Shibuya twenty to thirty yards behind, then Lieutenant Tate's squad, the squads of Lieutenants Hagiuda and Matsumoto, the radio and phone squads of Captain Shibuya's communications unit, and finally the squad of Provisional Lieutenant Wada. The communications squads resumed laying telephone wire as they moved along near the rear of the party.[18]

The two guides passed out of view of the others just after regaining the coastal road. A curve in the track had taken them past a grove of trees that obscured them from view of Shibuya and Tate's squad, now only some ten meters behind the scouts. They had closed the distance between them and the scouts after having halted and waited for the navy men to return to the coast road.[19]

About halfway to the village with the orange grove, 2nd Lt. John Jachym was leading the eight men in his first squad under Cpl. Bill Jones as they approached another village known to the natives as Papangu. Suddenly, one of Clemens's guides who had been scouting ahead of them came running back to Jachym and excitedly shouted one word: "Japs!" Cpl. Forrest Wild—Jachym's platoon guide who was following just behind the two scouts—had sent the guide, Daniel Pule, back to Jachym with the surprising news that they had encountered a group of

Japanese proceeding on the government track heading towards them. They had run into each other where the trail turned in a sharp elbow to their right. After being fired on by the scouts and Wild, the Japanese were seen leaving the track and seeking cover in the thick jungle to their right.[20]

Following behind Jachym and his first squad, the men of the three other squads dived into the jungle on the other—their right—side of the trail. Jachym ordered his runner, Pvt. George Grazier, to report the startling information to Capt. Charley Brush, who was proceeding along behind Jachym's squads. Then Jachym left the track to go into the surf with a borrowed Thompson submachine gun, followed by the men of his first squad. Jachym began firing at the Japanese not more than fifty yards away in the jungle off the track. Struggling to keep the unfamiliar weapon from jumping up from the target, he wildly sprayed fire in the direction of the hapless enemy, but with limited accuracy, unmindful in that unexpected situation of the fact that he was an easy target for return fire.[21] Joining in were the men of his squad, firing their bolt-action Springfield rifles and single BAR.

As Captain Shibuya, 1st Lieutenant Tate, and Tate's squad of four men followed the bend in the track behind their two navy scout guides, they were suddenly greeted with the "tat-ta-tat" of bullets whizzing by them. Corporal Akasaka instinctively yelled, "Enemy!" as the middle and rear ends of the reconnaissance party about thirty to forty meters behind also began taking fire. Immediately they hit the ground and looked for cover. The fire was coming from about one hundred meters in front of them.[22]

But Shibuya had misjudged the situation. "They're friendly! Our Navy men have come to welcome us! Not enemy!" he yelled to the others. Then he called out, "Yama! Yama!" But when no answering password came back, Shibuya, joined by Tate, shouted the other password for the Ichiki detachment, "Kawa! Kawa!"

This time there was a response: the "ta-ta-ta-ta" of fire from single-shot rifles tearing into the hapless Japanese. Lying prone on the ground, Shibuya made a sound, followed by an effort to stand up, then fell over, uttering something like "uun." Also getting up, Tate took several hits from an automatic rifle or a submachine gun, twitched two or three times, then fell back down, motionless.

Right behind Tate, Corporal Akasaka called out, "Captain Shibuya! Lt. Tate!" Neither responded. He realized that both had been killed instantly. The two navy guides leading the party were also dead. It was about 1315.[23]

Akasaka also had been hit by the fusillade, one bullet through his right shoulder and another through his lower left thigh. Severely wounded, he could neither walk nor crawl. The next minutes were a blank to him, though he did manage to squirm over to the cover of underbrush.

Heading off the track into the jungle, some ten yards to their right, that separated them from the shoreline, the still-shocked survivors in the main body wildly sought concealment in the undergrowth too. Each tried to make use of any cover from which to spot movement of the "100-some" Americans in their dark green uniforms and to fire back at them. But as they lay on the ground, the return fire from their bolt-action Arisaka rifles seemed to be having little effect against the enemy, who were armed with automatic weapons as well as their bolt action rifles. "Bullets plopped around us like drops of rain. We were pinned down," Akasaka would later recall.[24]

As soon as Capt. Charley Brush got word from Pvt. George Grazier that the native scouts in front of him had run into a group of Japanese that had veered off the government track into the jungle in the direction of the beach after being fired on, he decided to order a flanking movement. Two of Jachym's squads were to turn sharply left from the government track to block any forward movement of the Japanese group, while the other two should move forward along the track and then position themselves slightly off the track to line up against the left flank of the Japanese. But Grazier would not be the one to pass the order to Jachym—Jachym's runner had decided on his own to stay behind and join Brush's headquarters and attached machine gun and mortar men in the fighting.[25]

When Jachym got the order, he led Corporal Jones and his first rifle squad out of the surf and ten yards inland into the jungle from the beach to take positions next to Cpl. Dave Edwards's second rifle squad. He also ordered his third rifle squad and his BAR squad further down the track to flank the Japanese on the enemy's left. With the ocean beach on their right, the Japanese group would now be trapped on three sides.[26]

But for Jachym, the situation he found himself in "was horribly frightening, uncertain, and confused." The Japanese seemed to be all around, yet were hard to see until they "popped up" out of the undergrowth just yards away. Facing his first combat experience just four months out of reserve officer training class, the twenty-four-year-old platoon leader kept firing his Thompson submachine gun "whenever one of them came into view."[27]

In the meantime, on the government track side of the Japanese, Jachym's third and BAR squads were seeking positions from which to fire on the Japanese opposite them in the jungle. Cpl. Henry Grimes and the other eight men of his third rifle squad were crawling along under cover of the undergrowth with their Springfield '03s and the BAR in front of them, using their weapons to push through the brush. Next over from them, Cpl. Ernie Dobbins's eight-man BAR squad was keeping as low a profile as possible. Although he and his men were in a good position to spot the Japanese, they realized that the Japanese by the same token could see them better, too, as they hunkered down just off the government track.[28]

Whang! Something crackled in Grimes's ear, and the twenty-eight-year-old squad leader from Philadelphia fell flat on the jungle floor. Venturing to look up, he was shocked to find a Japanese not more than eight feet from him, in a camouflage net and looking like a tree. Both frozen in their tracks, they stared at each other, then Grimes raised his Springfield and fired. The Japanese fell to the ground, "hit squarely between the eyes." But others were now appearing, on their knees and also camouflaged. Kneeling himself, Grimes began picking them off. They fell "without a scream or wail or groan."[29]

But why weren't they firing on me? Grimes wondered. Had they discarded their Arisaka rifles in order to carry the boxes they seemed to have been lugging? What was in those boxes that was so important to them?

A cracking sound next to his ear interrupted his thoughts. A .25-caliber bullet had barely missed his helmet and dug into the tree six inches from his head. *Snipers!* he thought. After lying unmoving for the next five minutes, Grimes began to crawl forward, rifle in his right hand. Then he spotted the first of the boxes that the Japanese had been carrying about twenty feet away. Still crawling along the edge of the trail, he then saw two Japanese also crawling out of the jungle heading for the boxes. As one of the Japanese began dragging one of the boxes into the underbrush, Grimes fired, and the Japanese fell to the ground next to the box. But before Grimes could get a bead on the second enemy, the Japanese leapt behind the body of his fallen comrade and fired ineffectively on the Marine. Then, with a wild scream, he jumped toward Grimes, bayonet fixed. Suddenly, a shot rang out, and the Japanese fell at Grimes's feet. Turning slowly around, Grimes saw Corporal Dobbins crouched near him, grinning as sweat ran off his face. "I owe you for that one, fella!" Grimes said to his savior, like him also twenty-eight years old.[30]

But it was not over yet for Grimes. As the two corporals crawled back to join their men, gunfire broke out somewhere behind them and "something awful" hit Grimes's legs, stunning him and throwing him to the ground. "They got him through the legs," Dobbins told the men near them. Grimes tried to lift himself up by his elbows but lacked the strength; his legs were numb. Dobbins broke out Grimes's medicine kit and dusted his legs with sulfa powder to prevent infection. Then the two battalion corpsmen who had accompanied the patrol came up. "We'll have you out of here in a jiffy," the red-faced one assured him. They placed him on a stretcher and carried him back along the trail.[31]

To the right of Grimes and his squad, the men of Dobbins's BAR squad had been engaged with Japanese just yards in front of them, shots ringing out from both sides. One of the two BAR men in the squad, Stub Morse, facing combat for the first time, only now was realizing that "there are people out there who would kill me if they could." Clutching the Episcopal medal he wore around his neck, Morse fought his "acrid fear," his adrenalin pumping, and charged through the underbrush as Dobbins yelled for his men to move off the track and in closer to the Japanese in the jungle.[32]

Suddenly, Morse tripped and fell flat on his face. Seeing that he had a loose shoelace, he stooped down to tie it just as squad mate John Buckhalt stepped in front of him, heading for the cover of trees. Morse then heard a rifle shot from his left and saw that Buckhalt had been hit in the left arm. As blood gushed from Buckhalt's wound, Morse yelled to him to get down. Motioning to the treetops, Buckhalt shouted, "The bastards are in the trees!" Morse knew they weren't and reached to pull him down, but Buckhalt pulled away and rose to his knees. As Morse was looking right at his twenty-year-old buddy from Dowling Park, Florida, a second shot hit Buckhalt right in the temple. He slumped back against the tree, uttered a little moan, and died.

In acute shock, Morse could not believe what had happened. He wanted to "wake up and discover it was all a bad dream," to "crawl into a hole and cry, . . . to die himself and get it all over with." But his overwhelming desire was "to kill the Jap who did this to Buck."[33]

Not far from where Buckhalt was shot, assistant squad leader Bob Cutshall had come over to the side of his dying squad mate, too, joined moments later by the squad leader. Like Morse, Dobbins "almost went off his rocker with sadness and anger," "screaming with his guts while at the same time asking the Lord for help." To his comrades around him, he "called out for strength that was greater than our own to see us through."[34]

Driven by a "nauseating, gut-wrenching hatred," Morse moved forward as his squad regrouped. He spotted the body of a dead Japanese. Someone had beat him to his ardent desire for revenge, he thought, assuming that this was the Japanese who had killed Buckhalt. But just a few yards further on, he ran into another body, and this was that of a comrade. Pvt. Charley Major in Corporal Grimes's third rifle squad was lying on the jungle floor with a hole in his back. A Japanese bullet "had opened him up, along with a can of corned beef hash in his pack." Fortunately, the wound—extending from his back to his right shoulder—was not fatal for the seventeen-year-old kid from Kentucky.[35]

With the loss of Buckhalt, Dobbins's regrouped BAR squad was now down to six men: four riflemen and the two BAR men, not including Dobbins himself. It seemed to them that the Japanese were now throwing firecrackers at their buddies on the other flank to torment them—these were the shots that the squad had heard. But now on an order to his squad, Dobbins and his men shifted their position to circle around to the right flank of the Japanese group, cutting off the enemy from any possibility of escape eastwards, the one side that had still been open to them.

"Crossfire!" As soon as the order was received, Dobbins directed his squad to commence firing. Stub Morse at one end and Henry Kent at the other opened up with their BARs, sweeping the target area from right to left, then left to right from their twenty-round magazines in a crisscrossing pattern, while the squad's four supporting riflemen between Morse and Kent let loose with single shots from their '03 rifles. The "chub-chub-chub" of the .30-caliber fire from the BARs filled the air, intermixed with the cracking sound of the Springfields. There was no return fire from the trapped Japanese, who apparently were overwhelmed by the devastating firepower of the BAR squad. To Dobbins "it was like shooting on the range that we had practiced over and over again on maneuvers." He was proud of his squad for its teamwork; his men performed like a "well-oiled machine."[36]

Pinned down with the other five men in their wire communication section near the tail of the Shibuya reconnaissance party, Pfcs. Yuichi Masako and Tadao Katayama decided to try to reach a low place outside the line of the enemy's flanking fire. It was about 1350. However, just as they began to make their move, a rifle bullet pierced Katayama's helmet and penetrated his skull. Without a word being uttered, his head slumped down to the jungle floor, his body lifeless. Masako rose up slightly and began returning fire, joined in by two comrades nearby, Ldg. Pvt.

Hikotaro Yamada and Pfc. Shigeo Nakahashi, both of whom appeared to Masako to be in a trancelike state. But every shot they fired with their Arisaka bolt-action rifles seemed to result in twenty bullets in response from the Americans.[37]

Then, just after Nakahashi was raising his arm to fire, he suddenly threw back his head and looked up to the sky. Masako could see a hole in the left side of Nakahashi's chest, blood rushing from it and dyeing his uniform red. "Pfc. Nakahashi—hold on!" Masako called out to him. It seemed to Masako that Nakahashi gave a slight nod in response, then he moved no more. Masako knew that his comrade was dead. Leading Private Yamada was also dead, turned over and lying prostrate behind Masako.

It appeared to Masako that anyone hit by a bullet would throw back his head and fall stretched out on the jungle floor. The volume and intensity of fire from the enemy was simply too great. Even as the return fire from the others in the reconnaissance party gradually was decreasing, there was no letup of fire from the Americans.

Behind the two communications sections, at the very end of the Shibuya party's column, Prov. 2nd Lt. Shigeru Wada and the four men of his reconnaissance squad had heard someone yell "Disperse! Take cover! Fire!" at the outset of the fighting. But with their backs to the sea after moving off the track, and the enemy on their flanks, Wada knew that the advantage of position was against them. Now some thirty to forty minutes later, two of Wada's men lay dead: his squad leader, Cpl. Hiroshi Mizuno, and Ldg. Pvt. Takeshi Someya. Besides himself, only Pfc. Katsujirō Tamano was still able to keep fighting.[38]

"We are all doomed," Wada thought. There was no doubt in his mind that the officer reconnaissance party was being overwhelmed by the superior firepower of the enemy. Just as this conclusion sank into his head, a bullet struck Wada's right shoulder. The young platoon leader from Ichiki's Engineer Company fell backward and hit the ground, in acute pain with his shoulder pierced all the way through.[39]

Little by little, in small movements, Pfc. Yuichi Masako had managed to crawl to the beach from the location in the jungle where his wire communications section comrades lay dead, but now he was being fired on again. Bullets made holes in the sand all around him, impeding his attempt to retrace his steps along the route that had taken him from Tetere earlier that day. A feeling of calm overtook him. He could see some palm trees just one hundred meters in front of him, but his body seemed unable to move any further.[40]

Lying wounded at the rear of the Japanese column, Provisional Lieutenant Wada yelled an order to Private First Class Tamano of his reconnaissance squad. "Pfc. Tamano, go back! Report to the detachment commander that we are being wiped out!" Wada screamed. When Tamano remained immobile on the ground, intent on continuing to fight, Wada repeated his order. "Your duty now is not to die here but to make the report. Do not let your life be wasted!" Finally, Tamano responded and began crawling towards the beach, trying to evade American gunfire.[41]

After Tamano departed, Wada was left all alone. Should he remain on the ground and face an ignoble death or get up and despite his wounds attempt to charge the enemy in a more glorious way to end his life? Wada rejected both courses of action. He would try to escape and take refuge in Koli village. With bullets flying all around him, he began creeping up towards the beach and managed to reach it safely.[42]

Meanwhile, at the front of the column, Cpl. Kiyonobu Akasaka also had been left lying on the ground, severely wounded. Looking around, he saw that only one of the five members of his squad was unscathed by the torrent of American gunfire. Like Wada, he realized that someone should report back to Colonel Ichiki with the report of the destruction of the reconnaissance party, and he himself was unable to do so. But when he yelled to Ldg. Pvt. Masamitsu Ōkuno to report back about the death of Captain Shibuya and 1st Lieutenant Tate, Ōkuno barked back, "Ōkuno stays to fight to the end!" Only when Akasaka repeated his order did Ōkuno comply and begin making his way cautiously up to the beach.[43]

With the departure of Ōkuno, Akasaka began to reflect on his own situation. Was he going to accept death like this, waiting to be dispatched by the enemy, or should he try to prolong his life to go down fighting in a future battle instead? His left leg was useless, but with his right leg and one hand, Akasaka began with great effort to drag himself toward the beach. Keeping below the level of American gunfire, he avoided being spotted, and after crawling some three hundred meters he reached a thick growth of low palms and shrubs. Akasaka erased the marks he had made in the sand and crawled into the bush.

Suddenly he heard Americans talking loudly among themselves as they approached his hiding place. "If they find me here, I'm done for—I'll be captured," he thought, sweat streaming down his body. But the enemy soldiers passed by, then turned and came back, and finally withdrew towards the site of the fighting. His terror giving way to relief, his body drained of strength, and oblivious to the pain of his wounds, Akasaka fell asleep.[44]

With no more return fire, it seemed to the men of Jachym's platoon that the Japanese group had been wiped out. The sudden engagement had only lasted fifty-one minutes. However, concerned that other Japanese might be lurking in the jungle nearby, Captain Brush decided to post security to the east and south. He also put in a radio call to regiment with the news of the encounter and the successful outcome.[45]

Assured that the two medics accompanying his patrol were already attending to the wounded, Brush now cautiously moved into the Japanese pocket. His men following him were to thoroughly search the bodies of dead Japanese for personal belongings and documents.[46]

As Stub Morse in Jachym's BAR squad carried out his grisly duties, he ran across a body among a small pile of cartridges and a couple of BAR magazines. Shocked, he realized it was his old boot camp buddy, Pfc. Jack Gardner, like Morse also a BAR man. Morse knelt down to touch Gardner's face, then threw up. The wet he felt under him was Gardner's brains. The top of his head had been blown off.[47]

Morse now had personally experienced two dead among his platoon comrades: Gardner and Buckhalt. He did not know of the death of a third until the casualties were toted up. Jachym's runner, Pvt. George Grazier, who had remained behind with Brush after being sent by Jachym to report running into the Japanese party, had been shot and killed when he had run out on the exposed beach to fire on Japanese in the jungle who had pinned down Jachym's two squads on the left flank of the Japanese.[48]

Morse also knew first-hand of the wounding of one of the men, Pvt. Charley Major, who had been hit in the back by a rifle shot. He now found out that Corporal Grimes in Jachym's third rifle squad had also been wounded, hit in both legs, as had Pfc. Bill Watts, shot in the left foot. But none of these men had suffered life-threatening wounds.[49]

With six casualties among its forty-two men, Jachym's platoon had suffered 14 percent losses. The two native scouts assigned to Jachym who had participated in the flanking operation, Gumu and Beato, were also missing. None of the men in the units attached to the patrol—eleven in Brush's mortar platoon and twelve in D Company's machine gun section—had been hit by Japanese fire. Perhaps because of the suddenness of the engagement, Brush apparently never ordered them to set up their two mortars or two heavy machine guns to join in with the assault on the Japanese party.[50]

When the gruesome task of locating and examining the bodies of the fallen Japanese was completed, platoon guide Forrest Wild confirmed to Brush that there were thirty-three dead. With four identified as officers, Brush realized that this was no ordinary patrol; there were too many officers for its size. Such a heavy participation of officers suggested a singular importance for the party. Except for two navy guides, they all had the five-pointed star on their caps or helmets, showing that they were members of the Japanese army. And they all wore fresh uniforms, a sign that indicated that they had only been on Guadalcanal a short time. The significant amount of radio equipment found among the bodies of one contingent suggested that radio communications with other forces was an intended objective of the party.[51]

Flags, wallets, cigarettes, rifles, pistols, helmets, packs, and bayonets were hastily removed as souvenirs from the enlisted men's bodies, as well as bloody "belts of a thousand stitches." From the bodies of the four officers, in addition to binoculars, highly-coveted swords were taken, intended as victory gifts for Jachym, Brush, Lieutenant Colonel Cresswell, and Colonel Cates.[52]

But what was of greatest interest to Brush was the contents they removed from the brown leather map cases the officers carried. In particular, a map taken from the highest-ranking officer—a captain—"startled" Brush. Though he couldn't read Japanese, he could figure out that it showed the positions of the Marines at their defense perimeter on the Tenaru (Alligator Creek and, upstream, the Ilu) in surprising detail. That and other maps retrieved "showed our weak spot all too clearly": no defense at all to the right of Cresswell's 1st Battalion on the upper "Tenaru" (Ilu).[53]

As successful as the engagement with the Japanese party had been, Brush was concerned that nevertheless he had not completed the mission he had been ordered to carry out. He thus now intended to continue moving with his men eastward and attack the Japanese group at Taivu, the assigned target of his patrol. Only afterwards would he then return to the defense perimeter to file a report and turn in the documents they had rifled from the map cases. He would leave a squad behind to protect the wounded and send a runner back with information about the engagement.[54]

"We can't do that!" Jachym protested. "We've expended half our ammunition, we have three wounded guys, and we have all this information. And what if we have more wounded—how are we going to bring them all back? . . . Shouldn't we turn back?" Jachym questioned.[55]

Accepting the reasoning of his platoon leader, Brush dropped his plan of action. He would end the patrol now and send a runner ahead immediately to the perimeter with the Japanese documents.[56] Instead of readying themselves for further combat to the east, the men would prepare for the long trek back to the perimeter.

Shallow graves were now dug for the bodies of Grazier, Buckhalt, and Gardner. In lowering their comrades into the holes, the men left their boondockers sticking out to aid in the anticipated recovery effort. In order to transport Grimes, a stretcher was rigged from a poncho and cut saplings. The other two wounded men—Major and Watts—were considered "walking wounded" and thus not to be carried in such makeshift means of transport.[57]

With the native scouts Pule and Viru leading the way, the men of the Brush patrol began picking their way through the jungle on their return trip to the Marine perimeter. Alongside Captain Brush, Pule had been "scared stiff" during the fighting, but now he was more concerned about the other two scouts who had been with Jachym on the patrol. Both Gumu and Beato were missing.[58]

Some of the men were carrying captured weapons, gear, and ammunition, including swords taken off the bodies of the four Japanese officers killed in the encounter. The two navy corpsmen along on the patrol, assisted by two of the Marines, were lugging a poncho, one man on each corner, in which the body of wounded Cpl. Henry Grimes was making the poor substitute for a stretcher sag in the center. With his men "exhausted, grimy, dirty, feet blistered," Captain Brush would have felt justified in his decision to leave the bodies of Buckhalt, Grazier, and Gardner behind in their shallow graves instead of asking twelve of the men to haul their dead comrades back in three more ponchos. He must have realized, however, that he was going against Marine Corps tradition of "No man left behind."[59]

Despite the long and arduous trip back, no one was complaining. The men took gratification from the knowledge that they had performed well in their first combat. As he dragged along, Cpl. Ernie Dobbins was even humming, particularly proud of the work of his BAR squad. But he was not oblivious to the possibility of encountering more Japanese, and he kept his eye on the trees along the route, his Springfield '03 at the ready.[60]

Although severely wounded in both legs, Corporal Grimes was feeling no pain as he lay in the poncho. In fact, he was surprised to find that he had no feeling at all in his legs, as he explained to the red-faced medic of the two helping to lug him. The medics reassured him that he'd be okay again after they had gotten him to the division hospital.[61]

"How do you feel, Grimes?" someone asked who had come up alongside him. Turning, Grimes realized his questioner was Captain Brush himself. "Okay, sir," he replied.

"That was a nice job you did out there on those Japs," Brush added.

His curiosity taking over, Grimes asked, "What *was* in those boxes they had, anyway?"

"Radios," Brush replied, "Short wave radios, and powerful ones too." He opined to Grimes that the Japanese he had fired on were part of a "radio call party," evidently intent on setting up at the Tenaru.[62]

At the bivouac area of the Ichiki Detachment at Tetere, the security guard thought he heard a voice calling for the detachment commander. When another guard told him that he had heard the cry, too, the two of them headed out in the direction of the call. At about twenty yards from the government track, they spotted a single soldier staggering from side to side in their direction, rifle in his right hand. Approaching him, they heard him gasp, "Detachment Commander Ichiki—the officer reconnaissance party has been destroyed!"[63]

"What? You say the reconnaissance party has been destroyed?" the two stunned guards responded. With one guard supporting the soldier with an arm under his arm and the other putting his arm around the soldier's waist, the two half carried the runner as they headed to detachment headquarters. Other men of the detachment stood off at a distance, striving to hear what he was still calling out.

When Ldg. Pvt. Masamitsu Ōkuno—tottering and out of breath after his almost six mile sprint from Koli—appeared before Colonel Ichiki, he attempted to present arms but was unable to do so properly. Gulping water from the canteen proffered him by a comrade, Ōkuno then heaved a deep breath and tried to give his report to Colonel Ichiki. It was about 1530.[64]

Ōkuno told his commander that Captain Shibuya's reconnaissance party had encountered enemy that he estimated as numbering "about 100 men" and that Shibuya and Lieutenant Tate had been killed almost immediately. The others had dropped to the ground but were being picked off one by one, outgunned by the Americans. When his squad leader, Corporal Akasaka, was hit in the leg and lay wounded, he had ordered Ōkuno to report back to the detachment commander.[65]

Also listening to Ōkuno's report, Sgt. Sadanobu Okada of Ichiki's headquarters staff could see the shocked and worried look in the detachment commander's face as the magnitude of the disaster was laid out by Ōkuno. Ichiki had always been regarded by his men as a loving father, and now he had apparently sent more than thirty of them to their death. It was clear that he now felt that his plan to send out Captain Shibuya and the others in the party without adequate weapons with which to defend themselves had not been well considered on his part.[66]

But Ōkuno was not the only one of Shibuya's reconnaissance party to report back. Pfc. Katsujirō Tamano of Provisional Lieutenant Wada's squad from the Engineer Company now also arrived at the bivouac site, ordered back by Wada. But since Colonel Ichiki already had the report of Ōkuno, Tamano sought out 1st Lieutenant Gotō of the Engineer Company to give its commanding officer an account of what had happened to Wada's reconnaissance squad at the hands of the Americans as he had experienced first-hand. However, he explained that he did not know the fate of Wada, last seen lying on the jungle floor with a severe shoulder wound.[67]

After the immensity of the disaster had sunk in, Colonel Ichiki quickly decided to take action. He would dispatch an emergency force in company strength to rescue any survivors and send medics to treat any wounded. His adjutant, Captain Togashi, was ordered to have battalion commander Major Kuramoto and chief medical officer Capt. Takatomo Tasaka report immediately to him for instructions.[68]

When Kuramoto had been briefed by Ichiki on the purpose of the mission, he informed his commander that he would immediately send 1st Lt. Yusaku Higuchi's 1st Company to carry out the task. Ichiki then ordered Captain Tasaka to send a six-man medical aid team headed by 1st Lt. Yoshihito Nakai, the officer in charge of the detachment's medical unit, to provide emergency aid to any of the wounded who may have survived the encounter.[69]

Meeting with his company officers, Lieutenant Higuchi informed them of their mission and assigned responsibilities. The second platoon of 2nd Lt. Yūzo Kudō was to serve as the vanguard and to warn of any enemy detected ahead of the Company's march. Following behind would be Company headquarters with the remnant of 1st Lieutenant Tate's 1st Platoon, now under direct command of Lieutenant Higuchi. The company's 3rd Platoon, under 2nd Lt. Tadayoshi Uchizawa, was assigned to bring up the rear.[70]

Just as Lieutenant Higuchi prepared to leave with his company on its rescue mission, he was approached by the adjutant of Kuramoto's battalion. 1st Lt. Naoyuki Kondō suggested to Higuchi that he leave behind any of his men who were in poor physical condition, including any with sore feet. Higuchi agreed and authorized Kondō to go among his men and select those who should be sent back with him to battalion headquarters.[71]

It was now 1600 when Higuchi gave the order to head out to the Koli site of the Shibuya disaster. In ranks of four the column began marching in the blazing sun from their Tetere bivouac, heading west. Shortly before Higuchi's company left, 1st Lieutenant Nakai—a graduate of Hokkaido University Medical School—had led out his five medic enlisted men for the same destination.[72]

After Higuchi's men passed from view, Col. Ichiki ordered all remaining units of his detachment force to assemble at Major Kuramoto's battalion headquarters. There, Sgt. Sadanobu Okada, attached to Adjutant Togashi, began to read the order that Ichiki had prepared and given to Okada to present. It set 1700 as the hour for moving out, with "Lengo" as the destination.[73] The passwords were to be *uni* (see) and *riku* (land).

Okada then read out the order of march:

Capt. Tetsuroh Sawada's 2nd Company in the lead
Major Kuramoto's battalion headquarters
1st Lt. Toshiroh Chiba's 4th Company
Colonel Ichiki with his detachment headquarters
1st Lt. Shigenao Komatsu's Machine Gun Company
2nd Lt. Tatsuharu Hanami's Battalion Gun Platoon
1st Lt. Magozō Maruyama's 3rd Company
1st Lt. Hideo Gotō's Engineer Company[74]

On receiving their orders, the men reported to their respective units and began preparing for the march, chatting among themselves. Right on schedule at 1700, while it was still daylight, Captain Sawada led the detachment out of its bivouac area. In ranks of four, the men began their march in a long column, with their first stop Koli, where they were to meet up with Lieutenant Higuchi's company before continuing their westward movement.[75]

When the men of the Brush patrol reached the mouth of the (real) Tenaru River in late afternoon after their slog westward from Papangu, they found two trucks waiting for them on the government track. The two runners that Captain Brush had sent back to the perimeter after the encounter with the Japanese had been told to request transport for his three wounded to division hospital and to deliver the captured Japanese documents to headquarters.[76] The other men also boarded the trucks, but in the absence of a road going south from Alligator Creek, they would have to be dropped off at the creek's mouth and return by foot down the west bank to the 1st Battalion's bivouac area.

By dark, the truck transporting Cpl. Henry Grimes, Pfc. Bill Watts, and Pvt. Charley Major had reached the 1st Marine Division hospital just to the northeast of Henderson Field. Grimes was lifted out by the two corpsmen accompanying him and examined immediately by division doctors. He had been hit by two rifle bullets in the back of his right leg and four in the back of his left leg. With pain now beginning to overtake him, Grimes was given a shot of morphine and wheeled into a ward. For the first time in weeks, he sank back into a soft bed and immediately fell off into a deep sleep.[77]

For the others of the patrol, it was almost 2100 when they arrived at their A Company position at the far end of the defense line. Brush, Jachym, and Cpl. Forrest Wild immediately reported in to battalion headquarters. Stub Morse was "ever glad" to see Pfc. Murl Myers of the Company's weapons platoon among the first to welcome him and the others back. That night, Jachym's men, still traumatized from their first combat experience and the loss of three of their comrades, enjoyed the first hot meal with Myers and the rest of the Company they had had since landing on August 7. "The guys around us could read the story of the patrol in the face of every man who came back," Morse recalled years later.[78]

With 2nd Lt. Tatsuo Tanaka and his 3rd Platoon leading the way as the advance guard, Capt. Tetsurō Sawada's 2nd Company, ahead of the other units of the Ichiki Detachment, was moving along in ranks of four through the coconut groves bordering the long and narrow coastal road in late afternoon of August 19, heading westward from their bivouac area at Tetere. Lieutenant Tanaka in turn had put out Corporal Ōmori, Ldg. Pvt. Kaoru Aizawa, and Pfc. Masaharu Hayashi as point men for the platoon, three hundred meters ahead of Sawada and his company headquarters. Mindful of the fate of Captain Shibuya's reconnaissance party only hours earlier, the men of the Ichiki Detachment had a feeling of foreboding, though the coconut groves concealed them from aerial view.[79]

Even at this late afternoon hour, the tropic sun was hot as it beat down on the men of the detachment. Soon their uniforms were soaked through with sweat. Teeth clenched against shoulder pain, the men of Lieutenant Komatsu's Machine Gun Company were lugging gun barrels, mountings, and ammo boxes and were falling behind. Superior Pvt. Miura, carrying a fifty-six-pound ammo box on his back, was in particularly bad shape, falling flat on the ground every hundred meters then getting up through grim determination. Still steadily losing his position in the Company, he now found himself with the men of Lieutenant Maruyama's 3rd Company, next to the end of the whole column.[80]

Just behind the Machine Gun Company, 2nd Lt. Tatsuharu Hanami's fifty-man Battalion Gun Platoon was also struggling to keep up. Every man was loaded with more then sixty-six pounds of canteens, bundles strapped to their shoulders, two hand grenades, and clothing, with many also lugging the barrels, carriages, and platforms of their two disassembled 70 mm guns. Others were carrying shells for the guns. In their training they had experience in dismantling and transporting the guns, but then they used packhorses rather than just their bodies.[81]

Ahead of the main body of the detachment, the rescue company of Captain Higuchi, unencumbered by heavy weapons, had forded Cavaga Creek and the Metapona River and now before 2000 was nearing Koli village. Earlier they had caught up with Lieutenant Nakai's medical aid team and were continuing on together. Unexpectedly, they spotted someone making his way in the opposite direction, a Japanese soldier. He turned out to be Private First Class Masako, from the wire communications section of the Shibuya party. Masako confirmed to Higuchi that the officer reconnaissance party had been almost completely wiped out.[82]

Further along, just about three hundred meters east of the battle site, Leading Private Ōkuno, in the remnant of the 1st Company's 1st Platoon that Lieutenant Tate had commanded, in the bright moonlight spotted someone else lying under a low palm tree. On approaching, Ōkuno realized it was his squad leader, Corporal Akasaka, from Tate's squad in the Shibuya party. "Ah, ah, at last it's over," the wounded man responded to Ōkuno's call. Ōkuno told Akasaka that he had obeyed his order and made his report to Colonel Ichiki. "I feel guilty being wounded and unable to direct the squad," Akasaka explained. When Ōkuno immediately volunteered to take command of the squad, Akasaka accepted and told the other members around him to cooperate with Ōkuno.[83]

After entering the area of the scene of the destruction of the officer reconnaissance party, Captain Higuchi's men could see that there were no members of the party for Higuchi to rescue, other than Masako and Akasaka. Mindful of the disaster, Higuchi thought it important to secure the area, assigning Lt. Yūzo Kudō's 2nd Platoon to man outposts one hundred meters to the front and keep watch in all directions. His 3rd Platoon, under 2nd Lt. Tadayoshi Uchizawa, was to set up another outpost to patrol the periphery on the south side. All were to keep an eye out for the main body of the detachment coming up behind them. While awaiting its arrival, Higuchi and the others settled down in a coconut grove.[84]

Lieutenant Nakai and his medical aid team reported back to Captain Higuchi that they had found no wounded men to help. Depressed from finding the corpses of so many of their comrades, the officers and men of Higuchi's company had carried on identifying the bodies in silence. They were particularly distressed to find Captain Shibuya—his body not yet cold—and Lieutenant Tate, his body also still warm in its blood-stained uniform. While they were able to identify other dead members of Shibuya's party, many were not known to them and would have to await the arrival of the other companies of the detachment to determine who they were. In the meantime, Sergeant Major Yamazaki and remaining members of Ōkuno's squad were given the unpleasant task of collecting the corpses.[85]

It now remained for Captain Higuchi and Lieutenant Nakai to draft a report on their findings to be sent back to Colonel Ichiki and the main detachment making their way to Koli village. The note concluded that thirty-four of the officer reconnaissance party had been killed, of whom four were officers and thirty enlisted men. Corporal Akasaka survived, though wounded. "The rescue company and medical aid team have had no contact with the enemy and stand on guard west of Koli, awaiting your orders," Higuchi and Nakai added.[86]

Two runners were dispatched with the report. About one hour later they met up with the main body and gave the note to Colonel Ichiki. "Yes, understood," Ichiki replied simply after reading it.[87]

At about 2200 the main body arrived at the battle site and was reunited with

Second Lt. Kiyoshi Satō, 1st Platoon leader, 4th (Chiba) Company, Ichiki Detachment. *Courtesy of Akio Tani.*

Higuchi's 1st Company and the medical aid team. The 1st Platoon CO of 1st Lieutenant Chiba's 4th Company, 2nd Lt. Kiyoshi Satō, was put in charge of disposing of the remains of the Shibuya party, while each of the other companies sent members to help in the identification of those killed who were unknown to Higuchi's company.[88]

One of the men assigned to Lieutenant Satō—Pfc. Mamoru Mizuno from Captain Sawada's 2nd Company—identified the remains of 2nd Lieutenant Hagiuda and three enlisted men in his reconnaissance squad who had been assigned to the Shibuya party from Sawada's company. When added to the others identified and carried to the collection point, the number of bodies—including those of Shibuya and Tate—that the Satō group had gathered totaled fourteen.[89] But with thirty-four of the officer reconnaissance party recognized as killed, that meant that in the darkness they had been unable to locate the other twenty dead.

But there were also the bodies of three men that were much larger than the others and had been wrapped in ponchos. When they examined the remains more closely in light, they realized that these were the corpses of American Marines, not Japanese. They concluded that the Marine commander had left them behind in making a "hasty return" to the Marines' defensive position.[90]

After the gruesome task of collecting the bodies was completed, Captain Sawada's company again led off as the Ichiki Detachment continued its night march to the west. Left behind was Lieutenant Satō's platoon, charged with guarding the collection site and burial of the bodies in the morning. The young officer posted two sentinels at the site as well as a security detail around his platoon's bivouac area.[91]

"Sleepy and tired," Cpl. Tomoteru Asahi in Higuchi's company, which was following directly behind that of Sawada, was leading the fourteen men under him through the jungle, so dark that it was difficult for them to see ahead. The younger of his charges were practically falling asleep as they moved forward, becoming separated from the others. Asahi decided to have them tie a white towel to a strap on their backs as a guide for the men behind them, while others held hands to help them keep going.[92]

Fording the Nalimbiu River at Koli Point, the detachment moved southwest down the coast to a location just beyond Makile village, which they referred to as Lengo. It was now about 0430 as the men flopped down for the remainder of the night. Captain Sawada set up his lead position and had his men dig an antitank ditch in front of them as protection against any possible American tank attack. They reckoned that they were now only ten kilometers (six miles) from their objective, the airfield.[93]

Less than four miles down the coastline southwest of Ichiki's bivouac area, Pvt. Jim Couch, an eighteen-year-old from Power, West Virginia, and his eight G Company comrades were on outpost duty that night on the west bank of what they thought was the Ilu River (actually, the Tenaru). Under G Company's Plat. Sgt. John Robinson, who was lugging a radio, they had left the 2nd Battalion's defense perimeter one hour before sunset and on arriving at their designated position after dark had dug two-man foxholes. One man in each foxhole was to be awake at all times.[94]

It was very late into the night when Couch and the others began to "hear noises and see lights" from time to time to their east. Were there Japanese way in front of them? But as the hours dragged on, no one approached their position.

Shortly before daybreak Couch and his foxhole buddy started to crawl back in pitch darkness to join Robinson behind them for the return to their lines. But just as Couch reached Robinson's hole and started to whisper, "Sergeant Rob . . . ," a .45 pistol was jammed right in his face. "My God, Couch, I almost shot you!" Robinson blurted out. He apologized to an unnerved Couch as the squad began heading back.[95]

When Couch and his squad arrived back at their G Company positions that morning, they found that their company and the others in their 2nd Battalion were all on alert. Colonel Cates had given the regimental order to Lieutenant Colonel Pollock at 0400 before daybreak.[96] It was clear that Vandegrift's headquarters was reacting to the report of the Brush patrol submitted to it the night before.

6

"Was This Going to Be the Real Test?"

AT VANDEGRIFT'S COMMAND POST in the early morning of Thursday, August 20, the 1st Marine Division commander and his staff were making a reassessment of their position. Capt. Sherwood F. Moran—the highly qualified Japanese language translator of division intelligence—had gone over the captured documents and maps rushed to him by Captain Brush the afternoon before and provided Vandegrift with translations. The material was of great interest in its estimate of the Marines' numbers and situation, including the location of defenses, but it did not provide Vandegrift what he most needed to know: information on the size of the main Japanese force that had landed and when and where it planned to strike.[1]

At any rate, it was apparent to Vandegrift and his staff that an attack in force was imminent. But while they judged that it was more likely the Japanese would strike overland from the east rather than directly from the sea against the Marines' beach defenses, there was also concern that the force to the east might just be an advance element that was to cover arrival of a much larger force landing on the north beaches. Or might it be a combination of both?[2]

Based on this assessment, Vandegrift and his staff identified two courses of action. The first was to send the division reserve to the east with orders to destroy the Japanese forces they encountered, while the second was to limit any operations to the east to strong patrols and outposts and continue to build up defenses. The first option, an all-out attack to the east, was seen as weakening defense capabilities against any landing from the sea and from the west and would require greater expenditure of ammunition and fuel. Furthermore, it was doubtful that a single battalion from the reserve could handle the situation.[3]

In the end, the second option was selected as more consistent with the assessment and offering greater promise of a successful defense against any course of action the Japanese might follow. Additional native scouts would be sent out along the coast and strong patrols ordered to the east as far as the Nalimbiu River, four and one-half miles to the east of the Ilu (the real Tenaru), while listening posts would be set up one mile east of the defense perimeter along Block Four River and 1.3 miles further east along the Ilu (real Tenaru River) at night. All defenses, including those at Alligator Creek/the Ilu River, would be maintained at "stand to" during hours of darkness. At the line of defense against any Japanese thrust from the east, Lieutenant Colonel Pollock's Combat Group B of his Tenaru River subsector had already been ordered put on alert at 0400 that morning.[4]

At their bivouac near the village of Makile, the men of Colonel Ichiki's detachment were getting some rest this morning after their late-night arrival from the site of the Shibuya disaster the day before. They were camped near the beach, five and a half miles northeast of the mouth of the Nakagawa River (Alligator Creek). About two miles further down the beach, Capt. Tetsurō Sawada and his 2nd Company were also resting, positioned behind the antitank ditch the men had dug for protection. They had been assigned as the advance guard for the detachment.[5]

At noon, Colonel Ichiki assembled his company commanders and announced his orders for the attack on the Marines and occupation of the former camp of the 11th Construction Battalion. Assuming they would be successful in reaching the camp, the detachment's men would then prepare there to capture the nearby airfield.

With Sawada's 2nd Company in the lead, Ichiki fixed 2000 as the time the detachment would set out from their bivouac and begin marching down the beach toward their objective. Following behind Sawada's men would be the battalion headquarters of Maj. Nobuo Kuramoto, then 1st Lt. Yusaku Higuchi's 1st Company, followed by Toshirō Chiba's 4th Company. Colonel Ichiki and his staff would follow next, then 1st Lt. Shigenao Komatsu's Machine Gun Company, 2nd

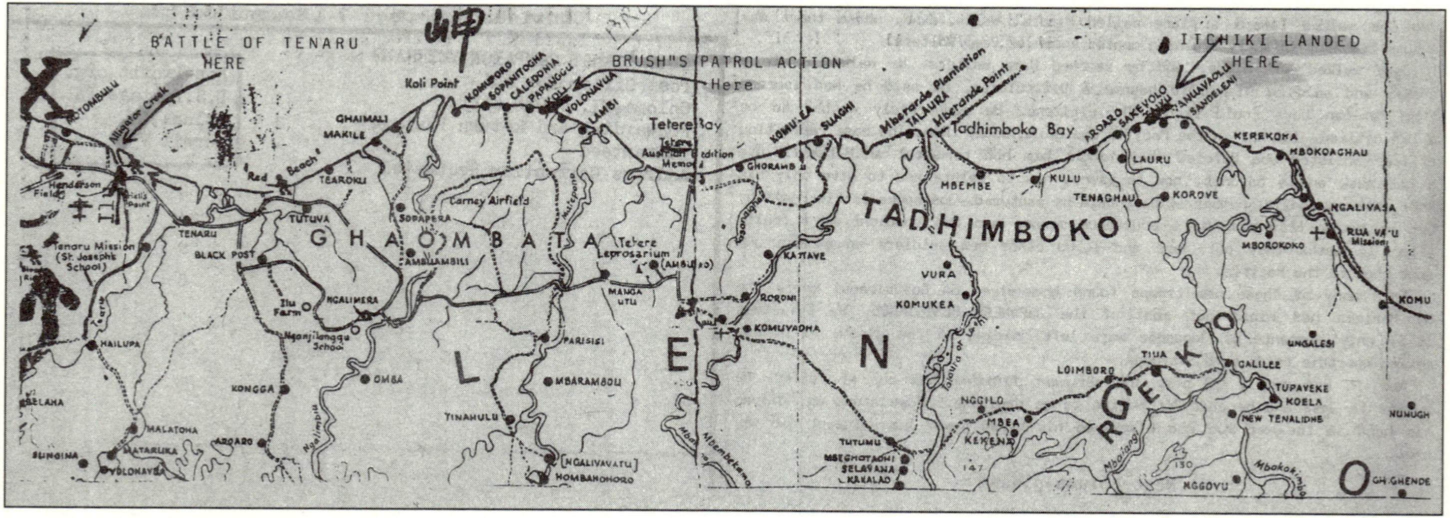

North coast of Guadalcanal showing the route of march of the Ichiki Detachment westward, Taivu to Alligator Creek, August 19–20, 1942. *Courtesy Akio Tani, in* Guadalcanal Echoes, *January 1986.*

Lt. Tetsuharu Hanami's Battalion Gun Platoon, 1st Lt. Magozō Maruyama's 3rd Company, and, bringing up the rear, 1st Lt. Hideo Gotō's Engineer Company.[6]

Ichiki indicated in his order that the detachment would reach the Nakagawa at 0030. After forming up, the men should begin the offensive four hours later, at 0430. The password was Yamakawa. They were not to load their guns before daybreak.[7]

However, before the detachment should set out from its bivouac, Lieutenant Gotō should send out a noncommissioned officer from his Engineering Company, accompanied by an interpreter and three native guides, in order to reconnoiter the Higashigawa River (the real Tenaru River) for a suitable fording location. The detachment would need to cross the Higashigawa, 3.2 miles down the coast, to reach the Nakagawa 2.2 miles beyond.[8]

Colonel Ichiki had hoped to obtain some information from a native scout captured that day by one of his patrols to add to what he knew about the Marines' defenses on the west bank of the Nakagawa. From the miniature American flag found on the scout's person, he was considered associated with the Americans and hauled before Colonel Ichiki for interrogation by the two civilian interpreters on the colonel's staff. After the scout refused to divulge any information, he was taken to the nearby village of Gaimale, tied with straw ropes to a tree, and beaten with rifle butts and slashed with a sword. Hung from the tree, he passed out from his wounds.[9]

Warily, 2nd Lt. Ed Craig was leading his F Company platoon eastward along the beach towards the "Ilu" (actually, the Tenaru) River on their patrol that morning. As ordered by Lieutenant Colonel Pollock at the 2nd Battalion command post, Craig was to report back the presence of any Japanese in the Ilu area, two and a quarter miles east of the battalion defense line at the "Tenaru" (Alligator Creek). In some places along their route, great tropical trees rose before them to a height of 150 feet, with vines and growth in the highest branches. Craig was wondering if a machine gun platform might not be concealed way up one of the trees.[10]

Second Lt. Edward J. Craig, 3rd Platoon leader, F Company, 1st Marines (as a first lieutenant in 1943). *Courtesy of Edward Craig.*

Their orders stipulated that if they should be hit by a superior force during the patrol, they were to stay in contact with each other and withdraw over the same route they had taken from their starting point. Some of the men visualized being captured alive and tortured to a slow death. Craig had told them that their best option if faced with such a situation was to be killed outright in combat.

When the Ilu finally appeared before them, tropical birds disturbed by their arrival rose noisily in the air. Cautiously, Pfc. Charlie Gambrell and the other men of Craig's platoon moved along the banks of the sluggish stream, sweating profusely in the one-hundred-degree tropical heat. It was very silent and had even become eerie when one of the men summoned Craig to come and examine fresh footprints he'd seen on the muddy shore. They were of a pattern made by a shoe with a split toe. Craig knew that Japanese snipers wore such shoes to help them climb trees.

It suddenly dawned on Craig that they had gone far beyond their own lines. Nervously, all eyes began searching the treetops, the men expecting at any moment to hear the whine of a bullet. But the silence continued.

As Craig's men made their way back to the Marine perimeter to report to Pollock and division headquarters, Craig wondered if, as he had read in history books, they were the last patrol to be allowed to return to their lines unmolested before the enemy attacked. At any rate, he knew that the "sneaker" tracks they had seen would be of great interest to division intelligence.[11]

When Craig returned afterwards to F Company's position in the Lever Brothers coconut plantation on the beach just west of the mouth of the Tenaru (Alligator Creek), he would have noticed much activity at the site. A small working party led by the assistant operations officer of Colonel Cates's 1st Regiment, 2nd Lt. Martin Holt, was busy removing barbed wire from the fences of the plantation. Because the stock of wire had never been landed from the transports before they were ordered away from the coast on August 9, Cates ordered the old, often rusted wire collected to string across the sand spit at the mouth of the Tenaru as part of the stepped-up defense arrangements against an impending Japanese attack from the east. For Pfc. Eben Babbidge of Pollock's quartermaster section, it was a difficult job loading the old wire into a truck for transport down to the sand spit.[12]

Further measures to improve the defenses around the sand spit and on the Tenaru River were keeping Pollock busy that morning. Accompanied by his company commanders, the 2nd Battalion commander was personally conducting the rearrangement of emplacements of heavy weapons—.30-caliber heavy machine guns, mortars, and 37 mm antitank guns—aimed at shifting more such weapons to the sand spit area and up the river. Such movements would shorten Pollock's battalion's beach front but give it stronger protection than before. Earlier work on the west bank of the Tenaru had created sufficient positions to permit the movement of one of his three infantry companies to occupy them in case of need.[13]

On the beach in the area assigned to 2nd Lt. Hugh Corrigan's H Company, 1st Platoon, "Lucky" Leckie and Lew Juergens were grumbling as they began to take apart their .30-caliber heavy machine gun. Nearby, their buddies Wilbur "Bud" Conley and Bill Smith were also disassembling their own gun. Their two squads had been ordered by Corrigan and acting platoon sergeant Frank Stewart to shift their guns past the sand spit and up the Tenaru River to a new defensive location.[14]

As they prepared to move out by foot, Juergens, his arms and legs stretched out, positioned the heavy iron tripod of the gun across his back while Leckie hoisted the barrel up on his own shoulder. Others in their machine gun squad picked up the water cans and ammunition boxes and, joined by the men in Conley's squad, lugged their number 3 and 4 guns toward the sand spit, where they found men of the 1st Special Weapons Battalion sandbagging a 37 mm antitank gun. Turning right to head up the Tenaru, they encountered Al Schmid and Jack Rivers of Lt. Bill Whorf's sister 3rd Platoon busy oiling their own .30-caliber heavy machine gun.[15]

After going past still another heavy machine gun paired with that of Schmid and Rivers and passing a bend in the river some 150 yards further upstream, the two squads arrived at the gun site that their H Company's master gunnery sergeant, James "Gunny" Blalock, had chosen for them. Lowering their heavy burdens to the ground, Corrigan's men, sweating and assailed by mosquitoes, ants, and flies, began to dig the emplacement for Conley's gun. It was now too late in the day to start work on the second emplacement for Juergens's gun, nor was there time to cut logs for the roof of Conley's dugout.[16]

Leckie and the others of Lieutenant Corrigan's section of two squads did not know that further upstream another machine gun section of two squads was also digging an emplacement for their own .30-caliber Brownings that afternoon. At the request of his H Company commander, Capt. James Ferguson, 2nd Lt. Bill Whorf had moved a section of two squads of his platoon with its two heavy machine guns up the Tenaru about five hundred yards south of the sand spit to a position picked by Ferguson on a small rise, with open land about fifty feet from their position and the river. The gunners of the two squads would have a good field of fire from this position, as there was not much cover on the other side of the river for an enemy. Under section leader Sgt. James Cross, the eight men of Cpl. Bill Wright's number 10 machine gun squad and the eight of Cpl. Perry Fridley's number 9 squad to Wright's left were hastily digging emplacements for their paired guns that would ensure some protection across the front of the gun pit, but there was not enough time left to provide overhead protection.[17]

Back at Whorf's other machine gun section, Captain Ferguson had paid a visit at the time he was inspecting the line of machine guns set up on the west bank of the Tenaru. He was disturbed to find Al Schmid's left leg nearly paralyzed from blood poisoning and had ordered Schmid to the hospital. Otherwise, Cpl. LeRoy Diamond's number 11 machine gun squad had passed muster. Its .30-caliber heavy machine gun was well protected in the pit, around which a three-foot-deep trench had been dug with room enough for three men and the ammunition boxes. There were sandbags on each side and in front of the gun, with coconut logs on top, covered with additional sandbags. With Diamond, gunner Jack Rivers, and assistant gunner Schmid in the pit, the other men of the squad were in individual foxholes dug in around the gun about ten feet apart, responsible for providing rifle protection for the gun crew against any attack by Japanese across the river. The tripod of the machine gun rested at ground level on a shelf of dirt. A shamrock was painted on the gun's water jacket for Schmid and the word *Chief* for Rivers. On each side of the gun, pointing out an opening below the log roof, final protective line stakes were stuck into the ground to serve as guides to the distance the gun could traverse left and right when its locking device was released, should no one of the gun crew be able to see to fire the gun.[18]

Some one hundred yards to the right and up the Tenaru from the Rivers-Schmid gun emplacement, the other .30-caliber Browning of Cpl. Ed Whatley's number 12 machine gun squad was in its own emplacement, paired with the Rivers-Schmid gun to provide traversing crossfire at targets across the river. In addition to Whatley, the gunner, Pfc. Jim "Bull" Warren, and the assistant gunner, Pvt. Joe Mills, were in the pit. Assigned from 2nd Battalion headquarters, navy PhM3c Robert "Doc" Day had also joined them. The other six men of the squad were in foxholes in a semicircle around the gun emplacement, sandbagged like that of Schmid and Rivers on each side and covered with logs and more sandbags. However, the gun sat lower than Schmid and Rivers's, positioned as it was on a defile that ran down almost to the edge of the Tenaru. With its top about level with the ground around it, the gun was not as visible from the other side of the river as that of Rivers and Schmid.[19]

From the standpoint of communications, Bill Whorf was unhappy that his two machine gun sections were so far apart from each other. He was particularly concerned that the Cross section was so far up the Tenaru. Neither his platoon sergeant, John Muth, in a foxhole back about fifteen feet from a point between the Rivers and Warren guns, nor Whorf himself, in a foxhole another fifteen feet behind Muth's, could communicate with Cross and his squad leaders Fridley and Wright except by the runner stationed with Muth.[20]

Unknown to Whorf, another machine gun platoon of four .30-caliber Brownings was dug in even further upriver than were the squads of Fridley and Wright. That platoon was not even assigned to Lieutenant Colonel Pollock, but instead to Lieutenant Colonel Cresswell's 1st Battalion, which had been preparing positions on the right of Pollock's 2nd Battalion for occupation if so ordered by Colonel Cates. Assigned as reserve to the Tenaru Sector a week earlier, 2nd Lt. John Speaks and his 2nd Machine Gun Platoon, D Company, were busy reinforcing the emplacements for their four machine guns with heavy logs and earth. Attached to B Company, Speaks's four squads under Plat. Sgt. George Pyles were stretched out along the upper reaches of the Tenaru.[21]

But except for Speaks's machine gun platoon, there were no other units of the 1st Battalion in prepared positions extending upstream beyond the 2nd Battalion's defense line. They were being held in division reserve to the right rear of Pollock's battalion.[22]

When Leckie's and Conley's squads were transferred to the Tenaru, 2nd Lt. Hugh Corrigan was left with just two of the .30-caliber heavy machine guns of his 1st Platoon on the ocean beach. Set up on Corrigan's left to the west, 2nd Lt. Bob "Porky" Molloy, with his intact 2nd Platoon, was also retained by Lieutenant Colonel Pollock and Captain Ferguson to provide defense against any possible Japanese landing from the sea. Under Plat. Sgt. Joe Bean, Molloy's four machine guns were sited some five hundred yards west of the mouth of the Tenaru.[23]

Cpl. Steve Boykin's number 2 machine gun of Corrigan's platoon was at the edge of the coconut grove overlooking the sand spit, like Rivers's gun in an emplacement dug four feet deep, surrounded by sandbags, and covered with coconut logs and more sandbags. The Browning gun, positioned at ground level, pointed out from a two-foot opening in the logs towards the spit, zeroed in on any Japanese who should try to cross over the mouth of the river to the Marines' lines on the west bank. Although it was not paired with Rivers's gun, the location of Boykin's gun would have allowed the two to provide a crossfire. Corrigan's other, number 1 machine gun, under the command of Cpl. Charles Daughtrey, was some thirty or forty yards behind Boykin's gun but positioned on the beach to fire out to sea instead.[24]

Also facing the sand spit, and just some twenty yards to Boykin's right at the corner where the mouth of the Tenaru met the sea, Cpl. Jim Olliff and his squad were busy sandbagging a 37 mm antitank gun when Leckie and his mates were passing by the corner on their way up the Tenaru with their heavy machine gun. Olliff and his men had dug an eight-foot by six-foot bunker, four feet deep, and covered it with logs and dirt, with an entrance on the north side that the squad members could use to crawl in and out. The gun itself faced out to sea, intended to oppose any Japanese troops landing from the sea in boats. Although it could traverse thirty degrees to the left and thirty degrees to the right, it could not be brought to bear sufficiently to completely cover the sand spit on its right.[25]

Leckie had noticed piles of cylinders stacked up behind the wheels of Olliff's gun. He recognized them as canister shells that, when fired by the antitank gun, would spray steel balls like a shotgun in a cone-shaped pattern. A stock of the canister had been delivered to Olliff and test-fired only a few days earlier. He and his squad were impressed with the deadly effect the canister fire would have on an enemy approaching from up to 150 to 200 yards.[26]

Under Capt. John P. Leonard, B Battery of the 1st Special Weapons Battalion was equipped with twelve of these 37 mm guns, assigned to Pollock's Combat Group B covering the Tenaru subsector as a form of heavy weapons support. Leonard had taken over B Battery only the day before, replacing its former commander, who had been relieved after shooting himself in the foot two days earlier. Leonard now moved the command post of the battery forward to within 150 yards of where his three platoons were deployed.[27]

When Pollock was rearranging the deployment of his heavy weapons that day, he instructed Leonard to shift two of the 37 mm weapons of his 2nd Platoon under 2nd Lt. Arthur Bell from their beach positions to a line where the beach met the mouth of the Tenaru. After further shifting the guns, the four of 2nd Lt. Jim McClanahan's 1st Platoon were now stretched out from the vicinity of the sand spit to positions up the west bank of the Tenaru. The four 37s of 2nd Lt. Jim Beatty's 3rd Platoon were left by Pollock and Leonard on beach defense,

Gun squad of Battery B, 1st Special Weapons Battalion, manning a 37 mm gun in an emplacement, evidently at Alligator Creek just after the Battle of the Tenaru. *National Archives, courtesy of Peter Flahavin.*

positioned to the left of the other two guns of Lieutenant Bell's platoon, also still on beach defense.[28]

Just to the right of Olliff's gun, Cpl. Glenn Campbell and his squad had prepared an emplacement for their own 37 mm gun, like that of Olliff also under Lieutenant McClanahan's command. As the first of the antitank guns sited up the Tenaru from the mouth of the river, it was pointing out across the sand spit and supplied with its own stock of canister shells. On Campbell's far right, Pfc. Elmer "Slim" Fairchild, in a two-man foxhole he shared with his assistant gunner, Pvt. Angelo Catullo, had positioned his .50-caliber air-cooled machine gun at the lip of the foxhole with just minimum forward protection. (Between each pair of the 37 mm guns, the battery had provided such a machine gun to defend the antitank gun crews, in addition to a similar .30-caliber light machine gun.) To Fairchild's right Cpl. Gaetano Mazzarella had prepared an emplacement for his own antitank gun, the fourth one in McClanahan's platoon.[29]

In addition to those of the 1st Special Weapons Battalion, Lieutenant Colonel Pollock had a 37 mm gun of his own battalion that he had also shifted to the riverbank defense. Although the antitank gun platoon of H Company's 2nd Lt. George Swinston had been equipped with two 37 mms, one had failed to be unloaded from the *Elliott* in time during the landing operations of August 7 and was lost when the transport sank. Under the command of Cpl. George Parker, the remaining gun had been moved on the orders of Plat. Sgt. Floyd Lowrence from its original beach position, some two hundred to four hundred yards west of the mouth of the river, to a new position to the right of Campbell's gun. Time was proving inadequate for Parker and his squad to prepare more than a rudimentary emplacement of coconut logs and sandbags for the gun and its shield, not a bunker as for the guns of the Special Weapons Battalion. With his stock of canister shells in the emplacement, Parker and his men were to defend a sector of fire extending from the right end of the sand spit on their left to a disabled LVT amtrac in the river on its right, but the gun could not traverse enough to the left to bear on the sand spit itself.[30]

Up on the ocean beach, 2nd Lieutenant Bell and Plat. Sgt. Tom McAnally had supervised the fashioning of pillboxes for their 2nd Platoon of Captain Leonard's B Battery. Using sandbags, coconut logs, and plate steel from Japanese dumps, they had provided for a blind entrance in the rear and a small opening in the front for each of their four 37 mm guns.[31]

For his own gun, Cpl. Mel Berge of Bell's platoon had to use the labor of his whole squad to drag one of the large steel plates to the emplacement dugout and hoist it up on and over the sandbags on each side of the gun. The heavy weapon itself had been dug in just enough to make it level with the ground, ready to be fired by his men from a kneeling or crouching position in the emplacement. Situated at the eastern end of the beach to the left of Corporal Boykin's .30 heavy machine gun, Berge had a clear shot to the sand spit.[32]

Near the positions of Berge and Boykin, Cpl. Tobe Cogswell of the Regimental Intelligence Section was high up in a coconut palm opposite the sandbar. From his perch—a plank nailed to the palm with a makeshift seat—he was keeping an eye out for any Japanese activity towards Tulagi across Sealark Channel, using a "spot-o-scope" telescope that afforded him a good view of any activity up to twenty miles away. Assigned with Cogswell were three other men from the section, taking turns in four-hour shifts after climbing the steps of boards leading up the palm tree. Wanting more mature men for the assignment, their Intelligence Section boss, 2nd Lt. George Hunt, had selected the twenty-four-year-old Cogswell and twenty-five-year-old Pfc. Stu Volan, along with Cpl. Tommy Dussault and Pfc. Jim Stone, for the job. They had not dug any foxholes and were sleeping on a blanket on the ground since their deployment to the observation post two days earlier following their transfer from their earlier OP located near the mouth of the Lunga to the west. They were to report anything of interest to Hunt on the telephone connected to Colonel Cates's regimental headquarters.[33]

Back at Cates's command post, a dug-in bunker roofed with coconut logs and topped with earth about a thousand yards inland from the beach, assistant R-3 (regimental operations officer) 2nd Lt. Martin Holt and his working party had finished salvaging the old barbed wire from the Lever Brothers plantation and had arranged for it to be delivered to E Company and G Company's 1st Platoon for stringing. Second Lt. George Codrea, his 1st Platoon deployed that day in the sand spit area, was finding laying the wire to be a "treacherous job" for his men. Lacking good cutting and splicing tools, they were forced to improvise.[34]

While they were erecting a low barrier of the wire on the section of the west bank of the Tenaru facing the sand spit, Codrea's men were interrupted in their work by a tall, older gentleman who approached them and was observing their performance. Without introducing himself, he asked Codrea to describe the specific tasks in stringing the wire. Nodding approval of the young officer's response, the visitor then began walking towards the upper Tenaru. Only later did Codrea realize that it had been Major General Vandegrift who had been querying him; he'd never seen his commanding officer before.[35]

It had come as a surprise to E Company's men when a jeep arrived in late afternoon, pulling a load of barbed wire. Their CO, Captain Rockmore, informed them that they were going to have to string the wire along the west bank of the Tenaru. As dusk approached, Pvt. Charley Royer and others of 2nd Lt. Dean Stover's 1st Platoon, joined by men in John Williams's 3rd Platoon and Harold Pierce's Weapons Platoon, began the disagreeable work. Cpl. Lugene Chesnut and his Weapons Platoon squad were "bitching" the whole time as they worked alongside the other E Company men and those of Codrea, setting up the apron in the sand spit area before moving upstream to string a single strand as the stock of wire began running out.[36]

No sooner had E Company's men completed the wire erection operation than Captain Rockmore designated two of the platoons to serve as the regular defense line that night along the Tenaru from the mouth as far upstream as the bridge that division engineers had recently constructed across the west branch of the river. At dusk 2nd Lt. Dean Stover and his acting platoon sergeant, Fred Wilburn, led the 1st Platoon's men upstream and spread them out in positions on the west bank up to the location of the bridge, while 2nd Lt. John Williams and his platoon sergeant, Arthur Simon, positioned the 3rd Platoon's men in two-man foxholes to the left of the 1st Platoon on the west bank in the area of the sand spit. Williams's platoon was to provide protection for the two machine guns of Rivers and Warren should the Japanese choose to come across the stream.[37]

But the E Company men were not the only riflemen moved to emplacements dug along the Tenaru for duty that evening. After finishing his late afternoon meal, 2nd Lt. Don Wheaton led some fifty men of his H Company mortar platoon down to foxholes on the west bank of the Tenaru along a three-hundred-yard front. The men selected for this "still patrol" were considered surplus to the needs of their four 81 mm mortar squads. After they were deployed, Wheaton relaxed and started writing a letter to his parents in the dim light. His foxhole faced out to the disabled amtrac in the river.[38]

The departure of Pfcs. Murray Battles and Clyde Lucas for the patrol duty at the Tenaru left their squad leader, Pfc. John Tatum, with just two men besides himself to operate their number 4 gun. That morning Tatum's crew, along with those of the three other mortars, had been shifted about 500 yards forward towards the Tenaru from their old position. Tatum now had about a 150-yard front for his base gun, on which the other three 81 mms were aligned. Set up near Tatum were Cpl. A. M. "Jack" Dalton's squad on number 3 gun, Cpl. Jim Young's crew on number 2 gun, and Pfc. John Mugno on number 1 gun with his men. All four mortar crews were now starting to dig new emplacements for their guns, around which they would be stacking Japanese sandbags to protect them.[39]

But before Battles and Lucas had headed out, the four mortar squads were startled—it was about 1600—by the deafening roar of aircraft overhead that made the earth tremble with their vibrations. Assuming they were Japanese, they all ran to their foxholes for safety. Then one of the men screamed, "American!" Sid Phillips looked up to see gray blue single-engine aircraft with the white star insignia under their wings and with the others "went absolutely wild with joy." The pilots and rear gunners had their canopies back and were waving at them as they banked in a circle, now very low overhead. "Our morale soared." They were not to be abandoned on the God-forsaken island after all, Phillips and the others realized.[40]

All up and down the Marine perimeter, the officers and men of Pollock's 2nd Battalion were standing and waving their hands, including Pollock himself, who was "so damn glad" to see the American planes. Lt. Bill Whorf was "overpowered by the joy of being able to fight those damn Jap bombers," he recorded in his diary that day. All the way west to the Lunga, regimental intelligence officer George Hunt had just scrubbed himself clean while bathing in the Lunga River when he heard the distant drone of aircraft becoming a "deep-throated roar" and looked up to see a flight of Grumman F4F Wildcats zooming over the coconut palms and banking steeply towards the airfield. Approaching higher, a flight of SBD Dauntless dive bombers then also circled and came in to land. Hunt mused that his boss, Colonel Cates, had won his five-dollar bet that American planes would arrive that day.[41]

In addition to the newly arrived Marine aircraft that could be used for attacking any Japanese force opposing them, Colonel Cates also had the support of the artillery of the 11th Marines' 3rd Battalion assigned to his 1st Regiment. The battalion's G, H, and I Batteries, each with four 75 mm pack howitzers, were positioned to the west of the upper Tenaru and south of the airfield. Earlier that day, the battalion reconnaissance officer, 1st Lt. John Frothingham, had run a survey from the mouth of the Tenaru back to the fire direction center (FDC) at battalion headquarters. With the topographic data collected, the FDC now could assign new targets to the three batteries to compute revised firing data. Provided with new registration points, Lt. Col. James Keating's battalion was now in a position to lay down fires in front of Pollock's 2nd Battalion dug in along the Tenaru.[42]

To ensure telephone communications with Cates, Pfc. William White and the others of his battalion wire section had double-routed a line from the battalion's FDC to the 11th Marines' liaison officer at Cates's command post, as well as a line to the forward observation post that 2nd Lt. Brooks Johnson of I Battery had set up on the west bank of Alligator Creek a few hundred yards upstream. But I Battery's other forward observer, 2nd Lt. Gil Small, was still in his post on the beach with Cates's 3rd Battalion. However, to Small's east, H Battery's Nat Mewhinney was positioned at his OP at the edge of the coconut grove just in from the beach, with the Tenaru on his right. H Battery's other forward observer, 2nd Lt. Herb Clark, remained at his post on the beach.[43]

For Sgt. Bob Askey and the other nine men of his I Battery anticipating an imminent Japanese attack, there was a "foreboding air" around their position that afternoon. Then at about 1600, on order from the battalion's FDC, I Battery's executive officer, 1st Lt. John Bradbury, called out, "Fire mission." Askey and the other three section chiefs of the four pack howitzers yelled back to Bradbury,

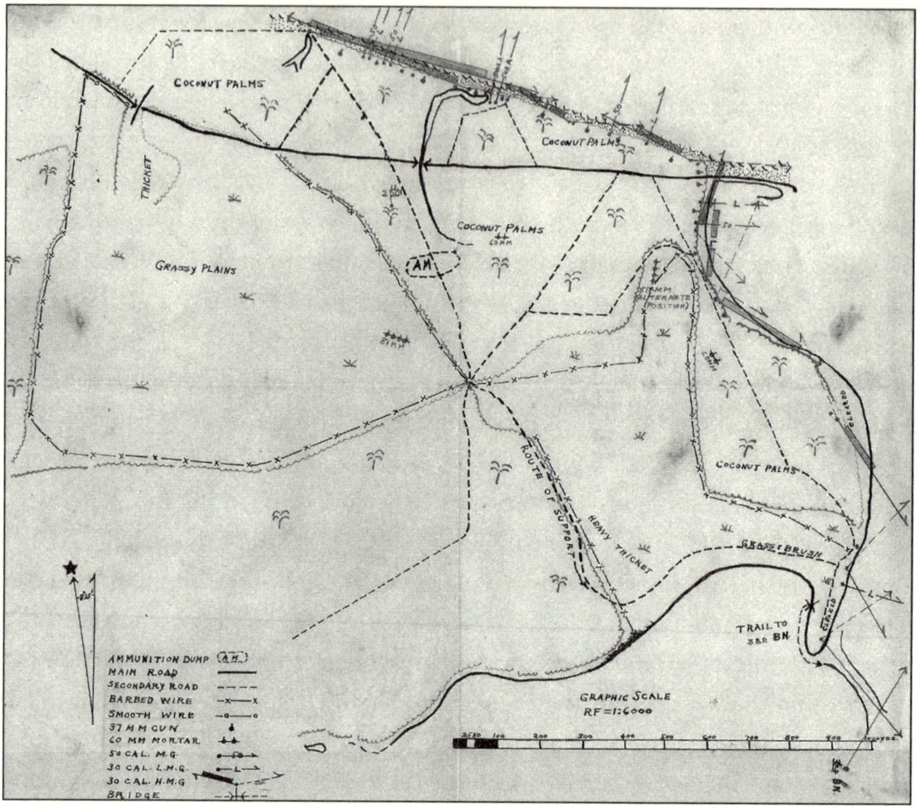

Hand-drawn overlay accompanying Bn-3 Unit Report for August 21–22, 1942, indicating Combat Group B's location of defensive weapons and route of support of 1st Battalion. *Courtesy former 2nd Battalion Operations Officer A. W. Larson.*

standing within earshot, that they were ready to fire. Earlier, Bradbury had laid Askey's number 1 gun on an azimuth of about 800 mills, with the others aligned on its axis. Askey's gunner fired six sighting rounds, then ceased fire. Satisfied with the test firing, Bradbury now ordered his section chiefs to stand down but remain on alert. Along with those of G and H Batteries, I Battery's 75 mm pack howitzers were now ready to be fired with effect on the numbered concentrations on the sand spit and across the Tenaru.[44]

Departing their bivouac area at Makile on schedule at 2000, Captain Sawada's men led the Ichiki Detachment's column as they proceeded down the north coast of Guadalcanal, heading west. After covering 3.2 miles, they arrived at the east bank of the Higashigawa (the real Tenaru River) and halted. It was now 2200 on a moonless night. There, the Japanese were met by the scout from Lieutenant Gotō's Engineer Company who had been reconnoitering the river as ordered earlier. The scout reported that one of the three native guides who had accompanied him had escaped.[45]

Colonel Ichiki was not getting much cooperation from the natives. The one they had captured at Makile and hung in a tree at Gaimale had refused to divulge any information about the Marines. At dusk, conscious again after his earlier beatings, he had been lowered from the tree and, with his wrists tied, taken with Ichiki's men when they left their bivouac at Makile for the attack.[46]

With Captain Sawada's 2nd Company still in the lead, Ichiki's detachment forded the Higashigawa at the point recommended by the scout. It was slow going as the long train of troops, stretched out about 380 yards, trudged along the beach in column in pitch darkness, heading west for the next river, the Hebigawa (Block Four River).[47]

At about midnight, having forded the Hebigawa, the lead platoon of Sawada's company, under 2nd Lt. Gorō Ohashi, reached a point about a hundred yards short of the mouth of the Nakagawa. Suddenly it was fired on by an automatic rifle. "A forward outpost!" Ohashi realized immediately. But before his men could return fire, the Americans began withdrawing "in a hurry."[48]

"Good! Attack them while they are pulling back. Follow me!" Ohashi ordered his men and took off running, the others following behind. But soon their feet began sinking in the sand, impeding their forward movement. Then they heard flowing water. "The river!" Ohashi realized.[49]

At that moment Ohashi saw something rise in the sky, turning darkness into bright light. "Lie down!" he ordered his men, all momentarily blinded. He figured that the Americans were aware of their approach and had sent up flares to illuminate them.[50]

Ohashi gave his platoon ten minutes to rest and to let their eyes adjust to the bright light. It was frustrating for him to see the flares still shooting up in the sky and lighting up everything in the area as if it were noon. He noted that towards its mouth the river before them seemed not very wide and figured the men of the American outpost must have crossed it at that point; "Surely we can cross it there too," he thought.[51]

But of course Captain Sawada and probably battalion commander Major Kuramoto would want to observe the location themselves before making such a decision. Accordingly, Ohashi dispatched a runner to go back and find Captain

Sawada. By the light of the flares, he could make out from his watch that it was now 0030.[52]

At midnight, asleep on the ground behind their foxholes, which extended from the sandbar up the Tenaru, Pfcs. Les Sapp and Cecil Powell and others in Lt. John Williams's 3rd Platoon, E Company, were suddenly woken by the sound of gunfire and screams coming from across the river. They had not been on alert that evening, but now they quickly got up and headed for their assigned foxholes, where they had positioned their packs and Springfield rifles. Privates Bill Moesner and George Turzai didn't need to move; with Moesner on guard duty, they had been in the two-man foxholes some twenty feet back of the Tenaru's west bank and two hundred feet upstream that they had dug earlier that evening. The gunfire and screams had awoken them, too, but now everything was quiet again.[53]

Some 750 yards west of Williams's men, at his command post, Lt. Col. Al Pollock knew what was up. He had received a report from his F Company commander, Capt. John Howland, that the men of Howland's two-man listening post on the other side of the Tenaru had just returned with the news that Japanese had run into their position. To Pollock, this was the first indication that the Japanese to the east would be coming. He had approved Howland's sending out men in rubber boats to set up listening posts across the Tenaru, but provided they "just listen and see if they could detect any advances by the Japanese"—a "scary operation," in his estimation. But evidently Pvt. Frank Wilson—whom they all called "Chicken" because of his diminutive size, which contrasted with the "great big BAR" that he carried—had fired on the Japanese who had approached him.[54]

Also in their foxholes somewhat further upstream than the men of Williams's platoon, the H Company men assigned to "still patrol" this evening under Lt. Don Wheaton had been ordered earlier to "stand by your guns." Pvt. Jim Donahue wondered, "Was this going to be the real test?" Buddy Pfc. Clyde Lucas, warned by his squad leader, Cpl. Charles Karp, that the Japanese would hit about 0030, was concerned that they would come across the river at the point where he had a good position to fire his '03 Springfield from his foxhole. Pvts. Claude Crotty and Harold "Punchy" Leygraff were also ready for action in their two-man foxholes lined with their ponchos. Like the others, they had heard the firing and noise emanating from downstream of their foxholes. It seemed to them that a sentry had challenged someone.[55]

All of a sudden, the moonless sky burst into blinding light that bathed the Marines in the sandbar area in an eerie, ghostly green brightness. "Flares!" they realized. Moments before it had been so dark that they could not see more than a few feet ahead, but now they could even make out men moving in groups on the other side of the river. "Who fired those flares," they wondered, "us or the Japs?" But all knew that the battle was on now.[56]

7

"F——k Babe Ruth"

AFTER MAKING HIS WAY FORWARD to reach the east bank of the Nakagawa River (Alligator Creek), Capt. Tetsurō Sawada crouched down next to his 2nd Platoon leader, 2nd Lt. Gorō Ohashi. In the light of the flares going off overhead, Ichiki's 2nd Company commander was trying to decide whether they should cross over. It seemed to Sawada that the water depth was shallower near the mouth of the river. Further up the Nakagawa, the flow was slow and it looked marshy, but did that mean it was shallow there, too? It was impossible to be sure of the situation just by observation.[1]

But Sawada would have to make a decision. Only by trying to ford the river would they know what conditions were like. He now opted for the mouth. Sawada ordered Ohashi and his men to cross over at the shallow point and rush the enemy position on the opposite bank. When Ohashi made it across in his platoon's assault, the rest of the 2nd Company would follow, Sawada added in his instructions to Ohashi.

Jumping up, Ohashi yelled to his men, "Forward! Follow me!" Sword in hand, he raced forward and plunged into the water at the mouth of the Nakagawa, the thirty-five men in his platoon following behind. The water was indeed shallow—only about a foot deep.[2]

Thinking only of attack as he joined the others, Pfc. Masaharu Hayashi surged ahead. Suddenly, the higher ground to their left on the opposite bank erupted in a cluster of sparks as flares once again lit up the night sky. A line of unrelenting machine gun fire was extending in an arc "like crimson blossoms" around the Japanese. Streams of tracer bullets "as bright as searchlights" illuminated the point as they cut into the hapless men. Hit, Hayashi fell in midstream. As he lay prostrate in the shallow water, three of his comrades following behind who had not been knocked down stepped on his back and jumped over him. The groans of the fallen filled his ears.[3]

Observing the scene from the eastern bank of the Nakagawa, Captain Sawada could make out that at least some of Ohashi's men had succeeded in running the gauntlet and had managed to reach the opposite bank despite the withering fire. Turning, he yelled to a member of his 1st Platoon detailed for training as a runner: "Private First Class Mizuno, cross over to the other bank! Find out the situation of Lieutenant Ohashi's platoon and report back to me!"[4]

After succeeding in getting across without being hit by gunfire, which had now died down, Mamoru Mizuno realized that the remnants of the platoon had turned left on reaching the opposite bank. He kept running in that direction and soon spotted Ohashi himself.

Mizuno called out, "Lieutenant Ohashi, sir!" He could see that Ohashi was wounded. Only a few members of his platoon were around him, the others apparently killed or seriously wounded. Mizuno himself had now taken a hit and was "pretty much out of it." However, he could understand that Ohashi was ordering him to report back to Captain Sawada that it was hopeless to attack this way against such a hail of fire. "Mizuno, quick, go back!" Ohashi yelled.

Second Lt. Gorō Ohashi, 2nd Platoon leader, 2nd (Sawada) Company, Ichiki Detachment, killed in action August 21, 1942. *Courtesy of Akio Tani.*

Sensing a lull in the firing, Mizuno made his way undetected back to the mouth of the river and crossed over. "Half-dead," he reported to 2nd Company headquarters that Ohashi's platoon was virtually wiped out.[5]

Sawada agreed with Ohashi's assessment as related to him by Mizuno. To continue attempting to force a passage in a column of four through the narrow throat against an enemy in established positions with heavy interlocking firepower would be

Capt. Tetsurō Sawada, commanding officer of 2nd Company, Ichiki Detachment, killed in action August 21, 1942. *Courtesy of Akio Tani.*

inviting another slaughter. Instead, he realized that a better approach would be to spread the troops in battle array along the east bank of the Nakagawa to draw fire from the opposite side so as to give away the positions of the enemy and disclose its strength and firepower at different points. And Sawada intended to press his argument before the battalion commander, Maj. Nobuo Kuramoto.[6]

But in his meeting with Kuramoto, Sawada failed to convince his battalion commander of the wisdom of his position. A methodical and earnest type, Kuramoto lacked any actual combat experience, unlike Sawada, who had fought at Nomonhan in 1939. Kuramoto wanted to make a personal reconnaissance of the crossing point used by Lieutenant Ohashi. Despite Sawada's protests that it was too dangerous for him to do so personally, Kuramoto was adamant. "Sawada Company will take cover and provide protective fire," he ordered.[7]

Accompanied by his adjutant, 1st. Lt. Naoyuki Kondō, and a runner, Kuramoto made his way quickly to the crossing point. In the light of flares overhead, the battalion commander and his adjutant studied the topography of the position. Sawada's men were providing them covering fire, but from the other side a continuous blaze of fire streaked across to their side.

Maj. Nobuo Kuramoto, battalion commander, Ichiki Detachment, killed in action August 21, 1942. *Courtesy of Akio Tani.*

Sawada, in the rear, was following the movements of his commander, now almost out of sight. Suddenly, he made out that Kuramoto had thrown back his head and fallen prostrate on the sandy bank. Kondō appeared to Sawada to have somersaulted and fallen head over heels next to Kuramoto.[8]

"The Major has been wounded!" Sawada cried out to his men. "We must carry him to the rear as quickly as possible! Sergeant Takeuchi, take some men and help the Major back. Everyone else, provide covering fire."

Crawling forward, with Takeuchi and his men following directly behind, Sawada reached the beach point where Kuramoto, Kondō, and the runner had fallen. He found them all dead, apparently killed instantly. Kuramoto had been hit in the chest, while Kondō had taken a round in his skull. Dragging Kuramoto's body, Sawada crawled back. When he reached a safe point, Sawada stood up and carried his commanding officer to his 2nd Company headquarters location, where he laid Kuramoto down. Viewing the body, Sawada's men were stunned to see that the life of such a prominent man had ended so quickly.[9]

Within seconds of hearing a rifle shot, Cpl. Glenn Campbell at his 37 mm gun position facing across to the sand spit was face-to-face with his platoon sergeant, Nelson Braitmeyer. "Follow me!" Braitmeyer ordered Campbell and Pvt. Fred Augustynowicz of his gun crew. Hurrying to the road that led to the sand spit, they ran into Pvt. Clair Hume of Corporal Olliff's gun crew, whose 37 mm gun was to the left of Campbell's. Hume told Braitmeyer that he had fired on someone while he was standing guard duty in his foxhole in front of his gun.[10]

To check out the situation, Braitmeyer, Campbell, and Augustynowicz turned to head out to their end of the sand spit, where they were confronted with the strands of barbed wire set up that afternoon. "The Russian" and Campbell went down on one knee as Braitmeyer crouched over them with his .45 pistol drawn. Suddenly, they heard a loud explosion behind them. Campbell could tell it was near his gun position.[11]

But now there came the noise of screaming men emanating from the far side of the spit. "Here they come!" Braitmeyer yelled. That was no place to be. The three men fired a few rounds in the direction of the onrushing Japanese, then ran back to the Marine line.[12]

In his two-man foxhole just to the left of the .30-caliber heavy machine gun position one hundred yards upstream, Pvt. Peter Martuscelli, a BAR man in Lt. John Williams's E Company platoon, had seen the Japanese, too, moving in groups on the other, lower, side of the river. As the Japanese began crossing the sand spit, Martuscelli heard them yelling, "Prepare to die, American Maline" and "F——k Babe Ruth!" "What did they have against Babe Ruth?" he wondered.[13]

To Martuscelli, it seemed everyone on the Marines' side now started to fire. The men on the Browning water-cooled machine gun to his right were firing tracers really close past his foxhole. It was unnerving, but Martuscelli realized that they had traversed their machine gun to the left to be able to fire on the Japanese crossing the spit.

Cpl. LeRoy Diamond and his gun crew on the machine gun were not worrying about Martuscelli when they pushed the sandbags away from the front of their machine gun to get a clear shot at the spit by tilting the gun downward in its tripod and traversing it to the left. Then Diamond yelled, "Fire!" and his gunner, Jack Rivers, opened up. To assistant gunner Al Schmid, the Japanese appeared as a "dark, bobbing mass"—"like a bunch of cows coming down to drink." As his gun chattered, raking the Japanese at a rate of 125 rounds a minute, Rivers could see that they were breaking up into a lot of " little shadows and shapes, screaming and running and flopping down" in the shallow water over the sand spit.[14]

Rivers soon realized that his was not the only machine gun firing at the Japanese crossing the spit. He could hear the "chug-chug" of the air-cooled machine gun to his left, firing .50-caliber rounds at a slower rate. Unprotected in his two-man foxhole dug in the ground except for a few sandbags, Pfc. Elmer "Slim" Fairchild of the 1st Special Weapons Battalion was directing his fire to the left across the sand spit, too, with Pvt. Angelo Catullo—sharing the foxhole with him—feeding belts of ammunition into the gun. The two men of the gun crew were pleased to see their tracers smoldering and lighting up the sand spit as they hit into the sand just below the water.[15]

And to Rivers's right—some one hundred yards further upstream—"Bull" Warren's .30-caliber Browning water-cooled machine gun had now also opened up on the Japanese. Paired with Rivers's team, Warren's gun crew in their covered emplacement had traversed the gun to the maximum to the left to be able to reach the easternmost part of the sand spit.[16]

Up on the corner of the ocean and the mouth of the "Tenaru," Pvt. Andy Dillman was also set to fire his water-cooled .30-caliber Browning, one of the four of Lt. Hugh Corrigan's platoon. His was in the best position of all the heavy machine guns of H Company to oppose the Japanese now charging across the sand spit directly opposite their gun. But when he pulled back the bolt and squeezed the trigger, nothing happened. Momentarily stunned by his gun's failure to fire, Dillman reacted quickly and opened the cover to check the ammo belt.[17]

Too late! In the darkness Dillman could make out a Japanese soldier with a bayonet on his rifle looking into the opening for the gun, then he felt a sharp jab in his left arm and shoulder. An explosion sent fragments flying in the narrow confines of the emplacement; the Japanese had thrown a grenade through the opening, too. Squad leader Cpl. Steve Boykin and assistant gunner Pvt. Joel Hogeland made for the exit of the emplacement, with Dillman last out behind

Covered emplacement, just on the Marine side of the mouth of Alligator Creek, of Pvt. Andy Dillman's Browning M1917A1 heavy machine gun, its barrel protruding from the dark opening. Photograph taken immediately after the Battle of the Tenaru. *USMC photo, courtesy of Peter Flahavin.*

them. Boykin was injured by the grenade, and Dillman wounded by it in the right knee.[18]

Dillman dove into his foxhole behind the gun emplacement and put his head down. He could not find his rifle. He could feel the warm blood from his arm, shoulder, and leg soaking through his uniform. Japanese were shouting all around him, and sporadic firing was coming from all directions.

Suddenly, a body landed right on top of him. Terrified, Dillman yelled, "Quill! Quill!" hoping the unexpected arrival was a fellow Marine.[19] "Are you okay?" his new foxhole mate asked. "No, I've been hit," Dillman replied. Without identifying himself, the Marine gave Dillman his first aid kit and moved on.

Dillman took out a bandage and tried to slow the bleeding from his shoulder wound. His leg hurt from the wound caused by the grenade. There seemed to be confusion all around, but he kept quiet and still in the foxhole. Some Japanese had managed to get across the spit and penetrate the Marines' line, but fortunately there were more Marine voices than Japanese.

Nearby, Hogeland was also hunkered down in a foxhole left unoccupied by squad mate Pfc. Jesse Baugh. He had fired Baugh's rifle to deter Japanese from trying to block the exit of Boykin and Dillman from the emplacement after the grenade explosion. Earlier, as Boykin and Dillman had been attempting to fix their gun before the Japanese assault, Hogeland had been firing a Reising submachine gun on the Japanese he had seen approaching before it jammed and he had joined his squad mates in getting out of the emplacement.[20]

Further back on the beach and to the left of Dillman's machine gun emplacement, Cpl. Mel Berge and his 37 mm gun crew had spotted the Japanese heading towards Dillman's gun and their own position. It seemed to Berge that there were "about 20 or 30 of them." He and his crew reacted quickly, loading and firing canister shells, mowing the enemy down before they could reach their rearward position.[21]

Some twenty yards to the right of Dillman's machine gun position, Pvt. Hugh Kay and Cpl. Jim Olliff in the dugout behind their own 37 mm gun emplacement heard a Japanese in front of their position yell "Quill!" and head for them. Both Kay, with an '03 Springfield rifle, and Olliff, armed with a Reising, fired, and the Japanese fell dead. To them it looked as if about three or four Japanese had managed to get across the sand spit despite the withering machine gun and canister fire ripping into them as they headed in Olliff and Kay's direction, directly opposite the spit. From his foxhole in front of the gun, squad mate Clair Hume was also firing on the Japanese with his rifle.[22]

As soon as Kay and Olliff felled the Japanese, they climbed out of their dugout and headed for their 37 mm gun. There they found Pvt. Patrick Sweeney, who had just shot two of the other Japanese who had penetrated into the gun emplacement. With Pvt. Irv Moore, Olliff, Kay, and Sweeney began firing canister from their gun, but could only partly bear on the spit; their gun was emplaced to fire out to sea and could not be traversed far enough to the right.[23]

But to their right, the 37 mm gun of Cpl. Glenn Campbell was in a direct line of fire to the sand spit, yet it wasn't firing. A grenade, apparently fired from a Japanese 50 mm "knee" mortar, had landed in the gun pit, spraying fragments among the crew.[24] Knocked down, Pfc. Tom Palmer was hit in the back in several places from the neck down to the knee. Pvt. Al Locke suffered wounds in his right leg and foot, while Pvt. Eugene Stevenson, like Palmer, was hit in the back. Palmer managed to climb out of the emplacement, but shortly afterwards a second grenade exploded, its pieces breaking his shoulder blade.[25]

Rushing back to their gun emplacement after the diversion to the sand spit,

Campbell and Fred Augustynowicz jumped into the pit only to find it empty. Trying to work the gun, they couldn't load it with the canister shells. The breech block handle was stuck, impossible to release. Campbell now realized that the explosion he'd heard behind him while at the spit must have been from a grenade landing in the pit.[26]

But where were the men of his gun crew? Asking around in the dark, Campbell was informed by someone that they were all dead or wounded.

Lying on the ground in the dark out of sight of Campbell, Palmer was in acute pain from his wounds. After "about five minutes," a corpsman came up to him and gave him a morphine shot. "This is going to hurt," the corpsman warned Palmer, who managed a weak smile in response. But he was then left lying on the ground.[27]

Up at the sand spit, eighteen-year-old Pvt. George Turzai of Lt. John Williams's E Company platoon was confronted with seven Japanese who had managed to evade the machine gun fire of Rivers, Warren, and Fairchild, as well as the canister fire of Berge, and had knocked down the barbed wire at the Marines' west-bank end of the spit. Working the bolt and trigger on his Springfield rifle as fast as he could, Turzai shot five of them with the five rounds in his rifle as he lay prone. But the two others were about to bayonet him. Rising, Turzai parried a bayonet thrust of the first one but nearly lost his left pinky in the action. Evidently confused in the darkness of the melee, the second Japanese inadvertently drove his bayonet into his comrade. Turzai smashed him in the face with his rifle butt, and he fell back into the river. With no more Japanese attacking him, Turzai turned back to his foxhole to get more ammunition.[28]

To the right of Turzai's foxhole, a bit further up the river, Pfc. Les Sapp and his foxhole buddy, Pfc. Jim Dolan, did not encounter any of the Japanese who had succeeded in crossing over the sand spit.[29] But others in Cpl. Elmer "Pappy" Potts's squad positioned closer to the spit, like Turzai, fired their five rounds from their rifles, then fixed bayonets to meet the onrushing enemy. Pvts. Gil Dolloff and Dean "Red" Wallace nearby were also firing at the Japanese who were coming at them through the shallow water over the sand spit.

In his foxhole at the mouth of Alligator Creek—right at what would soon be called Hell's Point—Pvt. Brady Wadsworth felt no fear, just anger, as he confronted other Japanese with his BAR. The twenty-year-old native of Lufkin, Texas, somehow managed to evade injury as his fast-firing automatic rifle tore into the onrushing enemy in short bursts. But he couldn't tell in the darkness how many he had felled.[30]

Pvt. Jim Edlin in Bob McMillan's squad was less fortunate. Only about thirty minutes into the fighting he was fatally shot by a sniper who had gotten through the defense line of Williams's platoon. The Japanese had climbed a coconut palm and hit Edlin in the back with a single shot from his Arisaka rifle.[31]

Still stunned by the deaths of Major Kuramoto and 1st Lieutenant Kondō, as well as the apparent annihilation of Lieutenant Ohashi's platoon, Captain Sawada left his 2nd Company headquarters position to look for Colonel Ichiki and report the disastrous developments. He did not have to go far to the rear. Ichiki had advanced his detachment headquarters to a location just behind Kuramoto's battalion command post.[32]

Sawada repeated the argument he had presented in vain earlier to Kuramoto. To charge the Marines' defenses en masse would just lead to a repetition of what had happened to Ohashi's men. Some had managed to get across the sand spit, but he didn't know of any success they may have had in attacking enemy positions before being felled by the Americans. The detachment would have to be reinforced to have any chance for victory. He pleaded with Ichiki to delay any further attack while considering the pros and cons of the situation.

Ichiki grunted noncommittedly as he listened to Sawada's appeal, his adjutant, Capt. Yokichi Togashi, at his side. "I fully understand your opinion, but no matter what, there is no choice but to attack," Ichiki then responded. Sawada swallowed his chagrin. He knew there could be no opposing the expressed will of a superior. Knowing Ichiki well, Togashi also elected to remain silent. Ichiki now declared that he himself would assume command of Kuramoto's battalion.

At this point, Sawada asked Ichiki if he would be allowed to show the detachment commander the Nakagawa crossing location. Sawada would be the guide. Ichiki acceded to his request and with Togashi and Sawada disappeared in the darkness, moving westward. The remaining units of the detachment remained assembled, waiting for eventual orders.

Observing the sandbar from his vantage point on the east bank of the Nakagawa, Ichiki felt this was the easiest way to get across to the other side. Single-minded in his determination to seize the airfield, no matter what stood in his way, Ichiki again dismissed Sawada's advice, apparently unconvinced of the deadliness of the Marine firepower that would be opposing his men. After all, it was infantry doctrine to march to the enemy's position and charge through any obstacle. Of course, some sacrifices would be inevitable, as in the case of Ohashi's platoon.[33]

Sawada had clung to his battle-tested argument that the enemy's firepower must first be suppressed with an artillery barrage for the Japanese to be able to close with the Marines in hand-to-hand combat, the latter the core of the fighting doctrine of the Japanese army. But Ichiki had dismissed Sawada's latest entreaty. He knew the only artillery his first echelon had was the two 70 mm battalion guns in the rear. His detachment's four 75 mm regimental guns had been left behind with the second echelon.[34]

His mind made up to cross over the sand spit, Ichiki had to decide which of his units should be selected to make the second attempt. Again, he felt a single platoon should suffice, despite the lamentable experience of Ohashi and his men.

At any rate, the platoon should not be from Sawada's company, Ichiki decided. Already it had lost the leader of its 1st Platoon, Lieutenant Hagiuda, in the Shibuya disaster and now the 2nd Platoon leader, Ohashi, and his men in the first attempt to cross over the Nakagawa. That left only 2nd Lt. Tatsuo Tanaka and his 3rd Platoon, and Ichiki did not want to run the risk of having Sawada's crack 2nd Company wiped out completely. No, he opted for one of the two remaining platoon leaders in 1st Lt. Yusaku Higuchi's 1st Company as the logical choice. Unlike 2nd Lt. Tadayoshi Uchizawa, 2nd Lt. Yūzo Kudō had combat experience at Nomonhan, and for that reason he was favored by Ichiki following an exchange of views between the detachment commander and Sawada.[35]

Approaching Lieutenant Higuchi, Ichiki informed the Company commander that Kudō and his 2nd Platoon had been selected to make the second attempt to cross the sand spit and seize Marine gun emplacements. Stoically, Kudō accepted his fate and bid farewell to Higuchi, then set out with his thirty-some men for the mouth of the Nakagawa. He knew he was confronting death, but he had no fear of it. Such was the tradition of the Japanese Army.[36]

Asleep in the tent at his battalion command post, some one hundred yards inland from the ocean beach, Lieutenant Colonel Pollock was awakened by the sound of gunfire to the east. Then, shortly afterwards, he had unexpected visitors. A member of his G Company, in reserve upstream that evening, had brought in a native through the lines. The badly wounded black man identified himself as Sgt. Maj. Jacob Vouza of the local police. At about the same time, coastwatcher

Martin Clemens arrived in his jeep, a dog riding on the hood. Clemens translated Vouza's pidgin English for Pollock. It was quite a story.[37]

According to Vouza, he had been captured by the Japanese the day before. They had tied him to a tree and tried to get information about the Marine defenses from him. When he refused to cooperate, they made him lie on a nest of red ants.[38]

When Ichiki's force moved forward that night, they took Vouza with them. The Japanese halted just short of the mouth of Alligator Creek. Still unable to force Vouza to provide information, the soldier serving as his escort thrust a bayonet under his armpit that exited his chest and into his throat, cutting his tongue. Then the Japanese jabbed his bayonet again under his armpit and into his chest. But Vouza was determined not to help the Japanese, even at the expense of his life. He was left lying down at the mouth of Alligator Creek, with Japanese soldiers stretched out next to him.[39]

As the Japanese began charging across the sand spit, Vouza, who was assumed to be dead, rose up and ran away in the dark. No one chased him; he was of little interest to Ichiki's men now. After working his way about a thousand yards down the eastern bank of Alligator Creek, he turned right and crossed over towards the American defense line on the other side. A Marine spotted him in the dark and challenged him, but when Vouza kept walking, Pfc. Wilbur Bewley shouted, "Stop where you are or you're a dead SOB!"

"No shoot, me no Japanese!" Vouza called out.

Bewley realized he was a native when he raised his hands. Not authorized to leave his two-man listening post, the G Company Marine turned Vouza over to his squad leader, Cpl. Elias Hontz, who took Vouza forward to the 2nd Battalion command post.[40]

Before he was taken away to a field hospital for treatment of his wounds, Vouza gave Clemens and Pollock a description of the Japanese force, including its numbers and weapons. He estimated that there were about two thousand of them.[41]

As Vouza related his experiences, the sound of firing to the east had died down. But when Clemens was telephoning the information provided by Vouza to division intelligence (to which he was attached) as he sheltered behind a tree, a bullet struck his jeep. The sounds of firing were picking up again. Pollock decided to go down to Alligator Creek to determine what the situation was.[42]

On arrival at Hell's Point, Pollock found that the gunfire of the Marines had ceased after the last of those Japanese who had managed to get through to the line in their charge across the sand spit had been dispatched. American wounded were being taken by medics back to the field hospital under the supervision of the battalion's surgeon, US Navy Lt. Robert Goldstein, whom Pollock had sent down to Hell's Point earlier. But anticipating a renewed attack, the defenders were now attempting to improve their defenses where possible.

In his 37 mm gun emplacement, Cpl. Jim Olliff—frustrated at being unable to have the gun bear on the sand spit rather than the ocean—ordered his crew to move the gun out and emplace it in a position where they would be able to fire on the Japanese should they come across the sandbar again. Olliff, Pat Sweeney, and Hugh Kay—joined by Cpl. Tobe Cogswell of regimental intelligence, who had come forward from his listening post—tore out the sandbags on the left flank and enough on the right to be able to pull the gun up and out of the emplacement backwards and turn it to the right to face the sand spit. But now the gun was in the open, its shield providing the only protection for his men.[43]

At the 37 mm emplacement of Cpl. Glenn Campbell to the right, there was nothing much that could be done to restore the gun to operating condition after the grenade explosion. Nor was there any crew to man the gun; almost all were wounded and subsequently evacuated (except for Tom Palmer, who was still lying unnoticed on the ground in the dark). With Fred Augustynowicz in the emplacement with him, Campbell was still trying to determine what damage had been done to the gun.[44]

Suddenly, Campbell was surprised to find the battery executive officer slithering down into the gun emplacement. "Follow me!" he ordered Campbell. The executive officer led Campbell and one other B Battery man upstream about seventy-five yards, then had them turn inland about one hundred yards to a big bomb crater. It turned out to be the special weapons battalion's B Battery command post, filled with noncombatant drivers, cooks, and communications people.[45]

To his amazement, Campbell found that he was being ordered to defend the makeshift command post and "shoot anyone who comes near." With Campbell's 37 mm gun inoperative, the executive officer evidently figured that Campbell was more valuable defending the command post than remaining on the line.

After drawing his sword, 2nd Lt. Yūzo Kudō stepped down onto the submerged sandbar at the eastern bank of the Nakagawa to lead the four squads of his platoon in a charge across to the other side. At that moment, machine gun tracers of streaking light zeroed in on the men. Unmindful of the enemy fire, Kudō pressed ahead amid the machine gun fire and shotgunlike sprays of steel balls from a gun or guns facing the sand spit. Ten, twenty, thirty meters and he was across to the opposite bank. But some of his men were wounded, and others had fallen on the sandbar, their blood staining the shallow water flowing over the sand spit. Suddenly, twenty-three-year-old Kudō himself was hit and fell back into the water, mortally wounded.[46]

Back at Hell's Point, the night was now being punctuated again by screams as a second group of Japanese (Kudō's) began their charge across the sand spit. Once more, Rivers, Warren, and Fairchild opened up on them with their machine guns, joined this time by Olliff's crew firing canister from their newly positioned 37 mm gun. In Lieutenant Williams's E Company platoon, the riflemen were shooting towards the sandbar, too. Brady Wadsworth began firing his BAR at Japanese who approached his foxhole, then seemingly turned back. Wadsworth was joined by Dean Wilson, who had remained out of his own foxhole and was also emptying his BAR on the Japanese.[47]

Unable to see well in the dark, and fearing that with his ten-foot radius of fire he might hit E Company men near the sandbar, Clair Hume only fired two rounds of canister. Olliff fired two more rounds before they stopped. The canister supply was also running low. But they could see the devastating effect of the steel balls being sprayed in a wide cone pattern at the hapless Japanese. It appeared to Olliff's crew that none of the enemy had made it into the Marine lines this time.[48]

After returning to his command post, Colonel Pollock instructed his executive officer, Maj. William E. Chalfant III, to go up to the front line to monitor the situation. But in the event, after spending only about ten minutes at Hell's Point, Chalfant returned and reentered his huge foxhole covered with coconut palm logs.[49]

After watching the failed attack of Lt. Kudō's platoon, Colonel Ichiki was beginning to think that Captain Sawada's advice might have had merit. Headlong rushing by lightly armed platoon-strength infantry alone into the Marines' defense line would indeed not succeed, as two attempts had proven. He would need firepower to suppress the machine gun and 37 mm gun fire of the Marines. This time, he would use the heavy machine guns of 1st Lt. Shigenao Komatsu's

Machine Gun Company and call up his battalion gun platoon with its two 70 mm guns to support a full-strength effort to cross the sand spit and break through the enemy line. He would also send an infantry company, supported by engineers, to cross over the Nakagawa upstream, also under cover of heavy machine gun fire. There was little alternative. If he pulled back, his men faced the prospect of starvation when their four-day rations were exhausted.[50]

8

"Crying, Praying, and Cursing All at the Same Time"

AFTER LABORIOUSLY MARCHING in the dark with their eight 7.7 mm Type 92 (1932) heavy machine guns from their rear position in Ichiki's detachment, the 109 men of 1st Lt. Shigenao Komatsu's company finally arrived at the coconut palms near the front, where they dropped, exhausted, to get rest. They could hear snapping sounds in the palms from gunfire flying by from the west. But it seemed only a minor engagement was going on.[1]

Their rest was short-lived. Orders had come from Ichiki to deploy their three machine gun platoons on the left wing of the detachment, extending south from the mouth of the Nakagawa. Komatsu gave the order to move out.

As the men slowly made their way through the coconut grove in darkness, they also began to reassemble their guns so as to be ready as soon as they reached their new positions. After finally emerging from the coconut plantation into an open area of the sandy bank of the Nakagawa, they found Colonel Ichiki standing there. He was waiting for Komatsu's men to set up their guns needed to suppress American fire in support of Higuchi's and Chiba's companies, which he had selected to cross the sand spit at the mouth of the Nakagawa again.[2]

Following Komatsu's order, the three platoon leaders gave instructions to their squad leaders to begin preparing emplacements for their guns. They were to be spaced four to five meters apart over about fifty meters of the Nakagawa's east bank in a line and extending from a point some seventy meters upstream of the mouth of the river.[3]

On the far right, 2nd Lt. Kōsaburō Osada's four squads of his 2nd Platoon, each of ten men plus the squad leader, set up their four machine guns, while to their left the 1st Platoon's 2nd Lt. Masao Inagaki positioned his two squads of one gun each. To his left, 2nd Lt. Zenji Itō's two squads of his 3rd Platoon had similarly emplaced their two guns. With all his guns emplaced, Komatsu took up his position at the center of the line and waited for each of the platoon commanders to report their readiness to commence firing at the Americans across the Nakagawa, only an estimated seventy to eighty meters away. None of the gun emplacements were protected from enemy fire, having been set up hurriedly.[4]

Ichiki had also ordered the Battalion Gun Platoon of 2nd Lt. Tatsuharu Hanami forward to provide further support for the main-force attempt to cross the mouth of the Nakagawa. However, due to difficulties in lugging the two dismantled 70 mm howitzers to the assembly area, only one of the Type 92 (1932) guns so far had arrived with its crew and Lieutenant Hanami. The second gun was stuck in the sandy soil, and its crew were still struggling to bring it forward. Other members of the fifty-man battery were spread out under the palms of the coconut grove.[5]

At any rate, Hanami had the number 1 gun in position to fire, under the command of Sergeant Tomita with his fourteen men. Observers moved out in front of their squat howitzer, prepared to guide the crew's fire. The platoon's fifteen-man ammunition squad was also in place, ready to feed 70 mm shells to Sergeant Tomita's gun.[6]

Poised to lead his 1st Company over the sandbar in the vanguard of Ichiki's main-force attack, 1st Lt. Yusaku Higuchi was going to attempt to move his men to the left once they had crossed over the Nakagawa's mouth. His company was considerably below its first-echelon strength of 105 men and officers, having lost 1st Lieutenant Tate and some men of his 1st Platoon in the Shibuya debacle and 2nd Lieutenant Kudō and his whole 2nd Platoon in the second charge across the Nakagawa. But his company headquarters and 2nd Lt. Tadayoshi Uchizawa's 3rd Platoon so far had sustained no casualties. They would also be joined by the remnants of Captain Sawada's 2nd Company, ordered to make a frontal assault after crossing the sand spit.[7]

But Sawada's men would not be with their commanding officer. Captain Sawada was being held back by Ichiki following the death of the battalion commander, Major Kuramoto. Instead, Ichiki had decided to put 1st Lt. Toshirō Chiba, the commanding officer of his 4th Company and a veteran of the Battle of Nomonhan, in charge of the whole attack force. Except for 2nd Lt. Kiyoshi Satō and his platoon, who had been left behind to dispose of the bodies of the Shibuya party, Chiba and his two other platoons now joined up behind Higuchi's and Sawada's men plus two platoons from the Engineer Company, awaiting the order to attack.[8] It was about 0300.

First Lt. Shigenao Komatsu, commander of the Machine Gun Company, Ichiki Detachment, killed in action August 21, 1942. *Courtesy of Akio Tani.*

First Lt. Yusaku Higuchi, commanding officer of 1st Company, Ichiki Detachment, killed in action August 21, 1942. *Courtesy of Akio Tani.*

Following behind the 2nd and 4th Platoons of 1st Lt. Hideo Gotō's engineers, some of whom carried flamethrowers, 1st Lt. Higuchi, shouting "Higuchi Company, Attack! Attack!" took the lead of his men and headed for the sand spit. In columns of four, the infantrymen, bayonets fixed, began rushing through the shallow water of the sandbar under the light of flares. At the same time, the grenade discharger squads of Captain Sawada's platoons began firing 50 mm projectiles into the American machine gun and 37 mm gun positions that they had targeted. The eight heavy machine guns of 1st Lieutenant Komatsu's men opened up with 7.7 mm fire against the locations of enemy gunfire opposite them. Joining in was Lieutenant Hanami's 70 mm howitzer.[9]

In Higuchi's company, Cpl. Tomoteru Asahi, squad leader in the 1st Platoon, now leaderless with the death of its commander, 1st Lieutenant Tate, in the Shibuya disaster, had been ordered to blow up the barbed wire at the American side of the Nakagawa's mouth. At the head of his squad, Asahi and his fourteen men plunged into the river just below the sand spit and waded across the waist-deep water, carrying a three-foot Bangalore torpedo to blow up the wire. Flares overhead illuminating their movement filled the night sky—fired by the Americans, they assumed. More than crocodiles, Asahi feared being attacked by sharks.[10]

None of Asahi's men attempted to return the American fire ripping into them as they made their way across the river. "Somehow" Asahi made it to the far bank and the barbed wire, but when he looked back for his men, he was dismayed to find only two had made it across safely; the others lay dead in the water. The man carrying the primer charge was one of those killed, so Asahi was obliged to drop his plan to destroy the wire. A Bangalore torpedo wouldn't work without a primer.

Asahi now decided to use the grenadelike charges his squad also carried, but as he and his two surviving squad members tried to blow up the wire, he was hit in the leg by American fire. Wounded but still mobile, Asahi told his men they should try to return to Taivu Point, where they had landed two nights earlier. Slowly, Asahi and the two others backed away into the river, then turned right to stealthily make their way to the ocean, where they would hide as the battle raged upstream from them.

Also in Higuchi's company, 2nd Lieutenant Uchizawa's 3rd Platoon brought up the rear. As Uchizawa led his men in the charge over the sandbar, he realized that many of his men were falling, hit by incoming fire. Then Uchizawa himself was struck several times and dropped down, mortally wounded. Up ahead, his commanding officer, Higuchi, also took hits and fell dead.[11]

On reporting to Ichiki that his company had completed preparations for firing their heavy machine guns, 1st Lieutenant Komatsu was ordered by Ichiki to commence firing. To Sgt. Masatoshi Mae, a squad leader in 2nd Lieutenant Osada's platoon emplaced to the far right of the line, it didn't make much sense firing in the dark when they couldn't see their targets. Although they had flash hiders on their guns, their firing triggered more flares being sent up, giving away their positions. But Komatsu's men continued to fire round after round from their eight machine guns, horizontally feeding fresh strips of thirty rounds of 7.7 mm bullets into their guns after each was exhausted, in a concerted effort to cut down the Marines' firepower against the troops crossing the sand spit.[12]

First Lt. Tōshirō Chiba, commanding officer of 4th Company, Ichiki Detachment, killed in action August 21, 1942. *Courtesy of Akio Tani.*

Under the cover of the concentrated machine gun fire from Komatsu's guns, 1st Lt. Tōshirō Chiba now led his 4th Company across the mouth of the Nakagawa. Merged into his force were other men of the engineer platoons of 1st Lt. Kiichirō Nakamura and 2nd Lt. Fumio Baba who had not crossed with Higuchi's company. In the face of devastating machine gun and 37 mm canister fire, many of the combined force still managed to get across the sand spit and through the barbed wire, thanks to the efforts of the engineers to cut an opening in the barrier. About ten men broke into the right wing of the Marines' defense line, throwing hand grenades at the 37 mm gun and covered machine gun positions. But Chiba and his two platoon leaders were dead, evidently mowed down by the murderous machine gun fire of the Americans.[13]

At Colonel Cates's regimental command post, 1st Lieutenant George Hunt, along with the others, was awakened sometime after 0300 by the sound of heavy gunfire, much louder than earlier that night. They could hear "the booming of mortars, the roar of 37 mm [guns], the loud crack of hand grenades." As far back from the Tenaru as their command post, machine gun tracers fired from the east were clipping through the palm trees around them.[14]

Cates's executive officer, Lieutenant Colonel Frisbie, immediately got on the phone to Lieutenant Colonel Pollock. "What's the dope, Al?" he asked. The 2nd Battalion CO told Frisbie that he had gotten a message from the front that "at least 500 Japs" were assaulting over the sand spit.[15]

"Sitting in front of his tent, a phone in one hand and a cigarette holder in the other," Cates began giving orders. "Hold till daylight, then we'll go get them," he told Pollock. To his 3rd Battalion commander, Lt. Col. Bill McKelvy, he ordered, "Throw a company into the reserve line." After consulting with Major Robert Luckey, the 1st Special Weapons Battalion CO, Cates at 0320 decided to call for an artillery barrage, too. He instructed Luckey to phone the 3rd Battalion, 11th Marines, for artillery concentration number 383, which would rain 75 mm shells down on the narrowest part of the sand spit near Pollock's defense line on the west bank of the Tenaru. After issuing all the orders, Cates "sat back in his chair and patiently waited for dawn."[16]

At his own 2nd Battalion command post, Pollock decided to call in reinforcements to counter the Japanese breakthrough. He sent a runner with a message for Capt. James Sherman, the commander of G Company, which was being held in battalion reserve, to meet him near the mouth of the Tenaru with one platoon of his men. At 0330 Pollock went forward again to wait for Sherman. But it seemed to be taking a long time for Sherman to show up with the platoon.[17]

Earlier that day, Sherman had called 2nd Lt. George Codrea to his company

First Marine Regiment Intelligence Officer George Hunt (*left*) with 1st Platoon leader, G Company, George Codrea in October 1942. *Courtesy of George Codrea.*

command post to inform him that G Company was being held in reserve and that Codrea's 1st Platoon was the Company's reserve platoon. Codrea then returned to his position in the coconut plantation about 250 to 300 yards west of the sand spit, with the coastal road on his right, and informed his NCOs of the order.[18]

Following Pollock's order, Sherman now sent a runner to Codrea with the order to move out. Sherman himself opted to remain at his company command post rather than accompany his platoon. Codrea and the men of his platoon spotted Pollock in the darkness, standing on the road with a runner and a radioman. With Sherman not with them, and not recognizing Codrea, Pollock asked who they were and what their orders were. When Codrea told Pollock, whom he identified in the darkness only by his voice, that his was the platoon ordered to the sand spit as soon as possible to plug any holes in the line and drive the Japanese back, Pollock replied, "That's correct, get going."[19]

As yet another wave of Japanese, this group much larger than the previous two, began streaming across the sandbar, Jack Rivers in Diamond's machine gun emplacement and Bull Warren on his Browning, one hundred yards to Rivers's right, again opened up on them.[20] But to their surprise, this time machine gun fire from across the river was streaking into their positions. This was no blind, suicidal charge across the spit unsupported by covering fire.

To the left of Rivers's gun, up on the ocean beach just to the left of the sand spit, Cpl. Jim Olliff and his crew on their 37 mm gun were also firing from their exposed position with canister shells on the new wave of Japanese. But as with the Rivers and Warren machine gun emplacements, they also came under counterfire from the Japanese machine guns positioned on the eastern bank of the river, with bullets bouncing off the steel shield of their gun.[21]

As their sister 37 mm gun, some one hundred feet to their right, was silent, knocked out during the first charge of the Japanese, Cpl. Glenn Campbell, the squad leader, was at the hole serving as B Battery's command post, ordered against his will to defend it. As the sounds of the renewed Japanese charge—this time punctuated by heavy machine gun fire—reached his ears, Campbell requested permission to return to his gun. "Corporal, you stay where you are, that's an order!" was the reply.[22]

Directly facing the Japanese who had succeeded in crossing the sand spit, the men of 2nd Lt. John Williams's 3rd Platoon once more opposed the enemy with BAR and rifle fire and hand grenades. Those not engaged in hand-to-hand fighting noted with relief that the Japanese machine gun fire seemed directed at H Company's machine gun positions and the 1st Special Weapons Battalion's 37 mm gun emplacements rather than at individual riflemen of their E Company.[23]

In his foxhole right across from the sand spit, Brady Wadsworth was again firing away with his BAR at this latest group of Japanese crossing over. Nearby, in the foxhole he was sharing with Pvt. Ray Roberts, Dean Wilson was also firing his BAR and Roberts his '03 rifle at them. But the Japanese kept coming, including some who tried to blow up the barbed wire at the end of the spit with Bangalore torpedoes. Wilson and Roberts began throwing hand grenades at them and soon used up a whole box of twenty-four grenades.[24]

Suddenly, Wilson's BAR jammed. Undaunted, the 6 foot 1 inch, 190-pound Marine dropped his useless gun and reached over to the machete he always kept in his foxhole, then climbed out with it. At the same time, Roberts also arose from their hole, carrying his rifle. But right in front of Wilson, a Japanese shot and killed his buddy.[25]

Enraged, Wilson attacked three of the Japanese in hand-to-hand fighting with his unorthodox weapon. Striking the nearest Japanese in the stomach, leaving him with his entrails spilling out on the ground, he then took on the other two with fatal consequences for both.[26]

In the meantime, Pvts. George Turzai and Bill Moesner had climbed out of their foxhole, too, and like Wilson and Roberts threw grenades at the approaching Japanese while also firing their rifles. They had been ordered to hold the enemy until reinforcements could reach them at daylight. Someone told them to get the 37 mm gun to their right operating again and that he knew how to operate it.[27]

As they made their way to the silent gun—unknown to them, that of Campbell—they ran into their platoon buddy Dean Wilson, crawling over dead Japanese. Moesner stabbed one of them to make sure he was dead.

On reaching the gun emplacement, they entered the unoccupied bunker and found three canister shells on the floor. Moesner showed Turzai how to put them in the gun and then fired one round into the coconut grove across the river, another down the beach, and the third into "about 20 Japs coming over the sandbar, blowing them all over."[28] Then they resumed firing with their rifles. A corpsman who approached informed them that the original gun crew were all wounded and were being treated behind the line.

Upstream, 1st Lt. Magozō Maruyama and his 3rd Company men had deployed along the eastern bank of the Nakagawa after being selected by Ichiki earlier as the Company to cross over the upper Nakagawa. They had observed the attack by Higuchi's company across the spit at the mouth of the river and watched as Chiba's company poised to follow Higuchi's men across. With a roar, Komatsu's machine guns emplaced near them again joined in the attack, firing across the Nakagawa.[29]

First Lt. Magozō Maruyama, commanding officer of 3rd Company, Ichiki Detachment, killed in action August 21, 1942. *Courtesy of Akio Tani.*

A cause for concern was that the crossing point chosen by Ichiki for the 3rd Company men was in deep water. Maruyama had ordered his three platoon leaders, 2nd Lts. Hiroshi Miura, Shigenori Niie, and Shōichi Matsuo, to be ready to move. Then as they saw Chiba's company to their right moving out for their attack across the sandbar, Maruyama gave the order to cross the river.[30]

Standing at the crossing point, Ichiki had called for volunteers from his headquarters to join

Maruyama and the engineers accompanying them in the attack. But when no one volunteered, Ichiki became angry and shouted, "Nobody? Nobody wants to join?" But then his clerk, Sgt. Sadanobu Okada, came forward, despite having no experience as a rifleman and expecting to be killed in what he felt was a forlorn effort.[31]

"Oh, you'll go with us?" Ichiki replied to Okada's offer. He told his clerk to ready himself to swim the river and to bring along only any others who could swim well. Three other men from headquarters now also volunteered. Okada left behind on the riverbank all but the most necessary items: two hand grenades, a pistol, and a sword. The others would be taking two hand grenades each, too, plus a rifle, a bayonet, and five rounds of ammunition for their rifles.

But just as Okada and the other volunteers were about to plunge into the river, Ichiki changed his mind. He ordered them to stop and wait a bit. He wanted to see if Komatsu's machine guns would succeed in suppressing Marine fire targeting Maruyama and the engineers. If not, Okada and his three comrades should join them.

Watching the men of the 3rd Company and the engineers struggling to get across the river, Okada was not optimistic. A wave of bullets was sweeping into them "like a broom."[32]

After receiving Lieutenant Colonel Pollock's order to take his 1st Platoon to the mouth of the Tenaru to stop the Japanese from breaking through E Company's defense line, 2nd Lt. George Codrea moved his men out in a column of squads along the dirt coastal road, heading east. But only halfway to their destination, "machine gun fire began zipping all around us," coming directly from across the spit and their right. They were caught in a deadly crossfire.[33]

Codrea halted his forward movement and told his men to crouch down on the road while he decided on a course of action. After a few moments' hesitation, he opted to deploy them in a two-pronged movement. Although he realized it was against Marine Corps doctrine, he would take the lead, feeling it was his responsibility "to lead and inspire his men." He also decided to go against doctrine and split his platoon, having full confidence in his platoon guide, Jim Hancock, promoted a week earlier, to lead half his force.[34]

Taking one squad with him and keeping as low as possible, Codrea continued up the road that would bring him just to the left of the sand spit. Hancock was instructed to take another squad and veer off to the right to protect the platoon's right flank. To stop any Japanese from breaking through them, Codrea kept Plat.

Sgt. Charlie Spakes some fifty yards behind him with the men of the platoon's third squad.[35]

Leading the rifle squad just behind Codrea, Cpl. Joe Faso had just gotten out of the hospital in time to resume his squad leader duties from assistant squad leader Pfc. Jack Shea, who had filled in for him in the meantime. With Charlie Spakes in the rear was Cpl. Robert Spillane and his squad. Moving forward to Codrea's right under Hancock was the squad of Cpl. John Oliveri. Each squad was oversized on Codrea's orders. He was missing several men from the forty-two assigned him and preferred to have three larger squads than four undersized ones.[36]

When Pvts. Andy Brodecki and Tom McLane in Faso's squad reached an embankment overlooking the Tenaru, they jumped into an abandoned foxhole and set up their BAR on its bipod. With McLane throwing hand grenades onto the sand spit when he was not feeding ammo magazines to the BAR, Brodecki worked his automatic rifle furiously against those Japanese charging towards their position who had managed to survive the machine gun fire of Jack Rivers's machine gun to Brodecki's right. As flares burst overhead, McLane could make out a Japanese officer waving his sword as he led his shrieking men into the positions of 2nd Lt. John Williams's E Company platoon lining the western bank of the river.[37]

Holding his fire until many of the Japanese had passed by him—as he believed Codrea had ordered—Pvt. Richard W. "Bill" Harding of Faso's squad, barely seventeen years old, from Ephrata, Pennsylvania, saw the Japanese as "small black shapes," all "jabbering to each other" as they came closer to his position. Harding pulled the pin on his grenade and like the others of his squad threw it. "There was a big orange-reddish flash, screams, and yells, the sand flying back to us like from a sand-blasting machine." As the apparently panic-stricken Japanese milled around, Harding and his squad mates fired into them with their Springfield rifles.[38]

But now new groups of Japanese were approaching and charging Codrea's men, firing their Arisaka rifles as they screamed and yelled at the Marines. Although many were felled, others were tossing grenades. Harding crawled into a nearby foxhole and continued banging away with his '03 rifle. Then he heard someone from a hole to his left yelling something in English. He recognized the voice as that of the assistant squad leader, Jack Shea. Shea seemed to be in trouble, so Harding, "plenty scared," climbed out of his foxhole and crawled over to the edge of Shea's hole and called out his name. "There's a dirty Jap bastard in here!" Shea exclaimed breathlessly. But Shea was okay now—"I got him."[39]

Shea had been lying on the ground near Codrea, firing a Thompson submachine gun at the onrushing Japanese, when it abruptly jammed. With Codrea's approval, he had crawled to a nearby foxhole, intending to get his weapon operational again, but had fallen on top of someone already in the hole. He felt a bayonet pierce his left leg twice. Instantly reacting, Shea pushed the Japanese against the side of the hole, but was stabbed again, this time in the thigh. Succeeding in releasing the bolt of his Tommy gun, Shea fired five rounds point blank into his adversary's chest.[40]

As Shea dragged himself back to Codrea after abandoning his foxhole, Harding crawled back to his own hole, fearing taking a hit from tracers "coming over like white bees." But as he was almost back to his refuge, a flare exploded behind him in the night sky. In the light of the flare, he could make out someone off to his left who was making for his hole. Sure that the other was a Japanese, Harding knew he would have to fight him for possession. After another flare went off, Harding crawled around to one side of the hole, gripping his rifle tightly. When the crawling Japanese was just about one foot away, Harding swung his Springfield at him, slashing his arms with the bayonet. Then he jumped on the Japanese and landed on his opponent's back. Harding managed to get the neck of the Japanese in the crook of his right arm and began strangling him as the Japanese struggled desperately to get loose. Finally, Harding let go, and the Japanese fell limp, dead.[41]

Turning to get into the foxhole, Harding made out yet another Japanese crawling past him. He lifted his rifle and shoved its bayonet into the enemy's stomach, eliciting a grunt then a scream from the victim. But as Harding struggled to pull the bayonet out, there was a sudden flash, the explosion throwing him on his back. His left hip was smashed, his left leg twisted, and his pants ripped at the knee.[42]

All around Codrea and his men, what seemed to be mortar shells began falling, followed by showers of hand and rifle grenades. Off to his right, Harding saw a motionless comrade lying down as if asleep, his faced turned away from him. And on his left, he could make out another Marine who could barely groan in response to Harding's call.

Codrea himself had been hit too, almost immediately at the beginning of the barrage. Shrapnel from what he surmised was a "knee mortar" had torn into his left arm in two places above the elbow. But he was determined to continue directing operations.[43] It was about 0430.

Codrea was in bad shape, covered in dirt and blood, his clothing in tatters.

When Andy Brodecki and Tom McLane saw his condition, they ran up to him. Brodecki shredded what was left of the sleeve of his dungaree jacket to make bandages and apply a tourniquet.[44]

One of the mortar shells had exploded very close to Cpl. Robert Spillane and his squad in Platoon Sergeant Spakes's group in the rear as they were moving forward to reinforce the men around Codrea.[45] Shocked by their first experiences in combat, Spillane's men were slow to get up. Wounded in the right knee by shrapnel, Pvt. Robert Flick, a rifle grenadier in the squad, got up with the intention of heading back, but when one of his comrades in rising up was hit with fragments in the throat, Flick decided to stay put. Then Spillane bellowed at them to get up and move forward, but to no avail. In front of them, Codrea realized he had to make a quick decision. Ignoring his wounded arm, he ran back to the front of Spillane's squad, gripping his .45 pistol with his good right arm, and ordered the men to get up and follow him.[46]

After moving forward, Spillane's squad formed a skirmish line, some distance from the edge of the ocean beach and not far from the sandbar, then dropped to the ground. Assistant squad leader Pfc. Jim Wilson felt like they were "sitting ducks," totally exposed without any cover. "Scared half to death," the men began to dig into the sand as deeply as possible. Then they began to attract sweeping machine gun fire from the east. Responding furiously, Wilson and others in the squad would squeeze off a .30-caliber shot from their Springfields, then open the bolt, eject the spent shell, and shove the bolt home for another shot.[47]

Suddenly, Wilson heard a *Wham!* and felt a burning, stinging sensation in his lower back at the same time as two or three other men in his squad were hit. Like Flick, Wilson resisted an impulse to get up and run back to the dugout in the rear to check out his condition, but at that moment he witnessed the fate of Pvt. Russell Butterweck on his right, who apparently intended to do just that. Wilson heard the bullets tearing into Butterweck's body as he stood up and knew that his comrade was dead.

"Lie still—wallow deeper into the sand—don't dare move," Wilson told himself. Japanese machine gun fire was "snapping in bundles" around him and "sand flying all around." Cries of "Corpsman! Corpsman!" added to the sounds of the battlefield. Not far from Flick, Pvt. George Tefertiller, the BAR man in the squad, had been shot dead in the machine gun fire.[48]

As he lay motionless in his shallow excavation, Wilson would spend the rest of the night "crying, praying, and cursing all at the same time."[49]

When Lieutenant Codrea had split his platoon after moving it forward as ordered, his platoon guide, Jim Hancock, formed a skirmish line and began moving to the right, heading upstream with the men of Cpl. John Oliveri's squad. Visibility was very limited in the darkness as the men made their way past the machine gun emplacement of Rivers and to the right of a 37 mm antitank gun. After some moving around to get better positions behind a fallen palm trunk, Pvt. Harry Horsman and his buddies, Pvt. Steve Arsenault and Pfc. Vinny Rogers, began firing their Springfield rifles across the river at Japanese attempting to cross over from the opposite bank. But moments later, the very popular twenty-two-year-old Rogers, from Wellesley, Massachusetts, so full of plans for after the war, was hit and killed instantly, a 7.7 mm machine gun bullet through his helmet.[50]

Some of the Japanese had managed to get up the higher bank of the river on the Marines' side and infiltrate the defenders' positions. One tore the back off of Hancock's shirt with his bayonet. Seeing Hancock's predicament, Pvt. Jim Boston rushed forward to place himself between the Japanese and Hancock. As the Japanese pulled back so as to be able to stab at Hancock again with his bayonet, Boston parried the thrust, then hit him with the butt of his rifle before shooting him in the head.[51]

Unknown to them, the 37 mm gun that Hancock's men had passed was that of Cpl. George Parker, from Lt. George Swinston's platoon in H Company. It was positioned in its bunker of coconut logs and sandbags directly facing the jungle on the other side of the river and could also traverse to the left about to the point of being able to fire on the sand spit and to the right where it faced the disabled LVT lying near the opposite bank of the river.[52]

When Parker made out shadows moving in the darkness on the opposite bank, he immediately called for canister. In response, Pvt. Deran Akullian would load the round into the breech, then yell, "Up!" to indicate the breech was closed and the gun ready to fire. Pvt. Harold Acker passed the canister to Akullian from boxes inside their bunker. Following this arrangement, Parker was traversing the gun to the maximum to allow for sweeping fire on the opposite bank. Outside their bunker, Pvt. Anthony Balestrieri was keeping an eye out for any enemy who might approach and was ready to fire on any unidentified person failing to give the password.

But Parker and his crew were concerned that the muzzle blast from their 37 mm was marking their position to the Japanese machine gunners on the other side of the river. Their fear was justified. Bursts of heavy machine gun fire were ricocheting off the gun shield and tearing into the sand bags around it, as were "knee mortar" shells and grenades. Some rounds or fragments were getting inside the bunker, pinning the men down momentarily. Parker was praying for the arrival of daylight so that he and his crew could locate the Japanese machine gunners better and fire more effectively.[53]

To Parker's left, the Japanese machine gunners had zeroed in on the .30-caliber machine gun emplacement of Lee Diamond, Jack Rivers, and Al Schmid. Their Browning's tracer fire—one round in six—had given away its position in the dark. Some of the enemy fire struck inside the emplacement, scattering chips of wood and dirt down the back of Schmid's shirt. Standing in the pit now instead of crouching, Rivers tried to spot the bursts of fire coming from the opposite bank. With the noise of their heavy machine gun making it impossible to hear each other, Diamond was trying to direct return fire by punching the arm of Schmid, who would then prod Rivers and point to the spot where Rivers should aim his fire next.[54]

Then they realized that Bull Warren's gun, one hundred yards to their right, was no longer firing in its crossfire pattern. They feared that Warren's crew had been hit and was no longer able to operate its heavy Browning.[55]

Almost at that moment, a burst of 7.7 mm bullets found the opening in their own emplacement and struck Rivers in the forehead. The Indian fell back into the dugout without a sound, blood spurting out of his head, killed instantly. Reacting quickly, Schmid pushed the body of his buddy away and took over the gunner position. Trained for such situations, no words exchanged, Diamond shifted over to be able to load .30-caliber belts into the gun.[56]

Using his left hand, Schmid coolly traversed the machine gun back and forth as he fired at Japanese trying to cross over the river in several places at once. He could tell that his slugs were hitting flesh as they hissed through the water. Easily visible in the moonlight, the wading Japanese made easy targets when they reached within fifty yards of the gun.[57]

But then one of the Japanese machine gunners succeeded in putting a burst through the water jacket of Schmid's Browning, just a few inches in front of his face. Water from the punctured jacket spurted out over Schmid's lap and chest. The gun "started to crackle and sputter." But even though it became red hot, for some reason it didn't cease operating, as would be expected of a water-cooled machine gun fired continuously without water in the jacket.

Some distance to the right of Schmid's emplacement, Pfc. Bob Leckie and

Pvt. Lewis "Chuckler" Juergens of Lt. Hugh Corrigan's 1st Machine Gun Platoon were taking turns firing their own Browning machine gun. Tracers were flying out of the dark from across the river, "dancing around." They figured that Japanese machine gunners had their gunfire spotted. "Chuckler, we'd better move—they won't be able to get the range that way," Leckie advised his buddy. Juergens pulled the tripod over himself as Leckie supported the gun on his chest, and they began to edge backwards.[58]

In their new location, the pair set up their gun again and once more commenced firing from their unprotected position on the ground. But they never knew if there were any Japanese where they were firing. While they could hear and feel Japanese bullets striking in their area, they couldn't make out their origin in the darkness. They were thus reduced to firing just at the sources of the noises they heard. After about fifteen minutes they shifted to yet another location and began firing again, a procedure of repeated moving and firing they would keep up the rest of the battle.[59]

Further upstream, two other H Company machine gun squads—those of Sgt. Cross's section of Lt. Bill Whorf's 3rd Platoon—had been ordered not to fire their paired guns unless any Japanese crossed the river in front of their positions. Nor were they to fire downstream; it would be too big a risk of hitting their own men in defensive positions to their left.[60]

But now they could make out Japanese moving out of the grove and heading for the river, walking rather than running. Pvt. Ed Manning, the eighteen-year-old gunner of Cpl. Perry Fridley's squad to the right of Cpl. Bill Wright's machine gun emplacement, began firing bursts into the grove when flares lit up the Japanese positions. His fire must have been effective, he thought, as no Japanese were attempting to cross the river in front of his position. With no overhead protection for their emplacements and only some sandbags in front of their guns, the men of both squads did not relish the thought of face-to-face combat with any Japanese who might succeed in getting across. Facing Wright's gun to Manning's left, some of the enemy had been trying to swim across, but when fired on by Wright's crew they were seen to turn around and head back to their side of the river.[61]

To the right of Fridley's crew, at the far end of the 2nd Battalion's defense line where there was a bend in the river, Pvt. John Joseph was wide awake at water's edge. He was the runner for G Company's Weapons Platoon and had been assigned listening post duty earlier that evening. He now heard a noise in the water. Slowly, there emerged the form of a man with a rifle, trying to climb the bank.

Machine gun crew of Cross section, Whorf platoon, H Company, re-positioning itself on beach, August 22, 1942. *Courtesy Mark Flowers at www.2gyrene.org.*

Rising from his sitting position on roots at the base of a tree, Joseph smashed the Japanese in the face with the butt of his rifle. His adversary fell back into the water and slowly drifted away.[62]

Excited, Joseph woke up his buddy, Ed "Shorty" Fahey, who was sharing listening post duty with him. As they looked across the river, a match lit up. They fired their rifles at the location of what they considered a careless Japanese, but in response a Japanese machine gun crew opened up on them with a long burst. It became quiet again. No more Japanese were coming across at their far end location.

On the right of Joseph, beyond the far end of the 2nd Battalion's defense line, the machine gun crew of Pfc. Bob Fincher, one of the four squads of 2nd Lt. John Speaks's 2nd Machine Gun Platoon, D Company, could also hear Japanese across the river in the grove. When flares went off, they could see them, too, to their left. They had come up to the edge of the riverbank on the other side of the Tenaru upstream.[63]

When Fincher started firing his .30-caliber heavy machine gun, the Japanese

Emplacement of 2nd Machine Gun Platoon, D Company, 1st Marines, at upper Alligator Creek/Ilu River, August 21, 1942. Pfc. Bob Fincher is holding his head. *Courtesy of Bob Fincher.*

"hunkered down" and began firing back. The crew of the other Browning paired with Fincher's joined him in a crossfire. But some of the Japanese were now in the river, trying to cross over to his side.[64]

While it was firing, Fincher's gun took a hit in the jacket, and the water soon starting boiling inside. His assistant gunner, Pfc. Joe Fontaine, passed Fincher the spare barrel. While Fincher was changing the barrel, another flare burst overhead. Fincher turned and saw a Japanese coming into his gun emplacement. Overcoming his initial shock, he reacted by hitting the unarmed man with the old barrel several times until he was sure his nemesis was dead.[65]

On the right flank of 1st Lieutenant Komatsu's Machine Gun Company, Sgt. Masatoshi Mae's squad of ten men was continuously firing from its Type 92 7.7 mm heavy machine gun into American positions in support of the Higuchi and Chiba Companies' attempts to cross over the sandbar at the mouth of the Nakagawa. The other three squads of 2nd Lt. Kōsaburō Osada's platoon, led by Corporals Nakamura, Kadoguchi, and Hanada, were also directing their fire across the Nakagawa when they made out the silhouettes of enemy soldiers.[66]

In the center of the line of Komatsu's machine gunners, Ldg. Pvt. Niide

Yoshimasa, in Sgt. Naoyuki Yamada's squad of 2nd Lt. Masao Inagaki's platoon of two machine gun squads, was shocked when American machine gunners returned their fire "like madmen," spraying bullets (evidently canister) all around their position. Immediately Lt. Inagaki took a direct hit and keeled over without a word. Sergeant Yamada now took charge of the platoon. Positioned right next to Yoshimasa, Lieutenant Komatsu was untouched and continued directing his company's fire. Then Yoshimasa himself was hit in the buttocks and forced to abandon his machine gun. He was carried to a depression in the ground where medics could treat him.[67]

On the far left of Komatsu's line of machine guns, the two squads of 2nd Lt. Zenji Itō began firing on the "big gun" across the river from them in support of 1st Lieutenant Maruyama's company of 105 men to their right, who were preparing to plunge into the Nakagawa. Immediately, the gunners began receiving devastating counterfire, mainly canister. "No. 5 hit, number 6 forward," Itō yelled. Then Itō himself was hit, too, his voice ordering the fresh crews forward fading out. Both guns were now knocked out of action.[68]

Maruyama's men were also met by a wave of fire as they tried to cross the river. As in the other platoons, the thirty members of Lt. Hiroshi Miura's 1st Platoon were taking hits as they struggled to get across the unexpectedly deep river. In the middle, the water was up to their chests, forcing them to dog-paddle to make progress. All the while, they were the targets of concentrated fire from the other side.[69]

Ldg. Pvt. Naokichi Nakayama, 3rd Squad leader in Miura's platoon, saw several of his comrades trying to take shelter behind an abandoned American "amphibious tank" in the river near the Japanese side. Nakayama concluded it was hopeless to continue trying to ford the river and decided to head back with his squad. There, on the eastern bank of the Nakagawa, he and his men reassembled and reorganized before once more plunging into the river in a renewed attempt. But with hand grenades flying in their direction and exploding among them, they all pulled back once more, still short some fifty to sixty meters from the American positions on the other bank.[70]

By the time of the third attempt, there were only about ten men left in Miura's platoon, including only one noncom, Nakayama. Leading his skeleton platoon in a final effort, Miura was hit in the head. Throwing back his head, he sank down in the water.

Now in charge of what remained of Miura's platoon, Nakayama realized they were in a hopeless situation. He ordered the remaining three or four men in the platoon to turn back and regain their bank of the river. There, the survivors found a hollow and took cover in it as the battle raged on. He wondered about the fate of the Company commander, Maruyama, as well as his other two platoon leaders, 2nd Lts. Shigenori Niie and Shōichi Matsuo, and the men under them. Did any of them make it across the river and penetrate Marine positions?

Unable to capture or even silence the big gun almost opposite the river fording point, several of Maruyama's men from a squad of Lieutenant Matsuo's platoon carried their Type 99 light machine gun into the water behind the disabled American amphibious tank and climbed up on it with their gun and cartridge boxes of detached ammo magazines, each holding a curved strip of thirty rounds of 7.7 mm bullets. After setting the "Nambu light" up on its bipod, they began firing at the emplacement of the enemy gun that had been causing such heavy casualties among the men of Maruyama and Gotō. The inability of American crossfire to zero in on their indistinguishable position in the darkness—abetted by the flash hider on their gun—was allowing them to continue firing throughout the night.[71]

Downstream, near the mouth of the Nakagawa, 1st Lt. Hideo Gotō, commanding officer of the Engineer Company of Ichiki's detachment, had observed the devastating fire from the "big gun" that was creating such havoc among Maruyama's men trying to reach the other side of the Nakagawa. Earlier he had ordered his 2nd and 4th Platoons to join the attack force of the Higuchi and Chiba Companies crossing over the mouth of the river, but he still had twenty men of his headquarters section and forty more of his 3rd Platoon available to join the battle. Now he ordered them to join him and head upstream to attack the Marines firing across the river at Maruyama's men in the water and capture their troublesome gun.[72]

But when Gotō's men arrived at the location on the left bank of the Nakagawa from where they intended to cross over, they were met by a hail of bullets. Superior Private Shimizu's flame thrower took a hit, fuel oil spurting out and blackening his face. Then the headquarters section chief, Warrant Officer Akira Takausa, was hit too, killed instantly.[73]

It was just before dawn before the men of Gotō's 3rd Platoon descended into the river, led by the Company commander himself. As soon as they reached midriver, they were spotted by the Marines, who began throwing hand grenades at them. Pfc. Takeshi Makabe and about twenty others clustered around Gotō.

The water was too deep to wade, so they began to swim. But now enemy fire was coming down on them "like in a rainstorm." Many of the men were hit, including Makabe through the shoulder. Lieutenant Gotō was dead, killed by one of the grenades thrown at them.

As he lay wounded in the water, Makabe realized that their plan to seize the gun had proven futile. Turning back, he managed to make it to the shelter afforded by the abandoned amphibious tank, where he was joined by Pfc. Kiichirō Sugawara. When the American fire let up a bit, they left their refuge and climbed back up the riverbank. There they found men of Maruyama's 3rd Company. They were reassembling behind Makabe and reloading their Arisaka rifles in preparation for another try to get across the Nakagawa after several failed attempts.

At the 1st Marines' regimental command post, Colonel Cates at 0347 decided to change the fire mission of the 75 mm pack howitzers of his 3rd Battalion, 11th Marines, following his initial 0320 order to put down an artillery concentration at the narrowest part of the sandbar. Cates was worried that the initial target area—as preregistered, based on 1st Lt. John Frothingham's survey—was too close to his men defending the mouth of the Tenaru. Shells would be falling within less than one hundred yards of them.[74]

Now he suspected (correctly) that Japanese were massing behind the opposite, east, bank of the Tenaru several hundred yards upstream, possibly bringing up reserves. He got on the phone to the executive officer of the 11th Marines' 3rd Battalion—at some thirty-five hundred yards west of the Tenaru in the best position of the battalions of the 11th Marines to lay down artillery fire on the Japanese. After being connected to Maj. George Wilson, Cates ordered him to shift the fire mission three hundred yards to the right and one hundred yards down.[75]

It was about 0400 when the new order reached Sgt. Bob Askey, section head for one of the four howitzers of I Battery, via the battery's executive officer, 1st Lt. John Bradbury: "Fire Mission, Azimuth 828, range 3500, Battery 10 rounds."[76] The firing order also went out to 1st Lt. Gerald Russell, executive officer of H Battery.

Askey and the other three section chiefs of I Battery reported back to Bradbury that they were ready to fire. The number two men on each howitzer had each rammed in a 75 mm high explosive shell, and now on Bradbury's command, "Fire!" the number one men yanked the lanyards. In just three minutes, beginning at 0403, forty shells from I Battery crashed down on the Japanese, each taking 8.6

seconds to reach the target. Ten minutes later, the four howitzers fired another forty rounds.[77]

But were any rounds falling short and hitting the defenders on the west bank of the river? Sgt. Bob White at the command post with Major Wilson had received word that "we're firing on our own people," but Wilson discounted the report and ordered firing to continue. Maj. Bob Luckey with Colonel Cates at the 1st Marines' command post also had received messages from the line that the 3rd Battalion's shells were falling on the Marines on the west bank, but Cates concluded that the fire allegedly falling short was actually from 50 mm Japanese "knee mortars."[78]

In their two-man foxhole some two hundred to three hundred yards upstream from the mouth of the Tenaru, Pvts. Claude Crotty and Harold "Punchy" Leygraff sometime after 0300 had noticed a lot of milling around across the river on the opposite bank and also heard a lot of excited "jabbering" in a foreign language. Two of the fifty men of H Company's mortar platoon assigned the night watch under 2nd Lt. Don Wheaton, Crotty and Leygraff were suddenly bathed in the "eerie green" light of a flare shot up from the opposite side. Then all up and down the defense line of the mortar men, machine gun fire sprayed around them, ripping past them into palm trees behind their line.[79]

Crotty figured that the machine guns on the opposite side were providing cover for Japanese intending to cross the river to attack them, and he was right. He shouted to his foxhole buddy to get ready for hand-to-hand combat when the machine gun fire let up. Sure enough, shadowy figures heading towards the defense line in "a peculiar crouched position" were climbing up the bank towards their position after having forded the river. Furiously working their Springfields, they yanked back the bolt after each shot, rammed it back with another round, and fired again.

In another foxhole thirty yards back of the Tenaru's right bank and eight to ten feet above the river level, facing the abandoned LVT Alligator, another of the mortarmen, Pfc. Clyde Lucas, was also the target of the sweeping machine gun fire, but fortunately for him the bullets were hitting the ground just below his foxhole. Then he saw the Japanese coming too—wading across the river under the moonlit night sky that was broken from time to time by fast-moving clouds. A sharpshooter from Tennessee, Lucas was excited to be in a good position to pick the Japanese off as they climbed up the riverbank. Those who succeeded in approaching him were felled with single shots from his '03 rifle.[80]

But some fifteen feet to the left of Lucas, a screaming Japanese officer was wielding his samurai sword against Cpl. Charlie Karp when from about twenty feet Crotty shot him in the chest as the assailant was silhouetted against the sky. It was too late; in his earlier swipes the Japanese had stabbed Karp through the face, neck, and stomach, then he had run his sword twice through Karp's shoulder. Earlier, Pvt. Ed DeJoinville had attempted to shoot the officer before he swung his sword at DeJoinville a second time, but his safety was on and all he could do was parry the blow. The first lunge had left DeJoinville with a badly cut leg.[81]

Even more disturbing to Lucas and the others was friendly artillery fire falling on their line. While they could ascertain that 75 mm shells were landing on the other side of the river where the Japanese were evidently bunched up, at least three exploded among the mortar men, "so close that we were covered in dirt," Pvt. James Donahue later recorded in his diary. Nearby, Pfcs. Arthur Atwood and Barney Sterling were less fortunate. A shell landed directly in the foxhole they were sharing about twenty feet to the right of Lucas. He heard "at least six" as they were fired from pack howitzers behind the line. With the shellfire sweeping to the left, Lucas figured the next round would fall on him. As a mortar man, he knew about such sweeping fire. But it was to his great relief that he realized seconds later that no more rounds were landing in the line.[82]

Right below Jim Donahue's position, some Japanese had succeeded in getting a Nambu light machine gun across the river and had set it up preparatory to firing. Pfc. Len Beer and Pfc. Art Dignan spotted the machine gun crew in a drainage ditch just across from them, but it was too dark to see them clearly as the Japanese opened fire. When it was a bit lighter, Beer and Dignan could hear them talking. The two mortar men climbed out of their foxhole, Dignan with his Springfield rifle and Beer holding a grenade he had picked up two weeks earlier. Moving to a favorable position, Beer tossed the grenade into the ditch. After the blast, the only response they received was "moans and groans."[83]

When Dignan returned to the foxhole, he realized that Beer had not joined him and was still near the ditch. Beer yelled to Dignan that he'd been hit in the back by fire from the machine gun and couldn't move. Hurrying to Beer, Dignan pulled him back to a place behind a small embankment that afforded some protection. His buddy feared that dropping Beer into the hole would hurt him. He figured it was preferable to wait for a corpsman to come and handle the situation better than Dignan could. Beer asked for water, and Dignan held his canteen for him to drink. But now Dignan realized that Beer was more badly wounded than he'd realized at first. It was quite a while before a corpsman could reach him.[84]

About two hours into the fighting, Donahue was relieved to see that reinforcements were coming up to the line. But only "ten minutes" after they had set up two light .30-caliber air-cooled Brownings, the two crews "were shot up" by Japanese machine gunners on the other side of the river. Donahue figured it was because they were not dug in—"not below the deck."[85] At that point, H Company Plat. Sgt. John Muth picked up one of the unmanned machine guns and began to run down the line with it, stopping at points to fire a burst across the river, then shifting to a new position.

But now a Japanese machine gun Donahue and the others figured had been set up on the abandoned LVT in the river began "throwing plenty of lead our way." A BAR man, Pfc. Verbon "Joe" Sanders, who had moved up behind Muth, suddenly shouted at Donahue, asking whether there was enough room in Donahue's foxhole for him. Figuring that Sanders would be killed by the Japanese machine gunner if he stayed on the deck, Donahue assented to Sanders's request, even though his foxhole was full with him and Murray Battles in it. The new arrival slid down into the hole as Donahue and Muth kept up the fire. But when Donahue asked Battles five minutes later why Sanders wasn't firing his BAR too, Muth replied slowly, "He's dead." Donahue reached over to check Sanders's pulse. "His face was sunken and there was no pulse." It was not evident in the dark to Donahue at the time, but Sanders was already badly wounded when he had called out to Donahue, hit in the head and chest by the Japanese machine gunner.[86]

9

"Goddamn, They Got Me in the Eyes!"

ABOUT FORTY-FIVE MINUTES AFTER George Codrea's 1st Platoon, G Company, had been ordered to the line, the 2nd Platoon's seventeen-year-old runner, Pvt. George Gibbs, reported to his CO, 2nd Lt. Bob Smith, with a message from Captain Sherman. The men were to leave their bivouac position in the coconut grove 75–100 yards inland from the ocean beach and head for the mouth of the Tenaru, 125–150 yards to the east, to give support for Codrea's men engaged in deadly combat with the Japanese who had crossed over the sand spit and into the 2nd Battalion's defense line. Plat. Sgt. John Robinson would be leading the first and second squads to the point, while platoon guide Sgt. Ed Claffey would angle off to the left to the beach side.[1]

With Cpl. Knight Farr in the lead and assistant squad leader Pfc. Al Schlemmer bringing up the rear, the platoon's first squad formed up as if for close-order drill and double-timed through the palms, followed by the second squad. But when about two-thirds to the mouth of the Tenaru, they were abruptly met by machine gun fire flying overhead through the palms. All nine men in Pvt. Jim Couch's second squad ran to shelter behind palm trees and piled up on top of each other. Recovering from the shock of first combat, the men of both squads spread out as they continued to move towards the Tenaru.[2]

When they neared the Japanese who had made it across the spit and were now rushing towards them, illuminated by the flares going off overhead, the Marines of the two squads responded by countercharging. But then their line buckled, lacking direction. "Out of the smoke and powder" came a blast from Platoon Sergeant Robinson: "Gawdammit, you're going the wrong way! What the hell is this, the Japanese are over there!" Regaining their courage in response to the "deep-throated blast" from their "jut-chinned" leader, the men of the two squads plunged forward and began engaging the bayonet-wielding Japanese in hand-to-hand combat.[3]

Corporal Farr in the first squad led the fighting with his four-man fire team. Pfc. Dick Stitt, a twenty-two-year-old former guard on the University of Pittsburgh football team, emptied his BAR's twenty-round magazine of .30-caliber bullets into the Japanese. While Stitt fired, Farr and the other two fire team members—Pvts. Tommy Lynch and Leo Carvalis—protected him with shots from their '03 Springfield rifles.

Among the group of second squad men, Jim Couch was firing his BAR as fast as he could, hoping it wouldn't jam. But when it got so hot it did stop firing, the eighteen-year-old from Power, West Virginia, jumped into a nearby foxhole to try to fix it. Succeeding, he climbed out and resumed firing. But a few minutes later, his assistant BAR man, Pvt. Jim Carlin, was shot in the shoulder and started screaming for the corpsman. Now Couch was virtually disarmed again; he had no assistant to pass him more twenty-round magazines to reload his BAR.[4]

In the meantime, Al Schlemmer in the first squad had come upon an abandoned 37 mm antitank gun emplaced to the right of the sand spit. With Pvt. Walt Wittmer and another squad mate, Schlemmer decided to take it over. He felt confident he could fire it, based on the information he had picked up on the 3-inch gun on the transport that had brought him to Guadalcanal. Someone told the men that the crew had gone to get ammunition for the gun, but they found two boxes of canister outside the gun pit. With Schlemmer firing the gun and the others passing and loading canister shells, they began spraying steel balls at the Japanese trying to cross the sand spit in the moonlight. But then "some people came from Special Weapons," and Schlemmer and his comrades vacated the pit and took cover, firing their own rifles instead.[5]

As dawn broke, Schlemmer found himself lying on the right side of the 37 mm gun on an up slope. Next to him, he saw Stitt with a nasty wound in his left bicep. He also saw a Japanese on the ground a few feet from Stitt, lying dead still. A few feet from his wounded platoon mate, he noticed one of the other men in Farr's fire team, Leo Carvalis, apparently dead from bayonet wounds.[6]

Schlemmer tried to bandage Stitt's wound, but the Tarentum, Pennsylvania, native resisted his efforts. Then Schlemmer realized that the "dead" Japanese was moving. "Stab him!" Schlemmer urged Stitt, who carried two yellow-banded knives on his right hip. Edging up to the Japanese, the muscular Marine sank the blade of one of the knives up to the hilt in the back of the man, who jumped up, screaming.[7]

Stitt rolled over towards Schlemmer, but too late. The frenzied activity had attracted the attention of the Japanese crew of a machine gun mounted on the abandoned LVT on the other side of the Tenaru. The Nambu light opened up, sending dirt and sand flying around them. Close by, Jim Couch heard a thud and a groan; Tommy Lynch had been hit, as had Stitt and the wounded Japanese, now all dead. Both Schlemmer and Couch were unscathed, but Farr, the fire team leader, was gravely wounded, having taken a bullet through his helmet. He was begging Wittmer, standing nearby, to finish him off.[8]

To their left and up on the beach side, Ed Claffey's third and fourth squads had suffered fewer casualties than had Robinson's two squads. The only man hit was Pvt. Amos Cooper, shot in the head by machine gun fire as his fourth squad had arrived on the beach destination area. His buddy, Pvt. Fred Metcalf, called for a corpsman to attend to Cooper, sprawled out on the ground. Cooper had not been wearing a helmet, and he would not survive his wound.[9]

But Bob Smith's platoon had lost three other men too: Pfc. Richard Holcombe and Pvts. John "Shorty" McHale and George Gibbs. Earlier that night, before the platoon had been called forward, the men had staged a birthday party for both McHale and Gibbs. Gibbs afterwards had been wounded while serving as the platoon runner, struck in the eye by a bayonet. He was being looked after behind a palm tree to the rear of Captain Sherman's command post by Pfc. George Miller, the G Company runner, when he was fatally hit by a machine gun burst.[10]

Not previously called in by Pollock to support the 1st and 2nd Platoons of G Company, 2nd Lt. Luther Jordan's 3rd Platoon had suffered no casualties. Then his squads were ordered by Pollock to "fill in the line where needed." The men left their reserve position and moved forward in what Pvt. Bill Finnegan of Cpl. Claude Hazen's squad felt was "not a well-organized way" to fill empty foxholes or position themselves behind trees several hundred yards upstream from the main fighting. However, at this late hour there were still some Japanese in Pollock's defense line. Finnegan fired his rifle in the cleanup operation, but neither he nor the others experienced any hand-to-hand fighting.[11]

The only remaining platoon in G Company's reserve location was 2nd Lt. Preston St. C. Malone's Weapons Platoon, but it was only at half strength. Early the previous evening its machine gun section had been ordered to leave its two .30-caliber light machine guns at their beach positions, obtain rifles from one of the rifle platoons, and head upstream for outpost duty. Pfc. Lou Imfeld and the other men of the section arrived at their designated position at the far end of the 2nd Battalion's defense line just before dark. It was too late for the men to look around and familiarize themselves with their surroundings.[12] The platoon's mortar section of two 60 mm mortars remained in their reserve position, awaiting daylight before they could be put into action.[13]

It was about 0430 when a runner yelling "Quill! Quill!" burst into the bivouac area of the 3rd Platoon of F Company. The men were in slit trenches facing the beach some two hundred yards inland of F Company's 1st and 2nd Platoons, which the 3rd Platoon had been assigned to support. After screaming the password, the runner approached the platoon leader, 2nd Lt. Ed Craig, and gasped, "Lieutenant, Col. Pollock says to report to him with the 3rd Platoon at Battalion Headquarters at once. Bring combat gear. I'll lead you back to the Colonel."[14]

Craig yelled to Plat. Sgt. John Ruth, platoon guide Cpl. Bill Wolvington, and his four squad leaders to have their men fall in and follow him closely. With the runner guiding them in the pitch darkness, all forty men were screaming "Quill" as they rushed blindly under the palm trees, their canteens and bayonets clanking together. The noise of combat was growing progressively louder and over-rounds were zipping about them as they double-timed down the dirt road in an eastward direction.[15]

Arriving at Pollock's command post, Craig found the battalion commander waiting for him in the midst of a knot of battalion headquarters personnel. "Such composure," Craig thought; "It was as if this were a war game back in North Carolina." In a cool voice, Pollock addressed him: "Craig, the Japanese have attacked our flank along the Tenaru and are breaking through our defenses. Tell Captain Sherman that I said for you to drive them back across the river, and good luck to you." From Pollock's order, Craig understood that Sherman and G Company were already at the river and needed extra support to fight off the Japanese who had penetrated the battalion's defense line.[16]

Craig directed his men to fix bayonets, as ordered by Pollock, then led them as they again double-timed through the palms. The over-rounds "were really whizzing about us," and the din of battle was growing increasingly louder as the platoon covered the approximately three hundred yards to the mouth of the Tenaru. It began to sink in to Craig that the Japanese were actually firing on them and that Pollock's order to fix bayonets meant that they could conceivably be running into a face-to-face confrontation with the Japanese.

It was nearly dawn when the platoon neared its destination.[17] Craig ordered his men to spread out and keep abreast in skirmish line formation. They advanced very slowly from palm tree to palm tree over the open ground amidst mortar explosions and machine gun fire overhead.

There was now very little communication between Craig and his men—a situation of "every man for himself." Nor did Craig know where his platoon sergeant was. He had not seen Ruth since the platoon had moved forward.[18]

Suddenly, only ten feet away, Craig spotted a dark human shape moving forward collapse to the ground. He fell almost at the feet of Pfc. Charlie Gambrell, the BAR man in Cpl. John McHugh's third squad. When Cpl. Clarence McCampbell in an adjoining squad turned to see if he could help him, the wounded man, hit in the chest, replied, "You go ahead, Mac—I'll be with you in a minute."[19]

But Craig did not want to leave the man there. Against standard Marine Corps practice to leave wounded to corpsmen while engaged in a firefight, Craig, with one of the men next to him, dragged the wounded Marine to the shelter of a tree. As he laid the moaning casualty down, Craig recognized him as Pvt. Bennie Jones. In shock, the seventeen-year-old was muttering, "Mama! Mama!" Craig told him he was safe and that a corpsman would be along shortly to dress his wound. Leaving Jones, Craig planned to return when the tide of battle permitted.[20]

With Japanese machine gun fire from the east bank picking up, Gambrell and the other men in the platoon dropped down to their knees and proceeded to crawl, looking for a suitable field of fire. While on his knees, Pfc. John Gildea, a Brooklyn boy, took a hit in the head, which killed him instantly. Then Pvt. Marion Nelson was struck by three machine gun bullets, one penetrating his abdomen. His wounds would not prove fatal, however. But including Jones, that made three casualties in Gambrell's squad.[21]

After leaving Bennie Jones, Craig and his runner, Pfc. Aneck Green, tried to move up about one hundred yards to where G Company was engaged in hand-to-hand fighting in order to give Pollock's message to Captain Sherman. But they never got even near G Company's location, where they assumed Sherman was fighting alongside his men. Despite "crawling like a snake," it was too dangerous to move, "with bullets coming in like thousands of bees" and the risk of being shot by fellow Marines as well as the Japanese.[22]

Dawn had now broken as Craig and Green headed back to the position of their platoon. With firing all around them, they dove into a large shell hole. But it turned out to be already occupied—by a dead Marine, a bullet hole in his head right between the eyes. Craig told his runner that whoever had drawn a bead on him was probably just waiting for them to show their heads. There were snipers in the trees. But comforted by the fragrance of a cigar Craig incongruously decided to light up, the two climbed out of the hole in a flash and darted from tree to tree, heading back to their platoon position, where the men were now occupying foxholes along the west bank of the Tenaru.[23]

Reunited with his platoon, Craig was saddened to learn that Bennie Jones was dead. So was Corporal Wolvington, whom he so admired for his daring and whom Craig had appointed as his platoon guide shortly before the battle. The muscular twenty-two-year-old native of Rockbridge, Pennsylvania, was seen to have picked up an abandoned .30-caliber Browning light machine gun. Firing the thirty-one-pound weapon from the hip, Wolvington had reportedly mowed down Japanese infiltrators charging forward, then trained the air-cooled gun on two enemy machine gun crews on the other side of the Tenaru before being shot dead.[24]

As knee mortar shells now began arcing into their position, Craig jumped into one of the drainage ditches scattered throughout the palm grove. Sniper and machine gun fire also had his men pinned down in the bright morning daylight. Craig reasoned it would be foolhardy to try to mount a counterattack to drive the infiltrating Japanese back across the mouth of the Tenaru, as per Pollock's instructions to him.[25]

But now a turn in the tide made it apparently unnecessary for him to have delivered Pollock's message to Sherman. Overhead, 75 mm shells from the pack howitzers were raining down on the Japanese on the other side of the river. The first barrage was fired at 0722, followed by another at 0742, then a third at 0851—although Craig did not note the times himself. The noise "was almost overwhelming" as Craig watched the shells exploding "a few hundred feet away" on the other side of the Tenaru. He was just hoping that the firing continued to be accurate, with no short rounds falling into the Marine positions on the west bank.[26]

Unknown to Craig, Colonel Pollock was also concerned about accuracy of the batteries of the 11th Marines firing in support of his operations. Evidently mindful of the short rounds fired in the initial barrage of 0403 (and at 0515?), Pollock had not permitted further artillery firing in the early hours after daylight. But with Japanese targets now in view of H Battery's Nat Mewhinney, who had shifted his forward observation post at first light to the mouth of the Tenaru, the twenty-three-year-old second lieutenant telephoned in to his 3rd Battalion headquarters Fire Direction Control for permission to adjust on Japanese positions. He was rebuffed. Pollock feared his battalion's men were too close to the enemy to risk artillery fire. But was Pollock's objection overruled later by Colonel Cates as regimental commander, and were the howitzers allowed to fire again at 0722, with positions called in to the FDC by another forward observer of the 3rd Battalion?[27]

In the meantime, F Company's 2nd Platoon had now arrived to join the fight from its reserve position at the beach. As daylight broke, 2nd Lt. Steve Ryan and Plat. Sgt. Norvell "Red" Mills had formed the platoon in a skirmish line as they continued forward some five hundred yards, disregarding rifle fire until Ryan gave the order to hit the deck.[28]

But they could not see any Japanese. Crawling on his hands and knees, .45 pistol in hand, Ryan approached near the position of Pvt. B. J. Wilson and yelled above the noise, "No firing! Friendly troops ahead!" He did not want to risk firing on Craig's 3rd Platoon men, not in their sight but known to be ahead of them.[29]

Off to his right, Wilson noticed an 81 mm mortar crew in a low draw and a reconnaissance truck unloading shells for their gun. At that point—about 0830—Wilson felt there was not much return fire from the Japanese across the river.

Suddenly, Wilson was surprised to see Lieutenant Colonel Pollock himself walking up from the mouth of the Tenaru towards him and the others in Ryan's platoon. Wilson also recognized the battalion's police sergeant, Russell Graddick, accompanying Pollock. While Graddick was armed, the battalion commander had no weapon at all, nor any cartridge belt, gas mask, or even a canteen, only his steel helmet. As Pollock passed by, he told Wilson—lying prone on the ground—to keep his head low. "And here was the battalion commander offering himself as an excellent target!" Wilson reflected.[30]

Earlier, about one hour before daylight, Cpl. Jim Olliff's crew on their 37 mm antitank gun, now turned to its right and facing the sand spit directly opposite its beach corner location, was still firing canister at the Japanese trying to cross over. However, their supply of the 14-inch canister shells was running low.

Suddenly, a Japanese machine gun opened up on them and succeeded in scoring a direct hit on the gun, riddling its traversing mechanism. The burst also nicked Olliff in the left arm and wounded Irv Moore and Clair Hume. Hume yelled to Pat Sweeney next to him, "Sweeney, I just got hit!" Sweeney saw that his comrade had been hit in the hip.[31]

Their 37 mm gun was now rendered useless, stuck facing up into the sky. The whole crew edged away from the gun emplacement and sought protection behind the sandbags. After dragging him out from behind the gun shield, Sweeney cut Hume's trousers to examine his wound. Hume had a bullet wound in the right hip, right down to the bone, but was not bleeding much. Ignoring their own wounds, Olliff and Moore joined Hume and the unscathed Sweeney in firing their rifles from behind the sandbags in the direction of the Japanese machine gun, but to little apparent effect.[32]

Then, near daylight, Sweeney suddenly screamed. He had been hit, though not from any Japanese around—there were none. Hume called over to him but could see right away that his buddy was dead.[33]

Hume himself was still in pain from his wound. He rolled over and waited for a corpsman to come. It was about an hour later before one did show up. After giving Hume a morphine shot, he extracted the slug from Hume's hip. But then another corpsman arrived and gave him yet another morphine injection. Now he was feeling no pain at all. But neither corpsman had proposed taking him to the medical station.

Finally, a field ambulance drove up. Along with other wounded, including Tom Palmer from Campbell's 37 mm gun crew to the right, Hume was placed on a stretcher for the ride to the field hospital. Jim Olliff had resisted being evacuated himself until so ordered by his B Battery platoon leader, 2nd Lt. Jim McClanahan. It was about 0900.[34] But before leaving the gun emplacement, Olliff was puzzled to observe the action of a corpsman who placed himself behind the 37 mm and somehow had managed to fire a round up into the palm trees on the other side of the Tenaru.[35]

It was still dark when Glenn Campbell arrived back at his 37 mm gun emplacement to the right of Olliff's. He had disobeyed the orders of the battery executive officer, who directed him to remain at the hole that was being used by battery headquarters and to defend its personnel, and instead he headed back to his original position. But on reaching the gun pit he was surprised to find a dead Marine lying on top of the sandbags, then two others to the right, only half visible to Campbell once he entered the emplacement. Even more surprising, he encountered four men of the 2nd Battalion, two firing their rifles and the other two "with a dazed expression on their faces."[36]

On the arrival of daylight, Campbell was now able to examine his gun to determine what had so damaged it as to knock it out of operation in the mortar explosion that night. He finally found that the detent in the gun's breechblock had come out. After locating it in the pit and reinserting it and the spring, Campbell was pleased to find that the gun was now back in working order.

With the infantry men serving as a substitute for his missing original crew, Campbell began firing canister again, targeting Japanese positions across the river. But every time he sprayed canister pellets at the Japanese, he was subjected to retaliatory fire. The infantry men were trying to determine exactly from where the machine gun fire was originating, but each one of them came up with a different opinion.

Campbell concluded that the bursts were coming from a machine gun set up on the abandoned LVT in the river. He traversed the antitank gun to the extreme right to zero in on the Japanese machine gun, leaving the left side of his emplacement exposed. Immediately, "there was a big flash and an explosion" to the left of the gun position. "A charge of electricity flew up my left arm to my neck," he recalled years later. He realized he had been hit.[37]

Soon a corpsman arrived, gave him a morphine shot, and bandaged him up. He had two wounds in his left wrist and a large piece of shrapnel lodged just below his left ear, almost on the jugular vein. The corpsman gave him the location of the battalion aid station and told him to get there as soon as possible. Campbell was considered "walking wounded." But it was some time before he began his trek to the station. In the meantime, his buddy Pvt. Fred "the Russian" Augustynowicz had jumped into his emplacement, asking what had happened.[38]

Just to the right of Campbell's gun emplacement, Slim Fairchild was firing his .50-caliber Browning air-cooled machine gun at Japanese crossing the spit when he became the victim of machine gun fire himself. The burst from across the Tenaru just before dawn that hit him in the hand emanated from a location almost opposite his position, not far from the abandoned LVT to his right in the river. Fairchild's blood splattered on the blouse of his loader, Pvt. Angelo Catullo, only a foot away from Fairchild in their hole.[39]

As soon as Fairchild took the hit, Catullo screamed for a corpsman, but none responded. Lying in their hole without help, Fairchild and Catullo waited for about an hour before anyone showed up. It was not a corpsman who finally appeared, but rather their platoon sergeant, Nelson Braitmeyer. He had been moving up and down the line, along with Lieutenant McClanahan, to support their B Battery men. After Braitmeyer succeeded in locating a corpsman and leading him to the gun position, Fairchild was treated and loaded in an ambulance for transport to the field hospital.[40]

Lying in an upper stretcher in the ambulance, Fairchild was dripping blood from his wound down to the lower stretcher. "Hey, you up there, quit bleeding on me!" the wounded man in the lower berth barked at Fairchild. Recognizing the voice of the complainer as that of a platoon buddy, Fairchild laughed and retorted, "Hey, Hume, I'll bleed on you all I want!"[41]

To the right of Fairchild's position, Pvt. Al Schmid was operating his Browning .30-caliber heavy machine gun by himself, the original gunner, Jack Rivers, lying dead in the pit. But Schmid was having big difficulties with fire coming from the machine gun mounted on the abandoned LVT Alligator some one hundred feet to his right across the river. The Japanese gunner had located Schmid's gun from the tracers it was firing in the predawn darkness, but it was proving impossible for Schmid to accurately get a bead on the Japanese. Then one of the rounds hit LeRoy Diamond in the arm, knocking his squad leader down in the dugout, partly across Schmid's feet. Now Schmid would have to load the gun as well as fire it.[42]

"Sweat pouring down his face," and talking out loud to himself, Schmid kept on loading and firing the Browning at Japanese across the river. Suddenly, there was a blinding flash and explosion in the gun pit. Instinctively touching his face, Schmid was shocked to feel only "wet, sticky pulp." Warm blood poured through his fingers. He fell backward in the pit. "Goddamn, they got me in the eyes," he cried out.[43]

Then Schmid realized that he had been hit not only in the face, but also in his left shoulder, arm, and head. It must have been a grenade that got him, Diamond and Schmid concluded. In exploding against the left stirrup of his gun, the projectile also had blown the water jacket off the Browning, rendering it useless.[44]

As dawn began breaking, Japanese machine gun fire was still being directed

Men wounded in the Battle of the Tenaru recuperating in a San Diego hospital, December 14, 1942. *Bottom bunk, left to right:* PhM3c Robert T. Day, USN; Pvt. Albert A. Schmid; and Leo Pambrun (USMC public relations). *Top bunk, left to right:* Pvt. Edward DeJoinville and Sgt. Frank J. Stewart. *US Navy photo, courtesy of Frank Stewart.*

at Schmid's emplacement. Both Diamond and Schmid were lying helpless at the bottom of the pit. Half delirious from his wounds and unable to see, Schmid started acting "kind of crazy," asking after Rivers.[45]

After "about an hour," squad member Pvt. Whitney "Jake" Jacobs approached and jumped into the pit. He poured some water from the spare jacket of the gun into Schmid's helmet, then Schmid immersed his head in it, drinking "sand, oil, blood and everything." As Japanese machine gun fire whizzed around them, Jacobs and Lt. Bill Whorf carried Schmid out on a blanket. Schmid felt himself losing consciousness, then dropped the .45 he held and passed out.[46]

At some distance to the right of the Schmid evacuation scene, Cpl. George Parker and his crew were still firing their 37 mm antitank gun across the upper Tenaru at any targets they could make out in the predawn darkness. The gun was hot from continuous operation. Empty canister shell cases were strewn around the emplacement.[47]

With the coming of daylight, Parker's prayers for better visibility were answered. But it cut both ways. The Japanese now had a good view of Parker's gun emplacement. Their machine gun fire now became more intense. The impact of the 7.7 mm bullets was shaking the bunker's logs and sandbags and bouncing off the protective steel gun shield. The heaviest volume of fire appeared to be coming from the machine gun mounted on the abandoned LVT just to the right and across from their position.[48]

Suddenly an explosion shook the emplacement, spraying fragments into all three men of the gun crew. Parker suffered multiple wounds to both hands, upper torso, and neck, as did Harold Acker in the pit with him, while Tony Balestrieri outside the emplacement also was hit in several places. Only Deran Akullian escaped injury. But despite their wounds, Parker and Acker exited the pit with Akullian and joined Balestrieri, then took up positions behind the sandbags, determined to fight back with their rifles.[49]

Unseen by Parker and his crew, two G Company Marines nearby noticed that the 37 mm antitank gun was not being fired. Pvts. Harry Horsman and Ed Carter had spread out on the west bank of the Tenaru, along with others in Sgt. Jim Hancock's group, as ordered earlier by Lt. Codrea. Horsman and Carter decided to enter the emplacement and see if they could get the gun operational again. On entering, they found the gun unattended.[50]

Despite his lack of experience with a 37 mm antitank gun, Horsman succeeded in firing it, with Carter loading it with canister shells they found lying in the pit. While the two were manning the gun, a lieutenant whom Horsman and Carter did not know came up to the emplacement carrying canister shells in an apron for the gun. Then Hancock himself joined them, along with Cpl. Larry DiPietroantonio.[51]

Unlike Horsman, Hancock was fully experienced on the 37 mm gun, having operated it during his five-year experience with the 11th Marines before switching to an infantry outfit, G Company. Displacing Horsman behind the gun, Hancock took over the firing position. But then a burst from the Japanese machine gun mounted on the LVT sent two 7.7 mm bullets tearing into his left forearm. Undaunted, Hancock with his good right arm managed to sight the gun and fired an AP (antipersonnel) round of canister at the offending machine gun emplacement, but missed. Shortly afterwards, he was wounded again, this time by a Japanese sniper, who hit him "right square in the chest." Fortunately for Hancock, the bullet hit on his dog tag, saving him from grievous injury.[52]

Hancock's perils were not over yet. A knee mortar shell exploded next to him, scattering fragments into his right hand and legs. Hancock was knocked back onto Horsman in the pileup following the blast. Determined not to be beaten, the resilient Hancock began to try to get up behind the gun to fire again, but his intentions were blocked at that point when Lt. Luther Jordan of F Company arrived on the scene and dragged Hancock out of the pit to a sheltered spot. It was about 0900. One of the other men took over firing the gun.[53]

After the 0515 artillery barrage fired by the 11th Marines' 3rd Battalion, and as daylight approached, Lieutenant Colonel Pollock decided to switch from the 75 mm pack howitzers to his battalion's 81 mm mortars. Visibility was now adequate for the crews of his H Company mortar platoon to see the bubbles in their sights for firing their guns. Just after 0530 he called into action the four guns of the platoon. However, of the two guns of the first section of the platoon, one proved unable to fire due to a cleaning rag inadvertently left in the tube, and the other misfired because of a missing firing pin. Apprised of the situation, Pollock then ordered the two remaining mortars of the second section forward from the platoon's position three hundred yards inland of the west bank of the Tenaru.[54]

Following orders from the platoon leader, 2nd Lt. Carl "Benny" Benson, the three remaining crew members of each of guns number 3 and number 4 broke down their weapons into their three components, strapped on the parts, and headed northeast through the coconut grove, "cursing our inability to see very clearly." (The rest of the crewmen were with the H Company line defense group at the Tenaru under Lt. Wheaton.) When they finally reached their new location, the two gun crews were greeted with shouts from F Company men: "Hurrah, here come the 81s!" The two crews set up their mortars about ten yards apart, careful to choose positions allowing for maximum clearance of the palm trees for their fire.[55]

Approaching gun number 4 of Pfc. John "Deacon" Tatum, Lieutenant Colonel Pollock asked the crew, "Who is the gunner here?" When Pfc. Sid Phillips responded that he was, Pollock told him "Aim on me—use me as your aiming stick." Pollock positioned himself about thirty yards in front of the mortar. The seventeen-year-old Phillips could see that his gun was lined up on the barely visible abandoned LVT across the river to his right. It was the source of harassing fire from a machine gun mounted on it that the men had complained about. With small arms fire still zinging around them, Phillips wondered if the battalion commanding officer "might be tired of living."[56]

Crew of number 4 gun, 81 mm mortar platoon, H Company, in October 1942. *Standing, left to right:* Cpl. John Tatum (squad leader), Pfc. Clyde Lucas, and Pfc. Paul Doyle. *Kneeling, left to right:* Pfc. Sid Phillips and Pfc. Carl Ransom. *Courtesy of Ed O'Soro.*

At such a short range, the mortar had to be fired almost perpendicularly. The heavy shell discharged by Phillips—at fifteen pounds the heaviest in use—shot up above the opening in the coconut palms and down near the LVT. After correcting range several times following more rounds fired, Phillips "put one right on it." The machine gun on the LVT, obviously heavily damaged or destroyed by the explosion, went silent. "A cheer went up like a touchdown at a football stadium," Phillips recalled.[57]

As Lieutenant Colonel Pollock continued to direct, both Pfc. Jim Moncrief's number 3 gun and Phillips's number 4 were now switched from direct to zone fire on the east bank of the Tenaru. Each gun fired three shells at one zone setting, sweeping right or left, then lifted the elevation fifty yards and swept back with three rounds per gun in the other direction. Passing through the coconut palms, the rounds with delayed action fuses detonated on the east bank in "bright, orange flashes." To the two gun crews, the pattern of fire appeared to have "a devastating effect" on the Japanese.[58]

But the supply of 81 mm shells was now beginning to run low. In response to the need of the two gun crews, a recon car showed up with wooden crates of the projectiles. The ammo men of Tatum's and Moncrief's squads struggled with shovels and rifle butts to pry open the boxes to dig out the tarpaper-wrapped canisters containing nine shells each. It was a job trying to keep up with the firing orders.[59]

However, the one-sided engagement was not to last. At "around 11:00" the two gun crews came under intensive shell fire. At first the rounds were falling about twenty-five yards in front of them, then the next just beyond their position. Pollock directed them to temporarily abandon their mortars. On section chief Albritton's command, Phillips yelled, "Abandon gun!" and pulled the gun sight as he headed for the rear. "We had to retreat nearly 500 yards to keep from being blasted off the map," Tatum recorded in his diary. Jim Moncrief feared a Japanese counterattack and capture of his gun. To Tatum, it seemed that "men were being blown to bits all around our position." He recorded in his diary that Jesse Phillips, the ammo man in Moncrief's crew who was with the mortar men sent to the line that evening, "got his head blown off."[60]

In the foxhole that Nat Mewhinney was using as his makeshift forward observation post near the mouth of the Tenaru, the H Battery officer did not know the big Marine on his right with whom he was sharing. Suddenly a knee mortar shell exploded close by, knocking Mewhinney to the bottom of the hole, fragments embedding his face, neck, right scapula, and lung and punching a hole in his helmet. But he was even further shocked when he looked up and saw that his Marine comrade was now headless. Reflecting later, he figured that the mortar explosion had detonated the two hand grenades the Marine had kept beside him on the edge of the hole and that his big body had shielded Mewhinney somewhat. Barely conscious, Mewhinney still managed to telephone the battalion's Fire Direction Control to tell them that he had been hit, but due to bleeding through his mouth and nose all he could produce was a garble. Moments later a corpsman showed up and put Mewhinney on a stretcher for a jeep ride to the aid station.[61]

Not far from Mewhinney's foxhole, other knee mortar shells were exploding at treetop level, showering fragments down on men of Lt. Craig's F Company platoon, who were lying prone. Other shells were throwing up dirt and sand when they detonated on the ground around them. Craig and Corporal McCampbell, now designated acting sergeant, rushed for cover in an irrigation ditch in the middle of the line of the platoon's men.[62]

Suddenly, as Craig swept the treetops with his binoculars, he was hit. "It felt like a batted ball hitting me in the chest while standing on the pitcher's mound," he recalled later. Craig surmised that he had been struck by a fragment of a mortar shell that had burst near the ditch. Looking down at his shirt, he could see a quarter-sized circle of blood that was gradually getting larger.[63]

"Mac, I've been hit!" Craig yelled to McCampbell. But McCampbell, not turning to face his commanding officer, blurted out, "Cut out the shit, Lieutenant." But when he saw Craig's blood-stained hand, he yelled, "Holy shit!" then "Corpsman! Corpsman, Christ, the Lieutenant's been hit!"

Craig let himself sink back to the bottom of the ditch, consciously trying to avoid going into shock. A few minutes later, a corpsman appeared, and Craig managed to climb out of the ditch. Laying Craig out on the ground, the corpsman worked on him with sulfa powder. Noting that the hole was very small and neat, the corpsman told Craig that he had been hit by a .25-caliber bullet, not by a shell fragment.

Craig felt "like a turkey on a platter" as he lay on the ground, exposed to sniper fire. But the morphine was beginning to take effect. Looking up, he saw the figure of Lieutenant Colonel Pollock hovering over him. "You all did a fine job, Craig," he told his young platoon leader. Then Captain Howland "appeared out of a fog." The F Company CO had driven right up to the front in his jeep.

A Japanese soldier demonstrating operation of the Model 89 (1929) 50 mm heavy grenade discharger. *USMC photo, in Henry I. Shaw, Jr.,* First Offensive: The Marine Campaign for Guadalcanal.

"Pick him up and follow me," Howland ordered the corpsman. Craig was assisted the one hundred feet to the jeep. Arriving at the 2nd Battalion's field medical station, he was deposited on the ground beside other wounded. Along with the corpsman, the two navy doctors assigned to the battalion were busy treating other patients. The battalion chaplain, Lt. (jg) Ansgar Sovik, was also with them.[64]

Suddenly, a mortar shell exploded nearby. Lt. Jacques Saphier and Sovik hit the deck, the doctor on top of the chaplain. "My God, they got me!" Saphier screamed. A piece of the mortar shell had lodged in his neck, severing the carotid artery. Saphier was bleeding profusely on Sovik, the upper part of Sovik's shirt soaked in blood. By the time Saphier was taken to the division field hospital, he was dead.[65]

Craig and the other wounded were also taken by ambulance to the field hospital, packed on stretchers like sardines. Blood dripped down on Craig from above. An old, white-haired commander of the Medical Corps supervised the unloading and carrying of Craig and the other wounded to a large tent. Inside, in the darkness, bandaged wounded lay on cots. Corpsmen were preparing two who had already expired for military burial. To Craig, it appeared that he was the only person in the group who was still conscious.[66]

Situated on the far right flank of Lieutenant Komatsu's line of heavy machine guns, extending south from seventy meters upstream, Sgt. Masatoshi Mae was experiencing a letup in the intense fire of the two "field guns" across the river that allowed his machine gun squad to resume its own fire. Suddenly, they were hit by a barrage of mortar shells. Mae and his squad members couldn't see even two meters in any direction from the dirt and dust thrown up. They left their exposed firing position and took refuge in the dugout nearby.[67]

When it seemed to Mae that the mortar fire was easing off, he led his squad back to their 7.7 mm machine gun and resumed firing across the river. But he realized that was a mistake; 81 mm mortar shells began falling again up and down the line. Clouds of stirred-up dust made visibility practically impossible for the gun crews. Trunks of coconut palms came crashing down on their gun positions, their fronds blasted off by the mortar bursts. During the next hours, only "about two or three" of the eight machine guns, including that of Mae, remained in a condition to fire back at the enemy. Mae's platoon commander, 2nd Lt. Kōsaburō Osada, lay dead nearby. Unseen by Mae, the Machine Gun Company commander, Lieutenant Komatsu, was also killed.[68]

10

"We Aren't Going to Let Those People Lay Up There All Day"

AT THE TENT COMMAND POST of the 1st Marine Regiment shortly after daybreak on August 21, Colonel Cates was huddling over a map with Vandegrift's operations officer, Lt. Col. Jerry Thomas. With a pencil, Cates was pointing out the location of the Japanese force on the opposite bank of the Tenaru left after its failed attempt to overcome the 2nd Battalion's defense line. "We aren't going to let those people lay up there all day," Thomas asserted to Cates. "We've got to get them out today," Cates replied.[1]

Now they were joined by "a grizzled man with a lined face," his shirt soaked in sweat as he entered the tent. Thomas immediately drew Cates's 1st Battalion CO, Lt. Col. Lenard B. Creswell, into the discussion. Pointing to the area of the Japanese on the division's D-2 map prepared on August 18, Thomas wanted to know if Cresswell thought that tanks could reach the Japanese over the terrain on the other side of the Tenaru, stretching north. When Cresswell stated that the dry ground through the woods would indeed make it possible, Thomas immediately told Cates that "we'll give L. B. a platoon of tanks" to support him in the plan the three senior Marine Corps commanders were developing to wipe out the remaining Japanese.[2]

Judging from the map, it was believed that the Japanese were concentrated in a small rectangular area just inland from the shore and extending eastward one mile from the mouth of the Tenaru to the mouth of Block Four River. Accordingly, they agreed that Cresswell would send his 1st Battalion troops, supported by a platoon of tanks, they hoped, across the dry bed of the upper Tenaru (actually, the Ilu), move eastward, then swing to the left and head north in an enveloping movement to push the Japanese into the sea. Any attempted escape to the west across the Tenaru by the boxed-in Japanese would be blocked by Pollock's 2nd Battalion.[3]

His oral instructions clear, Cresswell immediately took his leave and headed to his battalion command post to meet with his company commanders on the logistics of the operation. Responding to Cresswell's summons, A Company's Charley Brush, C Company's Nick Stevenson, and D Company's Ed Dzura were given their orders, along with Cresswell's executive officer, Major Marion A. Fawcett, substituting for B Company's CO, 1st Lt. Marshall T. Armstrong.[4]

Under the operation plan, all four companies would debouch from their jungle reserve position and cross over the dry riverbed to a grassy plain three thousand yards inland from the north shore. At that point, A and C companies would strike out north, A Company to the left of C Company, while B Company would veer off to the right on its northward movement, to bring it to the west of the "Ilu" (actually, the real Tenaru) in a position to block any Japanese trying to escape to the east. A and C Companies each would be reinforced by a machine gun platoon from D Company, but with the men following as riflemen only, leaving their heavy .30-caliber machine guns behind. D Company's mortar platoon would be deployed to the left of A Company to stop any Japanese attempt to escape from the Tenaru rear positions southward.[5]

At the newly operational airfield to the west of the Tenaru, now designated Henderson Field, Capt. Loren "Doc" Everton was warming up his Grumman F4F-4 Wildcat just before daybreak when Capt. John Smith, CO of VMF-223, which had arrived just the afternoon before, ran up to him with a map in his hands. Climbing up on the wing of the stubby fighter, Smith pointed on the map to an area where Japanese in several landing boats had been reported proceeding westward, just offshore. Division headquarters believed the boats were bringing reinforcements for their comrades fighting at the Tenaru and wanted the squadron's Wildcat pilots to check out the report and respond, if it were correct.[6]

Smith instructed Everton, on loan from VMF-212 to Smith's squadron because of his flying and leadership skills, to take several other pilots and fly out to the reported location of the boats and strafe any they found. Everton picked three others to join him on the mission and took off in the lead. As he was circling the field, a fellow VMF-212 pilot also on loan, Marine Gunner Henry "Tex" Hamilton, joined up on his wing. It was just after 0600.[7]

Flying low over the north coastline of Guadalcanal, heading east, they soon made out the landing boats, moving slowly offshore. Evidently having spotted the planes, the crews of the boats began heading for shore. As the boats reached land, it appeared that some of the Japanese were climbing out, but in an area unprotected by overhanging palms. Everton headed his Wildcat down in a dive, preparing to strafe the boats and the hapless Japanese.

In the small hours of the morning, Cpl. Kyonobu Akasaka was warming himself at Koli while the dead of Major Shibuya's ill-fated party were being cremated under the supervision of 2nd Lt. Kiyoshi Satō. Looking out to sea, he noticed three of the Type 95 collapsible boats that had transported the Ichiki detachment to shore at Taivu Point moving slowly westward, hugging the coast. When Akasaka yelled, "Engineers!" the crews responded by moving in to the shore.[8]

Akasaka waded out into the water and climbed on board the boat carrying a Sergeant Ogasawara, who turned out to be in charge of the little flotilla. In response to Akasaka's query, Ogasawara explained that that they were from 2nd Lt. Daizō Umeda's Boat Transport Unit and were taking medical and other supplies to Colonel Ichiki's men at the Nakagawa River. When Akasaka asked to join them, Ogasawara accepted, but he should get on board right away; they were in a hurry to get to their destination before dawn.[9]

It was slow going as the engineers rowed the plywood twenty-three-foot-long motorless craft, following the coastline. As the sky began to lighten, they heard gunfire and assumed they were near the Nakagawa. When the mouth of a river came into view, Ogasawara led the three boats into what he thought was the Nakagawa and had them proceed upstream about one hundred meters in search of Ichiki's men. But the river was becoming narrow and shallow, obliging them to come to a halt.[10]

Then two Japanese soldiers came alongside the boats. Pfc. Kiyoshi Saitō of Ogasawara's group recognized them as from his own Higuchi Company. Neither was carrying his rifle. Highly agitated, the soldiers yelled "Ichiki Detachment is annihilated! All killed!" They were carrying tiny remains of their dead comrades, wrapped in cloth triangles and stuffed into their backpacks.[11]

Some other soldiers on the bank of the river had descended into the water, evidently planning to wade across. Ogasawara's men disembarked from their boats into the knee-deep water and headed over to them. The soldiers told Saitō and the others what had happened at the Nakagawa. "We were all being killed, so we were ordered to go back."

Ogasawara now realized that his boats were not in the Nakagawa River after all, but in another river some distance to the east of their destination. But it now appeared pointless to try to deliver the supplies. He decided to turn the boats around for the sea and head back to Taivu Point, from whence they had set out.

However, as the boat crews proceeded down the river, the water was becoming even more shallow; the tide was going out. When they were still short of the mouth of the river, the water was too low to continue. Disembarking, they pulled their boats out of the river and dragged them over the beach thirty to forty meters to reach the ocean, all screaming "heave ho!" in unison as they manhandled the five-hundred-pound craft.

After succeeding in relaunching their boats in the water just offshore, the men were now confronted with another obstacle; artillery fire coming from the west was impacting near the boats.[12] But Ogasawara decided to keep going for Taivu Point; it was out of the question to turn around and go up that river again, where they would certainly meet death.

It was with relief that Ogasawara's men realized that at about one hundred meters offshore the American artillery fire had let up. Now they began rowing to the east for Taivu Point. But soon there was another threat, this from the sky: four single-engine planes that had appeared from the west were wheeling high over their heads.

In their first diving pass, Doc Everton and his three fellow pilots poured .50-caliber fire from their Wildcats' six wing guns into the wooden landing boats. They could see the Japanese scrambling to climb overboard and trying to swim to shore. It appeared to Everton that three of the boats were sinking. While it looked like some of the Japanese had made the beach, "we left plenty of them wriggling around in the water in circles," he recalled.[13]

On the second pass, Everton's "blasting fire" tore into those Japanese who had made it to the beach, precipitating a rush back to the water. It looked like other of the hapless men were using their dead comrades as sandbags to protect themselves from the stream of bullets raining down on them. "One machine gun opened up" on the strafers, but "Tex Hamilton dove on him, and that was that."[14]

With no more targets available after the gruesome business, Everton turned to lead the flight back to Henderson Field. Not one of the Wildcats had been hit. At about 0730, the last of the fighters touched down.[15]

When they spotted the planes diving down on them, Ogasawa's boat crews hurriedly turned around once more. Everyone put his back into rowing the boats back to the beach. Pfc. Saitō had never rowed a boat in his life and was thus considered of no help, but he nevertheless joined in and used his hands instead, to the rhythmic chant of the others.[16]

As soon as Saitō's boat reached the shore, the enemy planes swept in and sprayed his boat and its occupants with machine gun fire before the men could reach covering palms. Some of his comrades in the other boats had jumped into the water and tried to swim ashore, also targeted by the strafers. After this first pass, the Americans climbed back up, circled overhead, then dove down again for another strafing run at the boats and men.

Saitō and his boat mates managed to take cover under the branches of palms in the grove just inland as well as under the trunks of fallen trees. But the enemy pilots had spotted them and directed probing fire into the grove, the bullets striking around Saitō and sending up spurts of sand. Looking back, Saitō saw a comrade clinging to a palm, his whole body splattered with blood. He was crying out, "Help me!"

Saitō had not been hit by the strafers. He raised his head hesitatingly and looked around as quiet returned to the scene. The man he'd seen clinging to the tree was no longer there. His beached boat was shot full of holes. The supplies that it was transporting were bullet-ridden and rendered useless. Looking out to sea, Saitō saw that those boats that had not made it to shore were sinking.

Then Saitō was surprised to see fellow Japanese soldiers running past him, heading eastward. It seemed that he was the only one not moving. Picking up his rifle, helmet, and a bag of biscuits, he began to trudge towards Taivu Point, too.

In the coconut grove where he had taken shelter during the strafing attack, Corporal Akasaka also picked himself up. As he headed east for Taivu Point, he was saddened to see the bodies of twelve or thirteen of the men whom Ogasawara's men had encountered earlier heading east from the Tenaru battle. They also had been struck down by the gunfire from the American planes.[17]

To his astonishment, Akasaka spotted Lieutenant Hanami also withdrawing to the east. He knew Hanami well from the time both were called up to active duty. However, before Akasaka could greet him, a blood-splattered sergeant missing his left arm approached Hanami and cried out, "Lt. Hanami, sir, one of our battalion artillery guns is still operable and firing!" "What, firing now?" Hanami responded in disbelief. But at that moment Sgt. Mitsuo Abe, the leader of the second squad of their 70 mm battalion guns, collapsed on the ground, dead.

To Akasaka it appeared that Hanami had yelled something before turning around and running off toward the front. Akasaka noticed a mad gleam in Hanami's bloodshot eyes.

Sergeant Abe had been with a group of men being led back to Taivu Point by 2nd Lt. Kiyoshi Satō and others in Satō's platoon. They had been detached from Lieutenant Chiba's 4th Company for burial duties at the Papangu site of the ambush of the Shibuya party. Lieutenant Satō had encountered Abe and the others as he and his platoon were making their way westward to the Tenaru front after completing the burials the day before, but Satō decided to turn around and head back to Taivu Point when he realized from Abe and the others that the battle was lost. Like Akasaka, Satō was struck by the vehement response of Hanami in breaking away from the withdrawing men to head back to his gun crew at the Tenaru.[18]

Back at Hell's Point after daylight, Pfc. Masaharu Hayashi, lying in the water about thirty meters offshore of the mouth of the Nakagawa, looked back from the sea and saw that one 70 mm gun of Lieutenant Hanami's Battalion Artillery Platoon was firing. It was positioned about sixty meters to Hayashi's left at what he perceived to be the location of the remaining forward troops of Colonel Ichiki's detachment.[19]

Badly wounded, Hayashi had been swept out to sea after the tide reversed about 0300, carrying him and some fifteen corpses of men struck down while trying to cross the sand spit that was then covered with some 50 cm (20 inches) of water. He noted that no one was attempting to cross over the deadly sandbar any longer. But he could hear the sound of light machine gun firing by some of his comrades who had made it to the other side as well as the slower report of the heavy American machine guns.

A medical aid man from Hayashi's own Sawada Company now spotted Hayashi in the water and helped him ashore. The medic then turned his attention to another soldier who had been severely wounded, leaving Hayashi to attend to his own wound. Hayashi recognized the other man as Ldg. Pvt. Kaoru Aizawa of his company. But while the medic worked on Aizawa, he turned to Hayashi and informed him that company commander Sawada had told him that any of his men who had survived so far were free to return to Taivu Point and wait there for the expected arrival of Colonel Ichiki's second echelon.

But then the 3rd Platoon leader of Sawada's company, 2nd Lt. Tatsuo Tanaka, came up to the men around Hayashi with a contradictory order. He had a "weird, savage expression" on his face. "All able-bodied men, come with me!" Tanaka cried out. Ldg. Pvt. Yusaku Nakamura and about five other uninjured men heeded Tanaka's order and followed the platoon leader as he headed for the sand spit to rejoin the attack.[20] It was about 0700.

Left behind, Hayashi and Aizawa prepared to move east for Taivu Point. Hayashi had a wooden pole to support his wounded leg, and some men came to carry Aizawa, who was immobile due to his wounded upper thigh, on the stretcher his able-bodied comrades had made for him. But their trek was aborted when four American planes arrived on the scene and began firing at the stretcher bearers.

To save themselves, the men carrying Aizawa put him down and ran up to Hayashi to tell him what they had done. Hayashi turned around and headed back to Aizawa, lying on the stretcher. But with no one else around to help him carry the stretcher, Hayashi with deep remorse left his comrade to his fate.[21]

Another of Captain Sawada's men, Pfc. Mamoru Mizuno, had been lying near the shore in the same area where the medic had treated Aizawa but was too severely wounded to be able to withdraw under his own power. Furthermore, he had not heard of Sawada's order releasing his men, either wounded or able-bodied, to withdraw. Sawada himself had found shelter on the right flank of Komatsu's heavy machine gun emplacements, about ten meters in front of where Mizuno had taken cover. Mizuno noted that the forward command post of the detachment was set up somewhat behind him to the east.[22]

Immediately to the left of Sawada's position, Sgt. Masatoshi Mae was lying in the dugout near his heavy machine gun, wounded in the left side of his chest and upper right arm by mortar shell fragments. The gun position was covered by four coconut trunks that had fallen over it in a crisscross fashion. His trusty Juki machine gun, damaged by a mortar shell, was no longer operable. It didn't make much difference anyway; his supply of 7.7 mm ammo in the wooden boxes was exhausted.[23]

Mae was weighing whether he should just sit there and die or try to escape and keep alive. He was also wondering about the condition of the Nakamura gun squad just to his left and that of the other squads in Komatsu's company. As for

Dead Japanese crew of Lieutenant Komatsu's machine gun company lying next to their Type 92 Juki 7.7 mm heavy machine gun facing across toward the Marine side of Alligator Creek, August 22, 1942. *USMC photo, courtesy of Peter Flahavin.*

his own squad, seven men lay dead nearby, all killed earlier by the mortar fire of the Americans.

Peering out from between the fallen trunks, Mae became alarmed to see enemy soldiers climbing up palms. They were firing on the two remaining men of his squad. One of them, Pfc. Kiyoshi Ōno, took a hit from a rifle bullet in the left knee joint and could no longer move. Then the other, Ldg. Pvt. Tadaakira Saitō, had his right hand pierced by a bullet.[24]

Later, in the early afternoon, other Americans appeared from the south. Armed with rifles, they fired shots as they moved closer to Mae's position. Mae and his two surviving squad members lay like dead men under the palm trunks. When Ōno groaned in pain, Mae whispered to him to keep quiet or they all would be killed.[25]

Beyond the far left flank of Komatsu's machine gunners on the east bank of the Nakagawa, Sgt. Sadanobu Okada at daybreak had seen no more of the men of Lieutenant Maruyama's 3rd Company, nor of the Engineer Company, crossing the river. Colonel Ichiki had left Okada and his two comrades without ordering them across as he had originally intended to do. Ichiki instead had told them that he was going to head for the "sector front." Okada and the others should remain in their positions until his return.[26]

But by late morning the detachment commander had not come back. Okada was looking at the enemy positions across the river, easily visible now in the daylight, but realized the Americans could as easily see the Japanese on the other side. Whenever any of his comrades moved around, they were fired on by the American machine gunners. They made easy targets; there were no standing palm trees left or even brush that could provide protection; all had been knocked down by the devastating mortar and machine gun fire. Okada himself, unable to dig a hole in the hard earth without any tool, had taken refuge by lying down next to a palm trunk. He had been slightly wounded in the left buttocks by a mortar explosion in the trees but immediately had extracted the piece of shrapnel. He was thankful that at least the Americans had not tried to cross the river into their line.[27]

From a hole that he had managed to dig near Okada's position, Sergeant Shibutani began to cry out the name of each soldier in his Detachment Headquarters squad. "Are you alive?" he screamed. "You must hold out until dark! We will go back after sunset."[28]

After trudging eastward some fifteen hundred yards south of their bivouac position inland of the west bank of the Tenaru, the men of Lieutenant Colonel Cresswell's four companies reached the dry bed of the river, three thousand yards south of its mouth, and crossed over. It was 0950 when they began entering the kunai grass on the other side of the river bed to begin their enveloping action. On the left, the mortar platoon of D Company, the 1st Battalion's weapons company, was detached to proceed northwards to prevent any Japanese on the left bank of the river from breaking away and heading south to escape. A and C Companies struck out to the northeast, A Company to the left, to catch the Japanese situated just inland of the coast. To block any attempt to withdraw to the east by crossing over the "Ilu" (actually, the Tenaru) River, B Company swung to the right of C Company in a northeasterly movement.[29]

Just before the 1st Battalion men crossed over the riverbed, Colonel Cates called for another artillery barrage—this time from the 5th Battalion of the 11th Marines—to interdict the mouth of the "Ilu" (the Tenaru) and prevent the Japanese from withdrawing eastward across the river. At 0922, two batteries of the 5th

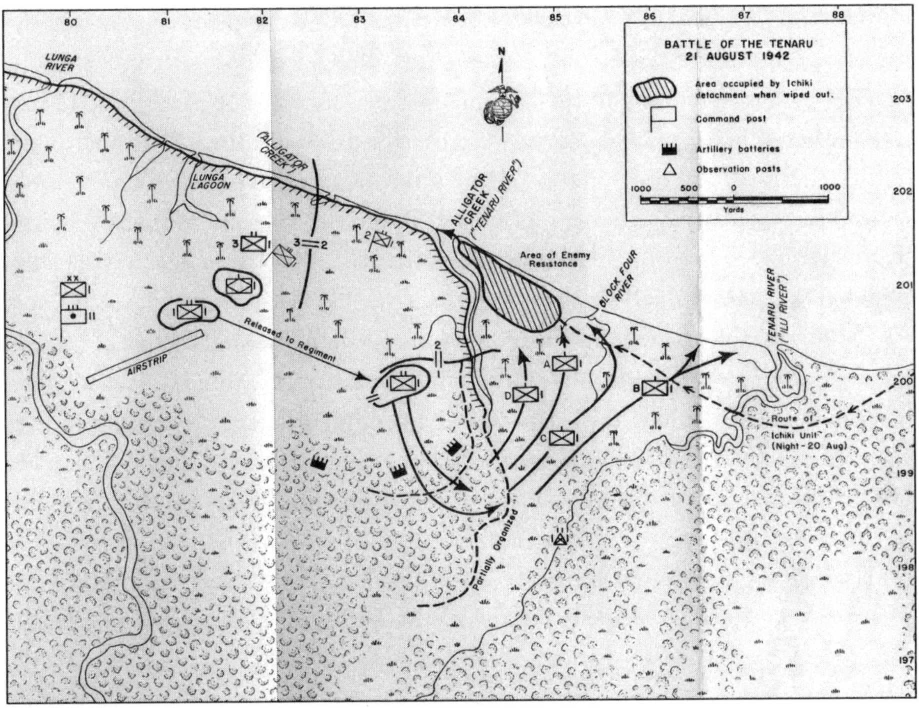

Direction of attack of A, B, C, and D Companies, 1st Battalion, in their enveloping action against the remnant of the Ichiki Detachment, August 21, 1942. *Courtesy John L. Zimmerman,* The Guadalcanal Campaign.

Battalion fired, raining 105 mm shells down on the rear flank of the Japanese. But at 0927 orders were received at 11th Marines headquarters to cease firing, as 1st Battalion men were about to move into the target area. The 0922 barrage would be the last artillery fired that day.[30]

Contrary to the plan, no tanks joined the battalion's men. Heading south from its encampment near the beach to the west of the Tenaru, the platoon of A Company's five M2A4 light tanks proved unable to continue to the dry bed due to the obstacles—irrigation ditches—in their way. One of them had fallen in such a ditch, from which the crew was unable to extricate it. Displaying initiative, Sgt. Earl Mowery drove his own tank up to the disabled tank and with the platoon leader's help attached a towing cable and pulled it from the ditch.[31]

Accompanied by a single rifleman, 2nd Lt. Joe Bushell, the assistant mortar platoon leader of D Company, was still puzzled why Cresswell's executive officer had ordered him to reconnoiter the area to his front at the head of the platoon's movement to the north. Soon Bushell spotted "about six or seven" Japanese moving around in a ditch directly in front of them. The Japanese spotted the Americans, too, and opened fire on them.[32]

Bushell ducked behind a palm tree and fired his .45 pistol at the Japanese, but to no effect. Looking around, he could not see his rifleman escort. He could make out the Japanese still moving laterally in the ditch, firing on Bushell as they shifted around. Then they threw several hand grenades that exploded near him. Shrapnel dug into his left thigh.

Falling to the ground in a prone position, Bushell pretended to be dead. The Japanese came out of the ditch but did not approach him as he lay next to a tree trunk, deciding to move away from their position instead. Soon other mortar platoon men were moving up. Bushell "yelled, whistled, and hollered" until they located him and carried him back to the battalion aid station. It transpired that his rifleman had returned to the rear and reported that he believed Bushell had been killed in the initial fusillade.

Following behind Bushell and his rifleman, Plat. Sgt. Michael Longazel, although just twenty years old and promoted to his position only six days earlier, was heading up an eleven-man patrol moving northwards too. As the men continued on their probing mission, they encountered a conglomeration of Japanese that immediately split into two groups, one turning left and the other right to confront the Americans. When one of the Japanese in the left contingent approached Pfc. Don Stiles, the Marine shot him in the shoulder with his '03 Springfield. To Stiles's astonishment, the wounded Japanese pulled off the bayonet from his Arisaka rifle and disemboweled himself. Stiles stepped backwards and finished the job by blowing his head off with a single shot. Pulling the bayonet out of the dead Japanese, Stiles wiped blood off of it, stuck it under his belt, and headed in the direction of his next adversary. Confronting the Japanese, Stiles fired a shot that he could see going all the way through his victim. "An incendiary round," he realized.[33]

But other members of the patrol were less fortunate. Pvt. Roy L. Barnes, an eighteen-year-old from Corbin, Kentucky, had shot a grenade from the hand of one of the Japanese as the enemy was preparing to throw it on a direct line into Longazel's men, but Barnes was then fatally shot in the head himself. Also both just eighteen years old, Pfc. Jim Smith (Cincinnati, Ohio) and Pvt. Freeman Blair (Milton, Pennsylvania) were felled and killed by Japanese gunfire, too. Three others were wounded in the engagement: Pfc. Gerard Cole and Pvts. Calvin

Schuler and Frank Huska. Only five survived unscathed: Longazel, Stiles, and Pvts. George Bono, Richard Swallow, and Lawrence Wattles.[34]

In the designated target area of D Company's mortar platoon, Pfc. Takeshi Makabe and Cpl. Shōji Setoda of Lieutenant Gotō's Engineer Company were seeking shelter as they heard the sound of gunfire nearby. Both were badly wounded, Makabe with blood flowing from his shoulder and head and Setoda's head cut by a piece of shrapnel. Just as Makabe spotted a ditch close by, five other comrades appeared, four of whom were also wounded. Setoda jumped into the ditch, followed by Makabe and the others.[35]

Scarcely after taking positions in the ditch, they spotted "seven or eight" enemy soldiers approaching. The uninjured member of the group at one end of the ditch fired his Arisaka rifle, as did Makabe from the other end, felling two of the Americans. As the others lay prostrate on the ground, the two Japanese threw five hand grenades at them. "Three or four" of the Americans got up and ran, dropping their backpacks, but those remaining fired at the Japanese, though without hitting anyone.[36]

Makabe and the uninjured soldier picked up two of the abandoned backpacks and brought them to their shelter to share with their wounded comrades. Eagerly, they opened the backpacks to find "a jumble of things—socks, flour, and a couple of cans of cheese." Opening one of the cans of cheese, they quickly devoured the contents, famished as they were.

With the sun now high in the sky, the seven decided on a course of action. Figuring that the enemy would be lying in wait for any Japanese survivors they thought would be heading south, Makabe and Setoda opted to head for the ocean shore. However, the other five set out for the south and the mountains as Makabe and Setoda struck out northwards, splitting the group.[37]

Back at the command post of the 1st Marines, Colonel Cates was on the telephone with Cresswell at 1115. The 1st Battalion commander was calling from his position with his headquarters company in the rear of his advancing men. Cresswell informed his superior that he was now beginning to attack, with his right flank positioned on the left bank of the "Ilu" River (actually, the real Tenaru River). But there were no tanks with his men, he informed Cates. They had evidently been held up "by some obstacle in terrain."[38]

Capt. Stevenson's C Company had moved forward through the tall kunai grass in full battle formation to reach the south edge of a coconut grove, with A Company abreast of it some four hundred yards to the left. Stevenson knew that they had now succeeded in setting the trap for the Japanese group, caught to their left. They were now about to spring it.[39]

Emerging from the kunai grass in skirmish line formation, 2nd Lt. Maurice Ahearn's 3rd Platoon, C Company, was in the lead, supported on its right by two light machine guns and two 60 mm mortars of 2nd Lt. Robert Fowler's Weapons Platoon. Following behind were 2nd Lt. Jim Wagner's 1st Platoon and 2nd Lt. Harold Jennings's 2nd Platoon. Stevenson was advancing in front of the 2nd Platoon to get a clear view of the operation.[40]

As C Company drew closer to the ocean, they could see Japanese moving around to their left, some 250 yards east of Block Four River and about 200 yards back of the beach. Stevenson assumed that they were the rear guard of the Japanese survivors, seemingly about thirty-seven men in platoon strength. With Ahearn in the lead, the 3rd Platoon wheeled to the left to engage the enemy. Fowler had his two light machine guns leapfrogging ahead, one replacing the other as they covered the beach on Ahearn's right flank to cut off any Japanese attempting to flee to the east.[41]

Ahearn's platoon, still in skirmish line formation, came under fire as it neared the Japanese, then the men hit the deck. They could make out the Japanese either lying prone behind coconut logs or crawling behind them. But when Ahearn was hit in the arm by a sniper as he led the charge, they realized that the Japanese were in the trees, too. With his leader wounded, Plat. Sgt. Lester Graham took command. Then nineteen-year-old Pvt. John Green was shot in the chest. He would die while being treated by a corpsman.[42]

After Ahearn was wounded, Jim Wagner's 1st Platoon moved up to provide support. Plat. Sgt. Reuben Pounder, a twenty-two-year veteran of the Corps, took the lead of two squads in a flanking movement, despite physical difficulties in keeping up. Fowler's two 60 mm mortars fired shells into the grove, but most of the projectiles exploded in the trees, although fragments showered down on the Japanese.[43]

Stevenson felt that the intensive exchange of fire would cost his company too much if it dragged on; already one of his men was dead and a platoon leader wounded. He decided to charge the Japanese with bayonets. The order to fix bayonets was passed to his platoon leaders. As the C Company men rushed the

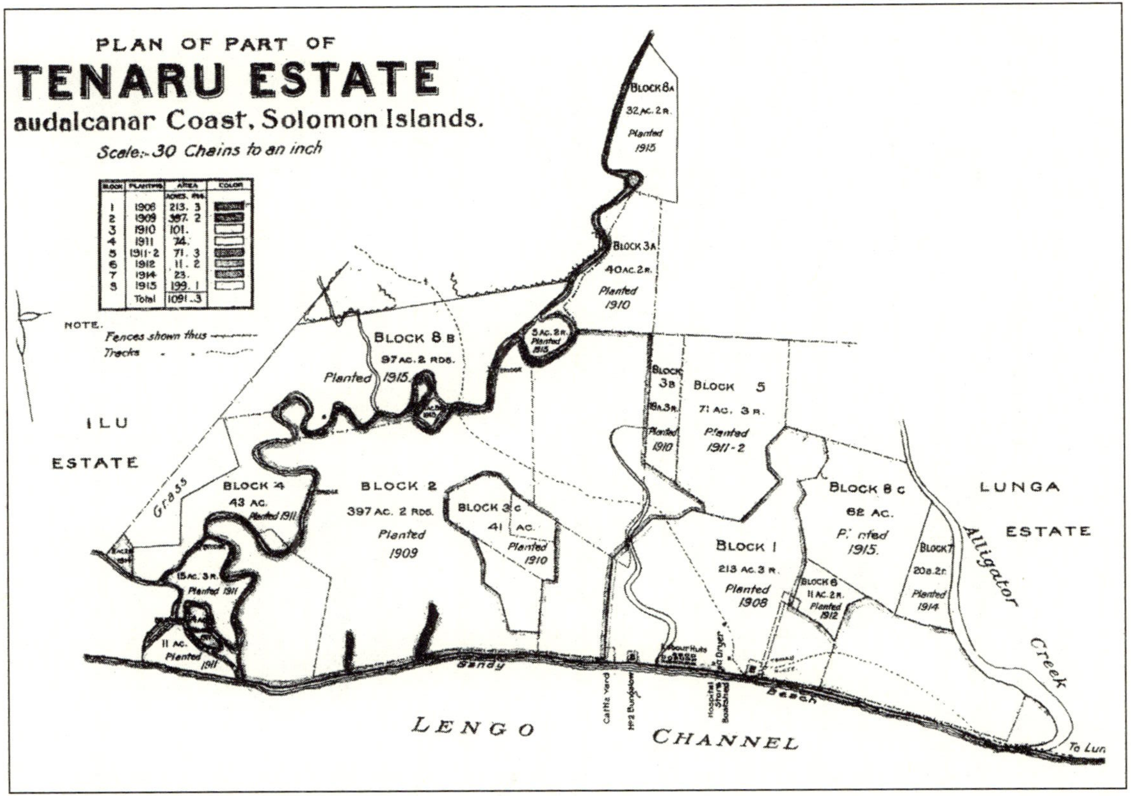

Tenaru Estate in 1925–26 by plantation blocks where Ichiki's men assembled for their attack across Alligator Creek. Block Four River (shown but not labeled) is the river immediately east of Alligator Creek, and the real Tenaru (not labeled) is the river further to the east. *Courtesy Unilever Archives, PIMB 1139, reel 3.*

Japanese positions, they were surprised at the reaction of their adversaries. Leaping up from behind fallen palms, the Japanese countercharged with fixed bayonets at Stevenson's men. In the vicious hand-to-hand combat, Japanese and Americans lunged, stabbed, and exchanged bayonet and rifle butt blows. "Horrible cries rose as cold steel tore through flesh and entrails," Stevenson recalled forty-three years later.[44]

The life-or-death struggle came to an abrupt halt. Stevenson and his victorious men stood over the bodies of the Japanese dead and wounded. They had suffered only one more casualty: Pvt. Frederick Clough was wounded.

Suddenly, Cpl. Frank D'Erico, standing near Stevenson, yelled, "Look out, he's got a grenade!" One of the Japanese lying on his stomach six feet away, and assumed dead, turned over, pulled the pin from a grenade, and flipped it at the two Americans. Stevenson and D'Erico hit the deck. The grenade exploded between them, spraying fragments. D'Erico's warning had saved them from death or injury.[45]

Recovering from the shock, Stevenson and D'Erico rose and approached the Japanese, who had resumed lying on his stomach. As D'Erico covered Stevenson, the C Company CO placed his .45 pistol against the head of the Japanese and fired. Then Stevenson rolled the now dead Japanese over and saw a samurai sword lying next to his body. Removing a wallet and some papers from the pocket of the blood-stained tunic, Stevenson also found a snapshot of his victim's wife and two children. A feeling of remorse momentarily overtook him. (Later, regimental intelligence informed Stevenson that the Japanese was Stevenson's opposite number and the commander of the rear guard of Ichiki's detachment.)[46]

Unseen by Stevenson, Colonel Cresswell's intelligence officer, 2nd Lt. Perry Perine, had come forward to situate himself behind C Company's position just before the bayonet charge. He had either been sent by Cresswell from his rear headquarters location to determine how the attack was progressing or had moved up on his own, presumably with the 1st Battalion commander's permission. Perine was finally getting the taste of combat he had craved. A single fatal shot from a sniper ended his aspiration.[47]

Meanwhile, about two hundred yards on C Company's left, A Company's 1st Platoon, under 2nd Lt. John Jachym, had the point ahead of the 2nd Platoon, under 2nd Lt. Vic Valente, and the 3rd of 2nd Lt. Charles Mackin as the men crossed over the grassy plain and entered the coconut grove to engage the Japanese from their southern flank. Also joining A Company's skirmish line was the

1st Machine Gun Platoon of D Company's 2nd Lt. Franklin Sills, but the men were acting as riflemen only, having stored their .30-caliber heavy machine guns before setting out.[48]

Scouts ahead of the Company were keeping Capt. Charley Brush apprised of the situation over their walkie-talkies as the men neared the Japanese. They warned that the Japanese had snipers up in the coconut palms. But one of Valente's squads decided that the platoon wasn't moving forward fast enough for it and took off ahead of the rest. Pfc. Carlton "Woodie" Woodward, a twenty-one-year-old from Bridgeton, New Jersey, was the instigator of the decision.[49]

As Woodward and his two best friends—Pvts. Patsy Campola and Jim Gorman—rushed into the coconut grove, they immediately became targets for snipers. A bullet bounced off Woodward's helmet, and all three hit the deck as more shots were fired from the trees at them. Spotting one of the snipers, Campola took a bead on him with his Springfield, and the Japanese fell from his sitting position and leaned over from the waist. Then Gorman made out the outline of another sniper tied in another palm and fired his rifle with the same fatal result for the Japanese.[50]

For the next few hours, A Company's men would advance a few steps, drop down when taken under fire by snipers, and try to locate and shoot at them. Word was passed over from C Company on their right flank that it had run into heavy opposition. Unlike Stevenson's men, Brush's company was experiencing very little hand-to-hand fighting.[51]

With no one in their squad having sustained a hit, Gorman and Woodward were wondering whether their luck would last, but not Campola. The feisty Italian-American was "in his glory, cursing Mussolini and the Japs and acting if he had eyes in the back of his head as far as snipers were concerned." But unknown to Campola, some of the Japanese were not tied in, but rather just sitting in the crotches of the trees.

Suddenly, Campola let loose with some choice swear words. An explosive bullet had struck the stock of his Springfield, ruining it. Worse, Woodward saw that his buddy's right arm was also bleeding, shattered by the same bullet that had hit his rifle. However, Campola was hopping mad about the destruction of his Springfield, not over his wound.

Ripping off a piece of his shirt, Woodward made a tourniquet for Campola's arm. In the next moment, Gorman, standing to their right, heard firing "all up and down the skirmish line, mixed with the yelling and curses of other A Company men he couldn't see." But then, "louder than anything," he realized that Campola was crying.

That wasn't like Campola! Looking to his left, Gorman was shocked to see tears streaming down Campola's face and Woodward lying flat on the ground, face up. He had made a perfect target as he tended to Campola.

"They got him, right through the heart," Campola blurted out, pointing to his best friend's body. Then he went into another fit of sobbing. Recovering and fighting mad, he bent over to pick up Woodward's rifle and, oblivious to his wound, began firing wildly into the trees at what he perceived were the forms of snipers, with Gorman joining in.

But then Gorman "felt a peculiar sensation" in his left arm, alternating hot and cold, followed by a terrible pain that sent him crumpling to his knees. He figured that a bone in his forearm had been shattered by an explosive bullet. Leaving their buddy lying dead on the ground, Gorman and Campola, now bleeding profusely, crawled behind some palm trees where they figured they would be out of sight of the snipers.

Lying motionless, both "about out of our minds with pain," Campola and Gorman waited for help. Finally, they heard footsteps approaching them. "American or Japanese?" they wondered. It was with relief that they recognized PhM3c Leroy "Doc" Preston from 1st Battalion headquarters.

As Preston waited impatiently to treat their wounds, Campola and Gorman got into an argument. Each wanted Preston to take care of the other first. Eventually both were taken to the hospital after being treated. Except for Pfc. Charley Crawford in Jachym's platoon, who was wounded, Woodward, Gorman, and Campola, all in Valente's platoon, were the only casualties suffered by A Company in the operation.[52]

Some eight hundred yards to the right of C Company's clash in the coconut grove, Major Fawcett had B Company's men positioned at the location designated for them to the left of the Ilu (actually the Tenaru) River in late morning. The 1st Battalion's executive officer had assigned squad-sized details along the east bank of the river as a rear guard to oppose any Japanese attempting to escape from the west. However, so far no enemy soldiers had presented themselves that far from where they were concentrated.[53]

Other members of B Company were approaching the area to their left where the extreme rear guard of the Japanese was believed holding out. Suddenly, a Japanese in the grove unexpectedly rose about seventy-five yards away and fired his Arisaka. The single rifle shot felled and killed Pfc. Bernard McCarthy only a few yards from seventeen-year-old Pfc. Robert Corwin. Both men were in 2nd Lt. Lawrence Smith's rifle platoon. Instantly, another member of Smith's platoon standing next to Corwin lifted his Springfield and shot the Japanese dead. Smith's men "took a good look" at the corpse, the first enemy soldier they had ever seen.[54]

Smith then ordered his platoon to flush out any other Japanese hidden in the grove. "Fix bayonets!" he yelled. Corwin and the others screamed wildly as they charged forward, egged on by Smith's shouts of "go get 'em, men!" To everyone's relief, they encountered no other Japanese.[55]

By 1230, A and C Companies were ready to start their westward movement, aimed at finishing off any remaining Japanese bottled up between them and the mouth of the "Tenaru." At 1315 they neared the end of the palm grove extending westward from the east bank of the river. Brush's and Stevenson's men were pushing the Japanese towards the 2nd Battalion's defense line on the opposite side of the Tenaru. Some of the Japanese were trying to escape by crossing over the beach and plunging into the ocean, but they were being picked off by Cresswell's men.[56]

Other Japanese in the grove were still fighting back, including the crew of a Nambu light machine gun that had been firing intermittently from the opposite bank at the mouth of the Tenaru into the Marines across the river. One of its victims was Pvt. Brady Wadsworth, hit by two 7.7 mm bullets in the left arm and groin from the machine gun as he continued to maintain his position with a Springfield rifle at the mouth of the Tenaru. Furious at the Japanese for wounding him in the genitals, Wadsworth screamed to his fellow E Company comrades at the spit, "If those bastards have ruined me, I'll kill every S.O.B. in Japan!"[57]

In a protected position nearby, Colonel Pollock and G Company CO Capt. Jim Sherman decided to take out the persistent machine gun crew once and for all with mortar fire. Available for the task was a 60 mm mortar of Sherman's Weapons Platoon that at the time was positioned at the end of the dirt road leading to the sand spit.[58]

With Sgt. Willis Accord positioned forward of the mortar as observer, the Japanese crew was located for Pfc. Paul Hanlon, practically on a line of sight for the gunner. All the increments were removed to allow for the short distance to the target, only some ninety yards away. With a "thwung," the first round fired by Hanlon arched upwards and exploded short. After the second 60 mm shell hit long, Accord yelled back to Hanlon and his two loaders, "Up fifteen!" The third explosion blew up one of the Japanese crew as he jumped up to escape the incoming shell, "a canopy of dirty gray smoke and debris" enveloping him. The three other members of the Nambu crew also jumped up in plain view but were cut down by rifle and machine gun fire from Pollock's men.[59]

It was about 1500 when the men of A and C Companies observed light tanks lumbering across the sandbar to their left. Although it was considered "risky," Colonel Cates had ordered the platoon of five M2A4 tanks under 1st Lt. Leo Case of A Company, 1st Tank Battalion, to mop up the remaining Japanese in the grove, where open spaces between the palms allowed them room for maneuver.[60]

War correspondent Richard Tregaskis on the 2nd Battalion side of the Tenaru mouth watched in fascination as "these awful machines" bustled around the palm trees, "pivoting, turning, spitting sheets of yellow flame." As they knocked down the trees, the tank crewmen fired canister from their 37 mm guns and .30-caliber bullets from their machine guns at Japanese running to escape.[61]

Suddenly Tregaskis saw a "bright red flash from amidst a cloud of black smoke" emanating from under the treads of one of the tanks. Crippled, it halted. (Actually, it had been disabled when one of the Japanese had stuck his rifle barrel into the tread). Case ordered three of his tanks to circle around it. Directly from behind, the crew of one of the tanks evacuated one of the four-man crew via the escape hatch in the bottom, then the men of the other tanks repeated the procedure until all four men were safely removed.[62]

Their rescue operation completed, the crews of the four remaining operational tanks continued the mopping-up exercise in the grove. Japanese survivors were running towards Stevenson's C Company men but were being shot as they tried to escape. Pvt. Dave Lynch in Jim Wagner's 1st platoon was having a field day, firing his BAR sidewise while kneeling behind a palm tree.[63]

Pvt. Julius Peebles in Hal Jennings's platoon was in a less fortunate position. A "dead" Japanese he approached as a point man for the platoon in the mopping-up operation had suddenly jumped up and knocked Peebles's rifle aside, then wrestled him to the ground and sat astride him. But Peebles managed to get a firm grip on both wrists of his adversary, preventing the Japanese from inflicting a fatal blow. By that time, platoon comrade Pvt. Bill Sadler, who had been covering Peebles forty feet to his rear, had dropped to one knee for a clear shot with his Springfield. With a single shot, the Japanese fell forward over Peebles. Sadler rose and ran to the scene. Raising his head, the young Japanese looked Sadler in the eyes. Slanting his rifle to avoid hitting Peebles, Sadler fired again, causing the Japanese to rise to his feet in an uncontrolled reaction. A third shot knocked him down on his back, this time dead for good.[64]

To the right of the right flank of what remained of the line of Komatsu's heavy machine guns, Captain Sawada was still commanding from his shelter in front of the detachment's forward command post when he saw tanks crossing over the sand spit and heading towards him. With no weapons capable of opposing them, Sawada realized he and his men were in a hopeless situation. Behind him, Pfc. Mamoru Mizuno, wounded earlier, was now hit again, this time in the knee joints by machine gun fire from one of the tanks. As he fell to the ground, he realized that he had no feeling in his feet. He watched helplessly as other tanks appeared, spraying canister and machine gun fire in all directions at his fleeing comrades. Falling one by one, they were calling out, "Mother!" "Toshiko!" and other female names in their final gasps. When he shifted his view to the front, he was shocked to see Captain Sawada lying on his back to the side of a ditch, lifeless, another victim of the tanks.[65]

Mizuno longed for his own death to come quickly. However, when the tanks headed towards him, their engines roaring, he abruptly changed his mind. Thoughts of his mother flooded his head as he lost consciousness.[66]

Some distance to Mizuno's left, Sgt. Masatoshi Mae and his two surviving squad members, Pfc. Kiyoshi Ōno and Ldg. Pvt. Tadaakira Saitō, lay pressed together under the palm fronds covering their machine gun position as the tanks approached. Americans on foot were following behind the tanks with their bayonets fixed. Despite their painful wounds, all three Japanese were keeping absolutely silent. Tree trunks lying on the ground were preventing the tanks from approaching close. The soldiers apparently assumed the threesome were dead. The Japanese drew no fire from either the tankers or the Marines on foot.[67]

Just before the tanks reached his position, Mae was surprised to see that one of the iron behemoths had come under attack from a surviving machine gun crew to his left, followed by fire from two other heavy machine guns that also had survived the mortar barrage earlier and had been turned to face other tanks to their right. But it was an unequal contest. Canister and machine gun fire from the tanks tore into the crews and silenced their Jukis. One of the tanks ran directly over one of the machine gun positions, crushing five men and flattening their gun.[68]

Sometime after the tanks had moved away from his position, Mae was still lying flat on the ground when he happened to look up towards his rear. "What the hell was that?" he exclaimed. He had seen a blaze in the distance sending up white smoke. "What kind of flame was that?" he wondered.[69]

As the tanks were pushing deeper into the detachment's rear, 2nd Lt. Tomokazu Itō was agonizing over a decision he would have to make as its color bearer. He could not allow the 28th Infantry Regiment's flag to fall into American hands. For Ichiki's men, the colors had an almost mystical significance: it was the same flag the regiment had carried at the time of its victory over the Russians at Hill 203 at Port Arthur in 1904.[70]

Abruptly, Itō took the black-lacquered staff flying the rising sun crowned with a chrysanthemum emblem from the hands of Sgt. Hidetatsu Kurugane standing next to him.[71] From a cylinder of magnesium incendiary compound he had been carrying all day in the event of such a need, Itō doused the flag after removing it from the staff and ignited it.

Instantly, there was a white flash followed by the bright glow of the flame. As the smoke rose into the late afternoon sky, Itō pulled the pin of a grenade he carried, placed it on top of the ashes of the flag, and threw himself on top of the remains. With this last sacrificial act, Itō had fulfilled his duty as the regiment's color bearer.[72]

Sgt. Sadanobu Okada had heard the clanging of the tanks as they headed from the grove down the riverside towards where he lay on the ground, upstream from the far left flank of Komatsu's machine gun line. As they approached his position, he could see that the top of their turrets was open, where gunners were directing their machine gun fire at anyone they spotted. To Okada, they seemed to be shooting blindly. However, to his satisfaction he noted that one of the tanks had been disabled, its crew apparently fleeing.[73]

When two of the tanks returned to Okada's location, he stretched out on the ground, partially under the root of a palm tree, pretending to be dead. Very slowly, one of the tanks approached him, but its gunner was not firing. Then as he lay helpless and terrified, the thirteen-ton vehicle passed over Okada's body. But he felt only some pressure on his back. Surprised to find he was still alive, Okada figured that he had been protected by the root of the tree.

But now he could see that the second tank following behind the first was moving towards him too. It stopped short, the crew taking no action. Okada suspected the crew was looking for Japanese, but somehow they had not spotted him. After a few minutes the tank started moving again, passing to his side and pushing up earth against Okada's body.

M2A4 light tanks of A Company, 1st Tank Battalion, weaving through palm trees on the east bank of Alligator Creek while returning to the west bank, August 21, 1942. Note the Japanese bodies on the ground. *USMC photo in author's collection.*

After what seemed to Okada like almost an hour, the tanks finally left the area around him. As he looked around, he could not see any other survivors except Sergeant Kurugane, a few meters away, like Okada from Ichiki's headquarters. Kurugane told Okada that he also had survived a tank going over him, thanks to the protection afforded by a deep hole in which he had sheltered.[74]

With the tanks now apparently gone and no more groaning voices of their Japanese victims heard, quiet prevailed around Okada and Kurugane. Their attention now turned to devising a plan to escape and get back to Taivu Point in order to warn the detachment's second echelon against any repeat of the "reckless rush towards the enemy." But they decided to wait until dark to set out.

Suddenly, someone cried out, "Tanks coming!"

"Not again!" Okada exclaimed. Apparently it was a survivor of Komatsu's machine gun company who had sounded the alert, he thought.

Looking to their right, Okada and Kurugane could make out three tanks approaching them, along with many soldiers firing at random, it seemed. This time Okada was sure he would be killed. As the deafening roar of the tanks came closer, mixed with the yells of the soldiers, Okada played dead again. The Marines passed a little to the left of where Okada lay, not stopping to examine Okada's body and firing into it as they did others lying dead nearby.

Okada found that Kurugane had also survived this latest incursion. Left alone in what they realized was now clearly enemy territory, they returned to planning for escape. But exhausted by the day's harrowing experience, they both fell into a deep sleep.

With dusk approaching following the withdrawal of the tanks and soldiers, Masatoshi Mae was also trying to figure out the best way for his two squad mates and him to escape. He finally decided to head northwards to the sea and told Saitō that should he be hit, to keep going himself. But Saitō was concerned that with Ōno unable to walk, they would be easy targets for the enemy.

"We have no choice but to leave it in the hands of the gods," Mae replied. Hefting Ōno onto his back despite his own wounds, Mae set out in the darkness with Saitō for the coast. Although Mae figured it was only about seventy meters in a direct line to the shore, he elected to move forward in a more circuitous way. But after having covered only some thirty to forty meters, it seemed that machine guns were firing on them. Thinking he had been hit, Mae dropped Ōno and fell down himself, Ōno screaming in pain. However, when Mae realized that no one had been shooting, he pulled Ōno back up again on his back and resumed his trek to the beach with Saitō. It was completely dark when the threesome reached the ocean without further incident.[75]

It was midnight when Kurugane shook Okada out of his deep sleep. To their great surprise, it seemed that the Americans were still shooting at this late hour. Figuring it would be too dangerous to try to escape together, they decided to head north separately, Kurugane first and Okada thirty minutes later. They would meet up at the Hebigawa River that they had crossed the evening before.[76]

But only a few minutes after Kurugane had set out, Okada heard what sounded like machine gun fire. Assuming that Kurugane had been the target and was undoubtedly dead, Okada decided to follow a different route to the sea than that taken by Kurugane. He figured that after reaching the ocean he would be able to swim eastward the two hundred meters or so to be safe from any American fire.

Despite intense thirst, Okada managed to crawl northward without incident and reach the beach. After drinking from the sea, he waded out until the water was neck deep. But when he turned and tried to wade eastward, the wind and tide impeded his movement. Abandoning his helmet and sword, Okada headed back to the beach, keeping a low profile. When he was some twenty meters offshore, he found that it was easier to wade in the shallow water and proceeded eastward to a point about three hundred meters from the Nakagawa behind him. Here there seemed to be no sign of the enemy. Figuring it was safe to return to the beach, he waded ashore and took refuge under a bush. After a brief pause, Okada then set out for the east on foot. After running some fifteen hundred meters, he reached the mouth of the Hebigawa, but searching the area, he could find no sign of Kurugane.[77]

As quiet settled over the killing field in late afternoon following the withdrawal of the tanks, the men under Brush and Stevenson were finally able to get some rest after some eight hours into the mopping-up operation. They were also hungry, not having had anything to eat since before setting out early that morning. Thus C Company's men were elated when an amtrac approached them and someone in the LVT began throwing cans of corned beef and hardtack at them. The belated lunch treat was courtesy of C Company Mess Sgt. Howard Ingerson, who had on his own initiative decided to bring food to the men.[78]

Sometime after they finished their meal, the order to return to their original positions arrived. Captains Brush and Stevenson led the men back across the mouth of the Tenaru. They were appalled by the sight of so many dead bodies of the Japanese littering the sandbar.[79]

On the other side of the mouth of the river, Pollock's 2nd Battalion men had been keen to fire on those Japanese who had made it to the ocean in fleeing the tanks and men of the 1st Battalion. Many E Company Marines had moved up to the spit and fired at targets of opportunity in the water.[80] However, at that distance the eager riflemen were not having much luck.

Finally, Pollock called up E Company's Charlie Angus, its master gunnery sergeant. A "grizzled, leather-faced" veteran of twenty-three years in the Corps, Angus was an expert rifleman. Attired in his shooting jacket and fingerless shooting glove, he began squeezing off single shots from his Springfield at the heads bobbing in the sea offshore. One by one they dropped beneath the water.[81]

At about 1700, with the fighting now apparently at an end, Pollock crossed over the sand spit, joined by many of his men determined to make sure that the Japanese lying sprawled on the ground were truly dead. Dick Tregaskis watched as the Marines pumped bullets into the prone bodies. The water offshore "grew brown and muddy," discolored from the blood of fallen Japanese littering the mouth of the Tenaru and the adjacent beach.[82]

But as Colonel Cates personally discovered earlier, the Marines' own west bank of the river was not entirely safe. He had been driven up in his jeep to the mouth of the Tenaru upon receiving word at his regimental command post that the enveloping action was nearly completed. Running up to a forward 37 mm gun position with his chauffeur, Pvt. Jack Strunk, Cates could hear rifle shots ricocheting through the palm trees in the grove on the other side. Nearby, the CO of his regimental weapons company, Capt. Harry Q. Findley, had also come forward to watch the finale. Suddenly, a single shot fired by a sniper struck Findley in the chest. To Cates, Findley's wound seemed only "fairly serious," but the captain would die two days later on the transport evacuating him from Guadalcanal.[83]

Epilogue

WHEN SGT. SADANOBU OKADA reached the mouth of Block Four River sometime after 0200 on August 22, he did not find Sergeant Kurugane waiting for him at the prearranged meeting place. Kurugane had left half an hour earlier that evening than Okada. Had he been killed on the way? Okada decided to search for Kurugane to the west of the river, but after two attempts failed to turn up any sight of the sergeant, he gave up and returned to the river to consider what to do. It would be disgraceful to escape and head back to Taivu Point without finding Kurugane, he felt, yet he was intent on surviving. He would try once more. Making his way three hundred meters further west towards the area now believed in American hands, he still could find no trace of Kurugane, so Okada decided to return and remain at the mouth of Block Four River until sunrise, then head east alone for Taivu Point.[1]

Unknown to Okada, the elusive Kurugane had reached the Block Four meeting place considerably before Okada, having taken a quicker route and easily passed through the area where the American tanks had been operating. He mistakenly assumed that Okada had followed the same route. After waiting for Okada for over an hour, he assumed that Okada had been killed and decided to strike out on his own for Taivu Point.[2]

That Saturday morning, correspondent Richard Tregaskis was one of the many who decided to visit the site of the vicious fighting that had ended late the afternoon before. He was appalled by what he saw and smelled. The stench of bodies strewn around the area of the mouth of the Tenaru and across the sandbar was nauseating. Some of the corpses were partially buried in the sand, while others at the edge of the beach "were already puffed up and glossy." The scene in the coconut grove across the sandbar was even more sickening. Bodies of many Japanese were ripped open, the entrails spilled on the blood-stained ground, arms and legs lying all around, heads blown off.[3]

Seemingly immune to the sight and smell as they walked among the dead Japanese that lined the beach on their side of the Tenaru early that morning, Pfc. Deacon Tatum and members of his mortar squad were searching through the packs on the bodies for souvenirs they could use for trading purposes. "We were especially interested in their German-made automatic rifles, machine guns, and bayonets," Tatum recorded in his diary.[4]

In the afternoon, Tatum and his whole squad—Phillips, Ransom, Lucas, and Battles—crossed over the sand spit to witness the "unbelievable carnage" in the coconut grove. They "could smell the stench of burned flesh" even before they reached the bodies, now covered with flies. But what drew their attention more than anything was the process being followed for burying the corpses that was underway.[5]

A bulldozer had been brought up from the lines and was excavating huge pits about twenty-five feet long, eight feet wide, and ten feet deep. In the ditch Tatum and his squad mates were looking at, bodies were already stacked up eight feet high. Japanese and Korean prisoners, "maybe 200," who had been brought forward were picking up and carrying the dead to the burial pits.

Earlier, when the POWs had come marching down the beach road, four abreast, in step, guarded by Marine MPs, they appeared to Phillips "like midgets" compared to the MPS, all of whom seemed to be over six feet tall. Armed with their submachine guns, the MPs were calling cadence from the flanks, a scene that to Phillips was reminiscent of Parris Island days. One big MP would bellow, "in cadence count," which was followed by "a chorus of oriental voices shouting 'Roosevelt good man, Tojo eats shit!'" Phillips and the others watching the procession nearly split their sides in laughter at the sight.[6]

Elsewhere in the grove, navy beachmaster Lt. Jack Clark watched as prisoners were loading trucks with dead Japanese. When some twenty bodies had

Corpses of Japanese lie half buried in the tidal sands of Hell's Point on early morning of August 22, 1942. *US National Archives photo 127-N-50963.*

Korean POWs carrying off the body of a dead Japanese soldier on the east bank of Alligator Creek, August 22, 1942. *USMC photo, courtesy of Peter Flahavin.*

Second Lt. Karl Soule of 1st Division headquarters inspects a 7.7 mm Type 99 Nambu light machine gun on the east bank of Alligator Creek, August 22, 1942. *USMC photo, courtesy of Ewan Stevenson.*

been piled on, the driver would proceed to a newly dug trench, into which the corpses were dumped or rolled off the trucks. "Parts of bodies were just kicked off into the trench," Clark noted. When a pit had been filled with some forty to fifty bodies, the bulldozers would push sand over them to fill up the hole. Clark did not notice markers of any kind set up that could identify the location of the burial sites.[7]

Near the collection sites, huge piles of gear of all kinds had been piled up, including many bullet-punctured helmets and gas masks. Tatum commented on the "piles and piles of grenades" that lay near where they had been taken off the bodies. Clark was impressed with the collection of flame throwers, knee mortars, machine guns, and rifles that had been recovered.[8]

To Lieutenant Colonel Pollock, burying the hundreds of Japanese dead was proving "quite a job" this day. He was surprised by how few Japanese had surrendered. Of the fourteen prisoners taken, all but two were wounded. The only officer captured was Prov. 2nd Lt. Shigeru Wada, a platoon leader of the Engineer Company, who had been left at the bank of the Tenaru.[9]

Pollock himself was personally involved in taking one prisoner. The Japanese had stepped onto the far end of the sand spit with his hands over his head. Pollock ordered cease-fire to allow him to limp to Pollock's position. The Japanese had a big hole in his leg. Pollock called the regimental command post for an interpreter. In response to the request, Capt. Fred O. Wolf reported to Pollock and began questioning the prisoner. When asked why he had turned himself in, the Japanese replied that he was "unable to withstand his thirst."[10]

Another of the Japanese wounded picked up that day was being sent to the rear for medical treatment, with Pvt. Harry Horsman serving as guard. As they sat facing each other in the rear of the truck, the Japanese "kept pointing to Horsman's rifle and then to himself." The G Company Marine realized that the prisoner was trying to get Horsman to understand that he wanted Horsman to shoot him. It was Horsman's introduction to the code of bushido, that to surrender was a disgrace to family, country, regiment, and Emperor.[11]

At Taivu Point the following day, Sergeant Okada finally arrived back after a trek of more than thirty kilometers from Block Four River. He found Sergeant Kurugane already there, each pleasantly surprised to find that the other had made it back safely. Of the NCOs, Sgt. Masatoshi Mae was there, too, along with Leading Private Saitō, whom Mae had helped on the long walk. Okada estimated that there were now about one hundred at the Taivu Point camp. They included some forty of 2nd Lt. Kiyoshi Satō's platoon who, too late for the fighting, had turned back short of the battleground after going forward belatedly following their burial duties for the Shibuya party.[12]

Although they had not been wounded, two officers also had returned from the front, but without orders. The detachment's communications officer, 1st Lt. Yoshiaki Sakakibara, had left the other headquarters staff at the time of the tank attack and made his way on his own back to Taivu Point, arriving by evening, August 21. Similarly, 2nd Lt. Toshio Habara, assistant adjutant to Maj. Nobuo Kuramoto, the battalion commander killed at the outset of the battle, had also reached Taivu Point after apparently fleeing the battleground.[13]

As the senior surviving officer of the Ichiki force, Sakakibara was faced with the responsibility of reporting the virtual annihilation of the detachment. Immediately after his arrival, he headed over to the navy's lookout station and asked the man in charge to send a message for the attention of Maj. Eiji Mizuno, the commander of the second echelon on its way to Taivu Point. At 1945 that evening, the following message went out to the navy's Rabaul Communications Section: "Ichiki advance force this morning failed to reach the airfield. On verge of annihilation. Inform Ichiki detachment commander on board *Boston Maru.* [signed] Navy East Lookout Station."[14]

When the Rabaul Communications Section received the message, it passed it to navy staff officer Matsumoto of the 8th Base Force, who immediately went to see the chief of staff of the Seventeenth Army at his Rabaul residence. It was 0130. Maj. Gen. Akisaburō Futami was on his way to bed when Matsumoto showed up. Stunned by the message, Futami hoped that it was false; Sakakibara had not included his own name on it.[15]

The wounded survivors who had trickled in to Taivu Point by August 23 wondered about the circumstances of Sakakibara's and Habara's leaving the battleground, apparently without orders. The two seemed in "an abstract state of mind." Neither was willing to discuss the matter with them.[16]

Now, two days after the battle had ended, it was clear to the remnant of the first echelon at the camp that there would be no survivors other than themselves among the 916 officers and men who had landed at Taivu Point. By Sergeant Okada's estimate there were just ten who had returned, plus the forty of the transportation unit who had remained behind and the forty of Satō's platoon.[17]

Okada did not know if any of the detachment had been taken prisoner, but this possibility would have been discounted. He felt that any men facing capture would have opted for suicide instead, given the disgrace such an act would have carried.[18]

A more widespread subject of discussion among the Taivu Point conglomeration was the fate of their commander. What had happened to Colonel Ichiki? Neither Okada nor any of the other survivors had seen him since he had gone to the forward command post with his adjutant Togashi the morning of August 21 to take personal charge. But he was certainly killed, they concluded.[19]

But one of the survivors who had reached Taivu Point believed he knew the fate of Ichiki, though he did not share his view with Okada, Kurugane, Mae, or the others. Separated from his unit, Ldg. Pvt. Masao Morihiro of Provisional Lieutenant Wada's platoon of engineers had seen from a distance someone near a large palm tree that was still standing in the coconut grove shoot himself in the head with a pistol. Then a second man also committed suicide, slashing his stomach with a sword. A third person next to them appeared to be dead already. "About five or six" soldiers immediately afterwards came forward and wrapped the bodies in blankets and tarpaulins that had been piled up at the site.[20]

At that point Morihiro approached the group and offered to help as the men prepared to bury the three bodies. On the east side of the tall palm, at its base, Morihiro and the others dug a shallow grave, into which they lowered the dead men, then covered them with sandy soil. Their work finished, Morihiro and the others separated, the men heading eastward for Taivu Point, while Morihiro remained on the field overnight before setting out at dawn for the same destination.

Since the three dead men he had helped bury were not wearing their tunics, Morihiro could not determine their ranks. However, the trousers of the two he had witnessed committing suicide were those worn by officers. Morihiro speculated that the two officers were Colonel Ichiki and his adjutant, Captain Togashi, and evidently a senior NCO of their headquarters staff was with them.[21]

Of more relevant concern for the small group at Taivu Point was the nonappearance of Ichiki's second echelon. According to Ichiki's plan, it had been scheduled to land at Taivu Point the day before, August 22.[22] There was a fear among the men that the Americans would come to finish them off before the second echelon could arrive and strengthen the defense. At present, they had only Satō's platoon with its three light machine guns and two grenade dischargers to protect them.[23]

On board the *Daifuku Maru,* 2nd Lt. Genjirou Inui was surprised to hear the air raid alarm sound on the transport just after he had finished breakfast on the morning of August 23, six days out of Truk. Running up to the deck, he spotted the source of the alarm: a large flying boat off to starboard, circling low around the three-ship convoy, in and out of dark clouds.[24]

Abruptly, the *Daifuku Maru*, along with the *Boston Maru,* carrying Maj. Eiji Mizuno, the second echelon commander, changed course, executing a U-turn. Anticipating that the enemy patrol plane would radio the sighting to American carriers assumed to be in the area, Rear Adm. Raizo Tanaka on board the escorting light cruiser *Jintsu* had ordered the convoy to evacuate to the north as quickly as possible, Inui learned. Inui and the other officers of his company on the *Daifuku Maru* were dismayed that the Imperial Japanese Navy with its fighting superiority was not coming to their rescue to "crush the enemy." They worried that they would be drowned before even having a chance to "carry out their duty" and reinforce the detachment's first echelon.

But would their effort already be too late? Inui had listened to a report on San Francisco's KWID short wave radio that a Japanese battalion had landed on Guadalcanal and had been "completely exterminated." "It's an old trick of the enemy" to spread such a rumor, he reasoned. He was sure the first echelon was still fighting.[25]

At the 1st Marine Division's command post, Vandegrift's operations officer, Jerry Thomas, and his assistant, Merrill Twining, were reacting to the news of the crushing victory. The outcome of what they called "the Battle of the Tenaru" due to the mislabeling of their July 1942 maps "was a great morale booster for the entire command," they felt. To Vandegrift, Japanese troops, comprising "a kind of mechanical juggernaut that swept inexorably through the Philippines, the Dutch East Indies, over the beaches of Guam and Wake Island, and through the jungles of New Guinea . . . no longer seemed superhuman." Vandegrift and his staff agreed that the men of Cates's 1st Marines had performed well, but they also acknowledged that "we were lucky," in their estimation aided by "gross enemy mistakes."[26]

However, victory had come at a cost. By 1st Marine Division calculations, the 1st Regiment had suffered one officer (Perine) and thirty-three men killed and seventy-five wounded. Casualties had been heaviest in Pollock's 2nd Battalion: twenty-five killed and forty-four wounded. Cresswell's 1st Battalion had lost seven killed (including Perine) and thirteen wounded in the mopping-up operation. Headquarters of the 1st Marines suffered three wounded, and its Regimental Weapons Company, one wounded: its commanding officer (who would die at sea on August 23). In Battery B, 1st Special Weapons Battalion, two had been killed and fourteen wounded.[27]

After surviving night attacks by American planes, Genjirou Inui and the others from his and two other gun companies of the second echelon finally reached their Taivu Point destination at 2230 on August 30, eight days behind schedule. But the men were not on the transports on which they had set out from Truk. The aerial attacks had obliged the convoy to reroute through the Shortland Islands to the west and the men to reembark on patrol boats—old destroyers converted into transports, each capable of carrying 250 men and their heavy weapons—for the fast run into Taivu.[28]

Without delay, the guns, ammunition, and men were unloaded into motorized Daihatsu landing craft that each patrol boat carried. Genjirou Inui's 8th Independent Anti-Tank Company landed its four 37 mm guns, while 1st Lt. Kakurō Wada's Regimental Gun Company came ashore with four 75 mm regimental howitzers, joined by 1st Lt. Yoshio Ōkubo and his four 37 mm antitank guns and personnel of his Rapid Fire Gun Company. Also landing was WO Kōsaku Nakao with the four remaining 7.7 mm Type 92 heavy machine guns and four squads of men from Komatsu's company left behind at Truk.

When the new arrivals assembled at the Taivu camp, they were greeted by 264 surplus men—66 from each of the 1st, 2nd, 3rd, and 4th companies—and their warrant officer commanders who had not been selected to join the first echelon at Truk and had landed as part of the second echelon at Taivu Point from two destroyers the night before.[29] Inui and his group also met some 130 men who were all that remained of the first echelon. The ranking officer, 1st Lieutenant Sakakibara, gave them the shocking news: Except for those standing before them, all the other officers and men of the 916 who had landed on the night of August 18 had been killed, either in Colonel Ichiki's failed bid to capture the airfield or earlier in the annihilation of the Shibuya party. Sakakibara confirmed that Ichiki himself "had died in action." So the American radio station report was true, Inui reflected.[30]

Suddenly, shells began flying over their heads. An American destroyer had appeared offshore in the dark from the direction of Lunga to the west and had begun firing furiously. Soldiers of Inui's company ran off in all directions, leaving only Inui behind on the beach. But the shells were exploding deep behind the shoreline, causing no damage. "If that shelling had hit us directly, the 8th Independent Anti-Tank Company would have been completely destroyed," Inui reflected after rejoining his unit.[31]

That night, as he bivouacked in the dark with his company, Inui felt quite relieved to be on terra firma again, rather than on the sea. But around Inui and the others of the second echelon, the survivors of the first echelon were spending another miserable night, half-starved with no rations left since August 25 and reduced to plundering native gardens for root crops. Wounded men were lying in crude huts, untreated because of the absence of medical supplies, all sent out with Ogasawara's boat unit nine days earlier.[32]

On the morning of September 1, Major Mizuno reported in to Maj. Gen. Kiyotake Kawaguchi, whose main force detachment had landed in eight destroyers without opposition the evening before. Earlier that day, a "fierce air raid" on the camp forced all to rush "in a panic" for the protection of coconut palms or the jungle. Bombing and strafing completely destroyed the Point Taivu native village.[33]

Kawaguchi informed Mizuno that the 658 men of the newly arrived second echelon were being assigned to a reconstituted unit, to be called the Kuma (Bear) Battalion, which would also include the survivors of the first echelon. A new offensive to retake the airfield would fall under his command. After being apprised of the circumstances of the fate of the first echelon, Kawaguchi praised its performance. However, he told Mizuno and the others that "it was a mistake that they jumped into the enemy's strongest point."[34]

At 1st Marine Division headquarters, Vandegrift's staff was also evaluating Ichiki's performance. Like Kawaguchi, Jerry Thomas and Merrill Twining felt it was a "gross mistake" for Ichiki to have "elected to attack us at our point of greatest strength, the mouth of the Tenaru." He had "ample knowledge of our position," they believed. Why hadn't he chosen to attack further upstream, where the cover would have provided an undetected approach, even if "slowed by the difficult jungle terrain"? Thomas and Twining still felt that they would have beaten them, given the Marines' greater numbers, albeit "only after a costly struggle."[35]

Similarly, Lt. Col. Sam Griffith, executive officer of the 1st Raider Battalion, later wondered why Ichiki had not reconnoitered the Tenaru a mile upstream. Had he done so, he could have ordered most of his men to cross at that (undefended) point, turned north, and taken the 2nd Battalion's defense line from the rear. Or was his information about the Marines' strength at the mouth of the Tenaru "faulty"?[36]

But a more basic question for Thomas and Twining was why had Ichiki attacked with only his first echelon at all, when intelligence later revealed that his second echelon was only delayed "a few days" and its arrival "certain." Why didn't he wait for its arrival to launch his attack? Was Ichiki "just an eager beaver who saw a chance to grab the glory?"[37]

Griffith blamed Ichiki for "his arrogant denial of reality, his obstinacy, his tactical inflexibility." But Twining concluded that Ichiki's decision to attack immediately could have been expected, a reflection of the Imperial Japanese Army's belief in its invincibility on land, "regardless of the size of the forces engaged," rather than any innate personality characteristic. It suffered from "victory disease."[38]

At any rate, the 1st Marine Division leadership did not question the combat characteristics of the individual Japanese soldier under Ichiki's command. With no previous experience in fighting the Japanese, Vandegrift was taken aback by the reports of his men that Ichiki's soldiers refused to surrender and that their wounded would play dead and blow themselves up to kill as many Marines as possible who approached to examine them. To Griffith, such alien behavior reflected the "willingness of the Japanese in moments of desperation to embrace with stoicism what fate had clearly ordained—to die gloriously for the emperor."[39]

Griffith's characterization indeed largely describes the attitude indoctrinated in the Japanese soldier, buttressed by centuries of cultural expectation of the Japanese people. All of Ichiki's men had originally been conscripted on reaching twenty years of age and subjected to a full year's brutal training before being assigned to combat duty with their home regiment, the 28th Infantry, at Asahigawa.[40] During their initial four months of training, absolute and unquestioning obedience and self-discipline were inculcated in the draftees, often through beatings. Conditioned since childhood to accept "the hierarchical social structure with its clearly defined ranks and status," they were taught that allegiance to their regiment was equated with allegiance to the emperor required in that structure. Their resolution to resist to the death in combat derived from the tenet of "death before dishonor" imbued in them by their culture and training. To act otherwise would be to bring disgrace to one's family and village—in the case of those of rural background, the majority.[41]

Such expectations of behavior of the Japanese Army applied to officers and noncommissioned officers as well as the enlisted men. For those responsible for command, the belief in the innate superiority of the Japanese race that served as the bedrock view of officers and men alike also informed the IJA's doctrine at the different levels of command to which Ichiki had been subjected from the time of his graduation in 1916 from the Imperial Military Academy. Progressing up the ladder of advancement, he was imbued with the IJA's command doctrine emphasizing "intense spiritual training and bayonet-led breakthroughs to compensate for opponents' material superiority." The only way Imperial Japanese Army commanders would be able to achieve victory would be to go on the offensive, attacking and annihilating enemy units and seizing territory. During his assignment as an instructor at the Infantry School in Tokyo from March 1938 to July 1941, Ichiki would have followed the tactical doctrine promulgated in the 1928 Infantry Manual (*Hohei soten*) stressing "night attacks, close combat, and shock actions to break enemy positions." However, following the release of the 1937 version, he would also instruct on the importance of supplementing bayonet-led attacks with the firepower of machine guns, field artillery, and tanks in combined arms formations, now accepted as IJA doctrine too.[42]

Ichiki assumed command of the 28th Infantry Regiment only in July 1941, when he was promoted to colonel. Thus, he did not experience the costly defeat of the IJA at Nomonhan in summer 1939, in which the 28th Infantry's 2nd Battalion suffered severe losses in fighting the Soviet army: 24 of 28 officers and 631 of 854 enlisted men killed or wounded.[43]

Returned in 1940 from Manchuria to its traditional home base in Hokkaido, the 28th Infantry experienced no further combat prior to being ordered to Guadalcanal. Nevertheless, it was considered an excellent unit with a storied past.[44]

The IJA's analysis of the reasons for the Nomonhan defeat resulted in confirmation of the need to complement infantry with increased firepower—particularly antitank weapons—but only as a supplement to the traditional doctrine that emphasized hand-to-hand fighting as the culminating point leading to sure victory. However, under the quite different jungle conditions faced by the army in Southern Asia following the outbreak of the Pacific War, the lessons learned at Nomonhan in 1939 would not be applied "in a practical manner with any zeal" by its commanders—contrary to the efforts of planners—as noted by an authority on the IJA. While the need for increased firepower as a complement was accepted, the IJA would continue to rely on "intangible factors to win battles," regarding the "magnificent display of traditional spiritual power," as evidenced at Nomonhan, "as the basis for modern warfare."[45] Colonel Ichiki clearly subscribed to this ideology as he took command of the 28th Infantry.

Taking into consideration the IJA's tactical doctrine as it did, or did not, influence Ichiki's command decisions at the Battle of the Tenaru, we can identify five of significant importance in contributing to the annihilation of his attack force.

1. *Ichiki decided to launch the attack immediately after landing at Taivu Point without waiting for the arrival of his second echelon.* First, was this decision taken on his own, or was it so ordered by Army General Headquarters in Tokyo and/or Seventeenth Army headquarters at Rabaul? Documentation indicates that the order to Ichiki from Army GHQ was vague, just calling for prompt action (see chapter 3) and leaving it to Seventeenth Army HQ to issue the operational order. Rabaul merely called for organization of a nine-hundred-man "spearhead unit" of Ichiki's detachment to be transported to Guadalcanal in six destroyers, but without referring to a second echelon and its role in the recapture of the airfield (chapter 4). It was left to a staff officer of Seventeenth Army headquarters to work out the details of how the assignment was to be carried out. Provided with conflicting assessments of the size of the American force on Guadalcanal, Ichiki took advantage of army GHQ's vagueness on the size of the force he should use and, exuding extreme self-confidence, argued for attacking immediately with his

nine-hundred-man "spearhead" rather than waiting for the arrival of the rest of his detachment, to be sent by slow transport and not scheduled to arrive until four days after Ichiki's first echelon. Although taken aback by Ichiki's impulsiveness, the Seventeenth Army officer did not overrule Ichiki's decision to employ such a small force. In the operational order Ichiki subsequently drafted and issued himself, he clearly indicated that his first echelon would carry out the initial attack, while the second echelon would join later following its arrival to together "annihilate" the rest of the defenders on Guadalcanal (chapter 4).

Ironically, Ichiki's headstrong decision may have proven the correct one to take. If he had awaited the arrival of his second echelon, he would have waited in vain. By the time it did arrive, on August 29 and 30, his first echelon men would have exhausted their four-day rations seven to eight days earlier. (They were to be replenished from stores the second echelon was bringing). Waiting for the second echelon thus would have left the men of Ichiki's first echelon to wither on the vine at Taivu Point, physically unable to march to Alligator Creek and launch an attack.

In retrospect, the pressure on Seventeenth Army headquarters at Rabaul to land troops as soon as possible on Guadalcanal contributed to Ichiki's fate. Use of destroyers as transport was the quickest way to get his detachment to its landing site from Truk, but that meant that his 37 mm and 75 mm guns could not be loaded, as they could not be disassembled and were thus too big to take on board destroyers. Furthermore, the six destroyers assigned could only carry a maximum of 150 troops each. If the patrol boats—former destroyers that could carry heavy guns as well as troops and that were eventually made available to Ichiki's 37mm and 75 mm gun units for their fast run from the Shortlands into Taivu Point—could have been put at Ichiki's disposal at Truk originally, instead of the slow transports, Ichiki's first and second echelons would have arrived together and been able to attack as a single unit if Ichiki had so wished.

2. *Ichiki decided to rely on his infantry to spearhead his attack.* Ichiki had even cut down his four rifle companies by 40 percent (105 men from 172) in selecting their most combat-fit men, a reduction forced on him, however, by the capacity limitation of the six destroyers assigned to him for the movement. Nevertheless, Ichiki was confident even with such a reduced number of infantry that they could lead his attack successfully. To Rear Admiral Tanaka, the bayonet-led attack Ichiki envisaged represented "bamboo spear" tactics and was doomed to failure against the modern weapons of the Americans. However, such a plan of attack reflected

IJA infantry doctrine in emphasizing "nonmaterial factors," though that doctrine was in this case carried to the extreme, a result of Ichiki's personality.

3. *Ichiki decided to attack at the point of the Marines' greatest strength.* Some sources have suggested that Ichiki knew of the disposition of the defenses at Alligator Creek before his attack, apparently including the buildup at the mouth of the creek facing the sand spit. Capt. Charley Brush recalled that maps taken from Shibuya's body indicated the position of the Marines' defense line "in surprising detail," while Lieutenant Colonel Pollock recalled thirty-five years later that the Japanese had an overlay of his 2nd Battalion's positions at the Tenaru. However, a 1st Marine Division document indicates that the captured papers from the Shibuya party reconnaissance included only an estimate of the Marines' situation accompanied by a map of Guadalcanal "apparently to be used to collect intelligence information along the Tenaru on the night of August 19/20."[46] Indeed, a Japanese author maintains that the purpose of the Shibuya reconnaissance was "to ascertain the enemy's strength, its disposition in the Lunga area, propose the best approach route, and indicate the jumping-off point."[47] These sources would seem to confirm that Ichiki did *not* know in any detail the disposition of the Marines' force on the other side of Alligator Creek, and clearly not the nature of the buildup at the mouth of the creek. The official Japanese war history asserts that "Ichiki did not know the enemy was on the west bank of the Nakagawa" (Alligator Creek).[48] Certainly, the fierce response of the Marines to the initial attempt of Ichiki's men to cross over to the other side of Alligator Creek via the sand spit came as a surprise to the Japanese.

However, it can be argued that Ichiki's deeply held belief in the invincibility of his infantry troops, regardless of any material superiority of the Marines opposing him, would have made any decision on his part on choice of attack route, dependent on intelligence or lack of it, largely irrelevant. Even after his first two platoon-sized attempts to cross over at the mouth of Alligator Creek ended in annihilation of his men, Ichiki persisted in retaining the sand spit as his main route of attack. And even Major General Kawaguchi, equally exposed to IJA doctrine, criticized Ichiki's decision to select the sand spit as his point of attack, referring to it as "a mistake" at the time he was giving orders to his troops (including those of Ichiki's newly arrived second echelon) for the next attempt to seize the airfield.[49]

4. *Ichiki failed to launch his main attack upstream, where the Marines were less strongly or not at all defended—or at least failed to have reconnoitered the area.* Such an attack point ideally would have had to be beyond the seventeen-hundred-yard

defense line of Pollock's 2nd Battalion. Up to that distance, extending from the mouth of the river, machine gun positions of Pollock's Weapons (H) Company, along with a 37 mm gun emplacement and those of a platoon of the supporting 1st Special Weapons Battalion, were positioned to fire across the river, while troops of E and H Companies were dug in along the defense line. Further upstream an additional fifteen hundred yards, only a platoon of four machine guns provided defense. Beyond thirty-two hundred yards from the mouth of the river, no defense line had been set up. Indeed, that area is where Kawaguchi ordered Ichiki's second echelon—now called the Kuma Battalion—to attack on September 13, 1942, but, fortunately for the Marines, K Company of the 3rd Battalion at that time was emplaced directly facing the Japanese and saved the day by repelling them. Indeed, if the Kuma Battalion had broken through, it would have been on a straight route to the airfield.[50]

So why didn't Ichiki consider such an upstream point of attack, or at least reconnoiter it? Apparently he was focused on the most direct route for his force, assembled on the north shore opposite the mouth of Alligator Creek. Opting to cross the river considerably upstream would have involved a delay in the prearranged time of attack because of the additional marching time to the south through unknown and possibly difficult terrain to reach the eastern bank of the river at such a location. Ichiki was in a hurry and would not have countenanced such a delay to enjoy his "inevitable victory."[51]

5. *Ichiki did not commit his heavy machine guns and two 70 mm battalion guns to reinforce his infantry troops at the outset of the attack.* Only following the failure of his two initial attempts to cross over the sand spit did he accept the entreaties of Captain Sawada, who recognized the importance of such additional weaponry from his Nomonhan experience, to call for heavy machine gun, battalion howitzer, and increased grenade discharger fire to suppress the Marines' heavy firepower, which had decimated two platoons. Integrating such additional weapons with bayonet-led infantry attacks had become part of the IJA's doctrine since 1937, yet Ichiki held to the IJA's earlier absolute faith in hand-to-hand fighting alone as the key to victory.[52]

While recognizing the tactical misjudgments of Ichiki that led to the disaster his troops experienced, one should also place blame on those Japanese planners who rushed such a small force to Guadalcanal in the first place. At Rabaul, Seventeenth Army staff members (except for Chief of Staff Futami) had grossly underestimated the number of Marines who were on Guadalcanal at the time and thus concluded that Ichiki's detachment was adequate to recapture the airfield. When the navy could put only six destroyers at Ichiki's disposal for quickly transporting his men from Truk to Taivu Point, Seventeenth Army headquarters reduced even further the size of Ichiki's force to 916 officers and men, now referred to as a "spearhead unit." The Rabaul army planners evidently expected Ichiki would wait for the arrival of the rest of his detachment, which was being sent in slow transports, before launching his attack, but they did not insist on it in formulating the operational plan with Ichiki.

Emphasis on the factors that resulted in the failure of Ichiki's detachment should not detract from those on the Marine side that secured the victory. A force of predominantly very young men—teenagers for the most part—whose training had been shortened at Parris Island and aborted in New Zealand and who had never faced combat before proved a match for the highly trained and indoctrinated Japanese soldier in fighting capability and acts of bravery often involving hand-to-hand combat, in which the Japanese regarded themselves as the masters.

Lt. Col. Edwin A. Pollock shows the strain of the Guadalcanal campaign, September 1942. *Courtesy of Edward Appel.*

But individual Marine performance as infantry only partly explains the annihilation of Ichiki's force. The vastly superior firepower of the Marine defenders, provided by their 37 mm antitank guns, 81 mm mortars, 75 mm pack howitzers, and .30- and .50-caliber machine guns, overwhelmed the Japanese attackers. Indeed, recalling events of forty-five years earlier, Colonel Pollock maintained that "our [81 mm] mortars did more damage to the Japanese than [the weapons of] any other unit," due to the mortar men's ability "to fire close in." He also felt that the platoon of 37 mm guns of the special weapons battalion's B Battery "gave us more defense than anything else." In giving credit to the 3rd Battalion of the 11th Marines and its 75 mm pack howitzers, he added that "the artillery supported us as well as it could."[53] Although he did not mention it in his interview, Pollock certainly would have intended to praise the performance of his H Company's 3rd Machine Gun Platoon, particularly that of the Diamond-Rivers-Schmid squad, whose valiant experience was so popularized during the war years.

Colonel Pollock was too modest to give credit to his own command leadership during the battle. Yet he was an inspiration to his men, literally standing with them at the front in the thick of the fighting while coolly directing fire. His example was followed by many of his young and inexperienced second lieutenant platoon leaders and older veteran NCOs who led their men at times during the desperate fighting when such leadership was critical for victory. The same was true for the leadership of the special weapons battalion's 37 mm gun platoon.

Although Pollock's 2nd Battalion and the division's 1st Special Weapons Battalion bore the brunt of the fighting the night and early morning of August 20–21, Colonel Cresswell's 1st Battalion and the 1st Tank Battalion should also be given credit for the success of their mopping up operation that followed late that morning and afternoon. In particular, the stellar performance of C Company, as led by its young commander, showed that Marines could best the Japanese in the bayonet charges their adversaries glorified. It was less of a contest for the Japanese to oppose the tanks; indeed, the havoc the armor wreaked was graphically documented by the few survivors of the afternoon onslaught.

With their overwhelming victory at the Battle of the Tenaru, the Marines wrote *finis* to the "victory fever" of the Japanese Army.[54] Although the Japanese continued to fight to the death in subsequent battles on Guadalcanal and on other Pacific islands, Japanese soldiers were no longer considered invincible by American troops—nor even by the Japanese themselves.

Emperor Hirohito had reached the same conclusion himself. When apprised on August 25 of the annihilation of the Ichiki Detachment, he questioned for the first time the vaunted superiority of the Imperial Japanese Army.[55]

While the Battle of the Tenaru was a relatively small action, "it was much more important than the mere numbers of men engaged would indicate," as Richard Frank has emphasized. "It set the terms of fighting for the rest of the war." The news of what happened at the Tenaru "really drove home what fighting the Japanese entailed": their refusal to surrender, even by the wounded, except in very rare cases. But the Marines had demonstrated that if the previously believed invincible Japanese soldier was ready to fight to the death, they were ready to oblige.[56]

POSTSCRIPT

In the fall of 1982, the executive director of Guadalcanal Campaign Veterans (GCV) was surprised to receive a request from the Washington bureau of the

Bones of dead soldiers of the Ichiki Detachment before being burned in a Shinto ceremony, November 19, 1982. *Courtesy of Y. Sagai.*

third largest newspaper in Japan. The *Sankei shimbun* wanted to know if the GCV could provide information and possible assistance in a matter of historical importance for a Japanese counterpart of the GCV, the Ichiki-kai (Ichiki Association), in the recovery of the remains of the Ichiki Detachment men killed at the Battle of the Tenaru.[57]

Since 1971, members of the Ichiki-kai had been traveling to Guadalcanal to try to locate the burial sites of their deceased comrades and exhume the remains for cremation and return to Japan. One of the members, former sergeant Sadanobu Okada, was at the time of the request conducting yet another fruitless search at the site where he had last seen his fellow men forty years earlier. By mid-December 1982 Okada and his team had dug in "about 200 different places" but hadn't found even "a scrap of bone." Despairing of ever finding remains, Okada "lay down and sobbed."[58]

Meanwhile, three members of the GCV—Harry Horsman, Andy Brodecki, and Hank Brunkhorst—were informed of the *Sankei shimbun*'s appeal for help. The three G Company veterans of Pollock's 2nd Battalion put aside their wartime feelings about the men they had fought against in the vicious battle so long ago.

Having themselves participated in the burial operations, they recalled the location of the mass graves and wanted to help the Ichiki-kai in retrieving the remains of their fallen comrades.[59]

On old maps the GCV veterans marked the grid coordinates of the locale of the graves on the east bank of the Tenaru and passed them to the GCV executive director for transmission to the main office of the *Sankei shimbun* in Tokyo.

The information arrived just in time. On Guadalcanal, Okada and the search team had given up hope in mid-December in their latest effort and were preparing to return to Japan the next day. But when the newspaper relayed the GCV information to them, they excitedly shifted their operation to the east of where they had been searching earlier to an oval-shaped area designated by Horsman and his buddies. Canceling their return plans, Okada and the others, "in a frantic and concerted effort," dug at the new location. In their first try, they found the remains of thirty-six of Ichiki's men, then nearby the bones of forty-four more.[60]

Then in March the following year, Okada and the others of the search team, now including the son of Colonel Ichiki, returned once more to continue digging the area. This time they managed to unearth the remains of 96 more men. By the time they finished work during the 1983 visit, they had succeeded in exhuming the bones of about 230 of the more than 700 men who had perished in the battle. A further search was initiated in 1984 in hopes of finding the remains of the rest of the fallen.

At improvised sites in the oval following each visit, the bones of the dead were piled up in a pyre for cremation in a Shinto ceremony. The ashes were then returned to their final resting place at the shrine at Asahigawa, the ill-fated 28th Regiment's home base.

In recognition of the assistance given by Horsman and the other GCV veterans, the area of the burials on the east bank of the "Tenaru" has been designated Horsman's Oval by the Ichiki-kai. In Horsman's words, "It is an honor not easily or commonly bestowed on a former foe."

APPENDIX A. OFFICERS, 1ST MARINE REGIMENT, COMBAT GROUP B (REINFORCED), TENARU RIVER SUBSECTOR, AUGUST 20, 1942

2nd Battalion, 1st Marine Regiment (37 officers, 853 enlisted men)

Headquarters and Service Company (9 officers, 58 enlisted men)

Lt. Col. Edwin A. Pollock	Battalion commanding officer
Maj. William Chalfant III	Battalion executive officer
1st Lt. William C. Ward Jr.	Battalion communications officer
2nd Lt. John R. Lesick	Battalion adjutant and company commanding officer
2nd Lt. Peter Bender	Battalion quartermaster
2nd Lt. A. William Larson	Battalion operations officer
2nd Lt. John R. Ridgway	Battalion asst. communications officer
2nd Lt. George M. Stratton	Battalion intelligence officer
2nd Lt. James N. Williamson	Battalion asst. quartermaster

E Company (6 officers, 178 enlisted men)

Capt. Martin F. Rockmore	Commanding officer
2nd Lt. Donald J. McCaffrey	Executive officer
2nd Lt. Dean E. Stover	1st Platoon leader
2nd Lt. Milton W. Karten	2nd Platoon leader
2nd Lt. John L. Williams	3rd Platoon leader
2nd Lt. Harold C. Pierce Jr.	Weapons Platoon leader

F Company (6 officers, 179 enlisted men)

Capt. John Howland	Commanding officer
2nd Lt. Roy W. Wallace Jr.	Executive officer
2nd Lt. James A. Moriarty Jr.	1st Platoon leader
2nd Lt. Stephen D. Ryan Jr.	2nd Platoon leader
2nd Lt. Edward J. Craig Jr.	3rd Platoon leader
2nd Lt. Ellis T. Paulk	Weapons Platoon leader

G Company (6 officers, 177 enlisted men)

Capt. James F. Sherman	Commanding officer
2nd Lt. George B. Mathews	Executive officer
2nd Lt. George Codrea	1st Platoon leader
2nd Lt. Robert B. Smith	2nd Platoon leader
2nd Lt. J. Luther Jordan	3rd Platoon leader
2nd Lt. Preston St. C. Malone	Weapons Platoon leader

H Company (10 officers, 261 enlisted men)

Capt. James W. Ferguson	Commanding officer
1st Lt. Alfred M. Lichtman	Executive officer
2nd Lt. William A. Murphy	Asst. executive officer
2nd Lt. Robert M. Port	Company officer
2nd Lt. Hugh Corrigan	1st Machine Gun Platoon leader
2nd Lt. Robert A. Molloy	2nd Machine Gun Platoon leader
2nd Lt. William H. Whorf	3rd Machine Gun Platoon leader
2nd Lt. Carl H. Benson	Mortar Platoon leader
2nd Lt. Don C. Wheaton Jr.	Asst. Mortar Platoon leader
2nd Lt. George Swinston Jr.	37 mm Gun Platoon leader

B Battery, 37 mm Anti-Tank, 1st Special Weapons Battalion (5 officers, 119 enlisted men)

Capt. John P. Leonard	Commanding officer
2nd Lt. Joe P. Beatty	Battery officer
2nd Lt. Arthur W. Bell	Battery officer
2nd Lt. James F. McClanahan	Battery officer
2nd Lt. Frederick H. Scantling	Battery officer

Source: 1st Marine Regiment, Operations Order 6-42, 14 August 1942; 1st Marine Regiment, 2nd Battalion, muster rolls, Headquarters and Service, E, F, G, and H Companies, August 1942, and muster roll, B Battery, 37 mm Anti-Tank, First Special Weapons Battalion, August 1942. Additional detail has been included by the author.

APPENDIX B. OFFICERS, 1ST MARINE REGIMENT, COMBAT GROUP B (REINFORCED), SOUTH SUBSECTOR, AUGUST 20, 1942

1st Battalion, 1st Marine Regiment (37 officers, 877 enlisted men)

Headquarters and Service Company (8 officers, 90 enlisted men)

Lt. Col. Lenard B. Cresswell	Battalion commanding officer
Maj. Marion A. Fawcett	Battalion executive officer
Capt. Burnace F. Brace	Battalion logistics officer (Bn-4)
Capt. Robert W. Noonan	Battalion communications officer
Capt. Rex G. Williams	Temporarily attached from division headquarters
2nd Lt. Levi Woodbury	Battalion personnel officer (Bn-1), company commander
2nd Lt. Irving V. G. Perine	Battalion intelligence officer (Bn-2)
2nd Lt. Donald K. Dayton	Battalion operations officer (Bn-3)

A Company (7 officers, 175 enlisted men)

Capt. Charles H. Brush Jr.	Commanding officer
2nd Lt. William L. Sewell Jr.	Executive officer
2nd Lt. James M. Rogers	Asst. executive officer
2nd Lt. John J. Jachym	1st Platoon leader
2nd Lt. Victor Valente	2nd Platoon leader
2nd Lt. Charles P. Mackin	3rd Platoon Leader
2nd Lt. Walter J. Ridlon Jr.	Weapons Platoon leader

B Company (6 officers, 173 enlisted men)

1st Lt. Marshall T. Armstrong	Commanding officer
2nd Lt. Joseph P. Daly	Executive officer
2nd Lt. Raymond C. Flynn	Platoon leader
2nd Lt. Charles F. Schlenker	Platoon leader
2nd Lt. Lawrence W. Smith Jr.	Platoon leader
Marine Gunner Theodore S. Bollack	Platoon leader

C Company (6 officers, 176 enlisted men)

Capt. Nikolai S. Stevenson	Commanding officer
2nd Lt. John N. Rentz	Executive officer
2nd Lt. James A. Wagner	1st Platoon leader
2nd Lt. Harold F. Jennings	2nd Platoon leader
2nd Lt. Maurice F. Ahearn Jr.	3rd Platoon leader
2nd Lt. Robert B. Fowler	Weapons Platoon leader

D Company (10 officers, 263 enlisted men)

Maj. Griffith W. Sherrill	Commanding officer
Capt. Edward S. Dzura	Executive officer
2nd Lt. James F. Lawrence	Reconnaissance officer
2nd Lt. Franklin D. Sills	1st Machine Gun Platoon leader
2nd Lt. John T. Speaks	2nd Machine Gun Platoon leader
2nd Lt. Everett P. Pope	3rd Machine Gun Platoon leader
2nd Lt. Henry T. Hillard	Mortar Platoon leader
2nd Lt. Joseph F. Bushell	Asst. Mortar Platoon leader
2nd Lt. George M. Dawes	Anti-Tank Platoon leader
Marine Gunner Charles J. Riley	Machine gun technician

Source: First 1st Marine Regiment, Operations Order 6-42, 14 August 1942; 1st Marine Regiment, 1st Battalion, muster rolls, Headquarters and Service, A, B, C, and D Companies, August 1942. Additional detail has been included by the author.

APPENDIX C. US MARINE CASUALTIES, BATTLE OF THE TENARU, AUGUST 21, 1942

Combat Group B (Reinforced), 1st Marine Regiment, Tenaru River Subsector

2nd Battalion, 1st Marine Regiment

Headquarters and Service Company

Lt. JG (MC), Jacques C. Saphier	KIA

E Company

Pvt. James P. Edlin	KIA
Pvt. Raymond F. Roberts	KIA
Pfc. Cecil C. Powell	WIA
Pvt. Joseph H. Davis	WIA
Pvt. James W. Maxwell	WIA
Pvt. George H. McNally	WIA
Pvt. James W. Sullivan	WIA
Pvt. George L. Turzai	WIA
Pvt. Joseph B. Wadsworth	WIA

F Company

Cpl. William H. Wolvington	KIA
Pfc. John Gildea	KIA
Pvt. Bennie C. Jones	KIA
2nd Lt. Edward J. Craig Jr.	WIA
Pvt. Marion H. Nelson	WIA

G Company

Cpl. Knight Farr	KIA
Cpl. Joseph J. Faso	KIA
Pfc. Richard H. Holcombe	KIA
Pfc. Vincent P. Rogers	KIA
Pfc. Richard A. Stitt	KIA
Pvt. Russell M. Butterweck	KIA
Pvt. Leo J. Carvalis Jr.	KIA
Pvt. Donald J. Davidson	KIA
Pvt. George R. Gibbs	KIA
Pvt. Thomas P. Lynch Jr.	KIA
Pvt. John J. McHale Jr.	KIA

Pvt. George E. Tefertiller	KIA
Pvt. Amos N. Coomer	WIA, died on board ship August 26
2nd Lt. George Codrea	WIA
Sgt. James W. Hancock*	WIA
Pfc. Louis Evers	WIA
Pfc. Robert M. Kavish	WIA
Pfc. John N. Shea	WIA
Pfc. James E. Wilson	WIA
Pvt. James D. Carlin	WIA
Pvt. Richard W. Harding	WIA
Pvt. Albert Eeckhout	WIA
Pvt. Joseph J. Ingrassia	WIA

H Company

Cpl. Charles C. Karp	KIA
Pfc. Arthur J. Atwood	KIA
Pfc. Jesse L. Phillips	KIA
Pfc. Verbon C. Sanders	KIA
Pfc. Barney Sterling	KIA
Pvt. Andrew F. Grabarczyk	KIA
Pvt. John Rivers	KIA
Pfc. Leonard T. Beer	WIA, died on board ship August 23
Pvt. Francis D. Ryan	WIA, died on board ship August 22
Sgt. Frank J. Stewart	WIA
Cpl. Stephen L. Boykin	WIA
Cpl. LeRoy Diamond	WIA
Cpl. George E. Parker*	WIA
Pvt. Harold Acker	WIA
Pvt. Anthony J. Balestrieri*	WIA
Pvt. Clayton A. Dillman*	WIA
Pvt. George A. Finger	WIA
Pvt. Joseph F. Gallagher	WIA
Pvt. Joel T. Hogeland Jr.	WIA
Pvt. Albert A. Schmid*	WIA

B Battery, 1st Special Weapons Battalion

Plat. Sgt. Nelson Braitmeyer	KIA
Pvt. Patrick J. Sweeney	WIA, died of wounds August 21
2nd Lt. James F. McClanahan	WIA
Sgt. Anthony F. Conti	WIA
Cpl. James A. Olliff	WIA
Cpl. Glenn C. Campbell	WIA
Pfc. Elmer E. Fairchild	WIA
Pfc. Alden T. Palmer	WIA
Pvt. Clair Hume	WIA
Pvt. Frank J. Kovach	WIA
Pvt. Albert C. Locke	WIA
Pvt. Irving W. Moore	WIA
Pvt. Eugene Stevenson	WIA
Pvt. Christian A. Wiegand	WIA

COMBAT GROUP B (REINFORCED), 1ST MARINE REGIMENT, SOUTH SUBSECTOR

1st Battalion, 1st Marine Regiment

Headquarters Company

2nd Lt. Irving V. G. Perine	KIA
Cpl. Raymond A. Negus	WIA
Pfc. Patrick A. Tierney	WIA

A Company

Pfc. Carlton Woodward	KIA
Pfc. Joseph J. Jarski*	WIA
Pvt. Patsy S. Campola	WIA
Pvt. Charles E. Crawford	WIA
Pvt. James J. Gorman	WIA

B Company

Pfc. Bernard J. McCarthy	KIA

C Company

Pvt. John C. Green Jr.	KIA
2nd Lt. Maurice F. Ahearn Jr.	WIA
Pvt. Frederick E. Clough Jr.	WIA

D Company

Pfc. James F. Smith	KIA
Pvt. Roy L. Barnes	KIA
Pvt. Freeman B. Blair	KIA
2nd Lt. Joseph F. Bushell	WIA
Pfc. Gerard A. Cole	WIA
Pvt. Frank Huska	WIA
Pvt. Calvin L. Schuler	WIA

UNITS OTHER THAN COMBAT GROUP B (REINFORCED), 1ST MARINE REGIMENT

Headquarters and Service Company, 1st Marine Regiment

Cpl. Theodore Cogswell	WIA
Cpl. Thomas W. Dussault	WIA
Pfc. James B. Stone	WIA

Regimental Weapons Company, 1st Marine Regiment

Capt. Harry Q. Findley	WIA, died on board ship August 23

A Company, 1st Tank Battalion

Pfc. Arthur A. Werz	WIA

Battery G, 3rd Battalion, 11th Marine Regiment

Pfc. Allen W. Tracy	WIA

Battery H, 3rd Battalion, 11th Marine Regiment

2nd Lt. Nathaniel S. Mewhinney	WIA

*Inadvertently not cited as WIA on August 1942 muster roll.
Source: Muster rolls for each unit listed, August 1942, in Marine Corps History Division, Reference Branch, Quantico, Virginia.

APPENDIX D. OFFICERS AND STAFF, FIRST ECHELON, ICHIKI DETACHMENT (916 OFFICERS AND MEN)

Headquarters (10 officers and 153 men)

Col. Kiyonao Ichiki	Commanding officer
Capt. Yokichi Togashi	Adjutant
Capt. Yoshimi Shibuya	Chief of communications unit
Capt. Takatomo Tasaka	Chief surgeon
1st Lt. Yoshiaki Sakakibara	Assistant communications officer
1st Lt. Tsutomo Shinohara	Paymaster
1st Lt. Yoshihito Nakai	Surgeon
2nd Lt. Tomokazu Itō	Regimental color bearer
2nd Lt. Kenji Matsumoto	Staff officer
2nd Lt. Daizō Umeda	Chief of transport (supply?) unit
Sgt. Kiyoshi Nakamoto	Runner
Sgt. Sadanobu Okada	Clerk
Mr. Kiichi Ōshima	Civilian interpreter

Headquarters, 2nd Battalion (3 officers and 20 men)

Maj. Nobuo Kuramoto	Commanding officer
1st Lt. Naoyuki Kondō	Adjutant
1st Lt. Toshio Habara	Asst. adjutant

1st Company (4 officers and 101 men)

1st Lt. Yusaku Higuchi	Commanding officer
1st Lt. Shōji Tate	Leader, 1st Platoon
2nd Lt. Yūzo Kudō	Leader, 2nd Platoon
2nd Lt. Tadayoshi Uchizawa	Leader, 3rd Platoon

2nd Company (4 officers and 101 men)

Capt. Tetsurō Sawada	Commanding officer
2nd Lt. Masami Hagiuda	Leader, 1st Platoon
2nd Lt. Gorō Ohashi	Leader, 2nd Platoon
2nd Lt. Tatsuo Tanaka	Leader, 3rd Platoon

3rd Company (4 officers and 101 men)

1st Lt. Magozō Maruyama	Commanding officer
2nd Lt. Hiroshi Miura	Leader, 1st Platoon
2nd Lt. Shigenori Niie (Arae?)	Leader, 2nd Platoon
2nd Lt. Shōichi Matsuo	Leader, 3rd Platoon

4th Company (4 officers and 101 men)

1st Lt. Tōshirō Chiba	Commanding officer
2nd Lt. Kiyoshi Satō	Leader, 1st Platoon
2nd Lt. Shigeru Konno	Leader, 2nd Platoon
2nd Lt. Tomosaburō Moriya	Leader, 3rd Platoon

Machine Gun Company (4 officers and 106 men)

1st Lt. Shigenao Komatsu	Commanding officer
2nd Lt. Masao Inagaki	Leader, 1st Platoon
2nd Lt. Kōsaburo Osada (Nagata?)	Leader, 2nd Platoon
2nd Lt. Zenji Itō	Leader, 3rd Platoon

Battalion Gun Platoon (1 officer, 49 men)

2nd Lt. Tatsuharu Hanami	Commanding officer

Engineer Company (Attached from 7th Division Engineer Regiment; 4 officers and 146 men)

1st Lt. Hideo Gotō	Commanding officer
1st Lt. Kiichirō Nakamura	Leader, 2nd Platoon
Prov. 2nd Lt. Shigeru Wada	Leader, 3rd Platoon
2nd Lt. Fumio Baba	Leader, 4th Platoon

Source: Akio Tani to the author, May 31, 1990; Hajime Yamamoto, in Itirou Inui email to the author, January 28, 2001; Stanley Jersey email to the author, February 13, 2003.

NOTES

PROLOGUE

1. A. A. Vandegrift, *Once a Marine*, 97; "Alexander Vandegrift," Wikipedia, http://en.wikipedia.org/wiki/Alexander_Vandegrift; Richard B. Frank, *Guadalcanal*, 46n5.

2. Abraham Felber, diary, 1941–45, February 17, 1942, in author's collection; George McMillan, *The Old Breed: A History of the First Marine Division in World War II*, 7; Vandegrift, *Once a Marine*, 97.

3. Kenneth W. Condit, Gerald Diamond, and Edwin T. Turnbladh, *Marine Corps Ground Training in World War II*, 158.

4. Ibid., 158–59, 162, 340.

5. Ralph R. Reber, "Memories of Military Service," memoir, 3, in author's collection; Kerry Lane, *Marine Pioneers*, 31; Vandegrift, *Once a Marine*, 98.

6. William Whorf to the author, July 16, 1999; Condit, Diamond, and Turnbladh, *Marine Corps Ground Training*, 57–58; Commanding Officer, Marine Barracks, Philadelphia Navy Yard, "Orders to Temporary Duty," March 23, 1942, in George Swinston, Jr., personal collection; Commandant, US Marine Corps to Below-named Officers, Marine Corps Reserve, Basic School, Marine Barracks, Navy Yard, Philadelphia, "Change of Station," April 13, 1942, in George Swinston, Jr., personal collection.

7. Condit, Diamond, and Turnbladh, *Marine Corps Ground Training*, 68, 83–84, 225; US Marine Corps, Seventh Reserve Officers Class, *The Gold Bar, April 1942*.

8. McMillan, *Old Breed*, 12; Frank, *Guadalcanal*, 40; Vandegrift, *Once a Marine*, 99.

9. 1st Marine Division, Headquarters, "Division Commander's Final Report on Guadalcanal Operation," 24 May 1943, Phase I: Events Prior to H Hour, 7 August 1942, in Folder A-7-1, Box 39, Geographic Files 1939–1949—Guadalcanal, Record Group 127, Records of the United States Marine Corps, 1775–1981, NARA, College Park, MD (hereafter cited as Phase I Report), 1–2; McMillan, *Old Breed*, 15; Vandegrift, *Once a Marine*, 100; Frank, *Guadalcanal*, 46; Merrill B. Twining, *No Bended Knee*, 11, 14; Denys Bevan, *United States Forces in New Zealand, 1942–1945*, 94. Twining, who was Vandegrift's assistant operations officer, recalled that the division was to prepare for "minor amphibious operations" (Twining, *No Bended Knee*, 11, 14).

10. Phase I Report, Annex A; Alan Millett, *In Many a Strife: General Gerald C. Thomas and the US Marine Corps, 1917–1956*, 159; Herbert Merillat, *Guadalcanal Remembered*, 10–11; Reber, "Memories," 5. Vandegrift recalled that he sailed on May 20 (Vandegrift, *Once a Marine*, 100).

11. Herbert C. Merillat, *The Island*, 5; Vandegrift, *Once a Marine*, 100; McMillan, *Old Breed*, 15; Lane, *Pioneers*, 32.

12. George C. Dyer, *The Amphibians Came to Conquer*, 243; John L. Zimmerman, *The Guadalcanal Campaign*, 5.

13. Zimmerman, *Guadalcanal Campaign*, 4, 5, 9.

14. Frank, *Guadalcanal*, 36; introduction to William H. Whyte, *A Time of War*, xviii.

15. The fact that the commander of the 2nd Battalion, 1st Marines, Lt. Col. Edwin A. Pollock, had been given the word just before leaving his transport to go ashore (see chapter 2) suggests that battalion and regimental commanders may also have been informed at that time.

CHAPTER 1

1. Bayard Berghaus, diary, February 2, 1942, in author's collection; Mary Anne Kampmann, e-mail to the author, February 25, 2010.

2. Berghaus diary, February 2, 1942; Kampmann e-mail; William Sager, e-mail to the author, February 27, 2010.

3. Berghaus diary, February 4, 1942; Kampmann e-mail. Before the war the program at the Basic School indeed extended over nine months, shortened to seven months just before the outbreak of war. But the February 1942 program Berghaus was attending was a special Basic School class of twelve weeks for reserve officers ordered to active duty (Kenneth W. Condit, Gerald Diamond, and Edwin T. Turnbladh, *Marine Corps Ground Training in World War II*, 57, 225, 227).

4. US Marine Corps, Seventh Reserve Officers Class, *The Gold Bar, April 1942*.

5. John Rivers to Betty (sister), February 18, 1942.

6. Rivers to Betty, January 19, 1942; Bill Freedman e-mail to the author, January 1, 2010.

7. Roger Butterfield, *Al Schmid, Marine*, 61; "2nd Battalion 1st Marines," Wikipedia, www.en.wikipedia.org/wiki/2nd_Battalion_1st_Marines.

8. Robert Leckie, *Helmet for My Pillow*, 23–24; "John Howland," entry in Harvard University, *Harvard Class of 1932: Twenty-fifth Anniversary Report*; Butterfield, *Al Schmid*, 61.

9. Leckie, *Helmet*, 24.

10. Sidney C. Phillips, "'You'll Be Sor-ree': The Memoirs of a US Marine Private during the Pacific Campaign of World War II," manuscript, 3, 7, 11, 15, in author's collection.

11. Condit, Diamond, and Turnbladh, *Marine Corps Ground Training*, 153; George McMillan, *The Old Breed: A History of the First Marine Division in World War II*, 6, 12; www.range95.com/Marines/regiment/1st, accessed January 18, 2011.

12. John Joseph to the author, October 14, 2001; "Capt. Sherman Tells of Fight at Guadalcanal," clipping from unidentified Massachusetts newspaper, no date, ca. 1943, copy in Harry Horsman collection.

13. Hugh Morse and George Head, *"A"-1-1: Pearl Harbor to Peleliu*, 10.

14. Ben Wofford and William R. White, *The Marine: A Guadalcanal Survivor's Final Battle*, 8, 10, 13.

15. Rivers to Betty, March 17, 1942.

16. Leroy Diamond to Harry Horsman, October 1, 1987; Butterfield, *Al Schmid*, 59.

17. Leckie, Helmet, 28; World Guns, Modern Firearms, Machine Guns, "Browning M1917 and M1919 machine gun (USA)," www.world.guns.ru/machine/usa/browning-m1917-m1919-e.html.

18. Frank Stewart, "Tenaru River Guadalcanal," in Ipswich WWII Celebration, Official Souvenir Program, August 13–September 2, 1995; Leckie, *Helmet*, 33.

19. Phillips, "'You'll Be Sor-ree,'" 15–16.

20. Leckie, *Helmet*, 33; Phillips, "'You'll Be Sor-ree,'" 15.

21. George Parker to the author, October 19, 1999.

22. Joseph to the author, October 14, 2001.

23. Wofford and White, *Marine*, 12.

24. Commanding Officer, Marine Barracks, Philadelphia Navy Yard, "Orders to Tempo-

rary Duty," March 23, 1942, and first endorsement by George Swinston, Jr., et al., in George Swinston, Jr., personal collection.

25. USMC, Seventh Reserve Officers Class, *Gold Bar*, 23.

26. Donald F. Moss, "What Was It Like in the Olden Days, Dad?—An Illustrated Memoir," no date, 20, in author's collection.

27. Ibid.; Dean E. Stover, untitled memoir, May 3, 2003, 1, in author's collection.

28. Condit, Diamond, and Turnbladh, *Marine Corps Ground Training*, 83; Headquarters and Service, A, B, C, and D Companies, 1st Battalion, 1st Marine Regiment, and Headquarters and Service, E, F, G, and H Companies, 2nd Battalion, 1st Marine Regiment, muster rolls, April 1942 (microfilm), Marine Corps History Division, Reference Branch, Quantico, VA; USMC, Seventh Reserve Officers Class, *Gold Bar*, 22–23; Stover, untitled memoir, 1.

29. Nikolai Stevenson, telephone interview with the author, August 4, 2010.

30. Stevenson, telephone interview with the author, August 1, 2010; C Company, 1st Battalion, 1st Marine Regiment (C-1-1), muster roll, April 1942 (microfilm), and K Company, 3rd Battalion, 7th Marine Regiment (K-3-7), muster roll, January 1942, both in Marine Corps History Division, Reference Branch, Quantico, VA.

31. K-3-7, muster roll, January 1942; A Company, 1st Battalion, 1st Marines (A-1-1), muster roll, April 1942 (microfilm), Marine Corps History Division, Reference Branch, Quantico, VA.

32. Nora G. Frisbie, "The Frisbie Family in the Revolutionary War," http://fffaa.info/PDF/bulletins/1960/Volume_XIII-No3-Jul1963.pdf, 5.

33. Brig. Gen. Edwin H. Simmons, "I Will Hold: An Appreciation of Gen. Clifton B. Cates," *Marine Corps Gazette,* November 2002.

34. Headquarters Company, 1st Battalion, 7th Marines, muster roll, January 1942 (microfilm), and Headquarters Company, 2nd Battalion, 1st Marines, muster roll, April 1942 (microfilm), Marine Corps History Division, Reference Branch, Quantico, VA.

35. Moss, "What Was It Like?" 20–21.

36. George Codrea, interview with the author, November 1, 1999; "Pvt. Charles F. Spakes," entry in Headquarters, Southern Recruiting Division, New Orleans, LA, muster roll, May 1935, at www.ancestry.com, US Marine Corps Muster Rolls, 1798-1958.

37. William H. Sager, e-mails to the author, February 26, 27, 2010.

38. Leckie, *Helmet*, 33–34.

39. Pollock biography in Pollock papers at US Marine Corps Museum, Parris Island, SC; Leckie, *Helmet*, 35; Headquarters Company, 2nd Battalion, 1st Marines, muster roll, April 1942 (microfilm), Marine Corps History Division, Reference Branch.

40. Leckie, *Helmet*, 35–36.

41. Ibid., 38–39; Phillips, "'You'll Be Sor-ree,'" 16. Earlier, in mid-March 1942, the 1st Regiment's 1st Battalion—along with the 5th Regiment and other units—had been transported up the Chesapeake Bay from Norfolk to Solomon's Island, Maryland, for more credible amphibious landing exercises—including one at night—using troop transports. (Jeter A. Isely and Philip A. Crowl, *The US Marines and Amphibious War*, 66; Ralph H. Reber, "Memories of Military Service," memoir, 4, in author's collection). The 2nd and 3rd Battalions remained at New River for their mock exercises.

42. Commandant, US Marine Corps, to Commandant, Navy Yard, Philadelphia, Pennsylvania, "Change of Station," 13 April 1942, George Swinston Jr., Personal Collection; A. William Larson, telephone interview with the author, November 9, 2009; H-2-1 muster roll, April 1942; Hugh Corrigan Jr., telephone interview with the author, January 6, 2010.

43. William Whorf to the author, August 13, 2001.

44. John Williams to parents, June 2, 1942; A. William Larson to the author, September 28, 2001.

45. C-1-1 muster roll, April 1942; author's assumption regarding Rentz's shift.

46. Berghaus diary, July 12, 1942.

47. Sager e-mail to the author, February 27, 2010.

48. Gilbert Small, Jr., journal, 1942, in author's collection.

49. John Collins e-mails to the author, February 6, 7, 2010; John Collins e-mail to Peter Flahavin, February 6, 2010; C-1-1 muster roll, April 1942.

50. Joseph to the author, October 14, 2001; Sager e-mail, February 27, 2010.

51. Joseph to the author, October 14, 2001; Sager e-mail, February 27, 2010.

52. Sager e-mail, February 27, 2010.

53. Gilbert Small to parents, May 5, 1942; Wofford and White, *Marine*, 19.

54. Alan Millett, *In Many a Strife: General Gerald C. Thomas and the US Marine Corps, 1917–1956*, 159; Herbert C. Merillat, *The Island*, 5; A. A. Vandegrift, *Once a Marine*, 101.

55. Genjirou Inui, "My Guadalcanal" (diary), May 19, 1942, www.nettally.com/jrube/genjirou/genjirou.htm; Itirou Inui e-mail to the author, January 24, 2001.

56. Information obtained from Japanese sources by Tom McLeod and e-mailed to the author, February 16, 2011; Edward J. Drea to the author, September 13, 2009.

57. Drea to the author, September 13, 2009; Saburō Hayashi and Alvin D. Coox, *Kōgun: The Japanese Army in the Pacific War*, 225; Edward J. Drea, *Japan's Imperial Army*, 191; Mark Peattie, Edward Drea, and Han van de Ven, eds., *Battle for China*, 127.

58. Inui, "My Guadalcanal," May 19, 1942.

59. Abraham Felber, diary, 1941–45, May 26, 1942, in author's collection; Leckie, *Helmet*, 49–50.

60. Moss, "What Was It Like?" 21; Phillips, "'You'll Be Sor-ree,'" 23.

61. Inui, "My Guadalcanal," May 28, 1942; Jonathan Parshall and Anthony Tully, *Shattered Sword: The Untold Story of the Battle of Midway*, 48; "Organization of Two Japanese Army Combat Teams," Intelligence Report Solomons–Guadalcanal, in Folder C-15-5, Box 46, Geographic Files 1939–1949, Guadalcanal, RG 127, NARA.

62. H Company, 2nd Battalion, 1st Marine Regiment, muster roll, April 1942, Marine Corps History Division, Reference Branch.

63. Thomas Barry, "Barry of the 1st Marines," in *Semper Fi, Mac: Living Memories of the US Marines in World War II*, ed. by Henry Berry, 94; Headquarters and Service Company, 1st Marine Regiment, muster roll, May 1942, Marine Corps History Division, Reference Branch.

64. Felber diary, June 3, 1942; Joseph to the author, October 14, 2001; Kerry Lane, *Marine Pioneers*, 32.

65. Condit, Diamond, and Turnbladh, *Marine Corps Ground Training*, 340.

66. Inui, "My Guadalcanal," June 4, 6, and 9, 1942.

CHAPTER 2

1. Genjirou Inui, "My Guadalcanal" (hereafter cited as Inui diary), June 13, 1942, entry, www.nettally.com/jrube/genjirou/genjirou.htm.

2. Inui diary, June 14, 1942, entry. On December 10, 1941, 4,900 men of the Japanese Army's South Seas Detachment and 370 of the Maizuru 2nd Special Naval Landing Force went ashore and faced a defending force of 271 weakly armed US Navy personnel and 122 Marines. After token resistance, the governor surrendered the same day. The Marines lost five men killed and the Navy eight (Gordon L. Rottman, *World War II Pacific Island Guide: A Geo-Military Study,* 389–90).

3. Henry Berry, *Semper Fi, Mac: Living Memories of US Marines in World War II,* 95; Gilbert Small, Jr., journal, 1942, in author's collection; Kerry Lane, *Marine Pioneers,* 32; Sidney Phillips e-mail to the author, March 21, 2010.

4. Bayard Berghaus, diary, June 13, 1942, and Abraham Felber, diary, 1941–45, June 9, 1942, both in author's collection.

5. Berghaus diary, June 13, 1942.

6. Sidney Phillips, "'You'll Be Sor-ree': The Memoirs of a US Marine Private during the Pacific Campaign of World War II," manuscript, 23, in author's collection; Edwin A. Pollock, diary, June 13, 1942, in author's collection.

7. Phillips, "'You'll Be Sor-ree,'" 23. Apparently NCOs—such as 1st Sgt. Abe Felber—were entitled to their own individual berths (Felber diary, June 9, 1942).

8. Felber diary, June 11, 1942.

9. Small journal; Berghaus diary, June 14, 1942.

10. Irving Perine to parents, June 14, 1942; Nikolai Stevenson, telephone interview with the author, August 4, 2010.

11. Berghaus diary, June 14, 15, 1942; William Sager e-mail to the author, February 26, 2010.

12. Inui diary, June 18, 19, 1942.

13. Berghaus diary, June 17, 18, 1942.

14. Ibid., June 18, 21, 1942. After being "practically plundered bare" to refit for bunks, the *John Ericsson* could carry 5,460 passengers, as against the 1,575 it transported as the *Kungsholm* (Roland W. Charles, *Troopships of World War II,* 291; http://thegreatoceanliners.com/index2.html).

15. Phillips, "'You'll Be Sor-ree,'" 24.

16. Hugh Morse and George Head, *"A"-1-1: Pearl Harbor to Peleliu,* 21–22.

17. Pollock diary, June 18, 1942; Phillips, "'You'll Be Sor-ree,'" 32.

18. George Codrea to Harry Horsman, February 27, 1998.

19. Berghaus diary, June 18, 1942; Small journal.

20. Berghaus and Felber diaries, June 22, 1942. The 11th Marines had arrived in San Francisco two to four days before the 1st Marines.

21. Berghaus and Felber diaries, June 22, 1942.

22. Berghaus diary, June 22, 23, 1942; Small journal.

23. Berghaus and Felber diaries, June 24, 1942.

24. Berghaus diary, June 26, 1942.

25. A. A. Vandegrift, *Once a Marine*, 103; Herbert C. Merillat, *Guadalcanal Remembered*, 15, 18; Merrill B. Twining, *No Bended Knee*, 28; John L. Zimmerman, *The Guadalcanal Campaign*, 7; Alan Millett, *In Many a Strife: General Gerald C. Thomas and the US Marine Corps, 1917–1956*, 165.

26. Vandegrift, *Once a Marine*, 103.

27. Ibid., 103–4.

28. Zimmerman, *Guadalcanal Campaign*, 6, and n25; 1st Marine Division, Headquarters, "Division Commander's Final Report on Guadalcanal Operation," 24 May 1943, Phase I: Events Prior to H-Hour, 7 August 1942, in Folder A-7-1, Box 39, Geographic Files 1939–1949—Guadalcanal, RG 127, NARA (hereafter cited as Phase I Report), 2; Vandegrift, *Once a Marine*, 104; George C. Dyer, *The Amphibians Came to Conquer*, 259; Millett, *In Many a Strife*, 165. The dispatch cited in Zimmerman—COMINCH to CINCPAC with information copy to COMSOPAC dated 25 June 1942—and used here as the source for the Ghormley-Vandegrift meeting is not included in the CINCPAC Gray Book of message traffic. The Gray Book does include a 24 June 1942 dispatch of COMINCH to CINCPAC (not copied to COMSOPAC) in which "arrangements are contemplated" as in the Zimmerman dispatch, including commitment of the 1st Marine Division. The first mention in the Gray Book of a target date for the operation is made in a 2 July 1942 dispatch from COMINCH to CINCPAC, info copy to COMSOPAC, citing the Joint Chiefs of Staff directive in which the target date "is tentatively set as August first 1942" (June 24 and July 2 dispatches are at American Naval Records Society, Nimitz "Gray Book": War Plans and Files of the Commander-in-Chief, Pacific Fleet, www.ibiblio.org/anrs/graybook.html).

29. Vandegrift, *Once a Marine*, 109; Millett, *In Many a Strife*, 165.

30. Phase I Report, 2; Twining, *No Bended Knee*, 28, 31; Merillat, *Guadalcanal Remembered*, 18; Millett, *In Many a Strife*, 165, 166; 1st Marine Division, Operation Order 5-42, Wellington, NZ, 29 June 1942, File B-2-1, Box 44, Geographic Files 1939–1949—Guadalcanal, RG 127, NARA (hereafter cited as Operation Order 5-42).

31. Berghaus diary, July 11, 1942.

32. Ibid.; Millett, *In Many a Strife*, 167.

33. Pollock diary, July 11, 1942; " History of the 2nd Battalion, 1st Marines," in Lt. Gen. Edwin A. Pollock Papers, Parris Island Museum, US Marine Corps Recruitment Depot, Parris Island, SC; Operation Order 5-42.

34. Phillips, "'You'll Be Sor-ree,'" 36.

35. Berghaus diary, July 12, 1942.

36. Small journal, July 12, 1942.

37. Ibid.; Operation Order 5-42.

38. Phillips, "'You'll Be Sor-ree,'" 36; Phase I Report, 6.

39. Phillips, "'You'll Be Sor-ree,'" 36, 37. For a thorough analysis of the dock worker problem, see Denys Bevan, *United States Forces in New Zealand, 1942–1945*, 105–10.

40. Berghaus diary, July 14, 1942; Phillips, "'You'll Be Sor-ree,'" 36.

41. Phillips, "'You'll Be Sor-ree,'" 36.

42. Ibid.

43. Ibid.; Small journal, July 13, 1942.

44. Small journal, July 15, 1942.

45. Ibid.

46. Millett, *In Many a Strife*, 166, 167, 168; Dyer, *Amphibians*, 272–75; Jeter A. Isely and Philip A. Crowl, *The US Marines in Amphibious War*, 101.

47. Merillat, *Guadalcanal Remembered*, 34; Zimmerman, *Guadalcanal Campaign*, 13; Small journal, July 15, 1942; Vandegrift, *Once a Marine*, 117–18; Millett, *In Many a Strife*, 167.

48. Merillat, *Guadalcanal Remembered*, 35; Pollock diary, July 11–21, 1942; "History of the 2nd Battalion." Merillat (34–35) gives July 19 as the date of the conference, but the 2nd Battalion history puts it as July 16.

49. Pollock diary, July 11–21, 1942; Zimmerman, *Guadalcanal Campaign*, 18; "History of the 2nd Battalion," 1.

50. A. William Larson to the author, September 7, 2001; E Company, 2nd Battalion, 1st Marines, muster roll, July 1942; Headquarters Company, 2nd Battalion, 1st Marines (Hq-2-1), muster roll, August 1942 (microfilm), Marine Corps History Division, Reference Branch.

51. A. William Larson to father, October 30, 1942; Larson to the author, September 7, 2001.

52. Small journal, July 16, 1942.

53. Berghaus diary, July 17, 1942.

54. Ibid., July 18, 19, 20, 1942.

55. Phillips, "'You'll Be Sor-ree,'" 37–38.

56. Berghaus diary, July 21, 1942; Small journal, July 19, 21, 1942. Three Australian and two American cruisers, plus eight American destroyers, had joined the transport and cargo ships in Wellington Harbor on July 19. The force was designated Task Force 44 (Denys Bevan, *United States Forces in New Zealand, 1942–1945*, 116).

57. John Tatum, diary, July 21, 1942, in author's collection.

58. Small journal, July 22, 1942; Berghaus diary, July 22, 1942; Merillat, *Guadalcanal Remembered*, 36; Felber diary, July 22, 1942.

59. Pollock diary, July 11–21, 1942.

60. Quote from Twining, *No Bended Knee*, 32. See also Zimmerman, *Guadalcanal Campaign*, 22; Phase I Report, 6; Millett, *In Many a Strife*, 166; John Miller, Jr., *Guadalcanal: The First Offensive*, 47.

61. Berghaus diary, July 23, 1942; Small journal, July 26, 1942.

62. Berghaus diary, July 23, 1942.

63. Ibid., July 24, 1942; Felber diary, July 24, 1942.

64. Perine to parents, July 27, 1942. Perine replaced 2nd Lt. Harold Jennings as battalion intelligence officer, and Jennings moved to C-1-1 as 2nd Platoon commanding officer while John Rentz shifted up to executive officer (Hq-2-1, muster roll, July 1942; Stevenson telephone interview, August 4, 2010).

65. Felber and Berghaus diaries, July 26, 1942; Small journal, July 26, 1942.

66. Berghaus, Felber, and Tatum diaries, July 27, 1942; Small journal, July 27, 1942.

67. Small journal, July 28, 1942.

68. Ibid.; Berghaus diary, July 28, 1942. For a detailed account of the Koro landing practice, see William H. Bartsch, " Operation Dovetail: Bungled Guadalcanal Rehearsal, July 1942," *Journal of Military History,* April 2002, 443–76.

69. Edward Craig to the author, August 9, 1999; Dean Stover to the author, December 16, 1999; Nathaniel Mewhinney to the author, May 12, 1999.

70. Phillips, "'You'll Be Sor-ree,'" 41; Tatum diary, July 28, 1942; John Tatum to the author, July 31, 1999.

71. USS *George F. Elliott,* deck log, July 29, 1942, US Navy Ships' Deck Logs, Record Group 24, National Archives and Records Service, College Park, MD; Tatum diary, July 29, 1942; Craig to the author, August 9, 1999; B. J. Wilson to the author, July 23, 1999.

72. Berghaus diary, July 29, 1942; Small journal, July 29, 1942.

73. Richard Tregaskis, *Guadalcanal Diary,* 10; 1st Marine Division, Headquarters, Wellington, New Zealand, "Operation Order 7-42," 20 July 1942, in Annex F, Phase I Report; Zimmerman, *Guadalcanal Campaign,* 20.

74. July 30, 1942, entries in deck logs of the USS *Elliott,* USS *Barnett,* and USS *McCawley,* US Navy Ships' Deck Logs, RG 24, NARA; Berghaus diary, July 30, 1942; Small journal, July 30, 1942.

75. Bartsch, "Operation Dovetail," 467–68; Berghaus diary, July 30, 1942, and Small journal, July 30, 1942.

76. Tatum diary, July 31, 1942; General Edwin A. Pollock, Oral History Transcript, interview with Maj. Thomas E. Donnelly, 1977, 121, Marine Corps History and Museum Division, Washington, DC.

77. Combat Team 5, "Operation Order 2-42," 28 July 1942, and Combat Group B, 1st Marines (Reinforced), Annex D to Operation Order 4-42, "Intelligence—Facts About Terrain on Guadalcanal Island," 29 July 1942, both in A. William Larson personal collection. See also map 3 (p. 52), which was prepared by Hunt's Intelligence Section, 1st Marine Regiment, July 31, 1942.

Unknown to Hunt and division higher-ups, the names of two of the rivers—the Ilu and the Tenaru—had been mistakenly interchanged due to either faulty information provided by the Australian source (according to Martin Clemens, *Alone on Guadalcanal: A Coastwatcher's Story,* 18) or an error of Thayer Soule of Vandegrift's staff according to Soule in his unpublished paper "Guadalcanal: The Desperate Gamble," cited in Tom McLeod, "How Did the Ilu River Become Known as the Tenaru River (AKA Alligator Creek)?" *Old Breed News,* April–June 2012, reprinted in *Guadalcanal Echoes,* Winter 2012, 11. The aerial photos may have been those taken by Lt. Cdr. Robert S. Quackenbush Jr., USN, in one of two B-17s that overflew Guadalcanal on July 23 and were flown by PBY to the *McCawley* two days later for use by Vandegrift's staff (Marine Corps Aviation Reconnaissance Association, MCARA War Stories, Quackenbush's Gypsies, South Pacific, 1942–1943, www.mcara.us/quackenbushs-gypsies.html).

78. Bartsch, "Operation Dovetail," 468, 469; Vandegrift, *Once a Marine,* 122.

79. Tatum diary, July 31, 1942.

80. Berghaus diary, August 1, 4, 1942.

81. George P. Hunt, "First Days on Guadalcanal," undated memoir, 1, in Lt. Gen. Edwin A. Pollock Papers, Parris Island Museum, US Marine Corps Recruitment Depot, Parris Island, SC; Tatum diary, August 2, 3, 1942.

82. Phillips, "'You'll Be Sor-Ree,'" 42.

83. Berghaus diary, August 5, 6, 1942.

84. Vandegrift, *Once a Marine,* 17–18.

85. Ibid., 18–19.

86. Inui diary, August 6, 1942; Hajime Yamamoto to Akio Tani, November 6, 1990.

CHAPTER 3

1. George P. Hunt, "First Days on Guadalcanal," undated memoir, 2–3, in Lt. Gen. Edwin A. Pollock Papers, Parris Island Museum, US Marine Corps Recruitment Depot, Parris Island, SC. The convoy had reached the transport area at 0651 (1st Marine Division, Headquarters, "Division Commander's Final Report on Guadalcanal Operation," 24 May 1943, Phase II: From H Hour to Evening 9 August, 1, Geographic Files 1939–1949—Guadalcanal, RG 127, NARA [hereafter cited as Phase II Report]).

Grassy Knoll was often erroneously referred to as Mount Austen in the literature covering the first days following the landing, but Gordon Rottman has clarified that 1,517-foot Mount Austen is actually two miles away from Grassy Knoll, a 450-foot ridge on the west side of the Lunga River (Gordon L. Rottman, *World War II Pacific Island Guide: A Geo-Military Study*, 108). It is likely that Hunt saw the much more prominent Mount Austen rather than Grassy Knoll.

2. 1st Marine Division, Headquarters, "Division Commander's Final Report on Guadalcanal Operation," 24 May 1943, Phase I: Events Prior to H Hour, 7 August 1942 (hereafter cited as Phase I Report), 10, and Annex F, "Operation Order 7-42," 20 July 1942, in Geographic Files 1939–1949—Guadalcanal, RG 127, NARA; John L. Zimmerman, *The Guadalcanal Campaign*, 44; Billy Wilson, "Guadalcanal 1942," *Richmond Times-Dispatch,* August 6, 1967, L8; Hunt, "First Days," 3; Merrill B. Twining, *No Bended Knee*, 52.

3. Lester W. Clark, *An Unlikely Arena*, 17–18; Roger Butterfield, *Al Schmid, Marine*, 71.

4. Robert Leckie, *Helmet for My Pillow*, 57–58.

5. Ibid., 58; Butterfield, *Al Schmid*, 72.

6. Sidney C. Phillips, "'You'll Be Sor-ree': The Memoirs of a US Marine Private during the Pacific Campaign of World War II," manuscript, 43, in author's collection.

7. Clark, *Unlikely Arena*, 18.

8. William H. Whyte, *A Time of War*, 27.

9. Hunt, "First Days," 4.

10. Ibid., 4–5.

11. Ibid., 5–6.

12. Phase I Report, Annex M, "History of the 1st Marines," 1; CO 1st Marines to Commanding General, message, 1431 August 7, 1942, 1st Marine Division, D-3 Journal, August 1942, Folder A-7-14, Box 41, Geographic Files 1939–1949—Guadalcanal, RG 127, NARA; John Miller, Jr., *Guadalcanal: The First Offensive*, 69–70; Phase II Report, Annex E 2, "Operation Order 7-42"; Combat Group B, 1st Marines (Reinforced), R-2 Section, "Northern Coast of Guadalcanal Island, Kukum to Tetere," map "traced from aerial photo," 31 July 1942, Australian National Archives. It is assumed that all three battalions of the 1st Marines received copies of this map. However, Whyte recalled over fifty years later that all he had as intelligence officer of 3rd Battalion was a "crude map drawn on mimeograph paper" (Whyte, *Time of War*, 27). The 1st Marine history annex gives the azimuth heading as 240, rather than 260, degrees.

13. Gen. Edwin A. Pollock interview with Maj. Thomas E. Donnelly, USMC Oral History Transcript, Washington, DC, 1977, 124; Zimmerman, *Guadalcanal Campaign*, 44.

14. Phase II Report, 10; Asst Division Commander to Vandegrift, message, 1635 August 7, 1942, D-3 Journal; "History of the 2nd Battalion, 1st Marines," 2–3, in Lt. Gen. Edwin A. Pollock Papers, Parris Island Museum, US Marine Corps Recruitment Depot, Parris Island, SC; Wilson, "Guadalcanal 1942," L8; Leckie, *Helmet*, 62. The August 1942 muster roll for

F Company, 2nd Battalion, 1st Marines reported McCutcheon as "missing in action" (muster rolls, Marine Corps History Division, Reference Branch).

15. William Whorf, diary, August 7, 1942, and William Whorf, "Cross Section at the Tenaru," November 30, 1998, both in author's collection; Butterfield, *Al Schmid*, 74–76.

16. Leckie, *Helmet*, 61–62.

17. Whorf diary, August 7, 1942; Leckie, *Helmet*, 60.

18. John Joseph to the author, June 16, 2010.

19. Clark, *Unlikely Arena*, 19.

20. Phillips, "'You'll Be Sor-ree,'" 43; "History of the 2nd Battalion," 3; Phase II Report, 10; Miller, *Guadalcanal*, 70; Twining, *No Bended Knee*, 55. Evidently it was the 1st Amphibian Tractor Battalion's B Company—charged with supporting the 1st Marines—that carried the materials for the bridge and provided its two amtracs as pontoons (Col. Albert F. Reutlinger, "A History of the First Amphibian Tractor Battalion, United States Marine Corps, during World War II," 15–16 [no date], in author's collection).

21. Bayard Berghaus diary and Gilbert Small, Jr., journal, August 7, 1942, both in author's collection; Robert F. Putnam, "Guadalcanal Memories," 1942, in author's collection.

22. Nikolai Stevenson, "Four Months on the Front Line," *American Heritage,* October/November 1985, 50; Putnam, "Guadalcanal Memories."

23. Commanding General to 1st Marine Division, message, 1601 August 7, 1942, D-3 Journal; Twining, *No Bended Knee*, 54; Herbert C. Merillat, *Guadalcanal Remembered*, 51; A. A. Vandegrift, *Once a Marine*, 123; Alan Millett, *In Many a Strife: General Gerald C. Thomas and the US Marine Corps, 1917–1956*, 174.

24. Vandegrift, *Once a Marine*, 124; Martin Holt, telephone interview with the author, October 23, 1999. The Advance Message Center had reported earlier that afternoon that "reliable communications not yet established with units" (Message to Commanding General, 1446 August 7, 1942, D-3 Journal). Because battalion command posts were on the move so much that day, pack radio sets "could be installed and operated for only brief intervals" (Phase II Report, Annex O, "Signal Communications"). Wire communications were impossible to maintain because of the telephone ground wires being cut by amtracs and trucks.

25. Twining, *No Bended Knee*, 51, 56; Vandegrift, *Once a Marine*, 124; Millett, *In Many a Strife*, 176. Division Order 7-42 had indicated that "Grassy Knoll" was only "four miles south of Lunga Point" (Phase II Report, Annex E). Twining refers to the crude map based on information supplied by the Australian former plantation manager and prepared on July 14, 1942 (reproduced in Zimmerman, *Guadalcanal Campaign*, 18), but the R-2 map of July 31, 1942, on which the location of Grassy Knoll was superimposed, should have been the one used by Cates's battalions. Grassy Knoll was actually 10 miles away from the Red Beach landing site, not 5.6 miles as indicated by the crude map or 6.5 miles on the R-2 map.

26. Vandegrift, *Once a Marine*, 124; Merillat, *Guadalcanal Remembered*, 51; Twining, *No Bended Knee*, 57.

27. Twining, *No Bended Knee*, 57; Asst Division Commander to Commanding General, message, 1635 August 7, 1942, D-3 Journal; Vandegrift, *Once a Marine*, 124; Millett, *In Many a Strife*, 176; Hunt, "First Days," 7; Phase II Report, Annex M, "1st Marines History," 1; Commanding General to Commander Task Force 62, message, 1024, and Cates to Commanding General, message, 1400 August 8, 1942, D-3 Journal. Three planes from the *Asto-*

ria were assigned to liaison duties for the Guadalcanal landings (Phase II Report, Annex K, "Aviation").

28. Hunt, "First Days," 6. Hunt in his memoir does not mention the reason for being sent out to Cresswell, but it would appear logical that it was for the purpose of giving him the new orders, given that the battalion early the following morning headed for the area south of the airfield.

29. Ibid. Cresswell afterwards apparently ordered Stevenson and his other company commanders to halt for the evening and head out for the airfield area in the morning. Stevenson and his men must have been quite far behind Cresswell and the rest of the 1st Battalion, as Hunt did not encounter them in his night search for Cresswell.

30. Leckie, *Helmet*, 62.

31. Putnam, "Guadalcanal Memories"; Nikolai S. Stevenson, "[C] Company History, June 14–December 22, 1942," n.d., Winston F. Fontaine Personal Collection.

32. Takushiro Hattori, *Dai Toa Senso Zenshi* [Complete History of the Greater East Asia War), II, Part IV, 9 (English translation, Library of Congress microfilm).

33. Ibid.

34. Ibid., 10.

35. Leckie, *Helmet*, 63; Headquarters Company, 2nd Battalion, 1st Marines (Hq-2-1), muster roll, August 1942. Leckie recalled that the medical corpsman had botched "Lilliputian" as the password, but that was not the password until August 15, according to the diary of John Tatum (in author's collection). Buchman was shot by a "very new" and "nervous" corporal, who was "weeping and wailing" afterwards over what he had done (Kathleen Valenzi, "Scouting Guadalcanal," *Military History*, August 1995).

36. Putnam, "Guadalcanal Memories"; Stevenson, "[C] Company History"; C Company, 1st Battalion, 1st Marines (C-1-1), muster roll, August 1942, Marine Corps History Division, Reference Branch.

37. William Sager e-mail to the author, August 3, 2010; Nikolai Stevenson, telephone interview with the author, August 3, 2010; Stevenson, "Four Months," 50. In response to Cates's request that afternoon for stretcher bearers to be sent by the 1st Medical Battalion to the 1st Battalion's aid station to evacuate casualties, twelve litter bearers and a medical officer were en route at 1650 to the station, but apparently only to pick up the battalion's wounded (messages, 1630 and 1650 August 8, 1942, D-3 Journal). Grover's body was never recovered, left at "an unknown site" (C-1-1 muster roll, August 1942).

38. Stevenson, "Four Months," 50.

39. Tatum diary, August 8, 1942; Phillips, "'You'll Be Sor-ree,'" 43–44; Sidney Phillips, e-mail to the author, June 11, 2010; "History of the 2nd Battalion," 3. Phillips recalled the mortar platoon crossed over on the first day, but Tatum documents the date as the second day.

40. Tatum diary, August 8, 1942; Phase II Report, Annex M, "1st Marine History," 1; Billy Wilson, "Guadalcanal 1942," *Richmond Times-Dispatch*, August 6, 1967; Clark, *Unlikely Arena*, 20.

41. Clark, *Unlikely Arena*, 20; James A. Donahue, "Guadalcanal Journal," 1942, in author's collection.

42. "History of Second Battalion," 3; Leckie, *Helmet*, 64; Luther Hayes, diary, 1942, in author's collection, August 8, 1942, and Whorf diary, August 8, 1942.

43. Putnam, "Guadalcanal Memories"; Phase II Report, Annex M, "1st Marines History," 1. Later, it was officially acknowledged that "much equipment was lost during the first two days simply because the individual could not continue on the march with the excessive gear." It was "excessive for jungle operations" (Phase II Report, 16, and Annex H, 2).

44. Berghaus diary, August 8, 1942.

45. Edwin A. Pollock diary, August 8, 1942, in author's collection; Pollock interview with Donnelly, 122, 126.

46. Pollock interview with Donnelly, 125.

47. Ibid.

48. Hunt, "First Days," 7. The D-3 Journal for August 8 includes a 1400 message in which Cates informed Vandegrift that he had not received a report from Pollock yet (erroneously recorded as August 7, 1942, in the journal), but at 1530 it records that Vandegrift had now received a situation report directly from Pollock for his Combat Team 5. No indication is made of how the report reached Vandegrift and why it was sent to Vandegrift rather than to Cates.

49. Hunt, "First Days," 7.

50. Ibid., 8.

51. Ibid.; Pollock interview with Donnelly, 126; Whyte, *Time of War*, 28; Berghaus and Small diaries, August 8, 1942.

52. Phase II Report, Annex M, "1st Marines History," 1; Stevenson, "[C] Company History," n.d.; Stevenson, "Four Months," 50. The two accounts by Stevenson differ in detail on the incident with the "Japanese," who may have been men of the 81st Guard Unit charged with protecting the 11th and 13th Construction Units originally located in the general area of the airfield.

53. Phase II Report, 12; James J. Gorman, "Behind the Lines with the Marines in the Solomons," draft manuscript for *Elks Magazine,* March 1943; Hugh Morse and George Head, *"A"-1-1: Pearl Harbor to Peleliu*, 31. The "Japanese" would have been Korean construction laborers who had been building the airfield.

54. Phase II Report, Annex M, "1st Marines History," 1; Pollock interview with Donnelly, 125–26; "History of the 2nd Battalion," 3; Berghaus and Small diaries, August 8 and 9, 1942; Putnam, "Guadalcanal Memories."

55. Hunt, "First Days," 9; Leckie, *Helmet*, 64–65.

56. Hunt, "First Days," 9; Leckie, *Helmet*, 65; Richard Tregaskis, *Guadalcanal Diary*, 62–63.

57. Tregaskis, *Guadalcanal Diary*, 62. In the ferocious night engagement off of Savo Island, seven Japanese cruisers and a destroyer clashed with an Allied force of one Australian and four American cruisers plus six American destroyers, resulting in the loss of the Australian and three of the American cruisers against only moderate damage to three of the Japanese cruisers. The human losses were even more appalling for the Allies: 1,077 killed and 700 wounded vs. only 38 Japanese seamen killed. The Battle of Savo Island was the "most humiliating defeat suffered by the U.S. Navy in World War II" (Richard B. Frank, *Guadalcanal*, 83, 121; Paul S. Dull, *A Battle History of the Imperial Japanese Navy, 1941–1945,* 187–92). For an excellent analysis of the causes of the disaster, see chapter 4 of Frank's *Guadalcanal,* 83–123.

58. Genjirou Inui, "My Guadalcanal" (hereafter cited as Inui diary), August 7 and 8, 1942.

59. Ibid., August 8, 1942; Frank, *Guadalcanal*, 145.

60. Inui diary, August 8, 1942.

61. Putnam, "Guadalcanal Memories," August 9, 1942; Berghaus diary, August 9, 1942.

62. Putnam, "Guadalcanal Memories," August 9, 1942; Small diary, August 9, 1942; Merillat, *Guadalcanal Remembered*, 67; Commanding General to Commander Task Force 62, message, 1024 August 8, 1942, D-3 Journal.

63. Phase II Report, 14; Millett, *In Many a Strife*, 178; Vandegrift, *Once a Marine*, 131; Herbert C. L. Merillat, *The Island*, 38.

64. Vandegrift, *Once a Marine*, 131; Zimmerman, *Guadalcanal Campaign*, 50; Whyte, *Time of War*, 33.

65. Vandegrift, *Once a Marine*, 132; Millett, *In Many a Strife*, 178.

66. Combat Group B, 1st Marines (Reinforced), Operation Order 5-42, 9 August 1942, File B-10-1, Box 45, Geographic Files 1939–1949—Guadalcanal, RG 127, NARA; Phase II Report, Annex M, "1st Marines History," 1–2.

67. Combat Group B, 1st Marines (Reinforced), Operation Order 5-42, 9 August 1942.

68. Phase II Report, Annex M, "1st Marines History," 2; Pollock diary, August 9, 1942; Pollock interview with Donnelly, 126–27; Whyte, *Time of War*, 34; Stevenson, "[C] Company History."

69. "History of the the 2nd Battalion," 3–4; Pollock diary, August 9, 1942; Pollock interview with Donnelly, 126–27.

70. William T. Coggin, "Guadalcanal 1942," August 9, 1942, memoir, 1998, in author's collection; Putnam, "Guadalcanal Memories," August 9, 1942; Joseph to the author, June 16, 2010.

71. Putnam, "Guadalcanal Memories," August 9, 1942; Leckie, *Helmet*, 66; Tatum diary, August 9, 1942.

72. Tatum diary, August 9, 1942; Putnam, "Guadalcanal Memories," August 9, 1942.

73. Tatum diary, August 9, 1942; Leckie, *Helmet*, 66; Phillips, "'You'll Be Sor-ree,'" August 9, 1942.

74. Leckie, *Helmet*, 66–67; Tatum diary, August 9, 1942; Phillips, "'You'll Be Sor-ree,'" August 9, 1942.

75. Putnam, "Guadalcanal Memories," August 9, 1942; Small diary, August 9, 1942.

76. Abraham Felber, diary, 1941–45, August 9, 1942, in author's collection.

77. Stevenson, "Four Months," 51; Stevenson, "[C] Company History," 1. The Japanese were probably men from the 81st Guard Unit that had arrived on Guadalcanal on July 1, 1942, charged with providing protection for the two construction battalions building the airfield. It became known as the Guadalcanal Guard Unit (Sankichi Kaneda, "Recollections of a Memorial Pilgrimage," memoir, in Japanese, 1969, in collection of Stanley Jersey).

78. Inui diary, August 9, 1942.

79. Bōeicho Bōeikenshūjo Senshishitsu [Japanese Defense Agency, War History Section], *Senshi sōsho* [Official war history], Vol. 14, *Minami-taiheiyo Rikūgun Sakusen, 1* [Port Moresby–Guadalcanal initial operations], 296 (trans. by Akio Tani).

80. Pollock diary, August 10, 1942; "History of the 2nd Battalion," 4; Zimmerman, *Guadalcanal Campaign*, 56. The 2nd Battalion history is in error in indicating the 37 mm guns were from C Battery; they were in B Battery.

81. Tatum and Whorf diaries, August 10, 1942; Phillips, "'You'll Be Sor-ree,'" 49.

82. Coggin, "Guadalcanal 1942"; Whorf diary, August 10, 1942; Leckie, *Helmet*, 67.

83. Putnam, "Guadalcanal Memories," August 10, 1942; Ben Wofford and William R. White, *The Marine: A Guadalcanal Survivor's Final Battle*, 53; Pedro Del Valle, "Marine Field Artillery on Guadalcanal," *Field Artillery Journal,* October 1943, 724, 726.

84. Del Valle, "Marine Field Artillery," 727; Small diary, August 7, 1942; Nathaniel Mewhinney to the author, May 12, 1999.

85. Leckie, *Helmet*, 67; Pollock diary, August 10, 1942; Pollock interview with Donnelly, 128–29; "History of the 2nd Battalion," 4–5; Whorf diary, August 10, 1942. The D-3 Journal, 1315 August 10, 1942, recorded that "25 heavy bombers . . . circled this area at thirteen thirty" but did not drop bombs.

86. Tatum diary, August 10, 1942; Ralph H. Reber, "Memories of Military Service," memoir, 10, in author's collection. Four (not three) Zeros flew low "on reconnaissance" at 1325 (1st Marine Division, Headquarters, "Division Commander's Final Report on Guadalcanal Operation," 24 May 1943, Phase III: Organization of Lunga Point Defense, 10 August–21 August, Annex F, "Intelligence," August 10, 1942, Geographic Files 1939–1949—Guadalcanal, RG 127, NARA).

87. Leckie, *Helmet*, 67, and Robert Leckie, *Challenge for the Pacific*, 105; Tatum diary, August 10, 1942.

88. Small journal, August 10, 1942; Putnam, "Guadalcanal Memories," August 10, 1942.

89. Leckie, *Helmet*, 68.

90. Hattori, *Dai Toa Sensō Zenshi*, 11.

91. Ibid.

92. Ibid.

CHAPTER 4

1. Robert Leckie, *Helmet for My Pillow*, 69; William Whorf diary, August 10, 1942, in author's collection.

2. George P. Hunt, "First Days on Guadalcanal," undated memoir, 12, in Lt. Gen. Edwin A. Pollock Papers, Parris Island Museum, US Marine Corps Recruitment Depot, Parris Island, SC.

3. Gen. Edwin A. Pollock interview with Maj. Thomas E. Donnelly, Oral History Transcripts, History and Museums Division, US Marine Corps, Washington, DC, 127–28; Hunt, "First Days," 12.

4. Hunt, "First Days," 12.

5. George Dennis, diary, August 10, 1942, in author's collection; John Tatum, diary, August 11, 1942, in author's collection. The only Japanese combat unit, the Guadalcanal Guard Unit, was deployed away to the west at the Matanikau River area, but may have sent out patrols to the east.

6. Leckie, *Helmet*, 69; Robert Leckie, *Challenge for the Pacific*, 105.

7. Gilbert Small, Jr., journal, August 11, 1942, in author's collection.

8. Alan Millett, *In Many a Strife: General Gerald C. Thomas and the US Marine Corps, 1917–1956*, 182–83.

9. "History of the 2nd Battalion, 1st Marines," 5, in Lt. Gen. Edwin A. Pollock Papers, Parris Island Museum, US Marine Corps Recruitment Depot, Parris Island, SC; Edwin A. Pollock diary, August 11, 1942, in author's collection; Pollock interview with Donnelly, 130.

10. Pollock diary, August 11, 1942; Hunt, "First Days," 12.

11. Pollock diary, August 13 [*sic*] 1942; Pollock interview with Donnelly, 131; Abraham Felber, diary, 1941–45, August 12, 1942, in author's collection; "History of the 2nd Battalion," August 12, 1942; Tatum diary, August 13, 1942.

12. Small journal, August 12, 13, 1942. Evidently as a consequence of the Japanese submarine's attack, Vandegrift at 0840 ordered artillery units to register at 1500 that day, with impact area "in sea about 2000 yards from beach" (Commanding General to all units, message 0840 August 12, 1942, 1st Marine Division, D-3 Journal).

13. Nathaniel Mewhinney to the author, May 12, 1999. The submarine would have been either the I-169, with a 3.9-inch deck gun, or the I-171, equipped with a 4.7-inch gun. They were the only submarines patrolling in the area in mid-August (Carl Boyd, *The Japanese Submarine Force and World War II*, 93; A. J. Watts and B. G. Gordon, *The Imperial Japanese Navy*, 326). However, Richard B. Frank, *Guadalcanal*, 143, suggests it may have been I-122 or I-123. Mewhinney doesn't indicate the date, but it is assumed it was not the only other possible date, August 15, 1942 (Tatum diary, August 15, 1942).

14. "History of the 2nd Battalion," 8; Thomas Brown to the author, November 5, 1998.

15. B. J. Wilson, "Guadalcanal," memoir, February 6, 1999, in author's collection.

16. Ibid.

17. "History of the 2nd Battalion," 8.

18. Hunt, "First Days," 12–13. Japanese records indicate no Guadalcanal Guard Unit members at the time to the east of the Matanikau, seven miles distant, except for seven men at the Point Taivu observation post, but the guard unit may have sent out patrols to the east.

19. Genjirou Inui, "My Guadalcanal" (diary), August 13, 1942; Bōeicho Bōeikenshūjo Senshishitsu [Japanese Defense Agency, War History Section], *Senshi sōsho* [Official war history], Vol. 14, *Minami-taiheiyo Rikūgun Sakusen* (1) [Port Moresby–Guadalcanal initial operations], 295, trans. by Akio Tani, April 29, 1990 (cited hereafter as *Senshi sōsho*).

20. Frank, *Guadalcanal*, 144–45.

21. Samuel B. Griffith II, *The Battle for Guadalcanal*, 79–80.

22. Pollock, Tatum, and Whorf diaries, August 14, 1942.

23. Combat Group B, 1st Marines (Reinforced), "Operation Order 6-42," August 14, 1942, File B-10-1, Box 45, Geographic Files 1939–1949—Guadalcanal, RG 127, NARA.

24. "History of the 2nd Battalion," 5; Leckie, *Helmet*, 72–73; Tatum diary, August 14, 1942.

25. Leckie, *Helmet*, 73–74.

26. Sidney C. Phillips, "'You'll Be Sor-ree': The Memoirs of a US Marine Private during the Pacific Campaign of World War II," manuscript, 52, in author's collection.

27. Tatum diary, August 14, 15, 1942; Tatum telephone interview with the author, July 31, 1999; Leckie, *Helmet*, 73–74. At that date there were no Japanese forces in their area, although the 81st Guard Unit could have sent out a patrol. Leckie did not mention any Japanese firing on his group.

28. *Senshi sōsho*, 296–97 (trans. by Akio Tani); Griffith, *Battle for Guadalcanal*, 79–80. Matsumoto's comments about the Marines are reflected in Ichiki's operation plan of August 15, 1942; see note 32).

29. *Senshi sōsho*, 297 (trans. by Akio Tani); Frank, *Guadalcanal*, 198.

30. *Senshi sōsho*, 295 (trans. by Akio Tani). Ichiki's operation plan, drafted a day later, confirms his intention of launching the attack with the first echelon only.

31. *Senshi sōsho*, 297 (trans. by Akio Tani). Numbers of officers and men assigned to the three companies and platoon are those at the time of departing Japan on May 18, 1942, for the attack on Midway, in "Organization of Two Japanese Army Combat Teams," Intelligence Report, Folder C-15-5, Box 46, RG 127, Geographic Files 1939–1949—Guadalcanal, RG 127, NARA.

32. Hajime Yamamoto (detachment assistant adjutant) to Akio Tani, November 7, 1990. I have compared figures of May 18, 1942, with 1st Echelon strength at August 15, 1942, included in Annex 1 of "Ichiki Detachment Operation Order A, no. 4," Truk, 15 August 1942, Intelligence Reports, Item No. 1231 (hereafter cited as Ichiki Detachment Operation Order), Folder C-15-5, Box 46, RG 127, Geographic Files 1939–1949—Guadalcanal, RG 127, NARA. An abbreviated form of the order can be found in William H. Whyte Papers, "Orders of the Ikki [*sic*] Detachment, Order No. 4," Truk, 15 August 1942, Item W 35, Marine Corps Historical Center, Washington, DC.

33. Allyn D. Nevitt, "Long Lancers," Imperial Japanese Navy Page, at www.combinedfleet.com/lancers.htm.

34. *Senshi sōsho*, 293 (trans. by Akio Tani).

35. Ibid.; Ichiki Detachment Operation Order. The Type 95 collapsible boat could carry sixteen troops plus a crew of three engineers (www3.plala.or.jp/takihome/vessel.htm).

36. Inui, "My Guadalcanal," August 15, 1942.

37. Tatum diary, August 15, 1942; Phillips, "'You'll Be Sor-ree,'" 50.

38. Leckie, *Helmet*, 74; Phillips, "'You'll Be Sor-ree,'" 50.

39. Tatum diary, August 15, 1942; 1st Marine Division, Headquarters, "Division Commander's Final Report on Guadalcanal Operation," 24 May 1943, Phase III: Organization of Lunga Point Defense, 10 August–21 August, Annex C, "Logistics," 4 (hereafter cited as Phase III Report), Geographic Files 1939–1949—Guadalcanal, RG 127, NARA. "Huge quantities" of unpolished rice in one-hundred-pound woven straw bags had been captured (ibid., Phase II: From H Hour to Evening 9 August, Annex G, "Intelligence," 80).

40. Phillips, "'You'll Be Sor-ree,'" 51; Vandegrift to Pollock, message, 1050 August 15, 1942, D-3 Journal. Alligator Creek continued upstream as the narrower Ilu River at about the 1,700 yard point (in my estimation), where the 2nd Battalion defense line was to end and the 1st Battalion to take over.

41. Messages 12, 13, and 14, August 14, 1942, D-3 Journal, cited in John L. Zimmerman, *The Guadalcanal Campaign*, 62. The D-3 Journal on perusal does not include these messages, and Zimmerman may be referring instead to August 15, which does include messages so numbered, with number 12 sent at 1250 by Vandegrift to Asst. Division Commander Rupertus on Tulagi, reporting "reliable information hostile forces approaching." On August 12, COMSOPAC Ghormley had informed Turner that the "large assemblage vessels Rabaul" reported to Ghormley "may indicate initiation expected movement against Cactus-Ringbolt area" (August 12, 1942, in Nimitz "Gray Book": War Plans and Files of the Commander-in-Chief, Pacific Fleet, www.ibiblio.org/anrs/graybook.html), and Turner apparently passed the information to Vandegrift.

42. Martin Clemens, *Alone on Guadalcanal: A Coastwatcher's Story*, 151, 237; Zimmerman,

Guadalcanal Campaign, 61–62; Phase III Report, 9. The intelligence report of the division indicated for August 10 that "friendly natives" had reported "a small force estimated at 10 or 12 men in the vicinity of Taivu" (Phase III Report, Annex F, "Intelligence," 1–2). The Japanese were actually seven navy men of the 81st Guard Unit deployed since July 5 at the East Observation Post set up at Taivu Point (Sankichi Kaneda, "The Battle for Guadalcanal," undated memoir, in Japanese, translation in collection of Stanley Jersey).

43. John J. Jachym interview with the author, December 1, 1998; John J. Jachym telephone interviews with Tom McLeod, ca. 2000; Eric Hammel, *Guadalcanal: Starvation Island*, 157; Zimmerman, *Guadalcanal Campaign*, 161–62; "Report on Guadalcanal Operation," (b) Intelligence, Folder C-18-1, Box 46, Geographic Files1939–1949—Guadalcanal, RG 127, NARA.

44. Hammel, *Guadalcanal*, 157–58; Zimmerman, *Guadalcanal Campaign*, 161–62; "Report on Guadalcanal Operations," (b) Intelligence.

45. Raizo Tanaka, "The Struggle for Guadalcanal," chapter 5 in *The Japanese Navy in World War II*, ed. David Evans, 55; *Senshi sōsho*, 296 (trans. by Akio Tani).

46. Tanaka, "Struggle," 55; *Senshi sōsho*, 296 (trans. by Akio Tani).

47. Tanaka, "Struggle," 55.

48. Ibid.; *Senshi sōsho*, 296 (trans. by Akio Tani).

49. Tanaka, "Struggle," 55.

50. Ichiki Detachment Operation Order.

51. Ibid. *Senshi sōsho*, 297 (trans. by Akio Tani) indicates that 916 men (not 900) were loaded on the destroyers: two additional men in the battalion gun platoon and fourteen more in Ichiki's headquarters.

52. *Senshi sōsho*, 296 (trans. by Akio Tani). Ichiki appears to be referring to his riflemen only, excluding those men carrying light and heavy machine guns. His operation order for the Guadalcanal attack indicated six hundred rounds of ammunition for each light machine gun and five boxes of ammunition for each of his heavy machine guns. Each man would also carry two hand grenades, while each grenade launcher squad in the rifle companies would be equipped with twenty rounds of 50 mm grenades. The order stipulated rations of four days of rice (for two meals daily), supplemented by dried bread for six days and canned goods for a third meal daily.

53. Ibid.; Tanaka, "Struggle," 55.

54. *Senshi sōsho*, 297 (trans. by Akio Tani); Tanaka, "Struggle," 55; Ichiki Detachment Operation Order; Sadanobu Okada, "Ichiki in Guadalcanal," memoir, June 4, 1984, in Japanese, trans. by Akio Tani, in author's collection.

55. Inui, "My Guadalcanal," August 16, 1942.

56. Small journal, August 16, 1942; Herbert C. Merillat, *Guadalcanal Remembered*, 74; Felber and Dennis diaries, August 12, 1942; Pollock diary, August 13, 14, 1942; Whorf diary, August 14, 1942; Tatum diary, August 15, 1942. Pollock notes that the morning following the night firing, they "buried seven cows" (Pollock diary, August 16, 1942).

57. Small journal, August 16, 1942.

58. Tatum diary, August 16, 1942; Tatum telephone interview with the author, July 31, 1999. One wonders who the "Japanese" were. None were reported to be in their patrol area that evening.

59. *Senshi sōsho*, 297 (trans. by Akio Tani).

60. Takushiro Hattori, *Dai Toa Sensō Zenshi* [Complete history of the Greater East Asia War], 12; *Senshi sōsho*, 289 (trans. by Akio Tani).

61. Inui, "My Guadalcanal," August 17, 1942.

62. Ibid.

63. Richard W. Harding, "Battle for a Foxhole," in *Out in the Boondocks*, ed. James D. Horan and Gerold Frank, 30; "History of the 2nd Battalion," 6; 2nd Battalion, 1st Marines (Reinforced), "Unit Report," 1800 16 August to 1800 17 August 1942 (hereafter cited as Larson Unit Report with dates), in A. William Larson personal collection.

64. Larson Unit Report, 16–17 August 1942.

65. Ibid.

66. Roger Butterfield, *Al Schmid, Marine*, 78.

67. Thomas D. Brown to the author, November 5, 1998.

68. "History of the 2nd Battalion," 5; Larson Unit Report, 16–17 August 1942.

69. Small journal, August 17, 1942.

70. Tatum diary, August 18, 1942; Larson Unit Report, August 17–18, 1942; "History of the 2nd Battalion," 6.

71. Butterfield, *Al Schmid*, 78.

72. Luther Hayes, diary, 1942, in author's collection, August 18, 1942.

73. Larson Unit Report, August 17–18, 1942.

74. Ibid.

75. Maj. Charles H. Brush to Commandant, Marine Corps, January 15, 1949, quoted in Zimmerman, *Guadalcanal Campaign*, 62; John Speaks to the author, October 19, 1999; George Dennis email to Peter Flahavin, in email to the author, February 5, 2011; Phase III Report, 10.

76. 1st Marine Division, Headquarters, "Division Commander's Final Report on Guadalcanal Operation," 24 May 1943, Phase III: Organization of Lunga Point Defense, 10 August–21 August, Annex I, "History of the First Battalion," Geographic Files 1939–1949—Guadalcanal, RG 127, NARA.

77. Larson Unit Report, August 17–18, 1942.

78. Outgoing message no. 14, August 18, 1942, D-3 Journal; Tatum, Pollock, and Whorf diaries, August 18, 1942; John Miller, Jr., *Guadalcanal: The First Offensive*, 25; Incoming message, 1300 August 18, 1942, D-3 Journal. The airfield was named in honor of Maj. Lofton R. Henderson, the commanding officer of Marine Scout Bombing Squadron 241, who was lost at Midway.

79. Jachym interview with the author, December 1, 1998; Jachym interview with McLeod, ca. 2000; Hammel, *Guadalcanal*, 162. The table of organization and equipment (TO&E) for Jachym's rifle platoon in July 1942 was forty-two men.

80. Jachym interview with the author, December 1, 1998.

81. Vandegrift to Rupertus, message, 1855 August 18, 1942, D-3 Journal, 55; Herbert C. Merillat, "The Ultra Weapon at Guadalcanal," *Marine Corps Gazette*, September 1982, 45–46.

82. CINCPAC to COMSOPAC, Info CTF 61, 62, 63, 17 August 1942, 2047, Nimitz "Gray Book," www.ibiblio.org/anrs/graybook.html. Unknown to all but Nimitz, the source of the intelligence was an intercepted and decrypted Japanese Navy message from Rabaul identifying the "Army shock troops" as the "Ikki Detachment," but a subsequent more detailed warning by Nimitz's intelligence, reportedly sent to US Naval commands in the Pacific indicating that it "now appears that 18th is date of arrival of Ikki Detachment . . . off RXI" (Guadalcanal code

name), apparently did not reach Vandegrift, in the view of Vandegrift's "in house historian" (Merillat, *Guadalcanal Remembered*, 87–88). However, it is questionable whether this warning message actually was sent out, as it is not recorded in the "Gray Book."

83. Ichiki Detachment Operation Order, Annex 1; *Senshi sōsho*, 225–26, 305 (trans. by Akio Tani); Okada, "Ichiki in Guadalcanal," June 4, 1984. All times cited in this book related to Japanese activity have been converted by the author from Japanese to Guadalcanal time, two hours later than the Tokyo time Ichiki's men followed.

84. Ichiki Detachment Order, Annexes I and II; Okada, "Ichiki in Guadalcanal," June 4, 1984; Hajime Yamamoto, "The First Battle on Guadalcanal: Annihilation of the Ichiki Detachment" (translated from the Japanese), in "Saiaku no semba" [The worst battlefield], *Maru* 5 (1987), 76.

85. *Senshi sōsho*, 295 (trans. by Akio Tani); Okada, "Ichiki in Guadalcanal," June 4, 1984; Phase III Report, 10. The 81st Guard Unit (west of Lunga) had sent Petty Officer 3rd Class Tan and five men, plus a radio operator, from its communications unit to Point Taivu to set up an East Observation Post, which began operating on July 5 (Stanley C. Jersey, *Hell's Islands*, 411; Kaneda, "Battle for Guadalcanal").

86. Ichiki Detachment Operation Order, Annexes I and II.

87. Okada, "Ichiki in Guadalcanal," June 4, 1984; *Senshi sōsho*, 305 (translation by Akio Tani).

88. Okada, "Ichiki in Guadalcanal," June 4, 1984; *Senshi sōsho*, 305 (translation by Akio Tani); Yamamoto, 'First Battle Guadalcanal."

89. Okada, "Ichiki in Guadalcanal," June 4, 1984; Stanley Jersey to Edward Rasmussen, February 24, 2004.

CHAPTER 5

1. Bōeicho Bōeikenshūjo Senshishitsu [Japanese Defense Agency, War History Section], *Senshi sōsho* [Official war history], Vol. 14, *Minami-taiheiyo Rikūgun Sakusen* (1) [Port Moresby–Guadalcanal initial operations], 306 (cited hereafter as *Senshi sōsho*) (trans. by Akio Tani). Of the total of 916 in Ichiki's first echelon, some forty of the supply/transportation unit had remained behind at Taivu Point (Stanley C. Jersey, *Hell's Islands*, 213).

2. Susumu Sugawara, *Ichiki Shitai zenmetsu* [Annihilation of the Ichiki Detachment], 94; road map of north coast of Guadalcanal, February 7, 1944, from Peter Flahavin. It is assumed that this coastal track was in existence in August 1942 too.

3. Ibid., 94; Okada, "Remembrance Ichiki on Guadalcanal," *Guadalcanal Echoes*, January 1986, 3.

4. Sugawara, *Ichiki Shitai zenmetsu*, 95.

5. Ibid., 94–95.

6. Ibid., 95–96; Jersey, *Hell's Islands*, 205; John L. Zimmerman, *The Guadalcanal Campaign*, 62.

7. Tomoteru Asahi, untitled memoir (in Japanese), n.d., translation in collection of Ewan Stevenson ; Sugawara, *Ichiki Shitai zenmetsu*, 102.

8. Sugawara, *Ichiki Shitai zenmetsu*, 96; Asahi memoir.

9. Sugawara, *Ichiki Shitai zenmetsu*, 96; September 1984 sketch by Akio Tani, *Guadalcanal Echoes*, January 1986; Jersey, *Hell's Islands*, 205; Asahi memoir; Sugawara, *Ichiki Shitai zenmetsu*, 109; 1st Marine Division, 1st Marine Regiment, "History of the First Marine Regiment," Phase

IV, 20 August–18 September, 9, File A-10-2, Box 42, Geographic Area Files—Guadalcanal, RG 127, NARA.

10. Hugh Morse and George Head, *"A"-1-1: Pearl Harbor to Peleliu*, 32; Eric Hammel, *Guadalcanal: Starvation Island*, 162; John J. Jachym interview with the author, December 1, 1998; John J. Jachym interview with Tom McLeod, ca. 2000.

11. John J. Jachym interview with Historical Section, US Marine Corps, Autumn 1944, in Zimmerman, *Guadalcanal Campaign*, 62; Jachym interviews with the author and with McLeod; Cpl. Henry R. Grimes, "The Empty Gun," in *Out in the Boondocks*, ed. James D. Horan and Gerold Frank, 49; Martin Clemens, *Alone on Guadalcanal: A Coastwatcher's Story*, 71, 206; Jersey, *Hell's Islands*, 205; Morse and Head, *"A"-1-1*, 32.

12. Morse and Head *"A"-1-1*, 32–33.

13. Chester Sliva e-mails to the author, March 28; April 3, 11, 2004.

14. Morse and Head *"A"-1-1*, 33; Jachym interview with Marine Corps Historical Section, interview with the author, and interview with McLeod; Hammel, *Guadalcanal*, 163. The village with the orange grove was evidently Koli.

15. Sugawara, *Ichiki Shitai zenmetsu*, 101.

16. Ibid., 102. Sugawara indicates that the village was Koli.

17. Ibid.

18. Ibid.; Jachym interview with Marine Corps Historical Section; Jachym interview with McLeod.

19. Sugawara, *Ichiki Shitai zenmetsu*, 103.

20. Jachym interviews with the author and with McLeod; Morse and Head, *"A"-1-1*, 33; Grimes, "Empty Gun," 50. Papangu, just to the west of Koli, is named as the village near where the Marines encountered the Japanese in the Navy Cross citation for Pvt. George Grazier. In his ca. 2000 interview with McLeod, Jachym recalled twelve men in his 1st Squad, but a rifle squad only numbered eight men. Grimes indicated that he was in front of the column, but [apparently] as squad leader of the 3rd squad, he would have been behind the 1st and 2nd Squads as well as the native scouts and Wild.

21. Grimes, "Empty Gun," 50; Jachym interviews with the author and with McLeod; Hammel, *Guadalcanal*, 33.

22. Sugawara, *Ichiki Shitai zenmetsu*, 103.

23. Jersey, *Hell's Islands*, 205; Sugawara, *Ichiki Shitai zenmetsu*, 103, 109.

24. Sugawara, *Ichiki Shitai zenmetsu*, 104.

25. Jachym interviews with the author and with McLeod. It is assumed that the men from the mortar section of Brush's weapons platoon and those from D Company's machine gun section remained under direct command of Brush in the engagement.

26. Jachym interviews with the author and with McLeod. For the positions in the flanking movement, see "Diagrammatic Sketch, Capt. Brush's Patrol, 19 August 1942," Annex A, "Defense Overlay," in Phase III Report.

27. John J. Jachym statement in *Guadalcanal Legacy: 50th Anniversary, 1942–1992*, 38.

28. Grimes, "Empty Gun," 50; Morse and Head, *"A"-1-1*, 33.

29. Grimes, "Empty Gun," 39–40, 50.

30. Ibid., 51–52. Grimes had apparently engaged the six men of Shibuya's radio squad near the tail of the reconnaissance party. He does not give the name of the corporal in his

wartime memoir, but the only corporal who could have been anywhere near him would have been Dobbins.

31. Ibid., 52.

32. Morse and Head, *"A"-1-1*, 33.

33. Ibid.

34. Ernest T. Dobbins, "A Squad on the Brush Patrol," *Guadalcanal Echoes,* March 1992, 31.

35. Morse and Head, *"A"-1-1*, 33; Grimes, "Empty Gun," 44; USMC records of casualties, Marine Corps History Division, Reference Branch.

36. Ernest T. Dobbins, "The Tenaru Patrol," *Old Breed News,* April 1992, 32, and Dobbins, "Squad on the Brush Patrol"; Ernest Dobbins Silver Star citation, *United States Marine Corps Headquarters Bulletin*, No. 212 (15 May 1943); Jachym interview with McLeod. It is assumed that Pfc. Henry Kent was the squad's other BAR man, as he was in November 1942 (A Company Roster, November 1942, in Morse and Head, *"A"-1-1*, 45).

37. Sugawara, *Ichiki Shitai zenmetsu*, 106, 109. Sugawara estimated that Lieutenants Hagiuda and Matsumoto were killed about 1350 (109).

38. Ibid., 107.

39. Ibid., 107, 109. Later, Sugawara (ibid., 162) contradicts himself by erroneously indicating Wada "was not involved in the fighting."

40. Ibid., 106.

41. Ibid., 107.

42. Ibid., 109.

43. Ibid., 108.

44. Ibid.

45. Jersey, *Hell's Islands*, 205; Samuel B. Griffith, *The Battle for Guadalcanal*, 82; Jachym interview with McLeod. In his 1944 interview with the Marine Corps Historical Section, Jachym indicated that the engagement had lasted fifty-five minutes (Zimmerman, *Guadalcanal Campaign*, 62), but in his interview with McLeod ca. 2000 he had reduced it to "about 45 minutes." Hammel, *Guadalcanal*, 163, gives thirty minutes only.

46. Jachym interview with McLeod; Griffith, *Battle for Guadalcanal*, 82.

47. Morse and Head, *"A"-1-1*, 33; Hammel, *Guadalcanal*, 163. Based on the fact that his 1st Rifle Squad was the only one in Jachym's platoon lacking a BAR man in November 1942, it is assumed that Gardner was in the 1st Squad up to the date of his death.

48. Herbert C. Merillat, *The Island*, 68; Navy Cross citation for George Grazier, *United States Marine Corps Headquarters Bulletin*, No. 213 (15 July 1943).

49. It is not documented to which squad Watts was assigned. The circumstances of his wounding are given in Marine Corps casualty records.

50. Clemens, *Alone on Guadalcanal*, 207; Jersey, *Hell's Islands*, 205. Chet Sliva, in an e-mail to the author, April 11, 2004, confirms that his machine gun squad did not participate in the fighting.

51. Jachym interview with McLeod; Phase III Report, 10–11; Griffith, *Battle for Guadalcanal*, 82; Clemens, *Alone on Guadalcanal*, 207. The figure for the number of dead accepted here that almost corresponds to Japanese figures (or thirty-four) is that of Jachym's interview with McLeod ca. 2000. In 1944 Jachym indicated thirty-one had been killed, while Jersey (*Hell's Islands*, 205) gives thirty-two dead.

One of the three Japanese lieutenants killed may initially have been only wounded in the exchange of firing, but from a story Richard Tregaskis heard at Vandegrift's command post the following day, he "had put his pistol to his head and killed himself" when approached by Brush (Richard Tregaskis, *Guadalcanal Diary*, 126). Such an incident is nowhere else reported in any account—including Japanese—the author has seen.

52. Jachym interviews with the author and with McLeod; Griffith, *Battle for Guadalcanal*, 82.

53. Maj. Charles H. Brush to Commandant, Marine Corps, January 15, 1949, quoted in Zimmerman, *Guadalcanal Campaign*, 62; Jachym interviews with the author and with McLeod. The map must have been taken from Captain Shibuya.

54. Hammel, *Guadalcanal*, 164; Jachym interview with the author.

55. Jachym interview with the author; Hammel, *Guadalcanal*, 163.

56. Jachym interview with the author; Hammel, *Guadalcanal*, 164; Brush to Commandant, quoted in Zimmerman, *Guadalcanal Campaign*, 62.

57. Hammel, *Guadalcanal*, 164; Morse and Head, *"A"-1-1*, 33; Jachym interview with McLeod. The August 1942 muster roll for A Company, 1st Battalion, 1st Marines (muster rolls, Marine Corps History Division, Reference Branch), indicates that Grazier, Gardner, and Buckhalt were buried in the "Hills" on August 19, but there was "no overlay for burial place."

58. Clemens, *Alone on Guadalcanal*, 206–7. Both scouts turned up safe two days later, reporting in to Australian Sub-Lt. Donald Macfarlan, who was working with Clemens (ibid., 211–12).

59. Dobbins, "Tenaru Patrol," 32; Jachym interview with the author. See "Traditions," www.marines.com/history-heritage/traditions and "222 Reasons to Love the Marine Corps," www.usmchangout.com/military/branches/usmc/misc/222reasons.htm#.Uxox1_ldV8E.

60. Morse and Head, *"A"-1-1*, 34; Dobbins, "Tenaru Patrol," 32.

61. Grimes, "Empty Gun," 53–54.

62. Ibid.

63. Sugawara, *Ichiki Shitai zenmetsu*, 112.

64. Ibid.

65. Ibid., 113.

66. Sadanobu Okada, "Ichiki in Guadalcanal," memoir, June 6, 1984, in author's collection; Sugawara, *Ichiki Shitai zenmetsu*, 113, 117.

67. Sugawara, *Ichiki Shitai zenmetsu*, 113. Four days later, on August 23, Wada was captured by four Marines on the left bank of the Tenaru as he was making his way on the government track towards Lunga in an attempt to rejoin his comrades (ibid., 114). He evidently did not know of the disaster that had befallen the detachment days earlier.

68. Ibid., 114.

69. Ibid., 115, 116.

70. Ibid., 116.

71. Ibid.

72. Ibid., 116, 126.

73. Ibid., 118–19. There is no place named "Lengo" on Guadalcanal, just a Lengo Channel off the northern coast in the Tetere area. However, it appears—based on the indication in the memoir of one of the detachment that the distance from "Lengo" to the airfield was ten kilo-

meters—that the area of Makile was the detachment's destination (Asahi, untitled memoir). In Okada's memory, the time the detachment was to set off was 1600, but 1700 appears more likely, as Higuchi had left at 1600, and it would have been some time later that the remaining troops would have been assembled and ready for departure.

74. Sugawara, *Ichiki Shitai zenmetsu*, 119; Hajime Yamamoto, "The First Battle on Guadalcanal: The Annihilation of the Ichiki Detachment" (in Japanese), in "Saiaku no semba" [The worst battlefield], *Maru* 5 (1987). Okada's reference to the order of battle ("Ichiki in Guadalcanal," June 7, 1984) is incorrect in that it includes the 1st Company, which had already left for Koli. It also differs substantially from the accounts of both Sugawara and Yamamoto, who are in agreement except that Yamamoto also erroneously includes the 1st Company.

75. Sugawara, *Ichiki Shitai zenmetsu*, 119–20.

76. Jachym interviews with the author and with McLeod; Brush to Commandant, quoted in Zimmerman, *Guadalcanal Campaign*, 62; Phase III Report, 10.

77. Grimes, "Empty Gun," 54.

78. Jachym interviews with the author and with McLeod; Morse and Head, *"A"-1-1*, 33–34. In the 1998 interview with the author, Jachym recalled being taken with Wild to "Headquarters." Most likely he was referring to battalion headquarters rather than division headquarters, and Brush would certainly have accompanied him.

79. Sugawara, *Ichiki Shitai zenmetsu*, 125.

80. Ibid., 119, 124.

81. Ibid., 120–21. Though it was not mentioned, the men were obviously also carrying 70 mm shells for the guns.

82. Ibid., 125.

83. Ibid., 126.

84. Ibid.

85. Ibid., 126–27.

86. Ibid., 127.

87. Ibid., 128.

88. Ibid.

89. Ibid., 127–28.

90. Evidently Sergeant Major Yamazaki's collection group had disinterred the bodies of Grazier, Gardner, and Buckhalt from their shallow graves. Marine Corps records confirm that Buckhalt's body was not recovered, nor were those of Grazier and Gardner, carried on American Battle Monument Commission records as "missing in action."

91. Sugawara, *Ichiki Shitai zenmetsu*, 129; Okada, "Ichiki in Guadalcanal," June 6, 1984.

92. Asahi memoir.

93. Sugawara, *Ichiki Shitai zenmetsu*, 129; Asahi memoir. Asahi gives 0200 (or 0400 Guadalcanal time) as the arrival hour, although Sugawara (129), *Senshi sōsho* (306), and Hajime Yamamoto, "The First Battle Guadalcanal: Annihilation of the Ichiki Detachment" [in Japanese], in "Saiaku no semba" [The worst battlefield], *Maru* 5 (1987), indicate 0230 (0430 Guadalcanal time).

94. James H. Couch, "A Marine's Story: My Four Years as a US Marine, January 9, 1942–January 15, 1946," memoir, n.d., in author's collection, 17.

95. Ibid. Colonel Pollock was sending out twenty-five-man patrols twice a day to inspect

the area between the Tenaru and Ilu Rivers (Combat Group B, 1st Marines (Reinforced), "Unit Report," August 19–20, 1942, in Larson personal collection). Robinson's group may have been part of the evening patrol.

96. Combat Group B, "Unit Report," August 19–20, 1942.

CHAPTER 6

1. Merrill B. Twining, *No Bended Knee*, 83; "Overseas Mission of the First Marine Division, Fleet Marine Force," File W2, Box 48, Geographic Files 1939–1949—Guadalcanal, RG 127, NARA; Herbert C. Merillat, *Guadalcanal Remembered*, 94; Richard B. Frank, *Guadalcanal*, 149.

How Ichiki knew about the defenses at the Tenaru and the artillery positions of the 11th Marines near the airfield is a mystery. It is possible that members of the 81st Guard Unit stationed earlier in the area contacted Ichiki with the information (Stanley Jersey e-mail to the author, July 30, 2004). Two had served as guards for the Shibuya reconnaissance and may have briefed Ichiki before he set out from Taivu Point.

2. Twining, *No Bended Knee*, 83; 1st Marine Division, Headquarters, "Division Commander's Final Report on Guadalanal Operation," 24 May 1943, Phase III: Organization of Lunga Point Defense, 10 August–21 August, Annex C, "Logistics," 10 (hereafter cited as Phase III Report), Box 39, Geographic Area Files—Guadalcanal, RG 127, NARA.

3. Twining, *No Bended Knee*, 83; Phase III Report, 10.

4. Twining, *No Bended Knee*, 83; Phase III Report, 11; Combat Group B, 1st Marines (Reinforced), "Unit Report," August 19–20, 1942, in Larson personal collection.

5. Susumu Sugawara, *Ichiki Shitai zenmetsu* [Annihilation of the Ichiki Detachment], 128.

6. Bōeicho Bōeikenshūjo Senshishitsu [Japanese Defense Agency, War History Section], *Senshi sōsho* [Official war history], Vol. 14, *Minami-taiheiyo Rikūgun Sakusen, 1* [Port Moresby–Guadalcanal initial operations] (hereafter cited as *Senshi sōsho*), 306, translated by Akio Tani for the author on April 29, 1990.

7. Ibid.

8. *Senshi sōsho,* 306 (trans. by Akio Tani, April 29, 1990); Yamamoto, "First Battle on Guadalcanal." Tani in a letter to the author of February 5, 1991, identified the Higashigawa as the (real) Tenaru River.

9. Sugawara, *Ichiki Shitai zenmetsu,* 123; Stanley C. Jersey, *Hell's Islands*, 208; Martin Clemens, *Alone on Guadalcanal: A Coastwatcher's Story*, 23, 209. The scout was Constable Sgt. Jacob Vouza, the most senior of Martin Clemens's scouts.

10. Edward J. Craig, memoir, 25; Edward Craig to the author, March 1, 1999; Charles Gambrell to the author, February 5, 2003.

11. Craig memoir, 25. Much later, when Craig was serving at division headquarters in Melbourne, he saw a Japanese report indicating that Ichiki had deliberately permitted a small American patrol that had reached the Ilu to return to the Marine perimeter (Craig memoir, 25; Craig to the author, March 1, 1999). It is likely that Craig had seen the tracks of a patrol from Captain Sawada's company bivouacked only about one mile to the east that morning. Curiously enough, a morning patrol of twenty-five men returning from an inspection of the area between the Tenaru and Ilu Rivers "had nothing to report" to Pollock (2nd Battalion, 1st Marines (Reinforced), "Unit Report," 1800 16 August to 1800 17 August 1942, A. William Larson personal collection).

12. John Howland, "Tenaru River Fight," letter, *Harvard Alumni Bulletin,* April 24, 1943; Martin Holt, telephone interview with the author, October 23, 1999; Eben Babbidge, telephone interview with the author, November 12, 2002; Gen. Clifton B. Cates, interview with Benis Frank, Oral History Transcript, 1973, 139–40; Edwin A. Pollock diary, August 19, 1942 (*sic*), in author's collection.

13. Combat Group B, "Unit Report," August 19–20, 1942; Robert Leckie, *Challenge for the Pacific*, 118.

14. Leckie, *Challenge*, 118; Robert Leckie, *Helmet for My Pillow*, 75; Frank Stewart, "Tenaru River Guadalcanal" (ca. 1944), in Ipswich World War II Celebration official souvenir program, August 13–September 2, 1995; Frank Stewart telephone interview with the author, July 5, 1999; Frank Stewart e-mails to the author, August 5, 1999.

15. Leckie, *Challenge*, 118–19; Frank Stewart telephone interview with the author, January 15, 2000.

16. Leckie, *Challenge*, 119.

17. William Whorf, "Cross Section at the Tenaru," November 30, 1998, in author's collection; William Whorf to the author, July 21, 1998, and March 3, 1999; Combat Group B, "Unit Report," August 19–20, 1942; Edward Manning to the author, August 3, 1998; Paul Leblanc to the author, September 12, 1998; William Whorf, telephone interview with the author, November 25, 1998.

18. Albert A. Schmid, "An Eye for Two Hundred Japs," in *Out in the Boondocks*, ed. James D. Horan and Gerold Frank, 22; Leckie, *Challenge*, 119; Whorf to the author, July 21, 1998; Roger Butterfield, *Al Schmid, Marine*, 97. There is some disagreement between Schmid and Leckie on the time of the hospital visit.

19. Whorf to the author, July 21, October 17, 1998, and March 3, 1999; Butterfield, *Al Schmid*, 97. Contradicting Whorf, Pvt. Joe Mills maintains that he, not Warren, was the gunner and Pfc. Ralph Hall was the assistant gunner, while not mentioning Whatley and indicating that Warren was the squad leader (Joseph E. Mills, "World War II—1941–1945," undated memoir, 10, in author's collection; Joseph Mills to the author, August 3, 1999). It seems unlikely that Warren, as a private first class rather than a corporal, would have been the squad leader.

20. Whorf to the author, July 21, 1998, and March 3, 1999.

21. Maj. Charles H. Brush to Commandant, Marine Corps, January 15, 1949, quoted in Zimmerman, *Guadalcanal Campaign*, 62; Combat Group B, 1st Marines (Reinforced), "Operation Order 6-42," August 14, 1942, File B-10-1, Box 45, Geographic Files 1939–1949—Guadalcanal, RG 127, NARA; John Speaks e-mail to the author, October 19, 1999; George Dennis, diary, August 20, 1942, in author's collection.

22. Brush to Commandant, in Zimmerman, *Guadalcanal Campaign*, 62 (see also 67).

23. Hugh Corrigan to the author, July 12, 1998; Stewart, "Tenaru River"; Joseph Repko to the author, June 30, 1998; Thomas Brown to the author, November 5, 1998.

24. Dale Lyth to the author, July 15, 1998; C. Andrew Dillman to the author, July 11, 1998; Stewart, "Tenaru River."

25. Leckie, *Challenge*, 119; Joel Hogeland to the author, July 3, 1998; James Olliff to the author, February 4, 1999; Clair Hume telephone interview with the author, January 27, 1999; Thomas McAnally to the author, December 6, 1999.

26. Leckie, *Challenge*, 119; Thomas McAnally to the author, June 4, 1999.

27. Col. John P. Leonard interview with Benis Frank, transcript, 46–47, History and Museums Division, Headquarters, US Marine Corps.

28. Combat Group B, 1st Marines (Reinforced), "Unit Report," August 19–20, 1942; McAnally to the author, June 4, October 18, 1999.

29. Glenn Campbell to the author, December 2, 1998; Glen Campbell, "August 21, 1942," memoir, December 10, 1998, in author's collection; Angelo Catullo to the author, February 8, 1999; A. Thomas Palmer to the author, January 27, 1999; Gaetano Mazzarella to the author, December 28, 1998. The author has not found information on the location of the third 37 mm gun of McClanahan's platoon or who crewed it.

30. George Parker to the author, September 11, October 19, and November 12, 1999; Whorf to the author, August 28, 1998; McAnally to the author, December 6, 1999.

31. McAnally to the author, June 4, 1999.

32. Mel Berge to the author, October 11, 17, 2002.

33. Theodore "Tobe" Cogswell to the author, January 1, 1999, and e-mail to the author, January 20, 1999; Cliff Fox to the author, January 12, 1999.

34. Martin Holt, telephone interview with the author, October 23, 1999; George Codrea to Harry Horsman, April 22, 1990.

35. Codrea to Horsman, April 22, 1990.

36. Charles Royer to the author, August 31, 1999; John Williams, "What Happened in World War II," memoir, n.d., 17, in author's collection; Don Moss, "Battle of the Tenaru," *Guadalcanal Echoes,* January 1993; Peter Martuscelli to the author, September 15, 1999; Cecil Powell, interview with the author, August 5, 1999; Lester Sapp to the author, September 19, 1999; A. William Larson to the author, October 1, 1999; Lugene Chesnut to the author, August 15, 2000; Anthony Kelly to Charles Royer, September 21, 1999.

37. Combat Group B, 1st Marines (Reinforced), "Unit Report," August 16–17 and August 20–21, 1942; Fred Wilburn to the author, December 18, 1998; Joseph Dusina to the author, September 9, 1999; Martuscelli to the author, September 15 and November 11, 1999.

38. Donald Wheaton to parents, November 14, 1942, published in *Central Hanover Observer,* March 1943, 1–2; Clyde Lucas to the author, January 29, 1999; Leonard Ray to the author, June 30, 1998; Lester W. Clark, *An Unlikely Arena*, 35; John Tatum to the author, March 25, 2000.

39. John Tatum diary, August 20, 1942, in author's collection; Edward O'Soro to the author, November 25, 1998; James Moncrief to the author, August 6, 1999.

40. Sidney C. Phillips, "'You'll Be Sor-ree': The Memoirs of a US Marine Private during the Pacific Campaign of World War II," manuscript, 11, in author's collection.

41. Gen. Edwin A. Pollock interview with Maj. Thomas E. Donnelly, Oral History Transcript, 1977, History and Museums Division, Headquarters, US Marine Corps, Washington, DC, 134; Pollock diary, August 20, 1942; William Whorf diary, August 20, 1942, in author's collection; George P. Hunt, "First Days on Guadalcanal," undated memoir, 18, in Lt. Gen. Edwin A. Pollock Papers, Parris Island Museum, US Marine Corps Recruitment Depot, Parris Island, SC. The planes were twelve SBD Dauntlesses of VMSB-132 and nineteen F4Fs of VMF-223 that had been catapulted off the little aircraft ferry *Long Island* 190 miles out to sea (Thomas G. Miller, Jr., *The Cactus Air Force*, 25).

42. Hand-drawn map by Robert Askey of location of batteries of 11th Marines, in Askey to the author, November 18, 1998; John Frothingham to the author, February 10, 1999; Ben Wofford and William R. White, *The Marine: A Guadalcanal Survivor's Final Battle*, 68; Pedro Del Valle, "Marine Field Artillery on Guadalcanal," *Guadalcanal Echoes,* January 1990, 19; War Department, *Field Artillery Field Manual FM 6-40*, 74.

43. Wofford and White, *Marine*, 68; Del Valle, "Marine Field Artillery," *Guadalcanal Echoes*, January 1990, 19; Nathaniel Mewhinney to the author, May 12, 1999, and August 4, 2003; Lester Clark to the author, June 26, 1999.

44. Robert Askey, diary, August 20 and 21, 1942, entries, in author's collection; Robert Askey e-mail to the author, December 17, 1999; Zigmund Gasiewicz to the author, August 4, 1999; Del Valle, "Marine Field Artillery," *Guadalcanal Echoes*, January 1990, 19; Samuel B. Griffith II, *The Battle for Guadalcanal*, 83.

45. *Senshi sōsho*, 306 (trans. by Akio Tani). The scout reported that he had killed the native when he ran away. Yamamoto also indicates the guide was killed, as he attempted to run away, by the Japanese scout's interpreter. However, there is no documentation (including Clemens's authoritative account *Alone on Guadalcanal*), that any native was killed, nor that any of his native scouts accompanied the Japanese.

46. Clemens, *Alone on Guadalcanal*, 209–10. The native was Vouza, of course.

47. Sadanobu Okada, "Ichiki in Guadalcanal," memoir, June 7, 1984, trans. by Akio Tani, in author's collection; Jersey, *Hell's Islands*, 209. Akio Tani (interview with the author, February 5, 1991) indicates the "next river" was the Hebigawa, the location of which corresponds to Block Four River.

48. Sugawara, *Ichiki Shitai zenmetsu*, 145; *Senshi sōsho*, 306 (trans. by Akio Tani); Yamamoto, "First Battle Guadalcanal."

49. Sugawara, *Ichiki Shitai zenmetsu*, 145.

50. Ibid. Sugawara's account may be incorrect. Jersey (*Hell's Islands*, 209) indicates it was the Japanese, not the Marines, who had set off the flares in order to see where they were going. Individual Marine accounts back up this assertion. According to a Marine intelligence report, the signal on Guadalcanal for a Japanese Army assault at night was "a flare fired (by a platoon leader) to hang over the objective" (M. Edson, "Notes on Japanese Tactics and Techniques," Miscellaneous Intelligence Report, File C-15-2, Box 46, Geographic Area Files—Guadalcanal, RG 127, NARA). Japanese troops were equipped with star shells fired from their Type 89 grenade launchers (War Department, *Handbook of Japanese Military Forces*, 322).

51. Sugawara, *Ichiki Shitai zenmetsu*, 145.

52. Ibid. Ohashi's watch would have indicated 2230 Japanese time, of course.

53. Lester Sapp to the author, September 19, 1999; Cecil Powell interview with the author, August 5, 1999; George Turzai, untitled memoir, 1999, in author's collection; Eric Hammel, *Guadalcanal: Starvation Island*, 167.

54. Pollock interview with Donnelly, 135–36; Albert Wilson to the author, January 6, 1999; Sugawara, *Ichiki Shitai zenmetsu*, 145.

55. Clyde Lucas to the author, October 9 and December 20, 1998; James A. Donahue, "Guadalcanal Journal," 1942, in author's collection; Clark, *Unlikely Arena*, 36.

56. Turzai memoir; Peter Martuscelli to the author, September 15, 1999; Donald F. Moss,

"What Was It Like in the Olden Days, Dad? An Illustrated Memoir," no date, 23; Charles Royer to the author, April 28, 2000; Tobe Cogswell to the author, January 1, 1999; Clark, *Unlikely Arena*, 36.

CHAPTER 7

1. Susumu Sugawara, *Ichiki Shitai zenmetsu* [Annihilation of the Ichiki Detachment], 145.

2. Ibid. At the time Ohashi crossed, it was high tide, when the sandbar connecting the two banks was under twelve to sixteen inches of water. Sugawara indicates that only 20 men were in Ohashi's platoon, but with a company strength of 105 men, and three platoons to a company, it would seem that the total in Ohashi's platoon would have been nearer 35 men.

3. As related by Hayashi in ibid., 146, 171.

4. As related by Mizuno in ibid., 146.

5. Ibid., 147. A relatively new addition to Ichiki's detachment and Sawada's company after being commissioned a second lieutenant, Ohashi would not survive the evening.

6. Ibid., 147; Sadanobu Okada, "Ichiki in Guadalcanal," memoir, June 7, 1984, trans. by Akio Tani, in author's collection.

7. Sugawara, *Ichiki Shitai zenmetsu*, 148–49. At the Battle of Nomonhan, the 2nd Battalion of the 28th Infantry suffered twenty-four of its twenty-eight officers killed or wounded (Edward Drei to the author, September 13, 2009). Sawada was one of the wounded.

8. Ibid.

9. Ibid., 149.

10. Glenn Campbell to the author, December 10, 1998; Glenn Campbell, "August 21, 1942," memoir, December 10, 1998, in author's collection; Clair Hume, telephone interview with the author, February 22, 1999.

11. Campbell, "August 21, 1942."

12. Ibid.

13. Peter Martuscelli to the author, September 15, 1999.

14. Roger Butterfield, *Al Schmid, Marine*, 96–97; Albert A. Schmid, "An Eye for Two Hundred Japs," in *Out in the Boondocks*, ed. James D. Horan and Gerold Frank, 20, 24; William Whorf to the author, March 3, 1999.

15. Angelo Catullo to the author, February 8, 1999.

16. Butterfield, *Al Schmid*, 97.

17. C. Andrew Dillman to the author, July 11, 1998. Later in the same letter Dillman writes that he was told by a squad mate that the firing pin on the gun was broken.

18. Ibid., and C. Andrew Dillman to the author, August 28, 1998; Joel Hogeland to the author, July 3, 1998, and entry in First Marine Division Association, *First Marine Division: Guadalcanal*, 159; Frank Stewart, "Tenaru River, Guadalcanal," in Ipswich World War II Celebration official souvenir program, August 13–September 2, 1995.

19. Dillman recalled yelling "Lucky Strike," but "Quill" was the password for the day.

20. Hogeland to the author, July 3, 1998.

21. Mel Berge to the author, September 18, 2002.

22. James Olliff to the author, February 4, 18, 1999; Hume telephone interview, February 22, 1999; Hugh Kay to the author, December 31, 1999.

23. Hume telephone interview, February 22, 1999; Olliff to the author, February 18, 1999; Kay to the author, December 31, 1999.

24. It is assumed that it was a "knee mortar" that had caused the explosion, as Ichiki's detachment had bought no real mortars with it. Each Japanese infantry platoon included a squad with three to four such weapons. Actually, the "knee mortar" was a Model 89 50 mm Heavy Grenade Discharger, which could fire an 11 pound 12 ounce high-explosive shell as well as a standard fragmentation grenade (Henry I. Shaw, Jr., *First Offensive: The Marine Campaign for Guadalcanal*, 45).

25. A. Thomas Palmer telephone interview with the author, January 27, 1999; USMC casualty reports, Marine Corps History Division, Reference Branch.

26. Campbell, "August 21, 1942." The detent in the breechblock had come out from the explosion of the grenade.

27. The corpsman was most likely PhM2C Jimmy Ury, attached to Palmer's platoon from 1st Special Weapons Battalion headquarters. Ury was awarded the Silver Star for risking his life to bring in wounded men of the platoon, probably including Locke and Stevenson (Headquarters and Service Battery, 1st Special Weapons Battalion, 1st Marine Division, muster roll, August 1942, Marine Corps History Division, Reference Branch; Herbert C. Merillat, *The Island*, 259).

28. George Turzai, untitled memoir, 1999, in author's collection; George Turzai to the author, September 16, 1999; Eric Hammel, *Guadalcanal: Starvation Island*, 167–68.

29. Lester Sapp to the author, September 4, 1999.

30. James Brady Wadsworth, untitled memoir, n.d., in author's collection; William Whorf diary, August 21, 1942, in author's collection.

31. Edmond Louisignan, telephone interview with the author, November 2, 2002; Robert McMillan, telephone interview with the author, October 29, 2002.

32. Sugawara, *Ichiki Shitai zenmetsu*, 151.

33. Ibid., 152–53. For an excellent analysis of Japanese Army infantry doctrine, see Edward J. Drea, "The Japanese Army on the Eve of War," chapter 4 in *The Battle for China*, ed. Mark Peattie, Edward J. Drea, and Hans van de Ven, 111–116, and Edward J. Drea, *In the Service of the Emperor*, 1–13, 63.

34. Sugawara, *Ichiki Shitai zenmetsu*, 153. Sawada apparently wanted Ichiki to wait for the two 70 mm guns to be brought up before launching another attack across the mouth of the river.

35. Ibid.

36. Ibid., 154.

37. Edwin A. Pollock diary, August 21, 1942, in author's collection; Gen. Edwin A. Pollock interview with Maj. Thomas E. Donnelly, Oral History Transcript, History and Museums Division, Headquarters, US Marine Corps, Washington, DC, 138; Martin Clemens, *Alone on Guadalcanal: A Coastwatcher's Story*, 209–10.

38. Clemens, *Alone on Guadalcanal*, 209.

39. Ibid.; "Jacob Vouza Tells What Happened," *Old Breed News*, April–June 2012.

40. W. F. Bewley, "The Night I led Vouza through the Lines," *Guadalcanal Echoes*, January 1985, 9.

41. Clemens, *Alone on Guadalcanal*, 210; Pollock diary, August 21, 1942; "Jacob Vouza Tells What Happened," *Old Breed News*, April–June 2012. It was well known that Guadalcanal natives were inaccurate in estimating numbers.

42. Clemens, *Alone on Guadalcanal*, 210; Pollock diary, August 21, 1942.

43. Olliff to the author, February 4, 18, and May 29, 1999; Hugh Kay to the author, December 31, 1999; Hume telephone interview, February 22, 1999.

44. Campbell, "August 21, 1942."

45. Ibid.

46. Sugawara, *Ichiki Shitai zenmetsu*, 154.

47. Olliff to the author, February 4, 1999; Wadsworth memoir; Dean Wilson telephone interview with the author, April 19, 2001. Behind Olliff's, Berge's 37 mm gun may have been firing, too.

48. Hume, telephone interview, February 22, 1999; Sapp to the author, September 19, 1999. The Japanese would have been the men of Lieutenant Kudō's platoon.

49. Pollock diary, August 21, 1942; Pollock interview with Donnelly, 138; Eben Babbidge, telephone interview with the author, November 12, 2002. Chalfant was replaced as executive officer on October 3, 1942 (John L. Zimmerman, *The Guadalcanal Campaign*, 182).

50. Sugawara, *Ichiki Shitai zenmetsu*, 154; Okada, "Ichiki in Guadalcanal," June 7, 1984. Ichiki evidently also decided that his infantry should use rifle fire instead of just their bayonets (and grenades) in combating the enemy.

CHAPTER 8

1. Susumu Sugawara, *Ichiki Shitai zenmetsu* [Annihilation of the Ichiki Detachment], 159.

2. Ibid., 160.

3. Ibid.

4. Ibid. List of platoon leaders in Akio Tani to the author, May 31, 1990.

5. Sugawara, *Ichiki Shitai zenmetsu*, 163.

6. Ibid.

7. Ibid., 155.

8. Ibid., 172, 174. Sugawara (ibid., 155) erroneously assumes that Satō's platoon joined up too.

9. Ibid., 156, 165; Mae, as related to Sugawara, ibid., 176.

10. Translation of Tomoteru Asahi's untitled memoir in Ewan Stevenson private collection.

11. Sugawara, *Ichiki Shitai zenmetsu*, 156

12. Ibid., 168–69; specifications for the Type 92 heavy machine gun (War Department, *Handbook on Japanese Military Forces,* Technical Manual E-30-480, 197).

13. Sugawara, *Ichiki Shitai zenmetsu*, 172, 174 (as amended by the author). Evidently the engineers were split between Higuchi's and Chiba's assault groups.

14. George P. Hunt, "First Days on Guadalcanal," undated memoir, 19, in Lt. Gen. Edwin A. Pollock Papers, Parris Island Museum, US Marine Corps Recruitment Depot, Parris Island, SC; Richard Tregaskis, *Guadalcanal Diary*, 127.

15. Hunt, "First Days," 19; Edwin A. Pollock diary, August 21, 1942, in author's collection; Gen. Edwin A. Pollock interview with Maj. Thomas E. Donnelly, Oral History Transcript, History and Museums Division, Headquarters, US Marine Corps, 138.

16. Hunt, "First Days," 19–20, 21; Gen. Clifton B. Cates, "My First at Guadalcanal: 7 Au-

gust–22 December 1942," unpublished memoir, 25, History and Museums Division, Headquarters, US Marine Corps.

17. Pollock diary, August 21, 1942; Pollock interview with Donnelly, 139; "History of the 2nd Battalion, 1st Marines," 6, in Lt. Gen. Edwin A. Pollock Papers, Parris Island Museum, US Marine Corps Recruitment Depot, Parris Island, SC; John L. Zimmerman, *The Guadalcanal Campaign*, 68; Combat Group B, 1st Marines (Reinforced), "Unit Report No. 13," from 1800 20 August to 1800 21 August 1942, File A-10-2, Box 42, Geographic Files 1939–1949—Guadalcanal, RG 127, NARA.

18. George Codrea to Harry Horsman, April 22, 1990.

19. Ibid.; George Codrea interview with the author, November 30, 1998.

20. Mills maintains he was the gunner (Joseph E. Mills, "World War II—1941–1945," undated memoir, 10, in author's collection; Joseph Mills to the author, August 3, 1999), but Whorf indicates the gunner was Warren.

21. Clair Hume, telephone interview with the author, February 22, 1999; James Olliff to the author, February 4, 1999. Berge's 37 mm gun may also have been firing at the new wave of Japanese.

22. Glenn Campbell, "August 21, 1942," memoir, December 10, 1998, in author's collection.

23. Lester Sapp to the author, September 4, 1999.

24. Eric Hammel, *Guadalcanal: Starvation Island*, 170; James Brady Wadsworth, untitled memoir, n.d., in author's collection; Dean Wilson, telephone interview with the author, April 19, 2001.

25. Wilson telephone interview.

26. Ibid.; Hammel, *Guadalcanal*, 170–71; George Hunt, "The Terrible Handful," *Mechanix Illustrated,* March 1944, 37.

27. George Turzai, untitled memoir, 1999, in author's collection.

28. Ibid. But this recollection conflicts with that of Campbell (see chapter 9).

29. Sugawara, *Ichiki Shitai zenmetsu*, 188.

30. Ibid.; List of Ichiki Detachment officers in Akio Tani to the author, May 31, 1990.

31. Sadanobu Okada, "Ichiki in Guadalcanal," memoir, June 7, 1984, trans. by Akio Tani, in author's collection; Adam Headley, "Sergeant Okada Survived the Bloody Tenaru Engagement on the Island of Death—Guadalcanal," *Military History,* March 1993, 63.

32. Okada, "Ichiki in Guadalcanal," June 7, 1984; Sugawara, *Ichiki Shitai zenmetsu*, 189. The fire was evidently canister from George Parker's 37 mm gun and the machine guns of Fridley and Wright.

33. Codrea to Horsman, April 22, 1990; George Codrea, interviews with the author, June 4, 1998, and November 1, 1999.

34. Codrea to Horsman, April 22, 1990; Codrea interview, November 1, 1999.

35. Codrea to Horsman, April 22, 1990; Codrea interviews, June 4, 1998, and September 29, 1999; Hunt, "First Days," 22; Hunt, "Terrible Handful," 37.

36. Jack Shea, telephone interview with the author, January 13, 1999; Hunt, "Terrible Handful," 37–38; Hunt, "First Days," 22; Hammel, *Guadalcanal*, 169–70; Harry Horsman to George Codrea, October 17, 1990, and October 16, 1998; George Codrea, telephone interviews with the author, November 25, 1998, and January 14, 1999; Codrea interviews with the author, November 30, 1998, and November 1, 1999.

37. Evan M. Wylie, "That Fearful Night on the Tenaru River," *Yankee,* August 1982, 76–77; Andrew Brodecki, untitled memoir, May 5, 1980, in author's collection.

38. Richard W. Harding, "Battle for a Foxhole," in *Out in the Boondocks,* ed. James D. Horan and Gerold Frank, 32–33.

39. Ibid., 33–34.

40. Hunt, "Terrible Handful," 37; Shea telephone interview, January 13, 1999.

41. Harding, "Battle," 35–36.

42. Ibid.

43. Codrea to Horsman, April 22, 1990; Codrea interview, September 29, 1999; Tregaskis, *Guadalcanal Diary,* 151.

44. Codrea to Horsman, April 22, 1990, and January 19, 1998; Codrea interviews, June 4, 1998, and September 29, 1999.

45. Hunt, "First Days," 22–23.

46. Robert Flick, telephone interview with the author, August 30, 2002; Codrea interviews, September 29, 1999, and November 1, 1999.

47. James E. Wilson, "Battle of the Tenaru River," *Old Breed News,* June 1999, 15.

48. Ibid.; Flick telephone interview with the author, August 29, 2002; G Company, 2nd Battalion, 1st Marine Regiment, muster roll, August 1942, Marine Corps History Division, Reference Branch. Tefertiller was a Native American.

49. Later, Wilson found that the bullet that hit him had cut the head strap of his helmet, shattering the back of the helmet, with pieces lodging near his spine that had made him numb from the waist down.

50. Wylie, "Fearful Night," 91; Luther Jordan to the author, December 8, 1998.

51. James Boston, untitled memoir, 1943, in author's collection; James Hancock, "Battle with the Enemy in the Solomons," letter to his mother published in an unidentified newspaper, ca. 1943.

52. George Parker to the author, October 19, 1999.

53. Ibid.

54. Roger Butterfield, *Al Schmid, Marine,* 97; William Whorf to the author, March 3, 1999.

55. Butterfield, *Al Schmid,* 97. Contrary to Schmid's recollection, assistant gunner Joe Mills maintains that Warren's gun "kept going all night" (Mills, "World War II," 10). Neither Warren nor Mills was hit by Japanese fire, according to H Company's August muster roll. Perhaps their machine gun was only temporarily out of action for some reason.

56. Butterfield, *Al Schmid,* 98; Robert Leckie, *Helmet for My Pillow,* 81.

57. Butterfield, *Al Schmid,* 99.

58. Leckie, *Helmet,* 82. Leckie doesn't indicate who must have been carrying boxes of belted .30-caliber ammunition for their gun.

59. Ibid.

60. Edward Manning to the author, August 3, 1998.

61. Ibid.; William Whorf, "Cross Section at the Tenaru," November 30, 1998, and William Whorf diary, August 21, 1942, both in author's collection.

62. John Joseph to Wilbur Bewley, August 1998.

63. Robert W. Fincher interview with Mike Miller, transcript, Alfred M. Gray Marine Corps Research Center, Marine Corps Base Quantico, VA, August 9, 2004; John Speaks, e-mail to the author, October 19, 1999.

64. Fincher interview with Miller.

65. Ibid. Speaks does not recall that his platoon, attached to B Company, was under direct fire, being positioned too far from the action taking place to its left. However, Fincher sixty-two years later had a vivid memory of his traumatic experience that evening.

66. Sugawara, *Ichiki Shitai zenmetsu*, 167–69.

67. As related by Yoshimasa to Sugawara, ibid., 178.

68. Pfc. Takeshi Makabe's account in ibid., 185.

69. Naokichi Nakayama's account in ibid., 190.

70. Ibid.

71. Stanley Jersey, *Hell's Islands*, 210; Sugawara, *Ichiki Shitai zenmetsu*, 191. Sugawara indicates that the machine gun was that of a "turret" of the "amphibious tank" rather than one of the Japanese weapons. However, it appears unlikely that this particular LVT still mounted its two machine guns on the cab and carried enough ammunition to fire for so long at the Marines. Jersey identifies it as a machine gun of Matsuo's platoon.

72. Sugawara, *Ichiki Shitai zenmetsu*, 192.

73. Takeshi Makabe's account in ibid.

74. Cates, "My First at Guadalcanal," 25; Hunt, "Terrible Handful," 36–37; Hunt, "First Days," 21.

75. Hunt, "Terrible Handful," 37; Hunt, "First Days," 21; Richard B. Frank, *Guadalcanal*, 153; Robert Lyon, telephone interview with the author, August 26, 2003.

76. Robert Askey, e-mail to the author, November 10, 1998.

77. Ibid.; Hunt, "Terrible Handful," 36–37; Hunt, "First Days," 21; Field Artillery School, *Abbreviated Firing Tables*, Table A, Fort Sill, 1942, 22; 1st Marine Division, Headquarters, "Division Commander's Final Report on Guadalcanal Operation," 24 May 1943, Phase IV: 20 August–18 September, Annex E, "Artillery," Geographic Files 1949—Guadalcanal, RG 127, NARA.

78. Lyon telephone interview, August 26, 2003; Hammel, *Guadalcanal*, 171.

79. Crotty, as related in Lester W. Clark, *An Unlikely Arena*, 36.

80. Clyde Lucas to the author, October 9, December 20, 1998, and as related by Lucas to Sidney C. Phillips in "'You'll Be Sor-ree': The Memoirs of a US Marine Private during the Pacific Campaign of World War II," manuscript, 58, in author's collection.

81. Clark, *Unlikely Arena*, 37; John Tatum, diary, August 21, 1942, in author's collection; James A. Donahue, "Guadalcanal Journal," 1942, in author's collection. The collar of the Japanese officer had an insignia of two stars, indicating a first lieutenant (Tatum diary, August 21, 1942). He must have been 1st Lieutenant Maruyama, the commander of the Third Company. Some of Maruyama's men—evidently including Maruyama himself—had managed to ford the river and hold a position on the Marines' bank, according to reports of wounded survivors who had managed to get back to the other side (Hajime Yamamoto, "The First Battle Guadalcanal: Annihilation of the Ichiki Detachment" [in Japanese], in "Saiaku no semba" [The worst battlefield], *Maru*, Vol. 5 [1987]).

82. Donahue, "Guadalcanal Journal"; Lucas to the author, January 29, August 4, 1999; Tatum diary, August 21, 1942; Edward O'Soro, diary, August 20, 1942, in author's collection; Leonard Ray to the author, June 30, 1998. The shells falling short must have been among those fired at 0403 and 0515 by the 11th Marines. Very near Lucas, Lieutenant Wheaton also "had a close call" when a "70 mm" exploded near his foxhole (Donald Wheaton, letter to parents,

November 14, 1942, printed in the *Hanover Observer*, March 1943), but it may have been from a 70 mm howitzer of Lieutenant Hanami's platoon rather than from a 75 mm pack howitzer.

83. Donahue, "Guadalcanal Journal"; Wheaton letter to parents, November 14, 1942; Arthur Dignan to the author, November 25, 1998.

84. Dignan to the author, November 25, 1998; Tatum diary, August 21, 1942. Beer died on August 23, 1942, on the destroyer evacuating him from Guadalcanal and was buried at sea (H Company, 2nd Battalion, 1st Marine Regiment, muster roll, August 1942 (microfilm), Marine Corps History Division, Reference Branch; "Leonard T. Beer, Jr.," www.wwiimemorial.com/registry/mia/search/pframe.asp?HonoreeID=740715&popcount=3&tcount=5).

85. Donahue, "Guadalcanal Journal." The two crews were evidently from the machine gun section of the weapons platoon of F Company. However, if so, none of the men were killed or wounded, according to the August 1942 muster roll of F Company. Don Wheaton wrote in his November letter home that another company "of about 150 men" reinforced the H Company mortar men and others with them in combat on the line during the night (Wheaton, letter to parents, November 14, 1942).

86. Donahue, "Guadalcanal Journal"; James D. Donahue e-mail to the author, August 5, 2012; Tatum diary, August 21, 1942.

CHAPTER 9

1. Albert Schlemmer, "August 21, 1942, as I Remember It or What I Can Remember," October 1998, in author's collection; Edward Claffey telephone interview with Albert Schlemmer; Albert Schlemmer to the author, February 7, 1999.

2. James H. Couch, "A Marine's Story: My Four Years as a US Marine, January 9, 1942–January 15, 1946," n.d., 18, in author's collection.

3. George P. Hunt, "First Days on Guadalcanal," undated memoir, 23, 25, in Lt. Gen. Edwin A. Pollock Papers, Parris Island Museum, US Marine Corps Recruitment Depot, Parris Island, SC.

4. Couch, "Marine's Story," 18.

5. Albert Schlemmer to the author, August 27, 1998, and Schlemmer memoir. Schlemmer and the others apparently took over Glenn Campbell's gun while Campbell was away and the other gun crew members were absent due to wounds. However, E Company's Turzai and Moesner have a similar recollection of taking over the gun themselves.

6. Schlemmer memoir; Schlemmer e-mail to the author, July 17, 2002.

7. Schlemmer memoir; Schlemmer e-mail to the author, July 17, 2002; Couch, "Marine's Story," 18–19.

8. Schlemmer memoir; Schlemmer e-mail to the author, July 17, 2002; Couch, "Marine's Story," 19.

9. Fred Metcalf, telephone interview with the author, November 20, 2002; G Company, 2nd Battalion, 1st Marine Regiment (G-2-1), muster roll, August 1942, Marine Corps History Division, Reference Branch.

10. Schlemmer memoir; Schlemmer e-mail to the author, July 22, 1999; G-2-1 muster roll, August 1942. The circumstances of the deaths of Holcombe and McHale are unknown.

11. J. Luther Jordan to the author, December 8, 1998; William Finnegan to the author, January 26, March 10, 1999.

12. Louis Imfeld, telephone interview with the author, December 9, 1998; Louis Imfeld to the author, December 13, 1998, and December 6, 1999. The section evidently manned the twenty-five-man night outpost cited in the 2nd Battalion's unit report prepared by Larson for the twenty-four-hour period, 6 pm August 19 to 6 pm, August 20.

13. Paul Hanlon to the author, January 26, 1999.

14. Edward Craig, memoir, 26; Charles Gambrell to the author, November 26, 2002.

15. Craig memoir, 26.

16. Ibid. From Pollock's order to Craig, it would appear that Captain Sherman had left his command post and joined his men in the combat area.

17. Gambrell to the author, December 11, 2002.

18. Craig memoir, 27, 29; Edward Craig to the author, March 1, 1999.

19. Gambrell to the author, January 5, 2003.

20. Craig memoir, 26.

21. Gambrell to the author, December 11, 2002, and January 5, February 5, 2003; J. Barrett Nelson, son of Marion Nelson, telephone interview with the author, January 28, 2003.

22. Craig memoir, 27.

23. Ibid.; Gambrell to the author, January 5, 2003.

24. Craig memoir, 29; Navy Cross citation for William Wolvington, *United States Marine Corps Headquarters Bulletin*, No. 213 (15 July 1943). It is not known where and from which weapons platoon machine gun section Wolvington had found the light machine gun. It may have been from one of the two crews of F Company's weapons platoon that are believed to have set up positions near the H Company mortarmen (as described by Jim Donahue in chapter 8) and from whom PlSgt John Muth took the other gun in an experience similar to that of Wolvington.

25. Craig memoir, 27.

26. 1st Marine Division, Headquarters, "Division Commander's Final Report on Guadalcanal Operation," 24 May 1943, Phase IV: 20 August–18 September, Annex E, "Artillery," Box 39, Geographic Area Files—Guadalcanal, RG 127, NARA; Craig memoir, 27, 28.

27. Nathaniel Mewhinney to the author, May 12, 1999; 1st Marine Division, "Final Report," Annex E, "Artillery" (for 0722 time). The Forward Observer of I Battery, 2nd Lt. Brooks Johnson, had set up his position "just two hundred yards" from the mouth of the Tenaru and was connected by telephone to the battalion's fire direction center (Ben Wofford and William R. White, *The Marine: A Guadalcanal Survivor's Final Battle*, 69.

28. B. J. Wilson to the author, December 19, 1998; B. J. Wilson, "Guadalcanal," memoir, February 1999, in author's collection.

29. Wilson, "Guadalcanal"; Wilson to the author, February 20, 1999.

30. Wilson, "Guadalcanal."

31. James Olliff to the author, February 4, 18, 1999; Clair Hume, telephone interview with the author, February 22, 1999; B Battery, 1st Special Weapons Battalion, 1st Marine Division, muster roll, August 1942, Marine Corps History Division, Reference Branch.

32. Hume telephone interview, February 22, 1999; Clair Hume to the author, March 4, 1999; Olliff to the author, February 4, May 29, 1999.

33. Hume telephone interview, February 22, 1999; B Battery, 1st Special Weapons Battalion, muster roll, August 1942.

34. Hume telephone interview, February 22, 1999.

35. Olliff to the author, February 4, 18, 1999.

36. Glenn Campbell, "August 21, 1942," memoir, December 10, 1998, in author's collection. Campbell's memoir clashes with the recollections of Turzai of E Company and Schlemmer of G Company, each of whom maintain that they were in Campbell's emplacement and firing the 37 mm gun. Schlemmer's memory more closely resembles that of Campbell in indicating that Schlemmer (and Wittmer) left the gun on the arrival of "some people from Special Weapons" (Campbell, apparently). (Schlemmer to the author, August 27, 1998, and Schlemmer memoir).

37. Campbell, "August 21, 1942."

38. Ibid. Campbell did not mention in his memoir what happened to the infantrymen serving as his new crew on the gun.

39. Angelo Catullo to the author, February 8, March 17, 1999.

40. Catullo, February 8, 1999.

41. Hume telephone interview, February 22, 1999.

42. Roger Butterfield, *Al Schmid, Marine*, 99–100. The Japanese machine gun may have been firing with a flash hider, making it difficult for Schmid to locate it.

43. Ibid., 103.

44. Ibid.; Albert A. Schmid, "An Eye for Two Hundred Japs," in *Out in the Boondocks*, ed. James D. Horan and Gerold Frank, 25; Wilbur Bewley to the author, August 19, 1998.

45. Butterfield, *Al Schmid*, 104; Schmid, "Eye for Two Hundred Japs," 25.

46. Butterfield, *Al Schmid*, 105.

47. George Parker, untitled memoir, 1999, in author's collection.

48. Ibid.; Richard Tregaskis, *Guadalcanal Diary*, 139.

49. Parker memoir. All four were given letters of commendations by the Marine Corps for their actions.

50. Harry Horsman to the author, September 17, October 16, 1998. From Horsman's description of the location of the gun and the circumstances, it appears the only 37 mm gun in action during the battle was that of Parker, although Parker does not recall anyone entering the emplacement after he and his crew left it.

51. Horsman to the author, June 10, September 17, December 18, 1998. The officer must have been 2nd Lt. Jim McClanahan, the CO of the 1st Special Weapons Battalion B Battery platoon operating the other 37 mm guns up and down the Tenaru.

52. "James W. Hancock," 11th Marines, 1937, 1941, Military Collection, USMC Muster Rolls, 1798–1958, Ancestry.com, www.ancestry.com; James Hancock, "Battle with the Enemy in the Solomons," letter to mother published in unidentified newspaper, ca. 1943; Horsman to the author, December 18, 1998.

53. Hancock, "Battle with the Enemy"; Harry Horsman to George Codrea, February 19, 1998; J. Luther Jordan to the author, December 8, 1998. Parker recalls that there was another explosion inside the bunker shortly after he and his crew had vacated it, which evidently was the one that knocked Hancock down.

54. John Tatum, diary, August 21, 1942, in author's collection; John Tatum, telephone interview with the author, July 31, 1999; Sidney C. Phillips, "'You'll Be Sor-ree': The Memoirs of a US Marine Private during the Pacific Campaign of World War II," manuscript, 57, in author's collection.

55. Phillips, "'You'll Be Sor-ree,'" 57; Sidney Phillips e-mail to the author, January 16, 1999; James Moncrief to the author, August 6, September 3, 1999; Tatum diary, August 21, 1942.

56. Phillips e-mail to the author, January 16, 1999; Tatum diary, August 21, 1942, n5.

57. Phillips, "'You'll Be Sor-ree,'" 57; John Tatum telephone interview with the author, July 31, 1999.

58. Tatum diary, August 21, 1942; Tatum to the author, October 2, December 21, 1999; Phillips, "'You'll Be Sor-ree,'" 57; Lester W. Clark, *An Unlikely Arena*, 40.

59. Phillips, "'You'll Be Sor-ree,'" 57.

60. Tatum diary, August 21, 1942; Moncrief to the author, September 3, 1999; James Young to the author, June 26, 1998; Phillips, "'You'll Be Sor-ree,'" 57; Clark, *Unlikely Arena*, 41. Tregaskis, *Guadalcanal Diary*, 133, gives between 1112 and 1115 as the time when he heard "loud bomp-bomp sounds like mortar shells exploding" near the Tenaru.

61. Mewhinney to the author, May 12, 1999. The Marine who shared the hole with Mewhinney must have been Pfc. Jesse Phillips, the only Marine killed that day in such a gruesome way and matching Tatum's description of his death.

62. Craig memoir, 29.

63. Ibid., 30.

64. Ibid.; Ansgar Sovik to the author, February 18, 1999.

65. Craig memoir, 30; Sovik to the author, February 18, June 6, 1999; John Howland, "Tenaru River Fight," letter, *Harvard Alumni Bulletin,* April 24, 1943. The other Navy doctor, Lt. Robert Goldstein, escaped injury in the explosion.

66. Craig memoir, 30–31.

67. Mae account, in Susumu Sugawara, *Ichiki Shitai zenmetsu* [Annihilation of the Ichiki Detachment], 238. The mortar shells would have been projectiles from Moncrief's and Phillips's tubes.

68. Mae account in Sugawara, *Ichiki Shitai zenmetsu,* 186–87, 238.

CHAPTER 10

1. Richard Tregaskis, *Guadalcanal Diary*, 130.

2. Ibid., 131.

3. Ibid.; John L. Zimmerman, *The Guadalcanal Campaign*, 69.

4. Nikolai Stevenson, "Four Months on the Front Line," *American Heritage*, October/November 1985, 52; Nikolai Stevenson, telephone interview with the author, August 13, 2010.

5. Zimmerman, *Guadalcanal Campaign*, 69. Lt. John Speaks's machine gun platoon would not be moving forward with the others. It remained deployed just beyond the far flank of Pollock's defense line on the west bank of the Tenaru.

6. Max Brand, *Fighter Squadron at Guadalcanal*, 66–67.

7. Ibid., 67; Stanley C. Jersey, *Hell's Islands*, 213–14.

8. Kyonobu Akasaka, as related in Susumu Sugawara, *Ichiki Shitai zenmetsu* [Annihilation of the Ichiki Detachment], 196.

9. Former private first class Kiyoshi Saitō and Akasaka, as related in ibid.

10. Akasaka, as related in ibid., 197. The boats had actually turned into Block Four River, some 1,600 meters short of the Nakagawa (Alligator Creek).

11. Saitō, as related in ibid., 197.

12. The fire must have been that of the 0722 barrage of the 3rd Battalion, 11th Marines, that morning.

13. Brand, *Fighter Squadron*, 67.

14. Ibid., 68. Neither Akasaka nor Saitō mention anyone in Ogasawara's group bringing a machine gun with them.

15. Ibid.; Jersey, *Hell's Islands*, 214; Capt. Kanae Monzen, commander, 11th Construction Unit, message cited in Sugawara, *Ichiki Shitai zenmetsu*, 251.

16. Saitō, in Sugawara, *Ichiki Shitai zenmetsu*, 197.

17. Akasaka, in ibid., 197.

18. As related by Lt. Kiyoshi Satō to Lt. Genjirou Inui, in Itirou Inui, e-mail to the author, January 15, 2001. Hanami's decision to return to the Tenaru battle proved fatal.

19. Hayashi, as related in Sugawara, *Ichiki Shitai zenmetsu*, 244.

20. Hayashi, in ibid., 245.

21. Years later, Hayashi learned that Aizawa had been picked up by the Americans in their enveloping action and spent the rest of the war as a POW in New Zealand (Hayashi, in ibid.).

22. Mizuno account related in Sugawara, *Ichiki Shitai zenmetsu*, 212.

23. Mae account related in Sugawara, *Ichiki Shitai zenmetsu*, 238–39. Juki was the common name for the *kyuni shiki jukikanju*, or "92 model heavy machine gun."

24. Mae, in ibid., 239. It is not known who these "snipers" recalled by Mae might have been. The incident does not fit any American account.

25. Mae, in ibid., 240. These Marines may have been members of Sgt. Longazel's patrol after their late morning encounter with seven Japanese members of the Engineer Company (described later).

26. Sadanobu Okada, "Ichiki in Guadalcanal," memoir, June 7, 1984, trans. by Akio Tani, in author's collection.

27. Ibid., June 7, 8, 1984.

28. Ibid. Although Okada did not indicate so, it would appear that Shibutani was in Ichiki's headquarters, as was Okada.

29. Zimmerman, *Guadalcanal Campaign*, 69; Stevenson, "Four Months," 52; Richard B. Frank, *Guadalcanal*, 154–55. See map 6 (p. 197) for the routes followed.

30. 1st Marine Division, Headquarters, "Division Commander's Final Report on Guadalcanal Operation," 24 May 1943, Phase IV: 20 August–18 September, Annex E, "Artillery," Box 39, Geographic Area Files—Guadalcanal, RG 127, NARA.

31. Oscar Gilbert, *Marine Tank Battles in the Pacific*, 42; Herbert C. Merillat, *The Island*, 72; Tregaskis, *Guadalcanal Diary*, 133; Lenard Cresswell Navy Cross citation, *United States Marine Corps Headquarters Bulletin*, No. 212 (15 May 1943); Earl Mowery Navy Cross citation, *United States Marine Corps Headquarters Bulletin*, No. 206 (15 November 1942). Mowery's citation incorrectly indicates that his action occurred during the later combat operation of A Company of the tanks.

32. Joseph Bushell to the author, November 3, 1999.

33. Donald Stiles to the author, November 16, 1999.

34. George Bono to Daphne Houze, October 10, 2004; D Company, 1st Battalion, 1st Marine Regiment (D-1-1), muster roll, August 1942 (microfilm), Marine Corps History Division, Reference Branch; Roy L. Barnes Silver Star citation, and Freeman B. Blair Silver Star citation, both in *United States Marine Corps Headquarters Bulletin*, No. 213 (15 July 1943). Details of this

engagement are from Stiles and Bono and differ markedly from the Navy Cross citation for Michael Longazel as published in *United States Marine Corps Headquarters Bulletin*, No. 206 (15 November 1942), which credits Longazel and his patrol, despite being outnumbered, with killing many Japanese in several groups as the patrol moved forward. Stiles recalled fighting only one group, and neither he nor Bono described their experiences as mentioned in the citation, which to the author appears overblown. Merillat's account (*Island*, 73–74) draws from Longazel's citation.

35. Makabe account, as related in Sugawara, *Ichiki Shitai zenmetsu*, 242.

36. Ibid. It would appear that the Japanese were attacked by the men of the Longazel patrol, despite the widely conflicting accounts by the two sides of the results of the clash. The American losses almost match in both accounts, although Makabe indicates no Japanese were killed, contrary to Stiles's recollection (and Longazel's Navy Cross citation). The Japanese account also corresponds to some extent to both the Bushell encounter (Japanese in a ditch) and that of the Longazel patrol (three Americans killed).

37. Makabe, in ibid., 243.

38. Tregaskis, *Guadalcanal Diary*, 133.

39. Stevenson, "Four Months," 52; Merillat, *Island*, 72; Andy Polinyi, "Col. Ichiki's Last Stand," *Guadalcanal Echoes,* April 1985, 8; John J. Jachym, interview with the author, December 1, 1998.

40. Stevenson interview with the author, August 27, 1991, and telephone interview with the author, August 13, 2010; Nikolai S. Stevenson, "[C] Company History, June 14–December 22, 1942," n.d., in Winston F. Fontaine personal collection; James A. Wagner, e-mail to the author, November 23, 1999; Merillat, *Island*, 73.

41. Stevenson, "Four Months," 52; Merillat, *Island*, 73; Nikolai S. Stevenson, Silver Star citation, *Military Times*, Hall of Valor, http://projects.militarytimes.com/citations-medals-awards/recipient.php?recipientid=38901; Stevenson, "[C] Company History."

42. James A. Wagner to the author, October 26, 1999; Stevenson, "[C] Company History"; Stevenson, "Four Months," 53.

43. James A. Wagner, telephone interview with the author, August 20, 2010; Stevenson, interview with the author, August 27, 1991.

44. Stevenson, "Four Months," 52.

45. Ibid.; Stevenson interview with the author, August 27, 1991; Stevenson telephone interviews with the author, August 11, 13, 2010.

46. Stevenson, "Four Months," 52; Stevenson interview with the author, August 27, 1991; Stevenson telephone interviews with the author, August 11, 13, 2010. Stevenson's victim was evidently 1st Lt. Yoshihito Nakai, a surgeon who was at the rear command post of the detachment at the time (Sugawara, *Ichiki Shitai zenmetsu*, 188). As the ranking officer of the rear group, and despite being a medical officer, he would have been in command and thus Stevenson's opposite number. Sugawara (115) indicates that Nakai—a graduate of Hokkaido University Medical School—was "fatally wounded in the head" and left a wife and a child.

47. Stevenson, "Four Months," 53; Stevenson interview, August 27, 1991; Stevenson telephone interview, August 13, 2010; Headquarters and Service Company, 1st Marine Regiment, muster roll, August 1942, Marine Corps History Division, Reference Branch.

48. James J. Gorman, "Biography of James Joseph Gorman," memoir, March 5, 1943,

www.justinmuseum.com/oralbio/gormanjjbio.html; Andy Polinyi, "Col. Ichiki's Last Stand," 8; Chester Sliva, e-mail to the author, March 28, 2004.

49. Gorman, "Biography"; Hugh Morse and George Head, *"A"-1-1: Pearl Harbor to Peleliu*, 36.

50. Gorman, "Biography."

51. Ibid.; Jachym interview with the author, December 1, 1998.

52. Gorman, "Biography"; A Company, 1st Battalion, 1st Marine Regiment (A-1-1), muster roll, August 1942, Marine Corps History Division, Reference Branch.

53. Zimmerman, *Guadalcanal Campaign*, 69; Merillat, *Island*, 73; Robert L. Corwin, interview transcript, Library of Congress, July 30, 2002.

54. Corwin in *Guadalcanal Legacy: 50th Anniversary, 1942–1992*, 39; Corwin, interview transcript, Library of Congress.

55. Corwin, *Guadalcanal Legacy*, 39. Other than McCarthy, who was killed instantly, B Company would suffer no other casualties in the enveloping action (B Company, 1st Battalion, 1st Marine Regiment [B-1-1], muster roll, August 1942, Marine Corps History Division, Reference Branch).

56. Merillat, *Island*, 73; Tregaskis, *Guadalcanal Diary*, 139.

57. Tregaskis, *Guadalcanal Diary*, 140, 145; Lester Sapp to the author, September 4, 1999.

58. Paul Hanlon to the author, October 18, 2001.

59. Tregaskis, *Guadalcanal Diary*, 140–41; Hanlon to the author, January 26, March 13, July 15, 1999, and October 18, December 26, 2001.

60. Frank, *Guadalcanal*, 155; Tregaskis, *Guadalcanal Diary*, 141–42; Stevenson telephone interview with the author, August 13, 2010; Gilbert, *Marine Tank Battles*, 42; Eugene Viveiros to the author, February 12, 2001.

61. Tregaskis, *Guadalcanal Diary*, 142.

62. Gilbert, *Marine Tank Battles*, 43; Tregaskis, *Guadalcanal Diary*, 142–43, 149.

63. Tregaskis, *Guadalcanal Diary*, 143; David J. Lynch to the author, September 22, 2010; Eugene Robbins to the author, September 13, 2010.

64. William Sadler to the author, September 13, 2010.

65. As related by Mizuno in Sugawara, *Ichiki Shitai zenmetsu*, 213.

66. Mizuno was subsequently captured and spent the rest of the war in a New Zealand POW camp (Mizuno in ibid., 214).

67. Mae, as related in ibid., 240.

68. Ibid.; Tregaskis, *Guadalcanal Diary*, 142 (see also 148).

69. Mae, in Sugawara, *Ichiki Shitai zenmetsu*, 215.

70. Yoya Kamakura to Harry Horsman, in "The Old Sarge," unpublished draft for *Guadalcanal Echoes*, ca. 1984.

71. Sugawara, *Ichiki Shitai zenmetsu*, 199, and Kurugane statement, 215.

72. Hajime Yamamoto, "The First Battle Guadalcanal: Annihilation of the Ichiki Detachment" (in Japanese), in "Saiaku no Semba" [The worst battlefield], *Maru* 5 (1987); Kurugane in Sugawara, *Ichiki Shitai zenmetsu*, 215, 216; Bōeicho Bōeikenshūjo Senshishitsu [Japanese Defense Agency, History Section], *Senshi sōsho* [Official war history], Vol. 14, *Minami-taiheiyo Rikūgun Sakusen* [Port Moresby–Guadalcanal initial operations] (1), cited in Sugawara, *Ichiki Shitai zenmetsu*, 241; Okada statement in Sugawara, *Ichiki Shitai zenmetsu*, 215.

73. Okada, "Ichiki in Guadalcanal," June 7, 1984.

74. Evidently Kurugane had earlier participated in the burning of the regiment's colors.

75. Mae statement in Sugawara, *Ichiki Shitai zenmetsu*, 241.

76. Okada, "Ichiki in Guadalcanal," June 14, 1984. The Hebigawa was known as Block Four River to the Americans. No Marines are known to have remained behind on the Japanese side of the Tenaru that night.

77. Okada, "Ichiki in Guadalcanal," June 14, 1984.

78. Stevenson telephone interview with the author, August 13, 2010; David J. Lynch response to author's questionnaire, September 2010.

79. Stevenson telephone interview with the author, August 13, 2010; Lynch to the author, September 22, 2010.

80. Sapp to the author, September 4, 1999.

81. Eric Hammel, *Guadalcanal: Starvation Island*, 177; Tregaskis, *Guadalcanal Diary*, 143–44; enlisted record for Charles Angus, US Military Collection. US Marine Corps Muster Rolls, 1798–1958, Ancestry.com, www.ancestry.com; E Company, 2nd Battalion, 1st Marine Regiment (E-2-1), muster roll, August 1942, Marine Corps History Division, Reference Branch.

82. Tregaskis, *Guadalcanal Diary*, 147; Gen. Edwin A. Pollock interview with Maj. Thomas E. Donnelly, Oral History Transcript, History and Museums Division, Headquarters, US Marine Corps, Washington, DC, 144; Edwin A. Pollock diary, August 21, 1942, in author's collection; 2nd Battalion, 1st Marine Regiment, "Unit Report," 1800 21 August to 1800 22 August 1942, A. William Larson personal collection.

83. Clifton Cates, "Battle of the Tenaru," *Marine Corps Gazette*, October 1943, 7; Regimental Weapons Company, 1st Marine Regiment, 1st Marine Division, muster roll, August 1942, Marine Corps History Division, Reference Branch; entry for Harry Quinby Findley, National WWII Memorial, Washington, DC, www.wwiimemorial.com/registry/mia/search/pframe.asp?HonoreeID=752050&popcount=1&tcount=1. The Regimental Weapons Company had not been employed by Cates in the battle.

EPILOGUE

1. Sadanobu Okada, "Ichiki in Guadalcanal," memoir, June 14, 1984, trans. by Akio Tani, in author's collection.

2. Sadanobu Okada, "Ichiki on Guadalcanal," *Guadalcanal Echoes*, July 1986, 15.

3. Richard Tregaskis, *Guadalcanal Diary*, 148; Jack Clark, "Beachmaster," *Guadalcanal Echoes*, October-November 1994, 30; George P. Hunt, "First Days on Guadalcanal," undated memoir, 25, in Lt. Gen. Edwin A. Pollock Papers, Parris Island Museum, US Marine Corps Recruitment Depot, Parris Island, SC; Edwin A. Pollock diary, August 22, 1942, in author's collection.

4. John Tatum, diary, August 22, 1942, in author's collection; Sidney C. Phillips, "'You'll Be Sor-ree': The Memoirs of a US Marine Private during the Pacific Campaign of World War II," manuscript, 58, in author's collection.

5. Tatum diary, August 22, 1942; Phillips, "'You'll Be Sor-ree,'" 58.

6. Phillips, "'You'll Be Sor-ree,'" 58–59.

7. Clark, "Beachmaster," 30.

8. Tatum diary, August 22, 1942; Clark, "Beachmaster," 30.

9. Pollock diary, August 22, 1942; 1st Marine Division, 1st Marine Regiment, "History of

the First Marine Regiment," Phase IV, 20 August–18 September, File A-10-2, Box 42, Geographic Files 1939–1949—Guadalcanal, RG 127, NARA (hereafter cited as "History of the First Marine Regiment"); Akio Tani to the author, September 21, 1991.

10. Gen. Edwin A. Pollock interview with Maj. Thomas E. Donnelly, Oral History Transcript, History and Museums Division, Headquarters, US Marine Corps, Washington, DC, 145.

11. As recalled by Harry Horsman, in Evan M. Wylie, "That Fearful Night on the Tenaru River," *Yankee*, August 1982, 92–93.

12. Okada in Susumu Sugawara, *Ichiki Shitai zenmetsu*, 241, 247.

13. Sugawara, *Ichiki Shitai zenmetsu*, 236, 248; Hajime Yamamoto, "The First Battle on Guadalcanal: Annihilation of the Ichiki Detachment" (in Japanese), in "Saiaku no semba" [The worst battlefield], *Maru* 5 (1987).

14. Bōeichō Bōeikenshūjo Senshishitsu [Japanese Defense Agency, War History Section], *Senshi sōsho* [Official war history], Vol. 14, *Minami-taiheiyo Rikūgun Sakusen* [Port Moresby–Guadalcanal initial operations] (1), 312, message dated August 21, 1942, trans. by Akio Tani, in Tani to the author, April 29, 1990; Sugawara, *Ichiki Shitai zenmetsu*, 250.

15. Sugawara, *Ichiki Shitai zenmetsu*, 248, 251. It was not until August 25 that the Japanese Navy confirmed that Sakakibara had sent the message (Sugawara, *Ichiki Shitai zenmetsu*, 251; *Senshi sōsho*, Vol. 14, August 21 and 25 entries, trans. by Tani, in Tani to the author, April 29, 1990).

16. Sugawara, *Ichiki Shitai zenmetsu*, 236.

17. Ibid., 246; Stanley Jersey, *Hell's Islands*, 213. Okada had underestimated the wounded who had returned, given as twenty-eight by Jersey (*Hell's Islands*, 213) and thirty by Sugawara (*Ichiki Shitai zenmetsu*, 245). On August 27 the East Lookout Post at Taivu Point reported to 81st Guard radio operator Kuichi Yamada west of Lunga that there were 128 remaining members at the Taivu Point camp (Kuichi Yamada diary, file 13, Box 15, Captured Japanese Documents, 1942–1945, RG 127, NARA).

18. Nevertheless, Japanese sources determined later that thirteen had indeed been taken prisoner, but only one as a result of being too severely wounded to resist (Sugawara, *Ichiki Shitai zenmetsu*, 246). More exact figures were reported by the 1st Marine Regiment: fourteen taken prisoner, including two who were not wounded, plus one Japanese who had surrendered ("History of the First Marine Regiment," 7).

19. Okada in Sugawara, *Ichiki Shitai zenmetsu*, 218, 219.

20. Morihiro account in ibid., 228–29.

21. Morihiro's account cannot be verified as fact, given the lack of corroborating evidence. It is not clear why he had not discussed his experience with the other survivors at Taivu Point. The official Japanese war history accepts that Ichiki committed suicide (noted in Sugawara, *Ichiki Shitai zenmetsu*, 241, and by Yamamoto in "First Battle on Guadalcanal") and that the NCO was a "Sgt. Kyoshi Nakamura" (Sugawara, 235), elsewhere referred to in 1958 as "Sgt. Kiyoshi Nakamoto" (Sugawara, 199). The Taivu Point lookout post had radioed to 81st Guard radioman Kuichi Yamada in the Lunga area on August 27 that Ichiki "had taken his life" and that the regimental flag and code books had been destroyed by the detachment (Yamada diary, August 27, 1942).

22. Yamamoto, "First Battle on Guadalcanal." As an officer with Ichiki's headquarters,

assigned to the second echelon, 2nd Lt. Hajime Yamamoto would have been knowledgeable about Ichiki's plan.

23. Ibid.; Sugawara, *Ichiki Shitai zenmetsu*, 247.

24. Genjirou Inui, "My Guadalcanal," diary, August 23, 1942.

25. Ibid., August 23, 1942; John F. Schneider, *Bay Area Radio*, Images of America, 101, 107.

26. Merrill B. Twining, *No Bended Knee*, 86–87; A. A. Vandegrift, *Once a Marine*, 142.

27. "Overseas Mission of the First Marine Division, Fleet Marine Force," File W2, Box 48, 35, Geographic Files1939–1949—Guadalcanal, RG 127, NARA; "History of the First Marine Regiment," 7. These casualty figures correspond to those of August 1942 muster rolls as presented by name in Appendix C, except for the wounded. Even counting the four wounded who subsequently died, muster rolls indicate sixty-four wounded only, versus seventy-five in the official reports, evidently due to incomplete recording by muster roll preparers. Not cited here are those killed (three) and wounded (three) of A Company in the earlier engagement of the Brush patrol with Captain Shibuya.

28. Inui, "My Guadalcanal," August 30, 1942; *Senshi sōsho,* Vol. 14, August 30, 1942, reference, 391, trans. by Tani, in Tani to the author, April 29, 1990. The Taivu Point lookout post radioed Kuichi Yamada on August 30 with the news of the landing of the second echelon (Yamada diary).

29. *Senshi sōsho,* Vol. 14, references for August 29 and 30, 1942, trans. by Tani, in Tani to the author, April 29, 1990. The distribution of infantry troops and the machine gun squads of the second echelon among the patrol boats and destroyers is based on author's assumptions. It is also assumed that all the men left behind from the four infantry companies joined up with the second echelon.

30. Inui, "My Guadalcanal," August 30, 1942. It is assumed that Sakakibara mentioned the losses sustained by the first echelon when he informed Inui and the others of the death of Ichiki.

31. Ibid. The author has been unable to identify the American destroyer referred to by Inui.

32. Inui, "My Guadalcanal," August 30, 1942; Sugawara, *Ichiki Shitai zenmetsu*, 247. "We are out of provisions," the Taivu Point lookout post had wired Yamada on August 25 (Yamada diary).

33. Inui, "My Guadalcanal," August 31, September 1, 1942; *Senshi sōsho,* trans. by Tani, 395, also in Tani to the author, April 29, 1990.

34. *Senshi sōsho,* Vol. 14, 395; Inui, "My Guadalcanal," September 1, 1942.

35. Twining, *No Bended Knee*, 86.

36. Samuel B. Griffith II, *The Battle for Guadalcanal*, 87.

37. Twining, *No Bended Knee*, 87.

38. Griffith, *Battle for Guadalcanal*, 87; Twining, *No Bended Knee*, 87.

39. A. A. Vandegrift, *Once a Marine*, 141–42; Griffith, *Battle for Guadalcanal*, 87.

40. Edward Drea, "The Japanese Army on the Eve of War," in *Battle for China*, ed. Mark Peattie, Edward Drei, and Hans van de Ven, 116; and Edward Drea, *In the Service of the Emperor*, 77–78.

41. Drea, *Service of the Emperor*, 76–89.

42. Drea, "Japanese Army," 112, 113; Edward Drea to the author, September 13, 2009.

43. Drea to the author, September 13, 2009.

44. Edward Drea, *Nomonhan: Japanese-Soviet Tactical Combat, 1939*, 62.

45. Drea, *Service of Emperor*, 11, 12; Drea, *Nomonhan*, 170.

46. Maj. Charles H. Brush to Commandant, Marine Corps, January 15, 1949, quoted in Zimmerman, *Guadalcanal Campaign*, 62; Pollock interview with Donnelly, 148; "Overseas Mission of the 1st Marine Division, Fleet Marine Force," File W2, Box 48, Geographic Files 1939–1949—Guadalcanal, RG 127, NARA.

47. Sugawara, *Ichiki Shitai zenmetsu*, 96. See chapter 5 in this volume.

48. *Senshi sōsho*, Vol. 14, reference for August 20, 1942, trans. by Tani, in Tani to author, April 29, 1990.

49. Inui diary, September 1, 1942.

50. For an account of K Company's valiant defense, see William H. Bartsch, "Crucial Battle Ignored," *Marine Corps Gazette,* September 1997, 82–90.

51. Twining refers to a diary Ichiki left behind that concludes with a premature (August 21) entry, "Enjoyment of the fruits of victory" (Twining, *No Bended Knee*, 87).

52. For example, in 1939 at Nomonhan, 70 mm guns were intended for use to destroy Soviet machine gun nests (Drea, *Nomonhan*, 43).

53. Pollock interview with Donnelly, 140.

54. "Victory fever," or "victory disease" (*senshobyou*) was the term used by the Japanese high command in reference to its sweeping victories over the Allies in the first six months of the Pacific War (Richard B. Frank, *Guadalcanal*, 22).

55. Translation of August 25, 1942, item in *Senshi sōsho*, 321, by Tani, in Tani to the author, April 29, 1990; Sugawara, *Ichiki Shitai zenmetsu*, 252.

56. Frank, *Guadalcanal*, 156–57; Richard B. Frank, email to the author, September 16, 2013.

57. Harry Horsman, "From the Old Sarge," *Guadalcanal Echoes,* January 1984, 6.

58. Tom Bartlett, "Japanese Warriors' Final Journey," *Leatherneck*, August 1985, 41.

59. Horsman, "Old Sarge," 6.

60. Bartlett, "Final Journey," 41; Horsman, "Old Sarge," 6.

GLOSSARY

A Company	Rifle Company of 1st Battalion, 1st Marine Regiment
amtrac	Amphibious tractor, LVT (US)
Arisaka	Japanese Type 36 6.5 mm or Type 99 7.7 mm rifle
Bangalore torpedo	Tube with explosive charge for clearing obstacles
BAR	Browning automatic rifle
battalion	Unit of a regiment, commanded by a lieutenant colonel and comprised of three rifle companies and a weapons company
B Company	Rifle Company of 1st Battalion, 1st Marine Regiment
Bn-2	Battalion intelligence section or officer
Bn-3	Battalion operations section or officer
C Company	Rifle Company of 1st Battalion, 1st Marine Regiment
CINCPAC	Commander-in-chief, US Pacific Fleet
CO	Commanding officer
COMINCH	Commander-in-chief, US Fleet
company	Unit of a battalion, commanded by a captain
COMSOPAC	Commander, South Pacific Area and South Pacific Force
coxswain	Naval person in charge of navigating and steering a landing craft
CP	Command post
D Company	Weapons company of 1st Battalion, 1st Marine Regiment
Daihatsu	Japanese motorized landing craft
E Company	Rifle Company of 2nd Battalion, 1st Marine Regiment
81st Guard Unit	Japanese security unit based on Guadalcanal
F Company	Rifle Company of 2nd Battalion, 1st Marine Regiment
1st Battalion	Unit of 1st Marine Regiment
1st Special Weapons Battalion	Unit attached to the 1st Marine Division
F4F	Grumman Wildcat fighter
fire direction control	Section of an artillery battalion controlling fire
1st Marine Division	Unit comprising the 1st, 5th, and 7th Marine Infantry Regiments and the 11th Marine Artillery Regiment, plus attached units
G Company	Rifle Company of 2nd Battalion, 1st Marine Regiment
Grassy Knoll	Knoll north of Mount Austen on Guadalcanal
Gunny Sgt.	Gunnery sergeant in a company
H Company	Weapons company of 2nd Battalion, 1st Marine Regiment
HA2C	Hospital apprentice second class, US Navy

H&S	Headquarters and service
Hebigawa	Japanese name for Block Four River
Hell's Point	Area around the mouth of Alligator Creek
Higashigawa	Japanese name for the Tenaru River
Higgins boat	American thirty-six-man landing craft
Hohei soten	Japanese 1928 infantry manual
Ichiki-shitai	Ichiki Detachment
Ichiki-tai	Ichiki Veterans Association
IGHQ	Japanese Imperial General Headquarters, Tokyo
IJA	Imperial Japanese Army
JCS	Joint Chiefs of Staff, US
Juki Model 92	7.7 mm Japanese heavy machine gun (kyuni shiki jukikanju)
K Company	Rifle Company of 3rd Battalion, 1st Marine Regiment
knee mortar	American misnomer for Japanese Model 89 50 mm heavy grenade discharger
L Company	Rifle Company of 3rd Battalion, 1st Marine Regiment
Ldg. Pvt.	Leading private, highest rank of private in the Japanese Army
LMG	Light machine gun
LVT	Landing vehicle tracked (amtrac; US)
M2A4	American light tank, later known as a Stuart
M3A1	37 mm anti-tank gun, weapon of B Battery, 1st Special Weapons Battalion, and of 37 mm gun platoon, H Company
mortar platoon	Unit of a weapons company comprised of four 81 mm mortar squads
Nambu light	Japanese Type 96 6.5 mm or Type 99 7.7 mm light machine gun
Nakagawa	Japanese name for Alligator Creek
NCO	Noncommissioned officer
OCC	Officer candidate class, Marine Corps
Operation Lone Wolf	Plan to send 1st Marine Division to New Zealand
Pfc.	Private first class (US and Japan)
Pioneers	Marine combat engineers
platoon	Unit of a company, led by a second lieutenant
platoon guide	NCO acting as assistant platoon sergeant (US)
PLC	Platoon leaders class
Plat. Sgt.	Platoon sergeant (US)

Red Beach	August 7 landing site of US Marines on Guadalcanal
Regiment	Unit of USMC comprised of three battalions and commanded by a colonel
Reising gun	.45-caliber submachine gun
R-2	Regimental intelligence section or officer
rifle company	Unit of a battalion comprised of three rifle platoons and one weapons platoon
rifle platoon	Unit of a rifle company consisting of three rifle squads and one BAR squad
Rikugun Shiken Gakko	Japanese Imperial Army military academy
ROC	Reserve Officers Class, Marine Corps
SBD	Dauntless scout bomber
Springfield '03	American 1903 model .30-caliber bolt action rifle
squad	Unit of a platoon
S.Sgt	Staff sergeant (US)
stovepiper	Slang for a mortar man
VMF	Marine fighter squadron
Watchtower	US code name for Guadalcanal operation
weapons company	Unit of a battalion consisting of three machine gun platoons, one 81 mm mortar platoon, and one 37 mm gun platoon
weapons platoon	Unit of a rifle company consisting of two machine gun squads and two 60 mm mortar squads
WO	Warrant officer (US and Japanese)

SOURCES

UNPUBLISHED OFFICIAL DOCUMENTS

Alfred M. Gray Marine Corps Research Center, Quantico, Virginia

Oral History Transcript, Robert W. Fincher, interviewed by Michael Miller, August 9, 2004.

Australia, National Archives.

Combat Group B, 1st Marines (Reinforced), R-2 Section. "Northern Coast of Guadalcanal Island, Kukum to Tetere," map, 31 July 1942. A 1196, 37/501/167, Attachment 7.

Author's Collection.

Whorf, William. "Cross Section at the Tenaru." Manuscript, November 30, 1998.

Fontaine, Winston F. Personal Collection.

Stevenson, Nikolai S. "[C] Company History, June 14–December 22, 1942." No date.

Larson, A. William. Personal Collection.

Combat Group B, 1st Marines (Reinforced). Annex D to Operation Order 4-42,"Intelligence—Facts About Terrain on Guadalcanal Island," 29 July 1942.

2nd Battalion, 1st Marines (Reinforced). "Unit Report," 1800 16 August to 1800 17 August 1942," and similar for 17–18, 18–19, 19–20, 20–21, 21–22 August 1942.

Combat Team 5. "Operation Order 2-42," July 28, 1942.

Library of Congress, Veterans History Project.

Transcript, Interview of Robert L. Corwin, July 30, 2002.

Marine Corps History Division, Reference Branch, Quantico, VA.

Company Muster Rolls, 1st Marine Division, 1941-42 (microfilms).

1st Marine Division, 1st Marine Regiment, 1st Battalion. Muster rolls, Headquarters and Service Company; A, B, C, D Companies; Regimental Weapons Company, April, May, July, August 1942 (microfilms).

1st Marine Division, 1st Marine Regiment, 2nd Battalion. Muster rolls, E, F, G, H Companies, April, July, August 1942 (microfilms).

1st Marine Division, 1st Special Weapons Battalion. Muster rolls, Battery B and Headquarters Batteries, August 1942.

1st Marine Division, 7th Marine Regiment, 3rd Battalion. Muster roll, K Company, January 1942.

Records of casualties.

Marine Corps History and Museum Division, Washington, DC.

Oral History Transcript, General Edwin A. Pollock, interviewed by Maj. Thomas E. Donnelly, USMC, 1977.

Oral History Transcript, General Clifton B.Cates, interviewed by Benis Frank, 1967.

Oral History Transcript, Col. John P. Leonard, interviewed by Benis Frank, 1983.

Pollock, Lt. Gen. Edwin A. Papers. Parris Island Museum, US Marine Corps Recruitment Depot, Parris Island, SC.

"History of the 2nd Battalion, 1st Marines."

Hunt, George P. "First Days on Guadalcanal," no date.

Swinston, George, Jr. Personal Collection.

Commandant, US Marine Corps, to Commandant, Navy Yard, Philadelphia, Pennsylvania. "Change of Station." April 13, 1942.

Commanding Officer, Marine Barracks, Philadelphia Navy Yard. "Orders to Temporary Duty," March 23, 1942.
US, National Archives and Records Administration, College Park, MD.
Record Group 24, Records of the Bureau of Naval Personnel, 1798-1991.
US Navy Ships' Deck Logs.
USS *Barnett.* July 29, 1942.
USS *George F. Elliott.* July 30, 1942.
USS *McCawley.* July 30, 1942.
Record Group 127, Records of the United States Marine Corps, 1775–1981.
Captured Japanese Documents, 1942–1945.
Yamada, Kuichi. Diary. Box 15, Folder 13.
Geographic Files 1939–1949—Guadalcanal.
Combat Group B, 1st Marines (Reinforced). "Operation Order 5-42," 9 August 1942. Folder B-10-1, Box 45.
Combat Group B, 1st Marines (Reinforced). "Operation Order 6-42," August 14, 1942. Folder B-10-1, Box 45.
Combat Group B, 1st Marines (Reinforced). "Unit Report No. 13, from 1800 20 August to 1800 21 August 1942," August 25, 1942. Folder A-10-2, Box 42.
Edson, M. "Notes on Japanese Tactics and Techniques." Miscellaneous Intelligence Report. Folder C-15-2, Box 46.
1st Marine Division, D-3 Journal, August 1942. Folder A-7-14, Box 41.
1st Marine Division. Operation Order 5-42, Wellington, NZ, 29 June 1942. Folder B-2-1, Box 44.
1st Marine Division, 1st Marine Regiment. "History of the First Marine Regiment." Phase III (10 August–20 August) and Phase IV (20 August–18 September). Folder A-10-2, Box 42.
1st Marine Division, 1st Marine Regiment, R-2 Section. "Intelligence Report," September 6, 1942. Folder C-8-1, Box 45.
1st Marine Division, Fleet Marine Force. "Combined Station List and Strength Report, Forward Echelon, 1st Marine Division and Attached Units, Sunday, August 2, 1942." Folder E-1-1, Box 47.
1st Marine Division, Headquarters. "Division Commander's Final Report on Guadalcanal Operation." 24 May 1943. Folders A-7-1, A-7-2, A-7-3, and A-7-4, Box 39.
Phase I: Events Prior to H Hour, 7 August 1942.
"Operation Order 7-42." 20 July 1942. Annex F.
Phase II: From H Hour to Evening 9 August.
"Aviation." Annex K.
"Intelligence." Annex G
"Medical." Annex H.
"Operation Order 7-42." 20 July 1942. Annex E.
Phase III: Organization of Lunga Point Defense, 10 August–21 August.
"History of the First Battalion." Annex I.
"Intelligence." Annex F.

"Logistics." Annex C.
"Signal Communications." Annex O.
Phase IV: 20 August–18 September.
"Artillery." Annex E.
"Ichiki Detachment Order A, no. 4," Truk, 15 August 1942. Intelligence Reports, Item No. 1231, Folder C-15-5, Box 46.
"Organization of Two Japanese Army Combat Teams." Intelligence Reports. Folder C-15-5, Box 46.
"Overseas Mission of the First Marine Division, Fleet Marine Force." Folder W2, Box 48.
"Report on Guadalcanal Operations." (b) Intelligence. Folder C-18-1, Box 46.
Whyte, William. Papers. Marine Corps Historical Center, Washington, DC.
Orders for the Ikki [*sic*] Detachment, Order No. 4. Truk, 15 August 1942. Item W 35.

UNPUBLISHED PERSONAL DOCUMENTS (IN THE AUTHOR'S PRIVATE COLLECTION UNLESS OTHERWISE INDICATED.)

Asahi, Tomoteru. Untitled memoir (in Japanese), no date. Translation in Ewan Stevenson collection.
Askey, Robert. Diary, 1942, entries for August 20, 21, 1942.
Berghaus, Bayard. Diary, 1942.
Boston, James. Untitled memoir, 1943.
Brodecki, Andrew. Untitled memoir, May 5, 1980.
Campbell, Glenn. "August 21, 1942," December 10, 1998.
Coggin, William T. "Guadalcanal 1942," 1998.
Couch, James H. "A Marine's Story: My Four Years as a US Marine, January 9, 1942–January 15, 1946," Memoir, no date.
Craig, Edward J, Jr. Untitled memoir, no date.
Dennis, George. Diary, 1942.
Donahue, James A. "Guadalcanal Journal," 1942.
Felber, Abraham. Diary, 1941–45.
Hayes, Luther. Diary, 1942.
Kaneda. Sankichi. "The Battle for Guadalcanal" (in Japanese), no date. In Stanley Jersey collection.
———. "Recollections of a Memorial Pilgrimage" (in Japanese), 1969. In Stanley Jersey collection.
Mills, Joseph E. "World War II—1941–1945." Memoir, no date.
Moss, Donald F. "What Was It Like in the Olden Days, Dad?—An Illustrated Memoir," no date.
Okada, Sadanobu. "Ichiki in Guadalcanal," memoir (in Japanese, trans. by Akio Tani), June 4, 5, 6, 7, 8, 14, 1984.
O'Soro, Edward. Diary, 1942.
Parker, George. Unitled memoir, 1999.
Phillips, Sidney C. "'You'll Be Sor-ree': The Memoirs of a US Marine Private during the Pacific Campaign of World War II." Manuscript, 2001.

Pollock, Edwin A. Diary, 1942.
Putnam, Robert F. "Guadalcanal Memories," 1942.
Reber, Ralph H. "Memories of Military Service," no date.
Reutlinger, Albert F. "A History of the First Amphibian Tractor Battalion, United States Marine Corps, during World War II," no date.
Schlemmer. Albert. "August 21, 1942, as I Remember It or What I Can Remember," October 1998.
Small, Gilbert. Journal, July 13–September 29, 1942.
Stover, Dean E. Untitled memoir, May 3, 2003.
Tatum, John. Diary, 1942.
Turzai, George. Untitled memoir, 1999.
Wadsworth, James Brady. Untitled memoir, no date.
Whorf, William. Diary, 1942.
Williams, John. "What Happened in World War II." Memoir, no date.
Wilson, B. J. "Guadalcanal," February 6, 1999.

MEDAL CITATIONS

Barnes, Roy L. Silver Star citation. *United State Marine Corps Headquarters Bulletin*, No. 213 (15 July 1943).
Blair, Freeman B. Silver Star citation. *United State Marine Corps Headquarters Bulletin*, No. 213 (15 July 1943).
Cresswell, Lenard. Navy Cross citation. *United State Marine Corps Headquarters Bulletin*, No. 212 (15 May 1943).
Dobbins, Ernest. Silver Star citation. *United States Marine Corps Headquarters Bulletin*, No. 212 (15 May 1943).
Grazier, George. Navy Cross citation. *United State Marine Corps Headquarters Bulletin*, No. 213 (15 July 1943).
Longazel Michael. Navy Cross citation. *United State Marine Corps Headquarters Bulletin*, No. 206 (15 November 1942).
Mowery, Earl. Navy Cross citation. *United State Marine Corps Headquarters Bulletin*, No. 206 (15 November 1942).
Stevenson, Nikolai S. Silver Star citation. *Military Times*, Hall of Valor. http://projects.militarytimes.com/citations-medals-awards/recipient.php?recipientid=38901.
Wolvington, William. Navy Cross citation. *United State Marine Corps Headquarters Bulletin*, No. 213 (15 July 1943).

BOOKS

Berry, Henry. *Semper Fi, Mac: Living Memories of US Marines in World War II.* New York: William Morrow, 1982.
Bevan, Denys. *United States Forces in New Zealand, 1942–1945.* Alexandra, NZ: Macpherson Publishers, 1992.
Bōeicho Bōeikenshūjo Senshishitsu [Japanese Defense Agency, War History Section]. *Senshi sōsho* [Official war history], Vol. 14, *Minami-taiheiyo Rikūgun Sakusen* [Port Moresby–Guadalcanal initial operations] (1). Tokyo: Asagumo Shimbunsha, 1968.

Boyd, Carl. *The Japanese Submarine Force and World War II.* Annapolis, MD: Naval Institute Press, 1995.

Brand, Max. *Fighter Squadron at Guadalcanal.* Annapolis, MD: Naval Institute Press, 1996.

Butterfield, Roger. *Al Schmid, Marine.* New York: W. W. Norton, 1944.

Charles, Roland W. *Troopships of World War II.* Washington, DC: Army Transportation Association, 1947.

Clark, Lester W. *An Unlikely Arena.* New York: Vantage Press, 1989.

Clemens, Martin. *Alone on Guadalcanal: A Coastwatcher's Story.* Annapolis, MD: Naval Institute Press, 1998.

Condit, Kenneth W.; Gerald Diamond; and Edwin T. Turnbladh. *Marine Corps Ground Training in World War II.* Washington, DC: Headquarters, US Marine Corps, Historical Branch, G-3, 1958.

Drea, Edward J. *In the Service of the Emperor.* Lincoln: University of Nebraska Press, 1998.

———. *Japan's Imperial Army: Its Rise and Fall, 1853–1945.* Lawrence: University Press of Kansas, 2009.

———. *Nomonhan: Japanese-Soviet Tactical Combat, 1939.* Fort Leavenworth, KS: Combat Studies Institute, Command and General Staff College, 1981.

———. "The Japanese Army on the Eve of War." In *Battle for China.* Edited by Mark Peattie, Edward Drei, and Hans van de Ven. Stanford, CA: Stanford University Press, 2011.

Dull, Paul S. *A Battle History of the Imperial Japanese Navy, 1941–1945.* Annapolis, MD: Naval Institute Press, 1978.

Dyer, George C. *The Amphibians Came to Conquer.* Washington, DC: Government Printing Office, 1971.

Field Artillery School. *Abbreviated Firing Tables.* Fort Sill, OK: Field Artillery School, 1942.

First Marine Division Association. *First Marine Division: Guadalcanal.* Paducah, KY: Turner Publishing Company, 1997.

Frank, Richard B. *Guadalcanal.* New York: Random House, 1990.

Gilbert, Oscar E. *Marine Tank Battles in the Pacific.* Conshocken, PA: Combined Publishing, 2001.

Griffith, Samuel B., II. *The Battle for Guadalcanal.* Philadelphia: J. B. Lippincott, 1963.

Grimes, Henry R., "The Empty Gun." In *Out in the Boondocks.* Edited by James D. Horan and Gerold Frank. New York: G. P. Putnam Sons, 1943.

Guadalcanal Legacy: 50th Anniversary, 1942–1992. Paducah, KY: Turner Publishing Company, 1992.

Hammel, Eric. *Guadalcanal: Starvation Island.* New York: Crown Publishers, 1987.

Harding, Richard W. "Battle for a Foxhole." In *Out in the Boondocks.* Edited by James D. Horan and Gerold Frank. New York: G. P Putnam Sons, 1943.

Harvard University. *Harvard Class of 1932: Twenty-fifth Anniversary Report.* Cambridge, MA: Harvard University,1957.

Hattori, Takushirō. *Dai Toa Senso Zenshi.* [Complete history of the Greater East Asia War.] Tokyo: Masu Shobo, 1953. (English translation, microfilm, Library of Congress.)

Hayashi, Saburō, and Alvin D. Coox. *Kōgun: The Japanese Army in the Pacific War.* Quantico, MD: Marine Corps Association, 1959.

Isely, Jeter A., and Philip A. Crowl. *The US Marines in Amphibious War.* Princeton: Princeton University Press, 1951.

Jersey, Stanley C. *Hell's Islands.* College Station: Texas A&M University Press, 2008.

Lane, Kerry. *Marine Pioneers.* Atglen, PA: Schiffer Publishing, 1997.

Leckie, Robert. *Challenge for the Pacific.* Garden City, NJ: Doubleday and Company, 1965.

———. *Helmet for My Pillow.* New York: Simon and Schuster, 1957.

McMillan, George. *The Old Breed: A History of the First Marine Division in World War II.* Washington, DC: Infantry Journal Press, 1949.

Merillat, Herbert C. L. *Guadalcanal Remembered.* New York: Dodd, Mead and Company, 1982.

———. *The Island: A History of the First Marine Division on Guadalcanal, August 7–December 9, 1942.* New York: Houghton Mifflin, 1944.

Miller, John, Jr. *Guadalcanal: The First Offensive.* Washington, DC: Department of the Army, Historical Division, 1949.

Miller, Thomas G., Jr. *The Cactus Air Force.* New York: Harper and Row, 1969.

Millett, Alan. *In Many a Strife: General Gerald C. Thomas and the US Marine Corps, 1917–1956.* Annapolis, MD: Naval Institute Press, 1993.

Morse, Hugh, and George Head. *"A"-1-1: Pearl Harbor to Peleliu.* N.p.: A-1-1 Book Committee, 1994.

Parshall, Jonathan, and Anthony Tully. *Shattered Sword: The Untold Story of the Battle of Midway.* Dulles, VA: Potomac Books, 2005.

Peattie, Mark; Edward Drea; and Han van de Ven, eds. *Battle for China.* Stanford, CA: Stanford University Press, 2011.

Rottman, Gordon L. *World War II Pacific Island Guide: A Geo-Military Study.* Westport, CT: Greenwood, 2001.

Schmid, Albert A. "An Eye for Two Hundred Japs." In *Out in the Boondocks.* Edited by James D. Horan and Gerold Frank. New York: G. P. Putnam Sons, 1943.

Schneider, John F. *Bay Area Radio.* Images of America. Charleston, SC: Arcadia Publishing, 2012.

Shaw, Henry I., Jr. *First Offensive: The Marine Campaign for Guadalcanal.* Washington, DC: Marine Corps Historical Center, 1992.

Sugawara, Susumu. *Ichiki Shitai zenmetsu.* [Annihilation of the Ichiki Detachment]. Tokyo: Narita Printing Company, 1979.

Tanaka, Raizo. "The Struggle for Guadalcanal." In *The Japanese Navy in World War II.* Edited by David Evans. Annapolis, MD: Naval Institute Press, 1986.

Tregaskis, Richard. *Guadalcanal Diary.* New York: Random House, 1943.

Twining, Merrill B. *No Bended Knee.* Novato, CA: Presidio Press, 1996.

US Marine Corps, Seventh Reserve Officers Class. *The Gold Bar, April 1942.* Quantico, MD: US Marine Corps, 1942.

Vandegrift. A. A. *Once a Marine.* New York: Norton, 1966.

War Department. *Field Artillery Field Manual FM 6-40.* Washington, DC: Government Printing Office, 1939.

———. *Handbook of Japanese Military Forces.* Technical Manual E-30-4880. Washington, DC: US Government Printing Office, 1944.

Watts, A. J., and B. G. Gordon. *The Imperial Japanese Navy.* London: Macdonald & Co., 1971.

Whyte, William H. *A Time of War.* New York: Fordham University Press, 2000.
Wofford, Ben, and William R. White. *The Marine: A Guadalcanal Survivor's Final Battle.* Annapolis, MD: Naval Institute Press, 2002.
Zimmerman, John L. *The Guadalcanal Campaign.* Reprint, Chicago: Lancaster Publications, 1949.

ARTICLES AND PUBLISHED LETTERS

Bartlett, Tom. "Japanese Warriors' Final Journey." *Leatherneck,* August 1985.
Bartsch, William H. "Crucial Battle Ignored." *Marine Corps Gazette,* September 1997, 82–90.
———. "Operation Dovetail: Bungled Guadalcanal Rehearsal, July 1942." *Journal of Military History,* April 2002, 443–76.
Bewley, W. F. "The Night I Led Vouza through the Lines." *Guadalcanal Echoes,* January 1985, 9.
"Capt. Sherman Tells of Fight at Guadalcanal." Unidentified Massachusetts newspaper, no date, ca. 1943, copy in Harry Horsman collection.
Cates, Clifton. "Battle of the Tenaru." *Marine Corps Gazette,* October 1943, 5–7.
Clark, Jack. "Beachmaster." *Guadalcanal Echoes,* October-November 1984, 30.
Del Valle, Pedro. "Marine Field Artillery on Guadalcanal." *Field Artillery Journal,* October 1943, 722–33.
———. "Marine Field Artillery on Guadalcanal." *Guadalcanal Echoes,* January 1990, 19.
Dobbins, Ernest T. "A Squad on the Brush Patrol." *Guadalcanal Echoes,* March 1992, 31.
———. "The Tenaru Patrol." *Old Breed News,* April 1992, 32.
Hancock, James. "Battle with the Enemy in the Solomons." Letter to mother published in unidentified newspaper, ca. 1943.
Headley, Adam. "Sergeant Okada Survived the Bloody Tenaru Engagement on the Island of Death—Guadalcanal." *Military History,* March 1993, 8, 62, 64, 66.
Horsman, Harry. "From the Old Sarge." *Guadalcanal Echoes,* January 1984, 6.
Howland, John. "Tenaru River Fight." Letter, *Harvard Alumni Bulletin,* April 24, 1943.
Hunt, George. "The Terrible Handful." *Mechanix Illustrated,* March 1944, 35–38, 157.
McLeod, Tom. "Jacob Vouza Tells What Happened." *Old Breed News,* April–June 2012. (Reprinted in *Guadalcanal Echoes,* Winter 2012, 8–11.)
———. "How Did the Ilu River Become Known as the Tenaru River (AKA Alligator Creek)?" *Old Breed News,* April–June 2012. (Reprinted in *Guadalcanal Echoes,* Winter 2012, 11.)
Merillat, Herbert C. L. "The Ultra Weapon at Guadalcanal." *Marine Corps Gazette,* September 1982.
Okada, Sadanobu. "Ichiki on Guadalcanal." *Guadalcanal Echoes,* July 1986, 2, 15.
———. "Remembrance Ichiki on Guadalcanal." *Guadalcanal Echoes,* January 1986, 2, 11.
Polinyi, Andy. "Col. Ichiki's Last Stand." *Guadalcanal Echoes,* April 1985, 8.
Simmons, Edwin H. "I Will Hold: An Appreciation of Gen. Clifton B. Cates." *Marine Corps Gazette,* November 2002.
Stevenson, Nikolai. "Four Months on the Frontline." *American Heritage,* October/November 1985, 49–55.

Stewart, Frank. "Tenaru River Guadalcanal." In Ipswich World War II Celebration official souvenir program, August 13–September 2, 1995.

Valenzi, Kathleen. "Scouting Guadalcanal." *Military History*, August 1995.

Wheaton, Donald. Letter to parents, November 14, 1942, *Central Hanover Observer*, March 1943, 1–2.

Wilson, Billy. "Guadalcanal 1942." *Richmond Times-Dispatch,* August 6, 1967, L8, L11.

Wilson, James E. "Battle of the Tenaru River." *Old Breed News,* June 1999, 11, 15.

Wylie, Evan M. "That Fearful Night on the Tenaru River." *Yankee*, August 1982, 72–77, 90–91, 93.

Yamamoto, Hajime. "The First Battle on Guadalcanal: Annihilation of the Ichiki Detachment" (in Japanese). In "Saiaku no semba" [The worst battlefield], *Maru* 5 (1987).

WEBSITES

Ancestry.com. US Military Collection, US Marine Corps Muster Rolls, 1798–1958. www.ancestry.com.

Archaehistoria. www.archaehistoria.org.

Dobbins, Ernest. Silver Star citation, March 18, 1943. http://www.hqmc.marines.mil/Portals/61/Docs/FOIA/WWII%20SS%20Citations/USMC%20WW%20II%20SS%20(Letter%20D)%20(DILL%20-%20DYER).pdf.

Frisbie, Nora G. "The Frisbie Family in the Revolutionary War." http://fffaa.info/PDF/bulletins/1960/Volume_XIII-No3-Jul1963.pdf.

Gorman, James J. "Biography of James Joseph Gorman," March 5, 1943. www.justinmuseum.com/oralbio/gormanjjbio.html.

The Great Ocean Liners. http://thegreatoceanliners.com/index2.html.

Guadalcanal Battle Sites, 1942–2013. www.guadalcanal.homestead.com.

Inui, Genjirou. "My Guadalcanal," diary. www.nettally.com/jrube/genjirou/genjirou.htm.

Marine Corps Aviation Reconnaissance Association (MCARA), MCARA War Stories, Quackenbush's Gypsies, South Pacific 1942–1943. www.mcara.us/quackenbushs-gypsies.html.

National WWII Memorial, Washington, DC. www.wwiimemorial.com.

Nevitt, Allyn D. "Long Lancers." Imperial Japanese Navy Page. http://www.combinedfleet.com/lancers.htm.

Nimitz "Gray Book": War Plans and Files of the Commander-in-Chief, Pacific Fleet. American Naval Records Society. www.ibiblio.org/anrs/graybook.html.

"2nd Battalion 1st Marines." Wikipedia. www.en.wikipedia.org/wiki/2nd_Battalion_1st_Marines.

Taki's Home Page, Imperial Army Home Page, Vessel. www3.plala.or.jp/takihome/vessel.htm.

"Traditions." www.marines.com/history-heritage/traditions

USMC, Hangout. http://www.usmchangout.com/military/branches/usmc/misc/222reasons.htm.

World Guns, Modern Firearms, Machine Guns. www.world.guns.ru/machine/usa/browning-m1917-m1919-e.html.

INDEX OF MILITARY UNITS
(according to organizational structure)

GENERAL INDEX

Page numbers with illustrations appear in *italics*.